Effective
Enterprise
Java

CW00434375

Effective SOFTWARE DEVELOPMENT SERIES ⋏

Scott Meyers, Consulting Editor

The **Effective Software Development Series** provides expert advice on all aspects of modern software development. Books in the series are well written, technically sound, of lasting value, and tractable length. Each describes the critical things the experts almost always do—or almost always avoid doing—to produce outstanding software.

Scott Meyers (author of the *Effective C++* books and CD) conceived of the series and acts as its consulting editor. Authors in the series work with Meyers and with Addison-Wesley Professional's editorial staff to create essential reading for software developers of every stripe.

TITLES IN THE SERIES

Elliotte Rusty Harold, *Effective XML: 50 Specific Ways to Improve Your XML*, 0321150406

Diomidis Spinellis, *Code Reading: The Open Source Perspective*, 0201799405

Effective Enterprise Java

Ted Neward

✦Addison-Wesley

Boston • San Francisco • New York • Toronto • Montreal
London • Munich • Paris • Madrid
Capetown • Sydney • Tokyo • Singapore • Mexico City

The publisher offers discounts on this book when ordered in quantity for bulk purchases and special sales. For more information, please contact:

U.S. Corporate and Government Sales
(800) 382-3419
corpsales@pearsontechgroup.com

For sales outside of the U.S., please contact:

International Sales
international@pearsoned.com

Visit Addison-Wesley on the Web: www.awprofessional.com

Library of Congress Cataloging-in-Publication Data

Neward, Ted.
    Effective Enterprise Java / Ted Neward.
        p.   cm.
    ISBN 0-321-13000-6 (pbk. : alk. paper)
    1. Java (Computer program language) I. Title.

QA76.73.J38N48 2004
005.13'3—dc22   2004012164

ISBN 0-321-13000-6
Text printed on recycled paper
1 2 3 4 5 6 7 8 9 10—CRS—0807060504
First printing, August 2004

Contents

Chapter 6   Presentation   285

Chapter 7   Security   321

Chapter 8   System   379

Foreword

Designing and implementing large-scale enterprise systems is hard. Building effective enterprise Java deployments is even harder. I see these difficulties on a daily basis. When consulting on enterprise projects, I see the real-world issues that developers are facing. I have also seen discussions, frustrations, and solutions to some of the issues on a daily basis on TheServerSide.com (Your Enterprise Java Community). TheServerSide.com really grew from the needs of developers faced with the new world of J2EE. It was the water cooler that allowed us to chat about solutions that worked for us, and it saw the growth of enterprise Java patterns.

Developing for the enterprise is a very different beast when compared to building smaller, standalone applications. We have to consider issues that we can safely ignore in the other world. As soon as we have to *share data* among multiple users, we start down the enterprise path. Then we start facing questions: What is the best solution for allowing concurrency to this data? How coherent and correct does it have to be? How can we scale up from 2 to 50 to 1,000 clients? These are all significant questions, and I don't feel that the average developer has enough help in answering them. Well, simply answering the questions may not be the correct focus. We need to be taught about the various issues involved and shown techniques that can help with the various problems. With Ted Neward's book, we are now armed with the knowledge that will allow us to come up with the right balance in the solution for each particular problem.

No book has attacked these problems quite like *Effective Enterprise Java* does. The most important part of this book is that it teaches you two things really well.

You will understand the general issues of enterprise computing.

These enterprise problems are far from new. Ted has been around the block, and he understands the core issues at work. A non-Java developer would get a lot out of this book for this very reason. What you learn here will be with you for as long as you develop enterprise solutions. The language and APIs may change, but you will understand the issues in building a good architecture, the options you have for communication, the choices for where to store state, the various security concerns, and so much more.

You will be able to attack the problems by using enterprise Java.

Although the book offers genuine insight into the general enterprise problems, it also gives you tools to solve them with enterprise Java today. You will understand more about where the various enterprise Java technologies fit together. When would you use Web Services? What can messaging do for you? What is EJB good for? This book provides answers to these questions.

It is great to have some answers to these common questions. The style of the book, in which you are given a set of "effective items," gets right to the point. Get stuck in, and enjoy the ride!

Dion Almaer
Editor-in-Chief, TheServerSide.com

Preface

Those who cannot remember the past are doomed to repeat it.

—George Santayana

These are heady days for Java programmers. Commercially available for less than a decade, Java has nevertheless emerged as the language of choice for enterprise systems on nearly all major computing platforms. Companies and individuals with challenging programming problems increasingly embrace the language and platform, and the question faced by those who do not use Java is often *when* they will start, not *if.* The breadth and scope of the specifications and libraries defined by and under the Java 2 Enterprise Edition Specification—which both dwarfs and subsumes that of the Java language itself—makes it possible to write rich, complex systems without sacrificing performance or implementing common algorithms or data structures from scratch. The Java language and virtual machines grow ever more powerful. Tools and environments for Java development grow ever more abundant and robust. Commercial libraries all but obviate the need to write code in many application areas.

Scott Meyers wrote much the same in his opening to *More Effective C++* [Meyers97] almost a decade ago. It seems a fitting tribute to use that paragraph, suitably modified, as the opening in this book. As a matter of fact, the two paragraphs are deliberately side-by-side similar. In many ways, we now find ourselves in a part of the Golden Age of Java, looking out over a landscape that stretches from horizon to horizon, with ample space and established borders that seem to have no limit. Just as C++ ruled the landscape in 1996, Java rules the landscape in 2004.

The chief aim in drawing these parallels is to recognize the scenario—not more than two years after Scott wrote that paragraph, C++ was toppled from its throne by this upstart named Java. Just as C++ developers had finally begun to "figure everything out," this new language and environment leapt forward into the fray, and almost overnight, it seemed, took over. In turn, Java now faces fierce competition from Microsoft's .NET platform. The natural concern, then, is to see that history doesn't repeat itself. To do that, Java developers must make sure that the systems they develop meet or exceed expectations set for them. To do *that,* Java developers need to know how to make the most of the language and platform they use.

It has been said, in many places by many people, that it takes about five years to "figure out" a technology and how best to use it. Certainly this was true for C++: in 1990, we looked at C++ as simply another object-oriented language, and therefore using it should mirror the best-usage practices discovered with Smalltalk. By 1995, we were well out of that world and starting to explore the uniqueness that C++ provides (such as templates and the STL). Certainly this was also true of HTTP: in 1995, when the browser debuted, we looked at HTTP as the means by which HTML was delivered. Now, we look at HTTP as a universal transport by which to transmit all sorts of data.

Thus, the timing is fortuitous for Java. It officially debuted in 1995; for all intents and purposes, however, Java truly entered the mindscape of the average developer in 1997 or so, having by that point built enough of a "critical mass" to win its way past the critics and skeptics. Almost a decade later, we have been writing Java applications for most of that time, and we're starting to see the practices and patterns that have emerged to assist (but not necessarily guarantee) successful deployments. As a community, we're just starting to hit our stride.

Some things aren't different from the C++ days. We have the same questions, modified for the Java world, as those we asked (and Scott answered) a decade ago about C++. As the language and platform have matured and our experience with Java has increased, our needs for information have changed. In 1996, people wanted to know *what* Java was. "It has something to do with the Internet, whatever that is" was a common explanation. Initially, developers focused on using applets, making rich browser clients, and harnessing Java's cross-platform portability. By 1998, they wanted to know *how* to make it work: "How do I access a relational database? How do I internationalize? How do I reach across physical machine boundaries?" Now, Java programmers ask higher-level questions: "How can I design my enterprise systems so they will adapt to future demands?

How can I improve the efficiency of my code without compromising its correctness or making it harder to use? How can I implement sophisticated functionality not directly supported by the language or platform?"

As if this weren't enough, a new dimension has arisen in the whole enterprise system arena, neatly captured in two words: Web Services. Even as Java developers are asking the hard higher-level questions about Java, they face the start of the cycle with Web Services—what is a Web Service, how does it work, and, perhaps most importantly, how does it relate to Java?

In this book, I answer these questions and many like them.

About the items

One thing I feel compelled to point out, before we get too deeply into it all, is that readers may notice a significant difference between the items in this book and those from books like *Effective Java* [Bloch] and *Effective C++* [Meyers95]. In particular, the scope of the items in this book is much larger than that in other similar books—in here, there's less focus on language and/or APIs and more on design-level constructs and/or usage patterns.

This is not an accident; in fact, I believe that this is in keeping with the larger scope of an enterprise application as a whole. Certainly, without question, all of *Effective Java* also applies to building enterprise applications, but to simply remain at that level misses the larger point, that enterprise systems have much more to worry about, things outside of the scope of the language or APIs.

For example, an unsuccessful EJB application usually begins not with misuse of a particular method call or interface but with the design of entity beans that are called directly from a client. This isn't so much an implementation problem as a design problem, and solving it requires a more "high-level" view of what the entity bean is trying to provide in general. (See Item 40 for more details about entity beans and their consequences.)

As a result, the items presented in this book strive to help developers recognize efficiency not at a language level but at a systemic and architectural level. Many of these items will be familiar ground to some; many will be simple codification of something some readers "always knew." That's OK—what's "intuitive" to one reader will be new to another, and vice versa.

In addition, I have carefully tried to avoid walking on familiar territory. A number of books have been released that discuss best practices and effective use of the virtual machine and/or the language; see the Bibliography for a complete list. As a result, discussions of material covered there won't be repeated here unless it has some particular relevance or application within the enterprise space.

Toward that end, I will refer frequently to patterns already established within the enterprise Java literature space; in particular, I will tend to lean heavily on Fowler's *Patterns of Enterprise Application Architecture* (Addison-Wesley, 2002), Hohpe and Woolf's *Enterprise Application Integration* (Addison-Wesley, 2004), and Alur, Crupi, and Malks's *Core J2EE Patterns*, 2nd ed. (Addison-Wesley, 2003), among others. (Again, see the Bibliography for a complete list.)

Where a pattern is cited by name, I use the standard Gang-of-Four pattern citation format, citing the pattern name with its page number in parentheses behind it; however, because these patterns come from different sources, I also put the author's names (or "GOF" for the Gang-of-Four book, *Design Patterns*) as part of the page citation. So a reference to the Data Transfer Object pattern from Fowler's *Patterns of Enterprise Application Architecture* book will be cited as "Data Transfer Object ([Fowler, 401])".

Acknowledgments

Authors have a tendency to spend a lot of time thanking people; there's a reason for that.

First and foremost, I want to thank my peers in the industry, most of all my fellow instructors at DevelopMentor. Kevin Jones, Brian Maso, Stu Halloway, Simon Horrell, Dan Weston, and Bob Beauchemin all served as sounding boards for the topics in this book at some point over its 30-month gestation. Tim Ewald, Don Box, Fritz Onion, Keith Brown, Mike Woodring, Ingo Rammer, and Peter Drayton all gave me insights into the Java platform by routinely smashing my preconceptions and assumptions in discussions that had nothing to do with Java. Outside of DevelopMentor, my fellow NoFluffJustStuff Symposium speakers Dion Alamer, Bruce Tate, Mike Clark, Erik Hatcher, Glenn Vandenburg, Dave Thomas, Jason Hunter, James Duncan Davidson, and Ron Bodkin, among others, all forced me to justify my assertions, questioned my conclusions, and offered suggestions and tips designed to make the book a stronger work. Thanks to Jay Zimmerman for inviting me to be a part of NoFluffJustStuff in the first place. Numerous other speakers at conferences far and wide (far too many to list here) played a similar role, known in the common vernacular as "keeping me honest."

Second, I must tip the hat to the staff at Addison-Wesley. This book took over twice as long as it was supposed to, and never once did Mike Hendrickson, the editor who started the project, nor Ann Sellers, the editor who inherited the project, use anything but polite language when asking if it was done—their patience far exceeded what mine would have been in their shoes. The reviewers, both of the content when it was hosted on the Web via my blog, as well as the more finalized manuscript drafts, did a Herculean job reading through the material and offering up copious corrections, suggestions, enhancements, and ideas. Thanks to Matt Anderson, Kevin Bentley, Dave Cooke, Mary Dageforde, Kevin Davis, Matthew P. Johnson, and Bruce Scharlau for all their help.

Writing this book has been both a labor of absolute love and an exercise in abject terror. While I've always looked for a project like this to let me rant about my thoughts on enterprise Java development, few books have "raised the bar" as the previous *Effective* books have done. With *Effective C++*, Scott Meyers gave me (and millions of other neophyte C++ programmers) the leg up I needed to start using C++, rather than just flailing around with it. Then Joshua Bloch wrote *Effective Java*, bringing the beauty of the item format to the Java platform. Elliote Rusty Harold further upped the ante with *Effective XML*. If ever an author were looking for an intimidating set of authors to follow, those three fill out the set admirably. Fortunately, help was available in the form of Scott Meyers, who spent almost as much time reviewing and criticizing (in the good sense) this book as I did writing it. His comments and insights helped transform a tolerable collection of suggestions into the book you see in front of you. Scott, I owe you a tremendous debt of gratitude, both for your help during the last year and your help 10 years ago as I struggled to understand C++. It has been a privilege and an honor to do this with you; thank you.

Finally, of course, I must thank my family and friends, those loving people who periodically staged interventions and dragged me, kicking and screaming, back into this thing they kept calling "the real world": parties, holidays, even just hanging out for a night or two relaxing over the

Nintendo64 or XBox. Though I'll never admit it out loud, they kept me sane in the face of the mounting pressure of writing this book during the last two years.

Reporting bugs, making suggestions, and getting book updates

I have tried to make this book as accurate, readable, and useful as possible, but I know there is room for improvement. (There is *always* room for improvement.) If you find an error of any kind—technical, grammatical, typographical, spiritual, *whatever*—please tell me about it. I will try to ensure the mistake is corrected in a future printing of the book, and if you are the first person to report it, I will happily add your name to the book's acknowledgments. Likewise, if you have suggestions or ideas on how to improve the book for subsequent revisions or editions, I'm all eyes and ears.

I continue to collect guidelines for effective enterprise programming in Java. If you have ideas for new guidelines, I'd be delighted if you'd share them with me. You can either find me on one of several public Java programming mailing lists, the predominant one being the ADVANCED-JAVA list at DISCUSS.DEVELOP.COM, or you can reach me at:

Ted Neward
c/o Addison-Wesley Professional/Prentice Hall PTR
Pearson Technology Group
75 Arlington St., Suite 300
Boston, MA 02116

Alternatively, you can drop me an email at ted@neward.net.

I maintain a list of changes to this book since its first printing (including bug fixes, clarifications, commentary, and technical updates) on the book's blog, http://www.neward.net/ted/EEJ/index.jsp. Please feel free to post comments and/or errata there if you wish to share them with your fellow readers.

Enough preliminaries. On with the show!

List of Abbreviations

ACID	atomic, consistent, isolated, and durable
AWT	Abstract Windowing Toolkit
BLOB	Binary Large Object
BMP	Bean-Managed Persistence
CMP	Container-Managed Persistence
COM	Component Object Model
CORBA	Common Object Request Broker Architecture
CSS	Cascading Style Sheets
DCOM	Distributed COM
DHTML	Dynamic HTML
DMZ	demilitarized zone
DNS	Domain Name System
DOM	Document Object Model
DTCs	distributed transaction controllers
EJB	Enterprise Java Bean
HTML	Hyper-Text Markup Language
HTTP	Hyper-Text Transmission Protocol
IDL	Interface Description Language
IIOP	Internet Inter-Orb Protocol
IPC	interprocess communication
J2EE	Java 2 Enterprise Edition
J2SE	Java 2 Standard Edition
JAAS	Java Authentication and Authorization Service
JAXB	Java API for XML Binding
JAXM	Java API for XML Messaging

JAXP	Java API for XML Parsing
JAX-RPC	Java API for XML RPC
JCA	Java Connector API
JDBC	Java DataBase Connectivity
JDK	Java Development Kit
JDO	Java Data Objects
JESS	Java Expert System Shell
JIT	just-in-time
JITA	just-in-time activation
JMS	Java Message Service
JMX	Java Management Extensions
JNDI	Java Naming and Directory Interface
JNI	Java Native Interface
JNLP	Java Network Launch Protocol
JRE	Java Runtime Environment
JSP	Java Server Pages
JSR	Java Specification Request
JSSE	Java Secure Sockets Extension
JTA	Java Transaction API
JVM	Java Virtual Machine
JVMDI	Java Virtual Machine Debug Interface
JVMPI	Java Virtual Machine Profiler Interface
JVMTI	Java Virtual Machine Tools Interface
LAN	local area network
MDBs	Message-Driven Beans
MIB	Message Information Block
MVC	Model-View-Controller
NAT	Network Address Translation
NFS	Network File System
OODBMS	object-oriented database management system
ORB	Object Request Broker
OSI	Open System Interconnection
OWASP	Open Web Application Security Project
POJOs	plain old Java objects
POP3	Post Office Protocol v 3

RDBMS	relational database management system
RMI	Remote Method Invocation
RMI/IIOP	RMI over IIOP
RMI/JRMP	RMI over Java Remote Method Protocol
RPC	Remote Procedure Call
SAX	Streaming API for XML
SMTP	Simple Mail Transport Protocol
SNMP	Simple Network Management Protocol
SOAP	Simple Object Access Protocol
SSL	Secure Sockets Layer
STL	Standard Template Library
SWT	Standard Widget Toolkit
TLS	Transport Layer Security
TPC	two-phase commit
TTL	time-to-live value
URI	Universal Resource Identifier
URL	Universal Resource Locator
URN	Universal Resource Name
VM	virtual machine
W3C	World Wide Web Consortium
WSDL	Web Services Definition Language
WS-I	Web Services-Interoperability
XML	Extensible Markup Language
XSD	XML Schema Definition
XSLT	XSL:Transformation, commonly also written as XSL:T

1 | Introduction

> *Before I came here, I was confused about this subject.*
> *Having listened to your lecture, I am still confused,*
> *but on a higher level.*
>
> —Enrico Fermi

This book shows how to design and implement enterprise-scope Java software systems that are more *effective:* more likely to behave correctly, more robust in the face of exceptions, more efficient, more performant, more scalable, harder to use incorrectly. In short, software that's just *better*.

In order to do this, however, I need to draw an important distinction between what this book covers and what it does not cover. In particular, this book is not a rehash of effective tips on how to use the language itself—that is the territory staked out by Joshua Bloch's excellent *Effective Java* [Bloch], which should be considered required reading for any Java programmer. Instead, this book aims for a higher scope, that of Java software written for enterprise systems; hence the name, *Effective Enterprise Java.*

As a result, it's important, at least for our purposes, to define precisely what an "enterprise Java" system is. For many developers, discussions of relational databases, business rules, transactional functionality, and scalability rule the day here. Any system that uses a majority of the specifications defined as part of the J2EE Specification is certainly a candidate. I tend to look at the answer from a slightly different perspective, however.

An enterprise system is one that has the following qualities.

- *Shares some or all of the resources used by the application:* The ubiquitous example here is the relational database(s) in which all application data resides. Sharing these resources adds some additional implied complexity: the data is shared because it needs to be available to multiple users simultaneously. As a result, the system must support user-concurrent access both safely and quickly.

- *Is intended for internal use:* "Internal" here means "the opposite of mass-produced software sold to end consumers." While the system may in fact be shared between the company and business partners, it is written with specific knowledge of the company, its business practices, and its specific requirements.

- *Must work within existing architecture:* With rare exception, the company already has a set of hardware and software in place that the system must be able to interoperate with. In particular, this implies that the application must adapt to the existing database schema (rather than the other way around). An enterprise system must be able to adapt to the heterogeneous environment in which it lives.

- *Will be deployed and supported by internal IT staff:* For most companies, the actual "production" machines remain out of the reach of developers. This is a good thing—most developers are not particularly interested in being awakened in the wee hours of the morning when their application fails. But it also implies that the deployment of the system will be done by hands other than theirs, and it implies that the staff responsible for the data center must have some way to monitor, diagnose, and fix problems short of writing code.

- *Requires greater robustness, both in terms of exception-handling and scalability:* Enterprise systems, particularly when made available over the Internet (the classic e-commerce system comes to mind), represent a huge investment for a company. Every minute the system is down means thousands, perhaps millions, of dollars of missed revenue. Every user turned away from the company Web site (or worse, forced to stare at the browser waiting for the login request to complete) leads to a loss of credibility and/or potential sales for the company.

- *Must fail gracefully:* In an application such as a word processor, an unexpected condition can be handled by throwing up an "oops" dialog, saving the user's work, and asking him or her to restart the program. An enterprise system can't afford to do this—if it crashes, millions of dollars go down the drain in lost productivity, sales, client perception, and so on. An enterprise system strives for "Five Nines Availability": total system uptime of more than 99.999% per year. That leaves downtime, scheduled or otherwise, of 0.001% per year, or roughly less than five minutes.

- *Must gracefully handle evolution over time:* Enterprise systems have long-lived lifecycles; the Y2K problem testified to that. As a result, a system must be able to accommodate the inevitable changes that occur within the company over time: mergers, sales promotions, policy shifts, corporate changes of direction, acquisitions, and so on.

Obviously, this is a large territory. Enterprise software spans the gamut, in size and scope, from one-person spreadsheets to multi-terabyte relational databases. Given the rise of wireless device usage within large corporations, you could even argue that writing code for a PalmOS device or cellular phone is enterprise development. For the most part, however, this book focuses on the traditional realm of enterprise computing, the PC connected against one or more servers.

Even that definition covers a large area. Enterprise applications may be for internal or external use and may run the complete range of "criticalness": some may be purely administrative in nature, such as a vacation reporting system for human resources, and some may be the core revenue stream of the company, such as an online e-retailer like Amazon.com. Business partners may use the enterprise system to place orders, check shipments, or submit invoices. Consulting firms may place technical content for customers to retrieve.

As a result, writing software that satisfies these needs can be difficult and time-consuming. Thus was the J2EE platform born.

The goals of J2EE

As the old saying goes, it helps to know where we've been (and why we got there) in order to know where next to go. I want to explain the "why" and "how" of J2EE, in order to make sure that certain concepts (like lookup, which is important in Item 16, for example) are clear.

Throughout the history of computer science, the overriding goal of any language, tool, or library has largely been to raise the level of abstraction away from details that distract us from the Real Work at hand. Consider the classic OSI seven-layer network stack, for example. It's not that when you "open a socket" you actually open something that directly pipes over to another machine; instead, that act serves as an abstraction over the four or five layers of software (and hardware, once you reach the physical layer) that each provide a certain amount of support to make all this stuff work.

In the early days of enterprise systems, layers were painfully absent—all data access was done directly against files of fixed-length records, and anything that happened to those records was your business and yours alone. No layering was present because the systems we ran on in those days didn't have much in terms of CPU cycles or memory to spare. Everything had to be as tightly focused as it could be.

As hardware capacity grew and demand for more complex processing grew with it, we found it necessary and desirable to have certain behavior guaranteed. So a layer of software was put on top of the traditional flat-file collection, and we called it a transaction processing system; it managed concurrent access to the data, making sure that the data obeyed the logical constraints we put into it via the code we wrote. Over time, this was formalized even further to include a powerful query syntax, and thus was the modern relational database, and SQL, born.

Then we started wanting to let end users work with the data stored in the database, rather than feeding to data processing clerks the stacks of paper containing the data to be entered. Not only did college students lose a viable form of employment over the summer, but a new form of programming, the client/server architecture, was born. A program executed on the client machine, responsible for presentation and data capture, and turned that into statements of work to execute against the database system. Typically this program is of the graphical user interface variety, written in some higher-level language built specifically for this purpose, customized to the particular system being developed for the company.

As the numbers of clients against these client/server systems grew, however, we began to run into a limitation: thanks to the internal processing that accompanies client action against a client/server database, the number of physical network connections (and the associated software costs) against the database have a definitive upper limit, thus placing an arbitrary cap on the number of users that can use the system at the same time. We can say that n clients was the upper limit of users against the system, where n was this maximum number of connections, and as soon as client $n+1$ wants to log in, we need a new database for him or her.

Even the largest Fortune 50 companies could accept this state of affairs for a short period of time because the largest number of users against an enterprise system usually didn't crest four digits; despite the costs involved in doing so, it's usually possible, though not desirable, to push a new installation out to a thousand internal clients. As soon as we started adopting the Web as a public interface to enterprise systems, however, the situation changed radically—the Web is all about extending the corporation's "reach," and that meant users could, virtually speaking, visit the corporation from all over the world, all at once. Where we used to have thousands of clients, the Web meant that now we had *millions*.

This exponential jump in the number of possible concurrent clients means that the old "one client, one connection" architecture isn't credibly possible anymore. A new breed of software architecture was necessary if this "bring the system to the end user via the Web" ideal was to have any chance of working.

An old maxim in computer science states, "There is no problem that cannot be solved by adding an additional layer of indirection." In this case, because client programs don't typically make use of the connection they hold to the server 100% of the time, the layer of indirection introduced was a layer of software in between the clients and the server. (Note the deliberate terminology; see Item 3 for details.) This layer of resource-managing software, after a few years of wrestling for a good name, came to be known as *middleware*.

Middleware and J2EE

Bernstein (as quoted in [Gray/Reuter]) defines the term *middleware* as a distributed system service that includes standard programming interfaces and protocols. He goes on to say that middleware services provide a layer of support above the operating system and networking layers and below industry-specific applications. A middleware layer, known in previous incarnations as a Transaction Processing Monitor, or TP Monitor for short, is "to *integrate* other system components and manage resources. . . . It interfaces to many different pieces of software, and its main purpose is to make them work together in a special way, a way that has come to be known as *transaction-oriented processing*" [Gray/Reuter, 240, emphasis added].

J2EE is an obvious inheritor of the TP Monitor/middleware legacy. The J2EE Specification itself welds a dozen other Java specifications into a coherent, definable whole, not so much describing any enhancements or addenda to those specifications as providing a stable and consistent base within which to build systems that make use of all of these specifications. Servlets, JavaServerPages, JDBC, Remote Method Invocation (RMI), Java Message Service (JMS), Java Transaction API (JTA), Java Connector API (JCA), and of course EJB—these specifications and more are all brought together into a mostly harmonious existence under the umbrella of the J2EE Specification.

Many if not all of the specifications unified by J2EE deal with resource management. For example, JDBC describes how to interact and deal with relational database systems. JMS covers integration with messaging-oriented middleware (there's that word again) systems. RMI is concerned with remote procedure calls; JTA with transaction management; JCA with "legacy" systems, other communication systems, and record-oriented data systems; and so on.

The idea for middleware in many ways came from the desire for integration. Too frequently, an enterprise finds itself in possession of a number of disconnected stovepipe systems that accomplish one particular purpose. (The name "stovepipe system" comes from the idea that the system is a very narrow, focused application: one database accessed by a single program, which, when viewed pictorially, looks like a chimney or stovepipe.) These systems were usually developed under the control of an individual department or division to handle that particular department or division's unique needs. A partial listing includes systems like accounting, inventory management, human resources, customer relationship management, order entry, and so on. Taken individually, each of these systems are usually quite successful—they satisfy the need the department had that drove the desire to build them in the first place.

Unfortunately, the needs of the enterprise as a whole don't end with the simple needs of the individual departments themselves. A secondary, intermediate set of needs stretches across the enterprise as a whole, and this was realized almost as soon as the "Internet revolution" struck. When corporations began to look at using the Internet as a new way to reach customers, alongside their traditional brick-and-mortar channels, the enterprise systems they'd developed over time were suddenly inadequate. Companies wanted to put everything online: order entry, order tracking, supply-chain management, and so on. They discovered very quickly that a system built for salespeople taking orders over the phone doesn't work when put behind an HTML form—when order entry suddenly becomes the responsibility of the customer, for example, much more validation is necessary than when done by trained corporate staff. New channels are also constantly being devised and explored; now, companies want to sell their goods and services over the Internet not only to customers but also to suppliers and business partners (the ubiquitous "business-to-business" channel). Mobile devices are fast becoming an area of interest, potentially allowing businesses to sell to customers over wireless PDAs, cellular phones, and other gadgets where traditional HTML won't fly.

As if the Internet and the rise of e-commerce weren't enough, corporations discovered that these stovepipe systems worked only as long as the department remained relatively static. As reorganization became a more common tool of corporate management, however, and departmental responsibilities and duties changed with each reorganization effort, the systems supporting the department needed to change accordingly. Where order entry used to be something handled by the sales department, suddenly sales and marketing coalesced into a single department, so the system supporting them had to integrate order entry and customer relationship management. Or, in some cases, the departments split, meaning the system was now being used by two different departments with differing agendas. These systems needed to be able to reach across to other systems and access and/or manipulate the data, provide processing not originally called for in the system requirements, and do it all quickly—even though that system originally was written in C++ and the one needing that access was being written in Java.

It's enough to make you want to quit and take up something a lot less stressful, like commercial air traffic control, organized crime, or auto loan repossession.

This is where middleware is supposed to step in. By providing a common baseline, the "glue," that all these different systems can talk to, IT developers can focus more exclusively on the domain-specific parts of the system. If we can somehow find the parts of the system that make it "hard" for programmers to build enterprise systems, we can put that functionality into a layer that's accessible from domain-dependent code. These parts of the system that are entirely domain-independent are sometimes referred to as *crosscutting concerns.*

A *concern* is a particular area of interest within a software system. In many respects, the driving goal behind most software architecture and design is to capture the related concerns into well-modularized constructs: for example, in an object-oriented system, the idea is to capture everything having to do with being a "person" in the system into the well-encapsulated, well-factored Person class. We then extend the concern Person to include people who study, calling the software type that represents them Student, and people who teach, calling their type Instructor, and so on. This is more formally known as the *separation of concerns*.

Unfortunately, concerns don't always stratify so easily. A whole host of issues cannot be easily refactored into base classes from which we can inherit or support classes we can simply compose or aggregate. For example, consider what otherwise seems like a relatively simple request: we want to emit a message to a diagnostic log every time a method is entered and subsequently exited. (If this seems like a trivial example, imagine instead that the desire is to begin a distributed transaction on method entry and commit it on method exit; the implementation will be almost identical.) This is a *crosscutting concern* because the concern stretches laterally across the static inheritance tree in a classic object-oriented system, cutting across inheritance lines, thus giving it its name.

The problem here is that, left unchecked, crosscutting concerns turn an otherwise well-factored codebase into a mess of spaghetti code and logic. Consider our simple example. Under normal Java language rules, there is no way to automatically provide this behavior to interested clients. If a class wishes its methods to log a diagnostic message, the Java developer must do this by hand: at the start of each method, do the "method entered" message, and at the exit of each method (actually, to be honest, at the end of each possible return point within the method), do the "method exited" message. It's an "opt-in" system; if a developer forgets to put the code in for a particular method, that method won't do the logging. This will get tedious and probably error-prone before too long. This is the kind of problem cut-and-paste reuse was born for, unfortunately bringing along with it all of its inherent problems and risks.

Crosscutting concerns are, in many ways, the parts that make software development hard. For example, consider this incomplete yet rather intimidating list of concerns that every enterprise developer has to face and solve somehow.

- *State management:* State management incorporates two related yet different elements—*transient state* and *durable state*—under a single name. In the case of transient state, while this is implicitly done in the case of rich-client or fat-client applications, it becomes more complex in thin-client systems. Having the system handle some of this reduces the complexity faced by the application programmer. Similarly, for durable state, data must be stored to the permanent data store and later retrieved. Usually this is a relational database, and because objects and relational databases don't exactly see eye-to-eye, this makes storing a rich object model to a relational model an exercise of extreme frustration. This is sometimes called the *object-relational impedance mismatch.*

- *Processing:* Although it seems like this should be naturally part of the domain itself being modeled, how we perform the system processing itself can be considered a crosscutting concern. For example, dealing with application-level failure can be a difficult task—it would be much easier if the system could handle failures in a more systematic way, particularly when dealing with external resources such as the relational database or messaging broker. Or, as a second example, it would be easier if the system could do some of the processing for us, evaluating the state of the data against a set of criteria that in turn identify which bits of code to execute.

- *Synchronization:* Enterprise systems are naturally multitasking, meaning that more than one client request can access a shared resource at the same time. Because not all resources can deal with this scenario, developers must explicitly write code to prevent simultaneous access (either at the Java code level or at the shared resource level) of that resource.

- *Remoting and communication:* Systems built out of components must somehow communicate with one another, and often that communication takes different forms depending on the circumstances of the system or component. Some communications need to be done in a message-oriented fashion, for example, while others need to use a request-response approach.

- *Lookup:* Once communication between processes was easily attainable, another problem became more and more obvious, that of how to *find* the other process/machine/object with which we desire that communication. As is usual, the first approach—simply hard-code the target into the codebase—is less than acceptable, and as a result, a new layer of indirection, one that allows for a mapping of a developer-friendly name to a resource, is necessary.

- *Object lifecycle management:* In an object-oriented enterprise system, the lifetime of objects becomes a particular concern. For example, in a system where a single object represents a single row in a database table, how that object is created, when it is created, and for how long that object remains in memory are critical concerns. Having too many objects at once creates a system with a much larger footprint than it needs to have, yet having too few objects means the system spends its time thrashing, swapping objects in and out of memory.

- *Resource management:* Threads, database connections, sockets, files—all of these resources are harder to manage than heap memory. They have lifecycles that stand outside the Java Virtual Machine and need to be acquired and released in a fashion that's friendly to concurrent use. More importantly, some resources may require some kind of pooling facility in order to most efficiently use them, rather than go through the expensive acquisition algorithm each time.

As you can see, this is far from a trivial set of concerns, and asking programmers to solve these problems each time we start a new enterprise project is more or less akin to asking carpenters to forge their tools each time they set foot on a new building site. Yes, it might be possible to build exactly the set of tools needed for the job, and perhaps even build a few tools uniquely suited to that particular job, but at what cost? Worse yet, it requires the carpenter also to be a blacksmith, a paired skill set that's fairly rare among carpenters these days.

The goal, then, is to find a way to capture these problem-domain-independent crosscutting concerns into a first-class construct, just as the goal of an object-oriented language and/or system was to find ways to capture related state and behavior into a first-class construct (a class, typically). In a middleware system, we look to these software processes running between the various nodes of the system to provide the support for these crosscutting concerns.

J2EE implementation

Several different techniques have been proposed over the years as ways to handle crosscutting concerns, including one that you should already be intimately familiar with: object-oriented software development. Objects (or, more particularly, inheritance) were seen as a way of extracting common code (crosscutting concerns) back into a single location, in this case a base class. And, while objects provide this capability admirably, we've since discovered that simple inheritance (or, to be more precise, implementation inheritance) isn't enough. I can't inherit from a base class that provides the tracing behavior in my derived classes, for example, because base-class methods are typically overridden in derived classes in order to provide the specialization that a derived class needs to provide.

One of the most interesting approaches to handling crosscutting concerns is the most drastic, that of extending the language (or simply inventing a new one) to better deal with crosscutting concerns at a first-class level. This is the purpose and motivation behind languages like Eclipse's AspectJ (aspect-oriented programming) and IBM's Hyper/J (subject-oriented programming), to name two of the more popular languages. Other, more research-oriented approaches include OpenJava and Javassist (both of which are meta-object protocol systems). As such, while interesting, they stand as examples that are completely outside of the "normal" Java spectrum, and as a result, they really don't fit within a book like this. I thoroughly recommend you take a look at each one of them, as well as others in the same space, on the grounds that something like this could easily be "the next big thing" in languages.

Another approach to handling crosscutting concerns is to take a class and, making use of Java's open ClassLoader mechanism (see Item 70), actually modify the compiled bytecode at load time to inject some additional code, usually to provide crosscutting concern behavior. For example, in the current Java Data Objects (JDO) Specification, JDO developers run an "enhancement" utility to modify a compiled class to inject persistence behavior into the class; runtime bytecode enhancement utilities/systems do this at runtime, from within the container, rather than forcing developers to do this at compile time. Several J2EE containers are flirting with this concept, and other open-source libraries, such as Nanning and AspectWorks, are working from this concept to explore its useful application in enterprise systems as well.

J2EE uses a classic technique, the *Interception pattern* [POSA2, 109], to capture these crosscutting concerns into first-class constructs. In an interception-based scenario, a request from the client is effectively "hijacked" by a third party (neither the client nor the programmer-written server logic) to provide some kind of behavior. For example, in EJB, when a component wishes to participate in a transaction in order to obtain Atomic, Consistent, Isolated, and Durable (ACID) semantics for its processing of client requests, an interceptor, a proxy generated at the deployment time to intercept the client call, will begin a transaction and then pass the call (along with, implicitly, the transaction it started) to the EJB bean the call was meant for. When the bean returns, the transaction will be committed, assuming the bean didn't abort the transaction explicitly, and the results of the bean's actions will either be permanently preserved to the database in the event of a successful commit or removed and thrown away in the event of a failure.

Transactional execution is just one example of J2EE's interception-based bag of tricks. In the case of EJB Entity Beans, for example, the EJB container not only will intercept the call to the bean in order to start a transaction but also will take that opportunity to reload the bean from the data store into memory (in order to ensure that it has the latest-and-greatest copy of the data from the data store). This means the interceptor has to know how to load (and store) the bean with data from the underlying data store, typically a relational database. In order to do this, EJB makes use of another classic technique, that of *code generation.* Again, at deployment time, it builds the proxy using information contained in the bean's deployment descriptor. Although you may be familiar with deployment descriptors simply as XML files, technically these are *declarative attributes* about the bean(s) in the component; these factual statements about the bean cannot otherwise be expressed easily in the Java code. Using this information, the container builds the proxy to know (for example) what sort of SQL needs to be generated to handle all the possible persistence operations for the bean against the data store.

Interception isn't reserved exclusively for EJB. The servlet container also intercepts an incoming HTTP request, examines the request to determine which Web application the request is headed for, and ensures that all the necessary resources for that Web application are loaded and ready to go to process the request. As an added bonus, in Servlet 2.3 and later containers, the servlet container will find all programmer-defined interceptors (filters) bound to that particular request and execute them as well. A filter thus essentially stands as a programmer-defined interceptor in front of whatever resource the Web application's deployment descriptor declares it to intercept, using URL patterns as the descriptive criteria. The servlet programmer builds the filter, optionally replacing the standard `HttpServletRequest` and `HttpServletResponse` objects with customized versions to provide whatever behavior is desired, such as encryption, compression, or potentially outright replacement of returned data. (Interception isn't restricted just to middleware containers, by the way; see Item 6.)

The J2EE Specification thus uses Interception [POSA2, 109], among other techniques, to provide support for the crosscutting concerns within an enterprise system. For example, JDBC captures the crosscutting concerns dealing with connecting to, authenticating against, and passing SQL queries to a relational database system. As the JDBC client, we simply write the familiar `connection.createStatement(...)` code, and the JDBC driver handles the details from there. More classic middleware scenarios are the servlet container and RMI plumbing: both deal with thread and connection management, receiving requests from clients and passing the request to your server-side processing code, then later passing the response back to the client again. The recently released JCA does much the same, providing the Common Client Interface APIs for interacting with systems that don't fit precisely into either the RMI or JDBC models, which include not only legacy messaging systems and legacy transactional processing systems but also large system components like SAP.

Quite possibly the most common middleware scenario, however, is the EJB container. It deals with not only the same sort of resource management that the servlet container and RMI plumbing handle, that of taking client requests, but also transactional processing. It handles obtaining a distributed transaction from a transaction manager, automatically enlisting resource managers (like the relational database) into those distributed transactions, and automatically trying to commit the transaction upon completion of the method call, all so that you and I don't have to worry about that sort of thing.

Unfortunately, the J2EE container doesn't intrinsically have all the knowledge it needs to build interceptors that will deal efficiently with all possible scenarios that we programmers can cook up. For example, for a given EJB Session Bean method, the EJB container can't know ahead of time what sort of transactional semantics it should enforce: should this method run under a transaction or not, should it borrow a caller's transaction (if present) or not, and so on. In some cases, one interceptor can be used for the entirety of the container (this is what happens inside the servlet container, for example), but the interceptor still needs additional information about how to process the request, such as which servlet and/or filters to invoke to handle the request itself.

This is precisely where developers need to help the J2EE system, and we do so by giving it that necessary information via *declarative attributes*. In the case of J2EE 1.4 and earlier, that's done via the deployment descriptor. In subsequent J2EE releases (after JDK 1.5), that will most likely be done via custom attribute declarations directly embedded in the Java source itself. Either way, the J2EE deployment utility will build or internally configure its interceptors based on that information, thereby giving us, in theory, exactly what we're looking for.

As a J2EE developer, you need to recognize one of the classic elements of middleware is its passivity, on a number of levels. A middleware system is client-driven, waiting for incoming requests from clients before taking on any additional action. A middleware system is a part of a larger system, managing resources on our behalf (see Item 73). A middleware system looks to bridge across other systems, which can incur additional performance and/or scalability costs, so be careful of accepting those costs by default (see Item 32). A middleware system is about tying multiple systems together for use by multiple clients and channels, so make no assumptions about your relationship to the data you're working with that won't hold true over time (see Item 45). Bear in mind the reasons middleware systems evolved the way they did, particularly with respect to the partitioning of code, and don't blindly follow advice that doesn't hold true anymore (see Item 3).

Most importantly, recognize that middleware has a feel that predates objects by an entire decade. Within J2EE, we use objects to build middleware solutions, but middleware solutions are not intrinsically object solutions. Certainly, J2EE does its best to bring the best of objects into the middleware environment—this is where we get servlets, session beans, and message-driven beans, for example—but at its heart, middleware is object-agnostic, and that forces an entirely new mode of thinking on the J2EE developer that may be unfamiliar and unfriendly territory. When recognizing that J2EE is middleware for Java, you buy into a whole class of problems that have already been solved many times in many ways. Don't make more work for yourself by ignoring the lessons learned in systems past—by understanding why middleware took the road it took, you deepen your understanding of how J2EE evolved the way it did, and ultimately how to build successful and useful J2EE systems.

The ten fallacies of enterprise computing

Unfortunately, while J2EE addresses and solves a number of issues, it also introduces a few of its own.

Building a distributed object system is hard. In fact, building a distributed system in general, never mind the object-ness of it, is difficult. Peter

Deutsch, a researcher at Sun, summed it up best with his long-recognized "7 Fallacies of Distributed Computing." James Gosling added one more to make it 8.[1] I've taken the liberty (and the arrogance, perhaps) of adding two more.

As Deutsch put it in the introduction to his original 7, "Essentially everyone, when they first build a distributed application, makes the following seven [ten] assumptions. All prove to be false in the long run and all cause big trouble and painful learning experiences."

1. *The network is reliable.* Face it, the network is hardly what we'd call reliable—it's still a reality of the Internet today that packets get lost, servers go down, routers get hacked and diverted to less-than-ethical purposes, and so on. While it may be true that *your* network will never go down, your network isn't the only one you need to consider—it's all those *other* networks you can't assume will remain active. That's why you need to be robust in the face of failure (see Item 7), as well as define up front what sort of performance and scalability your system will require (see Item 8), so that you can make sure the infrastructure you've got in place can handle it.

2. *Latency is zero.* Networks are not free—it takes time to transmit data across the wire (and across the many intervening devices that make up the Internet). Often, during development, the latency of the network is as close to zero as it will ever get, particularly if the development department is physically isolated from the rest of the company's network, as is often the case in larger companies. In fact, in many cases latency is as close to zero as it can possibly get because developers have a habit of running all the tiers—application server, browser, database, and anything else necessary—on one machine for convenience. Don't forget that, particularly in the case of Web applications, your clients may not be on 100- or 1000-megabit networks—some (shudder) may even still be on dialup, depending on your client profile. For this reason, make sure to minimize the amount of data being sent across as part of the presentation layer (see Item 52) or as part of your communications links in general (see Item 23).

---

1. See http://today.java.net/jag/Fallacies.html.

3. *Bandwidth is infinite.* Much as we'd like to pretend otherwise, the network does have a finite capacity for the amount of information it can send across at a time. Particularly as enterprise systems are exposed to the public, where some of our potential users are still running over slow dialup connections or saturated DSL connections ("What, you mean I can't use your application and watch streaming videos at the same time?"), the notion that we'll have the same kinds of bandwidth we see on quiet LANs is ludicrous. This is why sometimes it makes sense to remove as much from the wire as possible, preferring a rich client to the traditional HTML-based one (see Item 51).

4. *The network is secure.* Recent years have proven this fallacy over and over again, even within the corporate intranet. Not only can hackers crack your firewall pretty easily (firewalls don't protect against SQL injection attacks, for example), but in many cases you can't trust the people within the network—recent studies have shown that around 70% of all corporate loss is due to employee theft and/or fraud. Security is fast becoming a "big deal" in enterprise applications, meaning you need to think about security at all levels of your development process, instead of something you just "turn on" when the application goes into production (see Item 57). Some of the things you need to watch out for include user input (see Item 61), because that's the most common vector for a command or SQL injection attack, and to use role-based authorization (see Item 63) like Java Authentication and Authorization Service (JAAS) to ensure that users can't gain access to parts of the system they shouldn't be able to see.

5. *Topology doesn't change.* The one thing constant in any IT shop is change. Servers go up, servers go down, machines need replacement, hardware needs upgrading, and so on. We go to great lengths to keep up with the changes, but it would help if the software we write could automatically adjust to them as well (see Item 16).

6. *There is one administrator.* Mergers, acquisitions, and spinoffs are just part of the story—you also have people coming and going at an alarming rate, including your system administrator. Even if you have just one today, tomorrow is an entirely different story. For that reason, you need to remember administration (see Item 13), deployment (see Item 14), and monitoring (see Item 12) when building enterprise systems. Moreover, with the growth of the PC and the generalized distribution of do-it-yourself programs (like Microsoft Access, among others), not to mention the octopus-like partnership and alliance relationships becoming ever more common in business,

the assumption that any one team, department, or even corporation owns a program has shifted. It's now to the point where any application you build may turn into something an entirely different company depends on without you knowing it. You can't assume you own the database (see Item 45) or have free reign to change the component interfaces (see Item 2).

7. *Transport cost is zero.* Objects don't transport across the wire easily. In fact, nothing in Java, with the exception of the primitive types, is isomorphic to its wire representation. This means that beyond the costs of pushing the actual bits across the wire, you're still incorporating a huge hit just to marshal and unmarshal the data itself. For this reason, keep an eye on the number of network round-trips you're making (see Item 17), using techniques like passing data in bulk (see Item 23) to make each trip to the network count.

8. *The network is homogeneous.* When you stop to consider the rapidly growing pervasiveness of .NET, combined with the large number of existing systems written in Python, Perl, C++, and other languages, it becomes really easy to recognize that homogeneity at the software level is impossible to achieve, much less at the hardware level. For this reason you need to carefully consider vendor neutrality in your architecture (see Item 11) and realize that whatever you build today, you might not own parts of it later (see Item 45).

9. *The system is monolithic.* While this may have been true in older systems, the whole point of an enterprise system is often to integrate with other systems in some way, even if just accessing the same database. Particularly today, with different parts of the system being revised at different times (presentation changes but business logic remains the same, or vice versa), it's more important than ever to recognize that the different parts of the system will need to deploy, version, and in many cases be developed independently of one another. For this reason you'll want to favor component-based designs (see Item 1) and look to build loose coupling between components (see Item 2).

10. *The system is finished.* The enterprise is a constantly shifting, constantly changing environment. Just when you think you've finished something, the business experts come back with some new requirements or some changes to what you've done already. It's the driving reason why the topology changes or why the system can't remain homogeneous for very long.

On these 10 rules is much of this book built.

2 Architecture

In theory there is no difference between theory and practice.
But, in practice, there is.

—Jan L.A. van de Snepscheut

Architecture—it's that level above design where we get our first glimpse of what the system will ultimately resemble, how it will be built, the vision of the application and system as a whole.

By keeping the advice contained in the items that follow in mind when laying out the basic flow and design of your enterprise applications and systems, you'll make progress toward a noble goal: establishing an architecture that enables a high-performance, high-scalability enterprise system.

Item 1: Prefer components as the key element of development, deployment, and reuse

One of the difficulties many Java developers face when attempting their first J2EE-based project is that J2EE applications are built differently than traditional Java applications: rather than building applications, J2EE mandates the construction of components that plug in to an already-existing application, that being the J2EE container itself.

This may not seem like a large difference at first, but its implications are huge, in two different directions. First of all, this means that developers aren't really interested in constructing objects per se but in creating strongly encapsulated components that (in the case of J2EE) are made up of tightly coupled constituent objects. Second, it means that there are a set of stringent rules that must be obeyed over which we, as the component builder, have little to no influence.

Developers studying the object-oriented paradigm have, since the very early days, been repeatedly taught to promote encapsulation and data hiding. We've all memorized nuggets of wisdom handed down from on high, such as "Never use public fields; instead always create accessor and mutator methods (getters and setters, in JavaBeans lingo)," for example, or "Hide your implementation from client view," and so on. As a result, for every class ever written, we faithfully create get/set method pairs for every private data field, create a default constructor, and so on.

Unfortunately, this is hardly what the original proponents of object-orientation had in mind. Merely forcing clients to go through a get method to get a reference to some internally held data structure doesn't create encapsulation; this has long been documented in such books as *Effective C++* [Meyers95] and, more recently, *Effective Java* [Bloch, Item 24]. More importantly, it unfortunately leads developers to think at a scale too small for effective reuse, that of objects and classes, rather than thinking at a larger scale, such as what was originally intended by the JavaBeans Specification.

Not convinced? Consider a traditional collection class, say, an `ArrayList`. We can use the `ArrayList` as an independent object, but when it comes time to walk over the contents of the collection itself, another object, an `Iterator`-implementing object, becomes desirable, if not outright necessary. Thinking about reuse at the class/object level means we seriously consider reusing the `Iterator`-implementing class independently of the `ArrayList` it's bound to, which makes no sense. Instead, because the two are intended to be used as a pair, it means that we're looking at reuse at a higher level, what we refer to as a *component*. In practical terms, this usually means a standalone `.jar` file that contains, in this case, the pair of classes for `ArrayList` and its internal `Iterator` subtype. In the `Collections` case, it would also include relevant interfaces like `Iterator`, `Collection`, and `List` because they all help define the contract clients can place faith in.

This gets us into a discussion of coupling. The definition of Tight Coupling states that a given "thing" is tightly coupled to another "thing" if one has to change in response to changes in the other. In other words, consider `ArrayList`—if I change the definition of the `Collection` interface, will `ArrayList` need to change? Absolutely, since it implements `Collection` through `List`. If I change `ArrayList`'s internal implementation, will its internal `Iterator` implementation need to change?

Absolutely. However, will clients need to change? Not so long as they treat the `Iterator` as a general-purpose `Iterator` (and don't downcast). `ArrayList` is tightly coupled to its internal `Iterator`, and vice versa, but clients can remain loosely coupled by sticking to the interfaces. (Loose coupling is explained in greater detail in Item 2, but I need to forward-reference it here.)

Don't see the relevance? Run on over to the servlet-based Web applications. If we obey the traditional Model-View-Controller abstraction,[1] then we're building a minimum of two classes that are more or less tightly coupled to one another: the controller servlet that does the input processing on an incoming HTTP request, and the view JSP that it forwards to. The controller needs to know what data elements the view depends on, the view needs to know what processing has already been done by the controller so as not to duplicate that work, and the two have to agree on the names under which the data elements the view depends on will be bound. (The name-value attributes of `HttpSession` provide late binding but not loose coupling; again, see Item 2 for more.) In addition, both controller and view are themselves tightly coupled against the model classes, since they will need to know what data elements are present as part of the model(s) used. Ask yourself these questions: Is it really feasible to consider reusing the controller without the corresponding view and/or model classes? Could the view execute successfully without going through the controller servlet first?

Because the answer to this question is almost universally "no," it means that your classes within a given component, in this case your presentation-layer component, are implicitly tightly coupled to one another. That in turn yields a realization: where tight coupling already exists, we can enjoy a certain amount of relaxation of the traditional "encapsulate everything" rule that we obey so mindlessly. I'm not suggesting that you immediately run out and remove all your get/set methods in favor of direct field access, but I recommend that you think long and hard about what you're *really* protecting against. For example, if your model objects aren't used outside of the presentation layer (note the terminology; see Item 3) itself, does it

---

1. This is actually a misnomer—the appropriate pattern in question is really the Presentation-Abstraction-Controller [POSA1, 145], since the Model-View-Controller deals with multiple views and their update simultaneously, such as is commonly found in a GUI application like Excel or Word.

really make sense to put get/set methods in front of each field, particularly where the model objects are just thin wrappers over a collection of data, as with Data Transfer Objects [Fowler, 401]. Remember that encapsulation was designed to protect clients against implementation changes, not the component against changes within itself. (Few developers ever saw benefits in trying to encapsulate a class against itself; think of the component as a larger, more coarse-grained class, and you're not too far off the mark.)

Given that we have classes that tightly cooperate with one another to achieve some useful work, and that those classes need to be deployed together atomically or else not at all, we're looking for something "larger than objects" as the principal unit of deployment: in other words, we're looking for components.

The Servlet Specification has moved away from the idea of standalone servlets being deployed individually into the servlet container and instead embraces the idea of a *Web application,* a collection of resources like servlets, JSPs, model classes, utility libraries, and static resources (like HTML, images, audio files, and so on) that collectively work together to provide desired functionality. The Web application is deployed collectively under a single .war file, so that there is no possible way for (a) only part of the application to be deployed, or (b) the application to be version-mismatched between its collective parts. In essence, the .war file serves the same purpose that the Java .jar file did in making Java application deployments easier; if you did Java in the 1.0 days, you'll remember the "unzip the classes onto your CLASSPATH" style of deployment and agree that trying to deploy Java applications in those days was less than elegant. Instead, the atomic deployment provided by the .war file means that only those resources that are supposed to be part of the Web application actually show up in the deployed application.

That is, unless you deliberately screw that up by doing partial file-based deployments by copying individual files over into the deployed application directory.

There's a couple of reasons why this is a Bad Idea, not the least of which is the possibility of introducing version mismatches. While it may seem tempting to "only copy the stuff that changed" into the deployment directory, it's too easy for humans to lose track of exactly what has changed and, more importantly, to forget that the servlet container doesn't necessarily take the same view of what has changed as we do.

Enter the `ClassLoader`. Remember him? He's established by the servlet container to load your Web application from disk into the JVM. The servlet container is required to start a new `ClassLoader` each time the Web application "changes," which usually means "changes on disk in the deployment directory." But if you read the Servlet Specification carefully, you'll notice that when a new `ClassLoader` is started, it's established over the entire Web application, not an individual servlet. It does this so that each of those classes that form the Web application are all loaded by the same `ClassLoader`, since the container sees these as a single component. So it's entirely conceivable that each file copied into the deployment directory will yield a new `ClassLoader` instance, creating a whole ton of extra work for the container and yielding no tangible benefit.

By the way, make sure you understand what tangible effects this Class-Loading policy will yield to you directly by reading Item 70.

The point of all this is that the Servlet (and other J2EE) specifications expect you to build Web applications that combine to form components, not individual classes. The JSP Specification goes one step further: it promotes the construction and use of smaller components within and across Web applications by fostering the concept of reusable tag libraries. The specifications could care less what objects you create and use, so long as those objects that are handed back to the container itself obey certain contracts, as conveyed via interfaces, and certain out-of-band restrictions described in the specification itself.

It's more than just implementing existing interfaces, however. Part of being a component means that because you didn't write `main`, you don't necessarily know the environment in which your code is being executed. One classic mistake that bites servlet developers the world over as they move from one servlet container to the next is the simple assumption regarding "the current directory"—for some servlet containers, it's the directory in which the container's executable files are located (`tomcat/ bin`, for example). For other containers, however, they set a "work" directory in which bits and pieces of the Web application are assembled and called. The net result is that if you try to load a text file from your Web application's deployment directory by creating a `FileInputStream` with an argument of `../webapps/myapp/data.xml`, what works on one system will horribly break on another. For this reason, the Servlet Specification suggests using either the `ServletContext.getResource` or `ServletContext.getResourceAsStream` methods, both of which are also available on the `ClassLoader` for the Web application.

In fact, this concept of "context" takes on an important meaning in component-based environments—the context, such as the `ServletContext` in servlet applications, or the enterprise bean context (`SessionContext`, `EntityContext`, or `MessageDrivenContext`) in EJB, is the component's official "window to the outside world," and any and all access to that outside world should take place through the context. This gives the container the opportunity to intercept and redirect application requests to the appropriate place, if the container is doing something tricky under the hood hidden from the code's view. For example, when you want to do a forward from a servlet to a JSP, you are required to go through the `ServletContext` to get a `RequestDispatcher` to do the actual forward because a clustering container may have decided to put the JSP page on a different machine than the one executing the servlet. As a result, if you were to directly try to access the servlet instance inside the JVM, such as we used to via the `getServlet` call, the request would fail miserably.

In some respects, this is also why the Java Naming and Directory Interface (JNDI) was invented—to provide a common API for looking up resources rather than having to use per-specification APIs such as that provided by the RMI `Naming` class. It's no accident that the JNDI starting point is called an `InitialContext`.

As may now be apparent to you, writing components is different from what you may have expected from application development. In fact, when writing components you're not doing application development at all; you're writing libraries that are being called by an existing application. Part of being a component instead of an application is that your code must take on the same kinds of characteristics that make writing libraries (again, as opposed to applications) so much fun. For example, in order to best promote individual component flexibility, it's usually better to define types exposed to the library client in terms of interfaces, rather than actual concrete objects [Bloch, Item 16], particularly since that enables your components to provide an interesting "hook point" (see Item 6) for future use. Of course, in large measure this is already true for building components directly accessed by the J2EE container, such as servlets (remember `javax.servlet.Servlet`?) and EJBs (`javax.ejb.Session Bean`, `javax.ejb.EntityBean`, and `javax.ejb.MessageDrivenBean`). But this can also be true for your own domain classes, such as your

`HttpSession`-bound model objects, for the same reasons. Toward this end, you'll also want to pay careful attention to how clients construct your domain objects [Bloch, Item 1], whether you permit others to inherit from your domain objects [Bloch, Item 15], and what kinds of types you hand back from your components [Bloch, Item 34].

One important realization from this is the fact that J2EE components, with very little exception, are entirely passive entities; in other words, J2EE components must borrow a logical thread of control from the container in order to carry out any meaningful work. This notion of the logical thread of control, usually expressed as an actual thread itself (in other words, the container calls into your code using a thread that it created, usually in response to an end-user request somewhere back up the chain), is often called an *activity* or *causality*, and it means that you shouldn't write components that expect to do anything too obsessive with that borrowed thread—don't go off and calculate pi to the hundredth digit, for example—because the container expects to get that logical thread of control back at some point. If it doesn't, it could very well consider that your component has hung and decide to unload your component instance entirely.

This creates a bit of a quandary within the J2EE Specification because frequently tasks can't be accomplished in any reasonable fashion except by having a thread under personal control. Classic examples are the desire to poll some external resource every *n* seconds, to perform some kind of maintenance or nightly operation at midnight every night, and so on. This functionality is coming as part of the EJB 2.1 Specification in the form of the Timer Service, but for those working with containers that predate that specification, no standard J2EE solution exists, except to write a standalone application that calls into the container via HTTP request, EJB session bean call, or JMS message queue delivery, thereby giving the container that logical thread of control.

Ultimately, again, the key characterization of the J2EE application is its component-centric nature, and as a J2EE developer, you have to play into that model yourself. Failure to do so means swimming upstream against the decisions established by the J2EE container, and in many cases this results in a large amount of code that contradicts the policies established by the container; while you may be able to get away with it in today's version of the container, don't be surprised if tomorrow's version suddenly breaks your code. Instead, go with the current by embracing the component concept, and where you need to escape the container for some reason, do so by writing a standalone daemon process or application.

Item 2:   Prefer loose coupling across component boundaries

Loose coupling, like so many other terms in our world, is at once familiar and foreign—familiar in that we all know it's a goal we should be striving for, foreign in that we're not quite certain what loosely coupled code looks like. The fact that many programmers refer to code written by using Reflection (the `java.lang.reflect` libraries) as being "loosely coupled" code doesn't help matters. Before we get too far, we need to draw the distinction between tightly coupled, late-bound, and loosely coupled code.

To repeat our Definition of Tight Coupling from Item 1: a given "thing" is tightly coupled to another "thing" if one has to change in response to changes in the other.

Tightly coupled code is code that intrinsically depends on whatever it's using, whether that use be through a method call or a more rigorous protocol. For example, consider the following code:

```
Person p = new Person();
int age = p.getAge();
```

This code is tightly coupled to the definition of the `Person` type, in that if `Person` changes such that `getAge` changes its signature, our client code will break and will need editing and recompilation. Similarly, the Servlet API is tightly coupled to the HTTP protocol specification: if HTTP ever changes its rules, the Servlet API (at least the `javax.servlet.http` package) will need to change with it.

It's not quite as easy as that, though—the presence of an API (methods to call and such) doesn't necessarily indicate the presence or lack of tight coupling. Again, some have suggested that the following code is loosely coupled code, by virtue of the fact that the `Person` type and its `getAge` method never really appear directly in the code—therefore, the compiler won't complain if the `getAge` method on the `Person` type changes signature.

```
Class c = Person.class;
Object o = c.newInstance();
```

```
Method m = c.getMethod("getAge", new Class[] { });
int age =
   ((Integer)(m.invoke(o, new Object[] { })).getIntValue();
```

Unfortunately, even though we're not *syntactically bound* to the signature of the `Person` type, we're still *semantically bound*, in that this code will fail miserably if the `getAge` method, taking no parameters, does not exist or is not accessible on the `Class` object referenced by c. Worse yet, the error won't be caught until runtime, rather than at compile time, meaning that if you don't have a really good set of unit- or integration-test suites running to catch these errors, you're just begging to be embarrassed at the worst possible moment. This is not loosely coupled code. In point of fact, this is *loosely bound* code, meaning the method calls, or more technically the bindings behind them, aren't resolved until runtime. (This is why Java's dynamic method invocation mechanism is sometimes called *late-bound*—you don't know which method you invoke in an inheritance hierarchy of types until runtime, when you know the exact object you're working with.)

One way to think about loose coupling is to ask yourself if you're truly ignorant of what the "other party" is really doing. For example, JNDI uses a generic mechanism to convey initialization settings to the `Initial Context` (if it can't infer them from system properties) by asking for a `Hashtable` or `Properties` object to be passed in to the constructor—in other words, a simple collection of name-value pairs. From there, the `InitialContext` will look at the keys and values in that name-value tuple collection and figure out where to go next. This is so that you, as a programmer, don't need to worry about "keeping up" with all the possible configuration objects that JNDI Providers might require. JDBC operates in much the same way, using an arbitrary string to contain a "JDBC URL" that conveys all of that information.

Unfortunately, in this particular case, we're not *really* decoupled from the JNDI layer—if you don't hand in the exactly correct strings as part of the `Hashtable`, JNDI throws exceptions at best or silently accepts the strings and then fails with `NamingExceptions` when you try to do `lookup` calls later. It's up to you to hand in an object whose values match what the JNDI Providers are expecting—and you don't get any help from the compiler to make sure it's all correct. Once again, we're back in a loosely bound rather than loosely coupled scenario; if the Provider were to change its specific settings, our code would break.

Back up a second, though—what, precisely, is *wrong* with tight coupling?

In itself, nothing. Tight coupling permits a measure of efficiency in both the development and execution of code that can't be matched by loosely coupled code. Consider the Reflection-based example, above, and all the possible things that could go wrong in the execution. In fact, the code as written won't even compile because there are about a half-dozen different checked exceptions that need to be handled in those four lines that I've blithely ignored in the interest of keeping the code sample down to less than a page in size. None of those exceptions require handling in the first snippet because the compiler can, by virtue of the tight coupling of caller against target, ensure that everything's good long before we execute this code. And, as a result, the just-in-time (JIT) compiler can do a tremendous amount of work to make the call to the `getAge` method as efficient as possible.

In fact, to a certain degree, tight coupling is not only desirable but also absolutely necessary, such as within component boundaries. To create an `Iterator` that can navigate across a `Collection` without intrinsic awareness of the `Collection`'s implementation is a terribly difficult thing to do as well as a waste of your time and mine. I care only about the `Iterator`'s interface, not its implementation—so long as you write your `Iterator` implementation to obey the implicit contract defined by the `Iterator` interface, I can use it without worrying about how it works. In other words, I can remain loosely coupled to your implementation (of both the `Iterator` and the `Collection` itself, in fact) by sticking to the established contracts defined by the interfaces.

See how hard this is to nail down? No Reflection necessary, yet we're more protected against change than the Reflection-based code was.

Enterprise systems have a particular need for loose coupling due to the nature of the beast: enterprise systems are, by definition, systems that need to access and be accessed by other systems, both inside and outside of the company. While you might be able to control, for the first release, all the points of possible choice within the system, such as the client browser, by the time the second release is on the way, you'll find you're missing that exact level of control you used to have. Components tend to version independently of one another—that's what they're intended to do, as a matter of fact—and as a result, trying to keep a tightly coupled relationship when one side changes and the other can't is a great recipe for an early heart attack.

Put it in concrete perspective. Imagine that you've created a domain logic layer—whether exposed via EJBs, WSDL, or POJOs (plain old Java objects, as coined by Martin Fowler and company), the example still works in any case—that demands you pass three parameters to a `paySalary` method: a `Person`, an `Account`, and a `comment`. In Java interface definitions, this would probably look something like this:

```
public interface MyBusinessLogicInterface
{
  public void paySalary(Person p, Account a, String comment);
}
```

For the first release, everything's peachy, and several other departments get wind of the usefulness of your system and write clients to call in to pay employee salaries. Success!

After the initial euphoria, however, you find that changes need to be made. In particular, you need to take an additional parameter, the total amount the person should be paid, since some employees (contractors, perhaps, or other hourly workers) have a variable amount they're paid at each payday. How do you change this without breaking your clients?

Some have suggested that a new interface could be created, call it `MyBusinessLogicInterface2` or `MyBusinessLogicInterfaceEx`, which inherits from the old interface and provides the new `paySalary` method with the overloaded signature. Clients that want the new interface will explicitly look for it; those that want to stick with the old functionality will continue to use the old interface. Never mind that you'll have to be very careful to avoid duplicating common code in the implementation of these two methods if they're in two separate beans—after about the third or fourth revision, you're going to start running out of names: `MyBusinessLogicInterfaceEx3` is *not* an intuitive interface name. Think about any new partners who want to use the system, confronted with five interfaces that all seem to be identical in nature: What differentiates the most recent one from the previous four versions?

And please don't suggest that refactoring is the answer. Refactoring implicitly assumes that you control both ends of the spectrum, the caller and the recipient side. You can't arbitrarily force your clients to change their code, or you will be a very unpopular person after you tell them. Refactoring *within* a properly encapsulated component is absolutely your business—refactoring *across* component boundaries is almost always a Really Bad Idea unless all parties involved agree to it.

One approach would be to do as many legacy systems already do: subvert that `comment` field to your purposes by passing the additional parameter inside of it. In fact, you might even be tempted to use it as a mini hook point, passing the additional data inside the `comment` field for the recipient to parse out and process as necessary. "If the comment starts with 'amount,' then parse in all the digits you find until you reach the first semicolon. . . ." If this sounds like a good way to build maintainable, scalable code to you, please put down the book and check into the nearest mental health facility.

The problem here is that RPC-style interfaces, while convenient and easy to build (there's that efficiency argument again), create really brittle contracts that can't tolerate much change in the system. Anything that changes the contract between client and server requires new deployment to both sides, creating a ripple effect that can usually be found all across the enterprise. It's even possible that you won't be permitted to deploy the new code if it breaks too many (or too visible to upper management or the outside world) client systems.

One way to avoid the tightly coupled nature of remote components is to prefer data-driven interfaces rather than behavior-driven ones (messaging versus RPC, essentially), as described in Item 19. Critics will argue that this breaks the object-oriented nature of the component, but, as described in Item 5, that's not necessarily a Bad Thing. Keeping communications context-complete (as described in Item 18) will also help promote loose coupling.

For local components, it's less of an issue to be data-focused or context-complete because the cost of making local method calls is far less expensive than in the remote case. For example, the Servlet Specification can safely establish a `Context` object between the Web application and the container as a way to keep the container and component at arm's length from one another; for example, I don't have to assume anything about the container's deployment model if I can ask the `Context` for a file resource relative to my component (`getResource` and `getResource AsStream`).

The late U.S. Supreme Court Justice Potter Stewart once said that he couldn't define pornography, "But I know it when I see it."[2] In many respects, loose coupling is the same. It's not a clear distinction that follows a set of precise rules; it's more of a philosophical and stylistic approach. Usually it's pretty easy to spot systems that were tightly coupled—they're the ones that, after a few years, nobody wants to work on and everybody wants to rewrite from scratch. The goal is clear: to allow previously unrelated systems to interoperate with a minimum of technology adjustment on the part of any one system or program. You'll know you've reached a loosely coupled component state when another project/department/company can start using your components without having to worry about how you're doing what you do, sometimes even across technology boundaries. Or, from the opposite angle, with a loosely coupled component, you can completely change your implementation (perhaps moving from Java to .NET or vice versa) without clients being aware of the shift.

Item 3:   Differentiate layers from tiers

Anybody remember client/server systems? This was the dominant architectural style for enterprise applications in the previous decade and for years occupied a place in developer consciousness that was second only to object-orientation. Vendors offered toolchains that eased the construction of forms-based (and later GUI-based) programs that hid much of the grungy details of relational database access behind convenient programming constructs, and all seemed right with the world.

As time went on, however, we found a couple of problems with client/server systems.

The first problem was that of resource management. We found that client/server systems had an intrinsic flaw in their architecture that limited the scalability of the system to the highest number of connections the server could maintain at one time. Considering that most clients didn't use their individual connection more than (on average) 5% of the total

---

2. From *Jacobellis v. Ohio*, 378 U.S. 184, 197 (1964), as quoted at http://caselaw.lp.findlaw.com/scripts/getcase.pl?court=US&vol=378&invol=184.

time they held the connection open, it made sense to come up with some way for one client to "borrow" a connection from another client that wasn't using it.

The second problem came from developers. We found fairly quickly that enterprise systems are more than just dialogs and data, and that the rules surrounding the data (validation rules, for example), what we now call the domain logic, were often coded in the client half of the client/server system. The danger in doing so, as any good J2EE book will tell you, is that making updates to those rules requires a new deployment of the client program, which is difficult to do smoothly as the number of clients grows, particularly if new database changes need to be deployed at the same time. We found that if we could keep domain logic out of the code that goes onto the client system, we could minimize the number of client-side deployments needed.

At the same time, however, the only other place to put the domain logic in a client/server system is in the server half, and doing so meant writing code that was vendor-specific in some fashion. If the "server" was a trans-actional processing system like Tuxedo, then it meant writing code that was linked and compiled against Tuxedo libraries; if we were running clients against a relational database directly, then it meant that the domain logic was thus encoded in database-specific triggers and stored procedures. The concern at the time, which persists to this day, was that of vendor lock-in (despite the fact that few companies ever actually had to deal with this), in that porting your code to another RDBMS or middle-ware vendor would require actual work, rather than just a redeployment. (This drive to avoid vendor lock-in represents one of the great Holy Grails of our industry, and as with most Holy Grails, it is entirely impos-sible to achieve in a lossless manner; see Item 11.)

At first, both problems seemed solvable by placing an intermediary machine between the client and the server. We could host domain logic, written in some kind of standard form, in this intermediary, and clients thus could call into the domain logic in the intermediary, rather than storing it in the client itself. This results in a lower deployment cost, what we often refer to as a *Zero Deployment scenario,* since new domain logic only needs to be deployed to the intermediary, rather than every user's client machine. This also results in cleaner modularization of the code-base, since changes in the domain logic can not only remain cleanly partitioned away from the actual code needed to generate the display but also ensure that domain logic is centralized within the codebase, making maintenance easier and ensuring that the logic is consistently applied.

At the same time, if this domain logic is hosted in the intermediary, we can do resource management in a much easier fashion—the intermediary itself can manage database interaction, for example, thus sharing connections to the database across a much larger number of client requests. This amortizes the cost of the connection across more than one client, reducing the overall impact n clients have on the system, thus making it feasible to increase the upper boundary on the number of concurrent clients the system can support. (In fact, it becomes a question of how many clients the intermediary can support, and the total number grows substantially if we can have more than one intermediary talking to the server—this is the ubiquitous *clustering scenario* so frequently discussed.)

You know all this; why am I mentioning it now? Because there were two reasons for that intermediary, what J2EE refers to as the *application server tier*, and you need to recognize that at least one of those reasons has no particular need to require an intermediate machine in place.

One of the facets of Java that first gathered excitement in the development community is its inherent portability (to anywhere there's a JVM). Remember, our first experiments with Java occurred in the area of applets and the idea of mobile code—back then, we were thinking about shipping applets via Web browsers. The point, however, is the same: by changing the code stored on the server, we can silently distribute it to the client on any subsequent request. Without a doubt, applets had their drawbacks, but this intrinsic portability wasn't one of them. In short, Java code can migrate across the network in a pretty opaque fashion, thus providing a solution for pushing changes out to the client without requiring human intervention, whether through mechanisms like the applet, Java Network Launch Protocol (JNLP), URLClassLoader, and others. (See Item 51 for more details.)

Certainly, for the resource management and database connection pooling aspects, we can't really help but have some kind of intermediate machine in place—we need a "gather point" where we can throttle and coalesce client requests into a single funnel. But think about the traditional browser-servlet container-database flow, and count the number of machines in place. Although we don't normally think of it this way, the servlet container is, in many respects, that intermediate machine, coalescing client requests (HTTP, in this case) against the database. When combined with a JDBC driver that natively supports database connection pooling, we've already neatly achieved the goal of resource management without the need for an EJB server, which helps us keep EJB out of the picture for anything but transactional processing (see Item 9).

It's not like we can put all of our domain logic into the middle tier anyway; many domain-driven services, such as validation, need to be done at the client and/or at the server. Consider for a moment a Web application that chose to centralize all—and I do mean all—of its domain logic into its middle tier. This would mean that every form submission would have to make the round-trip back to the Web server (and possibly from there to the EJB container, if that's where the domain logic is implemented) to verify that the user entered a phone number correctly, thus earning one (or two) round-trips across the network and the commensurate cost in performance (see Item 17). Most of us would scoff at missing out on such an obvious case where JavaScript could do the same kind of validation without having to take the network hit. Consider this, though: another form of validation occurs when storing that data into the relational database, since the data needs to obey the relational database integrity constraints in order to be stored without complaint. The database schema, even when enforced by the validation rules in the presentation layer, is as much a part of your domain logic as the code you write by hand.

The point is that a real difference exists between *layers*, different parts of the software codebase that each cover a key responsibility, and *tiers*, physical machines in the network topography, and that we shouldn't confuse the two. Yes, frequently layers will map to a given tier, such as the database tier and the data layer, but simply assuming that one-to-one pairing as a given eliminates a wide variety of architectural possibilities that can have powerful performance and scalability ramifications, most notably in avoiding excessive time on the network stack between any two (or more) machines (see Item 17).

Consider the benefits when this distinction becomes clear. Take the ubiquitous order-tracking system, for example. The company's salespeople use the system to place orders from various customers, and the orders are passed to the shipping department to send out to the customers when the order is ready. Now consider Joe, a salesman who runs the order system off his laptop—if this is a traditional three-tier HTML-based application,

Joe needs a network connection in order to place an order. If Joe's out on the golf course with a CEO who's ready to buy, Joe's not going to be happy about waiting until he gets back to the office to place the order. If this is a million-dollar order, neither Joe nor upper management will be happy; Rule Number One of sales is to never give the customer a chance to change his or her mind. (This is why some are talking about "smart client" front ends; see Item 51.)

If, on the other hand, we design the system such that the presentation layer, domain logic layer, and parts of the data management layer are hosted on the client tier, and the rest of the data management layer stretches across the client tier, intermediaries (through some kind of Type 3 JDBC Network driver), and server tier, Joe can run the application entirely disconnected from the network, caching the data locally until the network connection becomes available for update against the centralized database (see Item 44). This idea becomes particularly powerful when we put messaging brokers on the client tier, in order to store messages locally until the network becomes available for delivery.

When thinking about your application architecture, make sure to delineate the various layers of your system (presentation, domain logic, and data management) from the traditional tiers in the network topology (client, intermediaries, and server) in order to find the best "sweet spot" between centralization and the cost of communication. Most importantly, never make the mistake of assuming presentation layers always go on the client, domain logic always goes on the intermediaries, and data management always goes on the server. It may turn out that doing so is the best architecture, but make that decision consciously, not as a matter of habit.

Item 4: Keep data and processors close together

It's a simple idea, but one that shows up time and again in a variety of guises and forms: when you want to work with something, keep it close to you so you don't have to go chasing all over the network to find it. This is why CPUs have on-chip cache, why video cards come with their own memory, and why performance experts suggest caching in your application as a way to speed up its processing.

In many respects, this is just another expression of Item 17 since there's really no intrinsic problem with keeping data in its permanent home (in

J2EE applications, typically the remote database), except that it costs so much to reach across the network to fetch that data every time we want to work with it. If round-trips were free, we wouldn't need to cache data. But they're not, so we do. We also need to make sure that caches don't get so big that they cause any sort of `OutOfMemoryErrors` (see Item 74). By the way, local and/or in-process databases (see Item 44) are also a great place to keep cached data.

Sometimes, however, the data can't come to you. One frequent reason is that doing so would require locks against the database for far longer than is desirable. This is part of the problem behind accessing entity beans even from a Session Facade [Alur/Crupi/Malks, 341], since the entity bean lives in the EJB container. As Item 23 discusses in more detail, passing data in bulk takes care of moving the data from the client to the EJB layer in a relatively inexpensive fashion, but the data still needs to be migrated from the database layer to the EJB container and back.

So, when the data cannot move to the processing, move the processing close to the data.

If you think about it, this is much of the stated reason for using a middleware technology in the first place: by placing the business logic on the server (and not the client), the middleware system could keep data close to the processing associated with it. Granted, those justifications were originally used for TP Monitors, but much of the current EJB product literature implies it: "Take full advantage of our product's caching" and so on. Unfortunately, as we've already discussed, since the data still has to end up stored in the relational database behind the EJB container, we're still looking at additional round-trips to put it there, and again, those round-trips don't come for free. (Note that in the scenario where the EJB container offers it, developers can flip a vendor-specific "exclusivity" bit to tell the EJB system that it is the sole owner of the database, and the EJB system now can cache and locally hold data as much as it wishes, thus avoiding a few round-trips. You lose vendor neutrality—see Item 11— when you do this, but sometimes the gain is worth the cost.)

You can keep data and processing close together in a number of other ways; one such way is to make use of every bit of the SQL language available to you. For example, if you need to calculate the average age of all people in the system whose last name is "Nelson," effectively you have two options: (1) either in a session bean or in your client code, pull all `Person` objects in the database with the last name equal to "Nelson" across to the client/session bean, do the calculation yourself, and return the results, or (2) let the relational database do the work by using the SQL-92 AVG function by executing SELECT AVG(age) FROM person WHERE last-name='Nelson'. This will return a single row containing a single column, a numeric value containing the average age of all the Nelsons in the database. In other words, all the calculations have been done on the server, where it was trivial to examine all of the rows in the database that met the predicate criteria, and no additional round-trips were required.

As another example, it's not uncommon to see newsgroups and mailing lists littered with a frequently asked question, "How can I know the number of rows in a ResultSet?" The short answer is, "You can't—there's no getRowCount function on ResultSet." Usually another response comes in to suggest that if you use a JDBC 2.x driver that supports scrollable ResultSet objects (see Item 49)—"You can move to the end of the ResultSet and see which row you're on"—but this has the unfortunate side effect of either pulling all the data across the wire or forcing the database to navigate to the end of the ResultSet on its side and send back that window of data to you. A better answer is to use SELECT COUNT() on your WHERE predicate first, before doing the actual SELECT for the data:

```
Statement s = . . .; // get the Statement from the usual
                     // places
ResultSet rs_count =
  s.executeQuery("SELECT COUNT(*) FROM person " +
              "WHERE last_name='Nelson'");
if (rs_count.next() == false)
{
  // Something went horribly wrong
}
int count = rs_count.getInt(1);

ResultSet rs =
  s.executeQuery("SELECT * FROM person
              WHERE last_name='Nelson'");
for (int i=0; i<count; i++)
{
```

```
// . . .
}
```

There is one small race condition—unless protected by a transaction, there is a small window of opportunity for another client to modify the contents of the `Person` table, thereby making the count incorrect. Either accept that the count could be off, or bracket the two statements with a transaction; either way, despite the transaction lock, this approach will yield better scalability than pulling all of the data across simply to count the number of rows, particularly if you end up not needing anything beyond the first set, such as in search results.

Functions such as COUNT, SUM, and others are sometimes called *aggregate functions* because they operate across a subset of the data in the table, producing an aggregate result based on that subset. In addition, thanks to the power of SQL's closure (see Item 41), these aggregate functions can be used over any relational result, such as views or nested SELECT statements. SQL-92 and its later cousin, SQL-99 or SQL 3, require a number of simple aggregate functions, such as COUNT, SUM, AVG, MIN, and MAX, all of which do exactly as you would expect, and a number of database products also offer vendor-specific hooks to introduce your own aggregate function capability. Many database vendors go well beyond this; for example, Microsoft SQL Server offers the ability to create a table whose definition includes a column that is in fact the result of a user-defined function:

```
-- SQL Server syntax; other databases provide something
-- similar

--
-- SQL Server syntax for creating a user-defined function
--
CREATE FUNCTION ConcatName(@LHS nchar(80), @RHS nchar(80) )
RETURNS nchar(161)
AS
BEGIN
    RETURN ( @LHS + ' ' + @RHS )
END

--
-- Create a table that defines a column that
-- uses the above function
```

```
--
CREATE TABLE Person
(
  ID int PRIMARY KEY,
  first_name nchar(80),
  last_name nchar(80),
  age int,
  full_name AS
  (
    dbo.ConcatName(first_name, last_name)
  )
)
```

When retrieving values from this table using a SELECT statement, SQL Server will call the ConcatName function to create the columnar data returned for full_name; this means that we can get the full names of all persons in the database whose last name is "Nelson" simply by executing this code:

```
SELECT full_name FROM person WHERE last_name='Nelson';
--
-- Assuming we have rows:
-- Row 1: 1, "Steve", "Nelson", 40, (ConcatName())
-- Row 2: 2, "Lori", "Nelson", 25, (ConcatName())
-- Row 3: 3, "Kirsten", "Nelson", 12, (ConcatName())
-- Row 4: 4, "Marnie", "Nelson", 7, (ConcatName())
--
-- Then the query above returns
-- "Steve Nelson","Lori Nelson","Kirsten Nelson","Marnie
-- Nelson"
```

Again, all of the processing is done on the server, so no additional work client-side is necessary. Contrast that with how the corresponding logic in the session bean would look, compound that with the fact that a session bean doing this concatenation on an entity bean would implicitly make round-trips to the database to obtain the first_name and last_name fields, and you start to see where this becomes so powerful. The drawback here, of course, is that this is horribly vendor-specific and thus a severe hindrance if you're concerned about portability across database products (see Item 11).

In fact, the ultimate expression of Item 4 is to use database stored procedures to do the processing—since the data lives in the database, and processing frequently is more complex than what can be expressed via an aggregate function or vendor extension, a stored procedure offers the ability to do a full procedural, step-by-step massaging of data before returning the results or modifying the data in the database. Stored procedures have two major flaws associated with them, however: they're written in a language other than Java (thus forcing you to learn a new language), and they're not portable to other database systems. Fortunately, help may be on the way here—as part of the SQL/J Specification effort, the various database vendors hope to standardize the use of Java in stored procedures, much as many of the "big name" database vendors, such as Oracle and IBM, have already done. This would address both problems, but seeing that in practical form could be years off. (On the other hand, depending on how complex your stored procedures are, porting them from one vendor's dialect to another may not be all that onerous.)

Ultimately, whether you cache data close to the processors or move the processing closer to the data, keep these two as closely bound as possible within your architecture, so as to minimize the amount of traffic that has to take place when processing occurs and to avoid the cost of moving that data across the network (see Item 44).

Item 5: Remember that identity breeds contention

Most programmers agree that an object is a unification of state (data) and behavior (methods), but there's a third element to any object-based or object-oriented language, too, and in many respects, this mysterious third element is what makes the object world go 'round. Look at the following code:

```java
public class Person
{
  private int age = 18;
  private String name;

  public Person(String n, int a) { name = n; age = a; }
  public void happyBirthday() { ++age; }
}
```

```
Person p1 = new Person("Cathi", 29);
Person p2 = new Person("Alan", 35);
p2.happyBirthday();
```

When finished, how old is Alan? Or, more accurately, what is the age of the object referenced by p2? Alan is 36, of course. So how does Java know how to differentiate the object named "Cathi" from the object named "Alan" and keep the ages straight?

It's not a trick question—even most inexperienced Java programmers can usually get this one right. The trick lies in the implicit this parameter that's a part of every object, that uniquely references the object in question. Former C++ programmers even go so far as to say that this is in fact a pointer to the object in memory, and since no two objects can occupy the same place in memory, the address of the object therefore makes it unique. (Java programmers, of course, know that there's no such thing as a pointer, despite the presence of the NullPointerException class in their language, and wish C++ programmers would just stop pretending otherwise.)

In truth, an object is made up of three things: state, behavior, and *identity*. Identity allows the Java language and platform to differentiate between the previous code and the following, where p3 and p4 both refer to the same unique object:

```
Person p3 = new Person("Stephanie", 10);
Person p4 = p3;

p3.happyBirthday();
  // How old is the Stephanie object at this point?
```

It seems like a pretty brain-dead concept, but stick with me.

Identity is fairly easy to spot in objects, but it appears elsewhere in a standard enterprise system, too. Given the following lines, where is the identity?

```
INSERT INTO person ("Cathi", 29);
INSERT INTO person ("Alan", 35);
INSERT INTO person ("Stephanie", 10);
```

Even without seeing the schema, we know that the relational database preserves a sense of identity because even those tables that lack a defined primary key can still differentiate between one row and the next—the database preserves the actual row's identity using some implementation-dependent scheme. (In Oracle, this is a silent column called the ROWID, for example.) Regardless of mechanism, it serves much the same purpose as the this pointer in C++ or Java, to provide a sense of identity. It allows us to write SQL expressions like the following and see that Cathi is now 30:

```
UPDATE person SET (age = age+1) WHERE name="Cathi";
SELECT name, age FROM person;
```

So why the concern? Objects have identity, rows have identity, what's the big deal?

One basic pillar of traditional object-oriented design has always been that abstract problem domain entities should map to a single object—in other words, that if we're representing Cathi with an object in the heap, then all references to Cathi should be done through references that refer to that same, individual object. Failure to do so can break code if we're not careful:

```
Person p1 = new Person("Cathi", 29);
Person p2 = new Person("Cathi", 29);
p2.happyBirthday();
  // So how old is Cathi?
```

In many respects, this is why the distinction between the == operator, which performs a test for identity, and the equals method, which performs a test for equivalence, is so crucial to Java programming, as shown here:

```
if (p1 == p2)
  System.out.println("It's the same object!");
if (p1.equals(p2))
  System.out.println("It's equivalent, but not identical.");
```

So thus far, we're still OK.

In fact, this concept of identity is so fundamental to our notions of how systems should be designed that we tend to mimic it in distributed object systems; fortunately, it's trivial to do given the mechanics of RMI (or CORBA, for that matter):

```
PersonManager pm = (PersonManager)
  Naming.lookup("rmi://localhost/PersonManager");
```

```
Person p1 = pm.findPerson("Cathi");
Person p2 = pm.findPerson("Cathi");
p1.happyBirthday();
   // Thanks to distributed object identity,
   // we have logical identity
```

When the RMI lookup occurs, we pull back some kind of "lookup" manager for `Person` objects, what in the EJB space is a `Home`, and subsequent lookups return remote stubs to the solitary object that lives on the server. So calling through `p1` to increment Cathi's age also implicitly does the same for `p2`, since they both reference the same *logical* object. (Remember that `p1` and `p2` are technically references to separate proxy objects, but since the proxy objects—the stubs—point to the same object on the server, they're logically the same object. This is why the remote stubs are carefully written to return `true` if you call `p1.equals(p2)`.)

In other words, identity in a distributed system is not just a function of memory addresses and logical mapping of behavior and state; in a distributed system, identity includes the hardware on which the object itself lives. And, to paraphrase the old Robert Frost poem, that makes all the difference in the world.

Consider the remote `PersonManager/Person` code again, this time with an eye toward identity as a factor of the machine on which the objects live. We presume that `PersonManager` can construct objects only on the local machine, so where, then, will each and every `Person` object reside? On the same machine as the `PersonManager`, of course, meaning that as the system scales up to include massive numbers of `Person` instances, we're intrinsically limited to the maximum work supported by that single machine. No matter how many additional machines we throw into the cluster, we can never have more `Person` objects in use at once than the one machine can support.

Worse, we run into the problem that we'll need to build in some kind of synchronization support to make sure that two accessors don't modify values concurrently and corrupt the data. After all, if an object has identity, it's possible that more than one client will want or need access to it simultaneously with another client. Locks mean that concurrent access by clients is impossible—that's what the locks are intended to prevent—which gets us to the lock window discussion of Item 29.

It's a simple observation: scalable access to a single shared object is impossible. If the contention inside the object's implementation doesn't kill you, and we haven't reached the implicit limit of work the underlying server can handle, the fact that it's a round-trip to the object in the first place (see Item 17) usually will. It begins to become more clear why Martin Fowler says that distributed object systems "suck like an inverted hurricane" [Fowler, 87].

Proponents of EJB are already getting ready to debunk this: "But in EJB, we have all sorts of enhancements to take care of this problem—passivation, for example." That's true, as long as some objects aren't in use by clients at the moment. Passivation works much like virtual memory at the operating system level—so much so that some have suggested that passivation should be tossed away in favor of just letting the operating system do it—and suffers from much the same flaws. If you have 100 clients, each of which is making active use of 100 objects, that's 10,000 objects that logically should remain active and unpassivated. But if the server's heuristics say that only 5,000 objects can remain active and the server passivates the other 5,000, then the server's going to spend a phenomenal amount of time in activation/passivation thrashing, just as your operating system does when you exceed physical memory. Forcing massive numbers of page faults (or activation and passivation of EJB objects) is a *really* quick way to kill performance.

The EJB proponents aren't finished: "But what about clustering? We can spread those objects around the network rather than host them on a single system." This presumes several things. For one, clients will want roughly evenly spread access to those objects; if any one object receives more than its fair share of attention from clients, then we're constrained once again to the maximum capacity for work of the system on which that singular object lives. (This is the danger of the Remote Singleton, by the way—regardless of how deeply you optimize your synchronization implementation in order to avoid holding locks longer than necessary—see Item 29—you'll always be constrained by the underlying remoting and/or networking plumbing.)

So where, exactly, does identity fit in the context of EJB?

In many ways, attempts to build identity-based systems in EJB will run into a brick wall. *EJB's understanding of identity is to rely on external forms of identity*—via the client or the external representation of the data in the database, for example—and *not* to rely on the commonplace identity mechanism we're so comfortable with in Java. This is why, for example, as an EJB programmer you can't assume that a request from one particular client will end up on the same actual object instance in memory. EJB explicitly throws away identity at the object layer, in order to preserve identity at the client or data layer. This is why an EJB container is so free to pool object instances. (This is also why attempts to build a Singleton in EJB are so painfully difficult—Singletons rely on object identity, and EJB takes object identity away from you.)

Stateless session beans are implicitly without identity. In fact, stateless session beans probably should have been called "anonymous session beans" because, while they can in certain circumstances maintain state, you can't be certain that you're invoking a method on the same bean instance you invoked last time—hence, they have no identity. This has led many pundits to call the stateful session bean the best horse to ride of those in the EJB stable because its implicit lack of identity allows the best scalability. (This isn't necessarily true, by the way, as some tests run by Mike Clark, of *Bitter EJB* fame [Tate/Clark/Lee/Lindskey], prove.)

Stateful session beans are objects whose identity is known (initially) only to the client that created them. Note that a stateful session bean isn't exclusive to that client—if you pass the handle to a different client, that second client can invoke methods on the same stateful session bean instance. As long as only one client accesses the bean, however, its identity remains a nonissue because little to no contention arises out of it. Interestingly, the EJB Specification requires that the EJB server implement a synchronization mechanism that prevents concurrent access of the entire bean instance by more than the client; unless the client makes multi-threaded access to the instance, this is unlikely. In essence, the synchronization on a stateful session bean effectively adds to the latency of the bean call itself; because the specification requires the container to throw an exception back to the caller in the event of concurrent access to the stateful session bean (EJB Specification, Section 7.12.10), at a minimum the container needs to check that there's not already a call in progress.

Transactional COM+ [Ewald] points out two interesting properties of the object-per-client model. First, if there is one object for each client accessing the system, then the number of objects in existence reflects the number of clients currently accessing the system; if objects are shared across clients, this information isn't easily available. Second, maintaining per-client state is much simpler because each object itself inherently acts as a cookie identifying the client, rather than relying on some external mechanism. So in general, it's best if stateful session beans aren't shared across clients (which further undermines the need for session beans to be synchronized in a per-instance fashion).

We really run into problems with entity beans because not only does an entity bean have identity, but that identity is well-known across the entire system, and thus each entity bean acts as a Remote Singleton. This is a necessary design—remember, the entity bean instance is trying to represent an entity in the system, and entities implicitly have identity, of the row in the database they represent,[3] if not an actual, physical thing. This means that if multiple clients need access to a single entity, they're all working against the same logical object. It also implies that at any given point, *two* identities need to be maintained: the identity of the entity bean object and the identity of the row in the database.

An entity bean (or other object-first persistence mechanism) can take two basic approaches to avoid the identity problem.

1. *Preserve the entity bean's identity, and try to cache like mad.* Unfortunately, the EJB Specification works against the entity in this case, since the specification clearly calls for transactional semantics around the bean's access—remember, the specification demands that should the EJB server crash, the entity's state *must* be preserved, and if the server tries to save on a round-trip or two by caching the data in memory, then it runs the risk that the process could die before the cache can be flushed. (This approach can't work for local entity beans, by the way, since local entities *must* be accessed within the same JVM; if the local bean in turn is a remote proxy to a remote entity bean, we've sort of lost the whole point of the local bean, haven't we?)

2. *Break the identity of the entity bean itself, choosing to define identity in terms of type, rather than object,* thus relying instead on the underlying database to hold identity. This essentially makes the entity bean an anonymous object that passes any state-manipulation logic directly to the database. (This is essentially the approach that Ewald

---

3. I should be more careful with my language here, since technically entity beans aren't required to be persistent to a relational database. (At a conference back in 1998 I heard the various OODBMS vendors raise a royal ruckus over the explicit phrase "an entity bean represents a row in your database" that appeared in the EJB 1.0 Specification.) Nevertheless, 99.5% of the world's entity beans are tied to an RDBMS, so I'll continue to use that assumption.

recommends, albeit for COM+.) This allows the server to create as many entity beans as necessary across the cluster, thus spreading the load of even the most highly accessed entity. Unfortunately, this means that caching is very unlikely, since the cache itself will have to have some kind of identity, meaning it's a singular place to which all the otherwise anonymous objects must come in order to exchange updates, and that in turn gets us back to the identity bottleneck. More interestingly, this effectively reduces the entity bean to a stateless session bean that has some SQL generated for it (in the case of Container-Managed Persistence (CMP) entities).

It's fair to ask at this point what, if anything, we gain from moving identity away from the objects themselves and into the database. It's simple: we gain the ability to move logic off the database and into a separate layer that can, if desired or necessary, run on a separate tier from the database or the client. It's not going to remove the possibility (eventuality, more likely) of a bottleneck within the database, but it will buy you a lot more room before you hit that ceiling. The process of removing just enough of the bottlenecks in a system to meet your throughput needs (which you clearly identified, per Item 8, right?) is the essence of scalable system design.

In the end, we can't eliminate identity completely from the system. Even if we could, it would be counterproductive to do so—after all, the data elements we want to work with have to be identifiable, otherwise we would be unable to tell one Customer from another. The trick is to recognize what forms of identity are acceptable, and where identity, and the necessary locking that has to accompany it, can be avoided. Get that right, and you're well on your way to a highly scalable architecture.

Item 6: Use hook points to inject optimizations, customizations, or new functionality

Almost every system, whether J2EE-oriented in nature or not, provides a number of "hook points" by which developers can "hook" into standard processing and influence what happens next. Within the servlet stack, for example, filters represent the most obvious hook point, allowing servlet developers the opportunity to block, redirect, or modify any incoming HTTP request or outgoing HTTP response. You can use filters to implement compression of the HTTP body, encryption of parts or all of the content, or any other authentication and/or authorization requests ladled into the HTTP message exchange.

Another such hook point presents itself within the RMI stack, via the custom socket factories that can be plugged into the RMI client and/or server. Secure RMI exchange can be added simply by replacing the standard socket factory objects with customized ones that force transmission over SSL/TLS sockets instead of the standard TCP/IP socket. In an all-Windows network, RMI could even use a custom socket factory to exchange data over a (faster) customized Windows named-pipe channel, for example, instead of TCP/IP entirely.

In each of these cases, *a hook point is used to add new behavior without requiring any client code changes; the additional processing is added at some point in the standard processing chain.* This additional processing can take many forms, either by providing an opportunity to pass some kind of out-of-band data, such as security context established from one tier and passed to another, or by consulting an external resource for shortcut processing (such as a cache for previously obtained immutable data, or perhaps an optimizer to rearrange SQL statements in optimal form), and so on. For example, the Java Data Objects Specification explicitly provides callers with the ability to pass a vendor-specific query to the JDO `PersistenceManager`, thus allowing the clients that wish to take advantage of proprietary vendor-value-added features (see Item 11 for why you might want to do this) to do so.

A classic way to provide a hook point is to use the Interception pattern [POSA2, 109]. After hearing how the J2EE containers make use of interception to add all this behavior around your code, interception may seem a deep, dark, mysterious secret that only programmers who are part of the Cult of the Container Implementor can understand. Rubbish. Interception isn't reserved exclusively for J2EE's own use. Starting with the JDK 1.3 release, Java provides *dynamic proxies*, which allow a programmer to build an anonymous object that implements an interface and wraps around another object implementing that same interface, thus receiving the calls bound for that original proxied object and providing additional behavior.

To put that into English, dynamic proxies permit you to write interceptors around normal Java objects, as long as they're referenced through interfaces.

For example, presume we're back to figuring out how we can add some diagnostic-logging behavior into code without requiring massive code changes all over the codebase. Instead of more exotic code-weaving mechanisms, we could capture this in a first-class concept using dynamic proxies in front of any object that exposes itself via a Java interface:

```java
public LoggingProxy
  implements InvocationHandler
{
  public static Object
    newLoggingProxyAround(Logger logger, Object obj)
  {
    return Proxy.newProxyInstance(
      obj.getClass().getClassLoader(),
      obj.getClass().getInterfaces(),
      new LoggingProxy(logger, obj));
  }

  private Object proxiedObject;
  private Logger logger;

  private LoggingProxy(Logger l, Object obj)
  {
    logger = l;
    proxiedObject = obj;
  }

  public Object invoke(Object proxy,
                       Method m, Object[] args)
    throws Throwable
  {
    Object result;
    try
    {
      l.info("Entering method " + m.getName());
      result = m.invoke(proxiedObject, args);
    }
    catch (Exception x)
    {
```

```
      l.warn("Unexpected exception " + x + " invoking "
          + m.getName());
      throw x;
    }
    finally
    {
      l.info("Exiting method " + m.getName());
    }
    return result;
  }
}
```

A `LoggingProxy` will thus wrap any object it is constructed around (using the `newLoggingProxyAround` factory method call) and write diagnostic messages for every method call that comes in through that interface. Using it would look something like the following:

```
public interface Person
{
  public String getFirstName();
  public void setFirstName(String value);

  public String getLastName();
  public void setLastName(String value);

  public int getAge();
  public void setAge(int value);
}


public class PersonImpl
  implements Person
{
  // other details omitted for brevity

  private String fname;
  private String lname;
  private int age;

  public String getFirstName() { return fname; }
  public void setFirstName(String value) { fname = value; }
```

```
    public String getLastName() { return lname; }
    public void setLastName(String value) { lname = value; }

    public int getAge() { return age; }
    public void setAge(int value) { age = value; }
}

public class PersonManager
{
    public Logger personLogger = ...; // some Logger instance
    public boolean loggingEnabled = false;
        // Set to "true" to turn on logging on objects

    public static Person
        getPerson(String firstName, String lastName)
    {
        Person p = new PersonImpl();
            // get Person from someplace; in a real system, we
            // would obviously do a database lookup or something
            // similar here
            //

        if (loggingEnabled)
            p = (Person)
                LoggingProxy.newLoggingProxyAround(personLogger, p);

        return p;
    }
}
```

To put this into words, when the static `PersonManager.getPerson` method is invoked, we'll go through the work of digging the appropriate person's data out of the database (or wherever it happens to be stored) and dump it into a concrete class representative of the domain object for `Person` instances. We do it through a static factory method [Bloch, Item 1], however, rather than a constructor, because we want to go one extra step of indirection from the client in constructing the object.

Remember, the point of all this was to get some diagnostic logging behavior "laced in" inside the objects in question. Since we can't (or rather, don't want) to modify the actual bytecode itself, we just want to spit out a diagnostic logging message at the start and end of each call we make. So we'll present an interceptor object in front of the actual `PersonImpl` object; the interceptor will keep a reference to the `PersonImpl` and forward all calls it receives on to the `PersonImpl`, but only after spitting out the diagnostic logging message.

The beauty of this approach is that regardless of the actual object type on the other side of the `LoggingProxy`, the method interception approach still works. The key is that the proxy requires all calls to the proxied object (the `PersonImpl` in this example) to go through an interface rather than a concrete class—this is why `PersonManager` returns a `Person`, as opposed to a `PersonImpl`. Better yet, there is no structural compile-time relationship between the `Person` implementation and the act of logging. Instead, it can be turned on or off at will, simply by changing the value of the `loggingEnabled` flag, which is presumably a hot-configured configuration item (see Item 13).

By building components instead of objects (see Item 1), we can make use of interceptors in whatever desired fashion to provide the behavior desired without changing any domain-specific or client-facing code. Use interfaces to define what clients will see outside of the component, use public static factory methods to provide construction facilities, and hide the actual object implementation returned behind one—or more—dynamic proxies that provide the desired crosscutting functionality. As a bonus, we get loose coupling (see Item 2) for free, too, since implementation can change without clients knowing or caring.

Not all hook points within the J2EE family of specifications are Interceptors [POSA2, 109], however. For example, the Serialization Specification (see Item 71) represents another such hook point within a J2EE system, since J2EE itself makes use of Serialization in a number of places, including marshaling of RMI method call parameters and (frequently, although this isn't a mandatory part of the specification) as a passivation mechanism for stateful EJB objects like stateful session beans and entity beans. In fact, for most normal Data Transfer Objects [Fowler, 401], the default Serialization logic is overkill, since most Data Transfer Objects don't require deep inheritance hierarchies or have extensive object references. Thus, for Data Transfer Objects that are used frequently, it might behoove you to replace the standard Serialization behavior by writing something extremely fast and customized for that particular Data Transfer Object—but only after profiling and determining that marshaling of this particular Data Transfer Object is a bottleneck in the communications stack (see Item 10).

While not all hook points within a system are defined as Interceptors, many of them are, owing to the passive client-oriented nature of J2EE systems in general (see Item 1). For example, the Java API for XML RPC (JAX-RPC) Specification, the Java side of WSDL-specified Web Services, defines Interceptors as `Handler`-implementing classes that are able to inspect SOAP packets coming back and forth between incoming requests and the outgoing responses. This permits developers to write vendor-neutral extensions to process new SOAP headers, such as those defined by WS-Security and/or WS-Routing, without having to change endpoint code itself. This will be particularly important as we begin to use EJB beans as Web Service endpoints, since your particular J2EE/EJB container may not support the latest-and-greatest WS- specification you're looking for.

It's unfortunate that one of the most widely known specifications in the J2EE family, the EJB Specification, provides no vendor-independent interception mechanism. This is a large part of at least one vendor's widespread popularity, since it exposes, in a vendor-specific fashion, a rich and powerful interception-oriented stack. Hopefully this can be corrected in future versions of the EJB Specification.

Item 7: Be robust in the face of failure

Every developer must squarely face the brutal fact that "stuff happens"—not only will code have bugs, but databases will run out of disk space, routers will go down, the power will go out (and the UPS will expire before it can come back on), servers will be hacked, and "absolutely safe" operating system patches will turn out to be anything but. Notice the very carefully chosen verbiage here: not "can" fail, but "will" fail.

In some circles, the term *defensive programming* comes to mind, the idea of never assuming that callers will in fact call your methods correctly, so you assert on every parameter, validate every return value, and so on, assuming that every caller of your method is pathological and wants to break the code. I don't necessarily subscribe to that particular mind-set;

I believe that most of the time, code within the component can be trusted to "follow the rules," but any call coming from outside the component (including user input in the case of a servlet/JSP) definitely needs to be validated six ways from Sunday before being passed on and processed. But it's more than just asserting every parameter.

At a microcosmic level, this means that *when writing code, you need to think about all possible failure scenarios:* what happens if the call to the EJB container throws a RemoteException, meaning the RMI plumbing had a problem satisfying the request, or the database throws a SQLException, or the parameters passed in to your session bean aren't within acceptable bounds? It's not just a matter of catching the exception and putting up a "something went wrong" message to the user—some kind of reasonable failure-recovery policy must be in place. For example, if the database throws a SQLException, is it because the SQL was malformed, or because the database didn't respond? If it's the former, it's probably OK to just tell the user something went wrong and try again; if it's the latter, it might be better to put the system into a kind of panic mode until the database can be reached again. At the very least, the system administrators need to be notified that the database was out for some period of time.

Part of thinking about failure in code means handling Java exceptions correctly.

First problem: we all know that any remote method called from an exported, remote object in Java RMI is capable of throwing a java.rmi.RemoteException; it's one of those things that RMI developers over the years have come to despise about RMI. It's actually a pity because a tremendous amount of information comes bundled in a Remote Exception, most of which is completely ignored when you write code like this:

```
try
{
  remoteObject.someRemoteMethod();
}
catch (RemoteException remEx)
{
  System.err.println("Error in calling RMI method!");
    // Beats the heck out of me what went wrong, but that's
    // OK, I logged it to the console, right? Besides, this
```

```
    // is just to keep the compiler happy, it's not like a
    // remote call will ever fail or anything...
}
```

When the `RemoteException` is thrown, all of the diagnostics carried as part of the exception are completely ignored. Was it a problem on the client, on the server, in between? Was the object you tried to call suddenly inaccessible? Was it a problem in marshaling, indicating that somehow the stubs and skeletons are out of sync? Or is it perhaps that the server specified in the lookup doesn't exist or can't be found, probably a failure of the TCP/IP stack?

For example, the `ConnectException` indicates that the client had difficulties finding the servant object on the server for some reason—assuming the underlying TCP/IP stack is still good (you can ping the other machine), this usually indicates the servant object is no longer available, usually because of a crash. This is not to be confused with the `NoSuch ObjectException`, which is most often thrown when the client holds an old reference to a servant object that no longer exists despite the stub's insistence that it should.

Catching the proper RMI exception can offer up a world of diagnostic information to the system administrator and/or support staff (that's often you, by the way) about what exactly went wrong where. Take a harder look at the RMI exceptions defined in the various `java.rmi.*` packages next time you've got a few moments between marathon coding sessions, and write catch handlers that react appropriately to each kind of RMI exception. (Bear in mind, too, that if you're working with a vendor-proprietary protocol stack, like BEA's T3 protocol, there may be new and/or different exceptions thrown there, too, and you'll want, if not need, to take a look at those as well.)

It's not just RMI that suffers from this programmer sloppiness syndrome of "catch the base class exception," either—JDBC frequently sees developers catching just `SQLException`, ignoring the exception itself, and doing some kind of super-generic error-handling code, like writing to a log file. Once again, while the JDBC Specification itself doesn't define a large taxonomy of possible exception types like RMI does, it does note that vendors are encouraged to do so for their own purposes, and in fact many do. Or, alternatively, the `SQLException` type defines a place for vendor-specific product error codes, which can in turn offer up much greater detail about what just went wrong. In addition, the SQLException type defines a "next exception" property, allowing SQLException instances to chain on top of one another as the need permits. When's the last time you actually reported this information to anybody but a log file? Considering that many system administrators also know something about database products, it might not be a bad idea to have specific error-handling logic for dealing with the common problems expressed by vendor product error codes.

Oh, and by the way, when's the last time you checked for SQLWarning instances on a Connection, Statement, or ResultSet? Or do you, like 99.9% of the other JDBC programmers out there, simply ignore their existence?

Inside of servlets and JSPs, in particular, exception-handling policies become particularly important, since the last thing you'll want is for your end users to see a stack trace when some unexpected error gets tossed out of your JSP. (This is important not only from a public-relations perspective but also from a security perspective—it's amazing how much information a single stack trace conveys about the architecture and general structure of a system, information that an attacker can put to effective use.) This means that every one of your JSP pages should have its error Page directive set, pointing either to a specific error page for that particular part of the application or else to a generic page that presents a message like "We're not sure what just happened, but we logged it, e-mailed the support staff, and automatically logged a $5 discount coupon in your name, so please don't hold it against us and try again, OK?" This also means that every one of your top-level servlets (i.e., servlets that were directly invoked by user actions, as opposed to servlets to which you chained from a different servlet) and filters must be wrapped in try/catch blocks that handle all possible exception scenarios—that means catching Throwable, by the way, not just ServletException. (J2EE 1.4—i.e., Servlet 2.4 and JSP 2.0—provide some container-managed error-handling facilities that can mitigate some of this; use them when you can.)

EJB, too, requires some careful exception-handling consideration. This time, however, it's not what goes on inside the bean that requires such sensitivity but how clients should react to exceptions thrown out of the bean. For example, we know that throwing an exception out of a Required-marked transactional bean method means that the transaction is implicitly rolled back, but what happens to the bean itself? Is the bean still good? Can we make further method calls on the bean to ascertain what, exactly, went wrong with that last call?

The EJB Specification draws a distinct difference between *application exceptions* (those exceptions that are domain-specific and inherit from neither `RuntimeException` nor `RemoteException`) and *system exceptions* (those that represent errors at a level below that of the application domain itself, such as underlying problems connecting to the database and such), and defines a new exception type, the `EJBException` class, which inherits from `RuntimeException` and stands as a kind of system exception wrapper.

When an exception is allowed to leave the call generated by an EJB interceptor, the EJB container takes some drastically different action based on the kind of exception thrown. When an application exception is thrown out of a transactional method, the container figures that the client needs to see the actual domain invariant that was violated and rethrows the exception back to the client. In this situation, the transaction itself is left alone, giving the client a chance to recover from the error scenario.

In the case of a system exception, the container is not nearly so forgiving—since the state of the bean itself is no longer certain (after all, an unexpected `NullPointerException` does wonders to reduce the stability of your code), the container rolls back the transaction and marks the bean instance as bad, thus forcing the container to discard it entirely. Now, depending on whether the caller is the "root caller" of the causality, the client will see either a returned `TransactionRolledBackException` or `TransactionRolledBackLocalException`, or else a `RemoteException` or `EJBException`. The situation gets even more interesting when we consider the Web Service endpoint behavior as described by EJB 2.1, since now we can't even pass an exception object back across the wire—instead, the client's going to have to suffice with a standard `SOAP:Fault` code, which can be pretty unspecific unless you know what's coming back and code your client accordingly.

(By the way, some J2EE books mention that you need to force your application exception types to implement `java.io.Serializable` because these exceptions will be carried across the network; as it turns out, you don't need to worry about this. The base `Throwable` class, ultimate ancestor of anything throwable in general, already implements the `Serializable` interface.)

But it's more than just thinking about code. *Enterprise applications have much more stringent uptime requirements than just about any other form of software* (with obvious exceptions, like embedded software controllers in airplanes and nuclear reactors, for example). At an architectural level, we need to think about failure scenarios at a more macrocosmic level: What happens if the database server goes down entirely? What happens if the EJB container does?

The J2EE vendors, in fact, will tell you that you don't need to worry about this because their feature-filled, incredibly-expensive-but-worth-it container will provide all sorts of fault-tolerance and failover capabilities for you. As much as I, more than anybody, would love to buy into that, the brutal truth is that the vendors don't—and can't—provide a complete, covered-from-every-angle sort of failure-recovery policy.

For example, take a simple scenario. In a Web application's servlet controllers (see Item 53), frequently the servlet needs to access parameters submitted by the HTTP request in order to figure out what programmatic action to take, even what JSP to forward to for output. What happens if that parameter isn't there, or isn't what's expected? If you're using session state to hold user-transient state, what happens when a user bookmarks a page deep inside the page flow, expecting to be able to come back to it tomorrow?

We also have to face the fact that despite our best efforts, despite how much time we spend trying to predict and prepare for every failure scenario, failures we never anticipated will still happen. None of us are perfect, and the possibility of bugs, missed use cases, or weird combinations of user actions leading to unpredictable behavior exists. Because we can't prevent those situations, we need to have a plan in mind for how to react to them: how to fix corrupt data, how to deploy a fix to the production environment (ideally without forcing a restart of the container or reboot of the server), even how to apply vendor patches to your servlet or EJB container to fix a vendor bug you've discovered.

As a corollary, however, once you read Item 60, you'll also realize that *in addition to "failing robustly," you also need to "fail securely"*—in other words, don't accidentally hand out information (like the complete stack traces in a servlet-based front end) that attackers can use to gain entry to the system. Make sure that any failures are reported (and in fact verified) and that repeated failures are brought to an administrator's attention somehow; repeated failures are often a sign that an attack is taking place.

Any and/or all of these things will happen to you. To stick your head in the sand and pretend otherwise, or to believe for even a moment that "those are things the system administrators have to worry about, not me" is a recipe for a very long night, struggling to figure out how to do all of the things mentioned above but without the luxury of time or experimentation. Don't sign yourself up for this sort of abuse unless you really like the idea of interviewing a lot.

Item 8: Define your performance and scalability goals

An ancient proverb holds that the journey of a thousand miles begins with a single step. That's not precisely true. The journey of a thousand miles begins with a single step and a destination; otherwise, it becomes a journey of two or three thousand miles, assuming it ever actually ends.

Developers are fastidious in dealing with customers and analysts when it comes to wanting to nail down exact requirements for the features and functionality of a given application. Field validation, use cases, class structure diagrams—all of these and more will be carefully and painstakingly ironed out into a document that stretches hundreds of pages long, yet nobody ever stops to ask, "Exactly how fast should this thing be?" And yet, this becomes one of the classic user complaints regarding a painstakingly architected application: "It's too slow." This of course brings back the immediate response, "Well, buy faster hardware."

The conversation deteriorates pretty quickly at that point.

The problem is that we developers need to know precisely what target we're aiming at if we're expected to hit it with any degree of success. Just as we need to know what the features must look like, how the pages must flow, and how the shopping cart must behave in the event of a VIP customer placing a $150 order over a holiday weekend, we need to know how fast the application has to be if we're to meet user expectations.

Unfortunately, this is easier said than done. Users speak in plain, simple terms: "It needs to be faster. It's too slow. It takes forever." As sympathetic as we may be to these sorts of reactions (c'mon, we've all felt the same way, sitting there impatiently at the Web browser, waiting for Amazon.com or some other Web site to finally respond), they don't give us much to go on. What we need is something quantifiable, rather than just gut-level intuition that, more often than not, doesn't exactly match up with what our users say they want.

What makes it worse is that the very things we need to identify and quantify are notoriously difficult to nail down. Terms like *performance, scalability*, and *capacity* get tossed around together in the marketing bowl to produce a stew that's wonderfully attractive but hideously difficult to identify. Popular myth holds that the terms *performance* and *scalability*, if not precisely synonymous, are close enough that improving one will quite naturally improve the other. What's good for performance must be good for scalability as well, right?

Not only do *performance* and *scalability* mean two very different things, but improvements to one often hurt the other. Other books may use different terminology, but for the purposes of this book, we'll define these and related terms as follows.

- *Performance:* Performance, to put it simply, is how quickly the system can respond to a given logical operation from a given individual user. If it takes so long for each page of the application to load when a user is ordering a product online that he or she gets frustrated and purchases the product from a competitor's site instead, obviously the performance of the application is less than optimal. The goal of a well-performing architecture is to achieve lower *latency* (the amount of time the system requires to respond to a user's request) so as to keep usability and the user's interest in the application high.
- *Scalability:* If performance measures the responsiveness of a system for a single user scenario, a "vertical" measurement, then scalability represents its polar opposite: the responsiveness of the system as more and more users enter the system concurrently. The goal of a scalable architecture is to achieve higher *throughput* (the number of logical operations that the system can process within a specific period of time: operations per second, if you will) as client demand grows, simply by taking advantage of additional hardware without redesign.
- *Response time:* This is a measure of the amount of time the system consumes while processing a user request. While frequently applied to the time consumed to respond to a user interface action (clicking a button, selecting a menu item, opening a window, and so forth), response time can also be used in a more granular fashion, as the amount of time consumed by a particular API call or system action

(such as processing a SQL call). Response time is made up of three things: latency, wait time, and service time.

- *Latency:* This is the amount of time spent processing overhead just to get to the point of carrying out a business action—it is the overhead associated with the system as a whole. Systems with high latency frequently fail because too much time is spent processing overhead and not enough processing actual work.
- *Wait time:* The time spent waiting for the server, or, once the server is executing, the time spent waiting for resources.
- *Service time:* The time needed to process the request when no waiting is involved.
- *Throughput:* This term describes a measurement of how much work can be done for a given period of time, such as transactions per second or bytes per second. Measuring throughput is typically a business-domain action because the concept of a business transaction can vary wildly among systems; most often, we discuss it in more abstract terms, simply as "you can achieve higher throughput by minimizing contention."
- *Load:* The current volume of work on the system, its load, can be measured in a variety of units, from coarse-grained (number of users currently using the system) to fine (bytes of memory consumed, CPU cycles used per second, and so on). Typically, load isn't measured in a vacuum—load is used as a baseline against which to measure some other statistic, such as throughput or response time: "When we see the server CPU pegged at anything less than 80% load, we get a response time of around 2 or 3 seconds; when it gets higher than that, however, the response time degrades pretty rapidly, to around 30 or 40 seconds at 90% load."
- *Concurrent load:* This term describes the load at any given moment. Load, for example, can be the total number of users a given system can support, where concurrent load describes the number of users that can be supported at a given moment. A servlet engine, for example, may have enough memory to hold 10,000 user sessions in memory before crumpling (load) but may accept only up to 2,000 simultaneous network connections (concurrent load).
- *Capacity:* This is the total load and/or concurrent load a given machine/system can handle before being "maxed out."

Frequently, optimizing a system for one of these will in turn help optimize for the other—for example, minimizing contention for resources will not only improve the application's scalability but also lower its latency (since now the system spends less time waiting for locks to be released). However, it's also possible to add enhancements to the system that benefit performance at the expense of scalability or vice versa.

For example, a developer may look at the current performance of a system and decide that it's running too slowly. He decides that the system is making too many trips to the database and that the solution is to cache data in the application server so as to eliminate network I/O if he can. (His first mistake is making this decision without consulting a profiler first; see Item 10.) So he writes a generalized caching mechanism, spends a month fine-tuning the cache algorithm, and starts caching data in the application server. Cue credits, we all go home happy, right?

Unfortunately, no—the story's not that simple. Because many people access the system all at once, the cache needs to be somewhat "global" in order to hold data for all of these users. And if the data has changed, we need to hold all the users at bay while we update the cache with the new data. The developer has perhaps improved *performance* by adding the cache but has also introduced a new contention point—access to the cache for data—and therefore hurt *scalability*. In some extreme cases, depending on usage and the synchronization policy of the cache lock, the time gained due to the removed I/O trip is more than lost due to the synchronization lock on the cache. Even worse, this cache-based implementation doesn't scale well; if the system later moves to run on clustered application servers, the cache must now be replicated across all of the nodes in the cluster, meaning that the system now takes *both* the latency hit of an additional I/O across the network (to check against the global cache) as well as the contention hit of the global cache lock.

Even if the cache has quite an efficient locking mechanism, such that the cost of checking the cache is zero (which will never happen, by the way), scalability is still affected: the cache now occupies memory on the machine, which in turn reduces the total number of concurrent clients that machine can process. The larger the cache, the fewer clients we can support; the smaller the cache, the less effective it becomes. (Sounds like the cache size should probably be hot-configurable; see Item 13.)

To be quite honest, *many of the performance problems in enterprise systems aren't, in fact, performance problems—they're scalability problems.* The system performs poorly because it's blocked waiting for access to some shared resource that everybody else needs, too. If the system does application-level audit logging to track users' actions in the system, and the developer simply uses the default isolation level (see Item 35 for details) when adding rows to the audit-log table, the database is taking out reader/writer locks on the table—meaning other writers are held at the gate, waiting for the one writer to finish before any others can get started. If we remove the unnecessary locking, the database pumps can add rows into the table much faster—thereby reducing the overall latency of the application.

The tradeoff in the caching example was one of performance for scalability. If the goal of the system is to minimize the response time for each particular user, even if that in turn reduces the capacity of the system, this was a successful step. If, however, the system needs to support as many concurrent users as possible, regardless of the response time for a particular user,[4] this was a terrible step to take and hurt the application's overall ability to meet its goals. So, in the final accounting, was this a successful optimization? That all depends on what the goals of the system are, and if those goals are never stated outright, as developers we'll never know which decisions to make.

At a practical level, this means a couple of things. First, make sure to optimize optimally (see Item 10) by ensuring you know which 20% of the operations and/or use cases your users are executing 80% of the time. Look for ways to ensure that the users' perceptions of the computer's activity are as short as possible. Note the peculiar phrasing of that last sentence; "the users' perceptions of the computer's activity" is the key here—use techniques and tricks to reduce the amount of time the user is physically unable to move on to the next task. Use multiple threads, use direct database access approaches, use whatever seems appropriate to minimize the user's sense of the system's performance. Find the hook points (see Item 6) that can provide the necessary optimizations if necessary. Or, in some cases, simply build a layer that moves the user out of the physical blocking call—spin off a thread, or post a message to a JMS `Queue` or `Topic` for further, asynchronous processing. Frequently, the solutions used here may not actually have an impact on *real* performance, but as long as the user feels it is fast enough, that's often good enough.

---

4. As with many things, most enterprise systems find themselves somewhere between these two extremes.

Performance and scalability are two obvious elements of importance in any enterprise system. Treat them as you would any other client feature request: document precisely what's meant by goals like "fast" and "acceptable performance" either through hard numbers or (more likely) some kind of reference point mutually acceptable to both developers and users: "It should have a user interface at least as fast as the system we're replacing." While that takes care of performance, nail down in concrete terms the expected loads and concurrent loads on the system; how many users are expected to use it during a 24-hour period, during a 1-hour period, and so on? Knowing these details at the start of the project will enable you to make better decisions about when to make the inevitable performance-against-scalability tradeoffs. Most importantly, though, having these goals explicitly stated tells you when you can *stop* performance-tuning, and that's just as important as knowing when to start.

Item 9: Restrict EJB to transactional processing

This flies in the face of over four years of advice and suggestions from almost the entirety of the Java and J2EE community, but the fact is that EJB is not the core of J2EE. It's not even the "first among equals" in the J2EE community, despite the large number of articles, books, and conference presentations on it. EJB is simply another way to go about building back-end infrastructure and should be seen in the same light as anything else: use it only if you need it.

EJB has been the *de facto* solution for anything in the J2EE space for several years now. Thanks to a combination of marketing hype and some really cool-sounding features, EJB became the latest technology to join the ranks of the "over-hyped and under-delivered," right alongside client/server, distributed objects, "push" communications, and UML modeling tools. Java programmers looked at using EJB on a project as a perk, something "cool" to put on their résumés, a mark of respect among other developers. Just as many years ago it was commonly held that "Nobody ever got fired for buying IBM," nobody ever got fired for suggesting EJB. After all, if performance on the project wasn't meeting your standards, your current EJB vendor was to blame, and you could just "swap out" the vendor for a better implementation (presumably a more expensive and thus obviously better one) that would solve all of your performance and/or scalability issues. What could be better, right?

The problem is that EJB has been sold on a promise that it simply can't deliver—it can't magically keep developers from making stupid mistakes or from having to think about underlying issues like ClassLoader *delegation trees, excessive network traffic, or lock contention.* To believe that your EJB container will somehow provide all this magic functionality is just wishful thinking.

Let's go back for just a moment to reexamine what EJB was supposed to deliver. In concrete terms, EJB was supposed to make building distributed systems simpler and easier, by creating a common set of services that could be used by components (written to follow a strict regimen of rules and restrictions), allowing developers to focus on the "core business" of the problem at hand. Containers were supposed to take on crosscutting concerns that show up in every enterprise software project: remoting, concurrency, persistence, object lifecycle management, transaction support, and so on. Couple this with the container vendors' promises to make it all perform well, scale out as far as you could ever want, provide fault tolerance and failover so developers could relax knowing the system had everything under control, *and* allow you to plug-and-play any vendor container into your back end based on your desired price-to-performance ratio (what's sometimes called "best of breed" purchasing), and you have a very high set of expectations. (It's a floor wax, and look! It's a dessert topping, too!)

To say that EJB failed at these expectations is somewhat anticlimactic. In particular, it failed on several points.

Part of the stated goal of the EJB Specification is to make building distributed systems simpler; this has not happened. If anything, EJB has created an entirely new branch of complexity that stretches far beyond anything else the Java community has produced this far. Complex things are still complex: witness the "ease" by which we can establish a simple one-to-n relationship between two entity beans using container-managed persistence. Or look at how "easy" it is to retrieve those bean instances—it involves the use of EJBQL, a language that's amazingly similar to but substantially less powerful than the language it's supposed to replace, SQL.

Worse yet, however, EJB makes simple things complex, too. Consider what has to be one of the simplest acts in an enterprise system: consulting a read-only table. Without EJB, the solution would be to create a simple class that scans the database for the data at startup and holds that data internally, never going back to the database again. Under EJB, however, there is no easy solution for this problem. If we create a CMP entity bean to hold the read-only data, the container will generate spurious and unnecessary calls back to the database to retrieve the data that hasn't changed (under transactions, no less). If we create a Bean-Managed Persistence (BMP) entity bean instead, the container will still make spurious and unnecessary calls to the bean's `ejbLoad` and `ejbStore` methods, except now we can trap those and do nothing. But you're back to writing SQL. To avoid the multiple store/load calls and/or trips to the database, we could read the data into a stateless session bean in its `ejbCreate` method and hand the data back when requested. It means holding multiple copies of the data, however, up to one per client (since session beans are tied to client identity—see Item 5). Ouch. As a result, J2EE "best practices" recommend going either directly against the database for read-only (or read-mostly) data, or else use BMP entity beans; either way, you're back to writing SQL by hand, which is pretty much what entity beans are trying to prevent, as described in Item 40.

It gets worse. Because an EJB component requires an EJB container to execute within (as do servlets), testing an EJB implementation is difficult to say the least. Where a plain old Java object can be tested in one of three different ways—via a unit-testing framework like JUnit, via an embedded `main` method, or via a simple test program that exercises some of the basic functionality of the component—an EJB component can be tested in a container only from outside the container, and as of this writing there are no "mock object" EJB containers that an EJB component can be tested within, as there are for servlets (like Cactus). This means that writing bulletproof EJB code, although certainly not difficult, is just that much harder.

Part of that difficulty comes because EJB deployment itself is an order of magnitude more difficult than anything else yet developed for Java. When deployed, an EJB container has a tremendous amount of work to do, and this means some of that work will bleed back onto you, the deployer. This means your production deployment (see Item 14) will be more complicated, plus your normal compile-test cycle suddenly got longer—now it's compile-deploy-test, and if that deployment step requires human intervention, it's going to be really hard to get developers to actually test their work. "Hey, if it compiles, it must be good, right? Besides, I hate deploying that thing. . . ."

EJB isn't the enterprise developer's dream come true; it is, however, a useful technology when viewed in a more realistic light. *The strength of the EJB Specification comes from its deep integration with the concept of transactional processing*, a role historically played by transaction-processing systems like Tuxedo. As a result, for doing transaction-processing work, EJB is pretty hard to beat; in particular, because the EJB container enjoys a tight relationship with distributed transaction controllers (DTCs), EJB is by far the best choice when working with multiple transactional resource managers, like multiple databases, JMS messaging systems, and/or `Connector` resource adapters.

With the 2.0 release, EJB also makes it much simpler to do asynchronous JMS message processing with the addition of the message-driven bean. While it's not all that difficult to create a JMS processing host (no more difficult than it is to create an RMI object host, in fact), using EJB to host message-driven beans, particularly if those beans want to execute under transactional semantics, makes a lot of sense. More importantly, however, writing a message-driven bean is quite probably the simplest part of the EJB Specification: write a single class that implements the `Message DrivenBean` interface, with no "remote" or "local" interfaces to worry about, just the deployment descriptor to describe the JMS `Destination` this bean should listen to, and the transactional affinity of the `onMessage` method (the sole non-EJB required method you have to implement). Coupled with the inherent flexibility messaging provides, an EJB container hosting nothing but message-driven beans makes a lot of sense and is scalable to boot.

In addition, many EJB vendor implementations offer extensions to make it simple to host RMI and/or CORBA object implementations, so while you may forgo the use of session, message-driven, and/or entity beans, don't necessarily throw the vendor's CD out the window just yet.

Again, the point here is that EJB provides a specific answer to a specific problem: providing transactionally aware middleware capabilities. To be more accurate, EJB provides distributed transactionally aware middleware, and if you're not going against multiple transactionally sensitive resource managers, it becomes difficult to see the real value proposition in using it.

Item 10: Never optimize without profiling first

The 80/20 rule, officially known as the Pareto Principle and one of the most famous (and most consistent) rules in computer science, states in its most common variation that 80% of a system's resources are used by about 20% of the code: 80% of the runtime is spent in 20% of the code, 80% of memory is used by some 20% of the code, and so on. The rule can be recursively applied to other aspects of the software development life-cycle as well—that 80% of the requirements document will cover only 20% of the necessary work, for example—but here the concern is focused on the 80/20 rule's application to software execution and engineering. This 80/20 rule has been repeatedly verified through examinations of countless machines, operating systems, applications, and enterprise systems; it's more than just a catchy phrase. The 80/20 rule is one of the few truisms about system performance that has both wide applicability and a solid empirical grounding.

Note that the numbers here are somewhat flexible, depending on your situation: your particular system may follow a split more like 90/10 or 70/30 for a given category than an 80/20 split. The point here isn't to focus on the actual numbers; the point is that the overall performance of your system is dependent on a *much* smaller percentage of the code than you might imagine at first.

As an enterprise system developer, striving to best enhance your system's performance and scalability, the 80/20 rule both simplifies and complicates your life. On the one hand, life is much simpler now—you can ignore most of the things you'd be tempted to do "to improve performance." Loop unrolling, using an array instead of a `Collection` class, manually inlining the code for a method call, all of these are optimizations that will yield benefits that are miniscule in nature; chances are 4 in 5 that this code *isn't* part of that core 20%. While it may feel strange to take that attitude, it will have the unintended benefit of keeping code somewhat clearer—more unreadable code is written in the name of performance than any other excuse. (After all, how many of us write crappy, illegible code just because we want to?)

Some people argue that the virtual machine is in a far better position to do that kind of optimization than the developer is because the JVM has the ability to perform method inlining, generate entirely different machine instructions based on usage patterns, and so on, but this is entirely JVM-specific and probably shouldn't be relied on if vendor neutrality is important to you and/or your organization (see Item 11).

The downside to the 80/20 rule, however, is that now it's up to us to find that 20% when performance problems do arise. You have to isolate and diagnose the 20% of the code that's being called 80% of the time, before you can tackle how to streamline it. What's the problem with this scenario? Most developers rely on their intuition (also known as "experience" or "the article I read the other day") to tell them where the bottlenecks and inefficiencies are. Developer after developer, when presented with a performance (or scalability) problem, will page randomly through screen after screen of code, then turn and with a solemn expression declare that the problem exists due to network delays, the JVM, the lack of aggressive optimization in the Java compiler, the operating system, or some bonehead manager's decision not to use EJB for this project. Quite frequently, the suggested solution centers around buying faster hardware, upgrading to the latest JDK, or rewriting the entire thing from scratch.

The problem with these pronouncements is that most developers' intuition sucks. Blind, random guesses often produce results similar to "experienced" developers' intuition. It's unfortunate, but the complex layers of interaction between the developer and the raw hardware mean that frequently the problem isn't where the developers' intuition leads them to believe it is. So if we can't trust our intuition, what can we trust?

Trust the system itself, of course; "Let the system tell you." Loosely translated, that means "run a profiler over the code."

Unfortunately, within the J2EE arena, this is easier said than done—Java profilers are barely mature, only really coming into usefulness in 2004. Worse yet, J2EE-based profiling is a difficult task, particularly since there are usually several machines involved. It's not *quite* impossible, just hard, to set up one Java profiler instance to run on the servlet container, another on the application server (if present) or any other Java-based middleware, and combine this with output from the database's own profiler tools and some network analysis tools to produce some good notions of where bottlenecks are occurring. With time, the J2EE profiler tools market will get stronger, and all-in-one profiling solutions will emerge to make this task simpler.

In the meantime, other tools offer much the same kind of data, and those tools are available right now.

First, and at the lowest level of the tools available, are the performance-monitoring tools available to your operating system, such as Performance Monitor (PerfMon) for Windows, or the /proc filesystem under Linux. While they can't tell you exactly how many Java objects are being created or how many classloads your JVM is being forced to undertake at startup, they can tell you equally important statistics like total memory footprint, the number of page swaps the process is going through as it uses the

Always Check The Profiler First

A VisualWorks (Smalltalk) customer was very concerned about the performance of their system. They were concerned that all the horror stories they heard about Smalltalk being too slow for real systems were true. It seemed that the fundamental section of their system was taking minutes to do anything, and they needed it to take seconds. They couldn't figure out what was taking so long no matter how hard they tried.

In a last-ditch effort to figure out whether their work could be salvaged, Dave Leibs, Smalltalk performance guru from ParcPlace Systems, Inc., was called in for a day of consulting. The customer quickly described an overview of what they were trying to do. Nothing stood out to Dave as anything that would bring Smalltalk to its knees. So, he said,

"Where did the profiler indicate most of the time was being spent?"

"What's the profiler?"

So he spent the next 30 minutes or so explaining what the profiler was and helping them install it.

He then ran the profiler on the section of code in question and found it was spending more than 98% of its time in `Date>>printOn:`. Dave thought for a second what might be so slow about `Date>>printOn:` and felt it should not cause so great a problem. So, he looked a little higher up the profile tree and examined the containing method.

He noticed the expression `'Date today printString'` inside of a loop. So he chose an Experiment and pulled the expression out of the loop, storing the value in a temporary variable that he then used inside the loop. Ten minutes after running the profiler for the first time, he ran the code again. This critical section of code that was central to the client's system now took less than a second.

Dave then turned to his hosts and said, "So, what are we going to do for the rest of the day?"[5]

virtual memory mechanisms available to it, and the number of threads being spawned.

For example, under PerfMon you can create counters that track not only the number of threads being spawned by the process but also the number

---

[5]. Quoted from an article written by Ken Auer of RoleModel Software and Kent Beck of Three Rivers Consulting; see http://www.rolemodelsoft.com/patterns/lazyopt.htm.

of context switches per thread and the amount of user, privileged (kernel), and processor time. This can be useful in tracking down threads blocked in native code inside the operating system, if your system happens to call into native code for some reason. The PerfMon Process counter allows you to track handle counts (a handle is roughly equivalent to a file descriptor in UNIX), thereby giving you a window into how many files and other kernel objects are being opened by the application server—a good way to track any "leaking" resources that aren't being finalized in a timely manner. The Process counter also tracks process Working Set and Working Set Peak sizes, giving you an operating system perspective as to how much memory the process consumes. This can be invaluable when choosing parameters to start the virtual machine itself (-Xms and -Xmx, for starters; see Item 68 for details). And the "Page faults/sec" statistic in the Process counter is also a good item to keep an eye on, since excessive numbers of page faults imply that your process is swapping to virtual memory a great deal and could be hurting performance terribly. (Determining what constitutes "excessive" numbers of page faults is always going to be a relative decision, however, and requires you to be vigilant about gathering a large statistical base before making any educated guesses about what's excessive and what's normal.)

PerfMon and most other operating system profilers also allow you to track these statistics over a long period of time, taking snapshots every *x* number of seconds, minutes, or hours, thus giving you the ability to examine the data over a long period of execution time. At the very least, set up these counters on your QA or development servers as soon as the application starts to get more routinely tested, so that by the time the application prepares for a production release, you can get a good idea of what's "normal" for this application. In addition, most profiling tools give you the ability to set alerts, so that if the application reaches beyond a certain threshold, system administrators can receive some kind of heads-up about a potential problem. For example, you can configure PerfMon to send a network message to a system administrator's machine whenever the thread count on the application server process or servlet container process broaches some magical value you set—typically a sign of either a malconfigured thread pool setting or an attempted denial-of-service attack that had better be dealt with pretty quickly. Best of all, this monitoring doesn't require any additional work on your part to use (see Item 12).

Don't ignore other operating system–specific tools, either. As much as Java and the JVM try to abstract away the underlying operating system, there are times when having a good view of what's going on underneath the JVM can be a powerful debugging and diagnostic tool. For example, a classic question that pops up on mailing lists is "When I run the servlet container as a standard process from the command line, everything works fine, but when I try to run it as a service under NT, nothing works. Now what?" The problem here is that most services, when installed, run as a lower-privileged account than you might expect (and this is a good thing—see Item 60), and as such don't have access to network file shares or may not have security rights to files on certain parts of the file system. Using ProcessExplorer or Filemon from Sysinternals.com can be a huge help here in diagnosing these kinds of problems. Similar tools exist in the Linux and other UNIX-based operating system spaces, either from the vendors themselves or from the open-source community—get to know them well before you need them.

Operating system profilers aren't your only option here, also—remember that in most enterprise IT applications, the other major player is the database itself, and keeping an eye on what's happening there can be just as instructive, if not more so, than watching the operating system process. Every major database ships with some kind of query analyzer or similar profiling and/or diagnostic tool, and it's definitely in your best interest to keep an eye on the database's execution behavior. Again, this falls into the "better to be comfortable with the tool before your project's life depends on it" category—far better to have profile traces running constantly on the production server *before* you get crushed with a burst load, so that any bottlenecks that might arise in such a situation can be identified quickly and dealt with.

The advantage of the database profiler tools is simple: they know only what the database knows and make no assumptions about what client tools are currently running. They can provide a powerful and useful view into what's being executed against your database—anything and everything ranging from SQL injection attack attempts (see Item 61) to badly generated CMP entity bean and/or JDO queries (see Item 50) will show up, along with the corresponding time required to execute each of those statements. It also serves as an important statistic when evaluating your application's execution performance—for example, if a given user request takes a full 60 seconds to execute in user time (from click to finished display results), knowing whether the database takes 5 seconds or 55 seconds makes a huge difference in where you start looking to optimize. More importantly, you can see exactly what's being executed against the database as part of that one user request—after all, it might not be any one particular query that's creating the bottleneck but the fact that you're running fifteen different "fast" queries, each from a different part of the code, that's creating the slowdown. And if you don't know what a full table scan is, somebody else on your team should; if not, it's time to crack open a good database profiling/optimization book.

Of course, nothing beats the ability to have a peek inside the JVM itself, and while this has historically been difficult due to a lack of a standard API across JVMs to provide profiling information—the Java Virtual Machine Profiler Interface (JVMPI), introduced in JDK 1.2.2, was never officially promoted beyond experimental status—two mitigating factors arise. First, JSR 174 (Monitoring and Management Specification for the JVM) will provide a number of Java Management Extensions (JMX) MBeans and SNMP MIBs over elements of the JVM itself, such as thread information, JIT compilation time, memory statistics, and other important JVM elements. Second, despite the current lack of a standardized API, a number of available commercial profilers provide most of the same information. Be careful with these commercial profilers, however—some of them require executing your Java code against their Sun-licensed-and-modified JVM implementation, which means that your execution could vary wildly on your production JVM—for example, the Sun 1.4.x JVM has seen some significant changes and enhancements just between 1.4.0 and 1.4.1. Other profilers gather their statistics by instrumenting your code (i.e., inserting additional bytecode into your compiled classes that gathers the profiling information desired), which can also throw off the profiling, in some cases significantly. A single-line method could be and usually is inlined by the JIT, but instrumentation inserted into that method could easily push the method out of the JIT compiler's heuristics for inlining, thus changing the performance of that method drastically.

Note that as part of JDK 1.5, Sun introduced a replacement for JVMPI and the debug equivalent—JVMDI—called the Java Virtual Machine Tools Interface (JVMTI), and this is expected to be the standard API for both profilers and debuggers. JDK 1.5 isn't scheduled to ship until late 2004, however, and even then, if it follows the same adoption patterns as its predecessors, it will be several years before it achieves widespread use.

Sun also makes a fairly low-level profiler tool available, called hprof, that will gather simple call-execution statistics over the lifetime of the JVM and dump them into a text file for you. While better than nothing, hprof output can be voluminous for J2EE applications, and it can be extremely difficult to sort out your application's execution path from that of the application server itself (assuming the application server is, as most are, written in Java). Still, it's better than making an "educated guess" or "intuitive decision."

You can always write your own "mini-profiler" against the JVMPI APIs directly, assuming you're comfortable with C++ and shared object libraries on your operating system. The JVMPI API is essentially a call-back-driven approach, where on startup you have the opportunity to register for certain events, such as object creation and/or destruction, classload and/or unload, thread start, stop, and wait, and so on. (This is not a path recommended for the faint of heart, however—be prepared to invest substantial time if you do this. It does permit you to be as specific and unobtrusive as possible about capturing only the data you're interested in, which for time-critical measurements could be an issue, but again, tread this road carefully.)

Regardless of the tools used, *make sure that the profiler has a fair chance to tell you what's going on within the system*—that means ensuring that the profiler isn't being misled by the data being fed through the system. When profiling, it's absolutely critical to run the system under normal load conditions, if possible, even if those conditions are artificially induced. Tools can be used to mock up client Web-browsing sessions. If your application uses a rich front end (see Item 51), focus on creating mock sessions against the middleware by instantiating client-side proxies directly and calling against the middleware. Remember that a profiler cannot tell you how your program behaves in general—it can only tell you how the program behaved on a given set of runs. Make sure the data the profiler sees is representative so it can tell you what parts are being executed 80% of the time, leaving you to focus on how to optimize those parts. And once you've identified the parts that need optimization, use the hook points (see Item 6) to bypass normal processing to put in the necessary optimizations.

Item 11: Recognize the cost of vendor neutrality

Just as Java holds portability (remember "Write Once, Run Anywhere"?) as a high priority, J2EE similarly holds vendor neutrality, or the ability to take a compiled J2EE application and run it within any vendor's J2EE container, as a high priority. Three of the eight stated goals in the front of the EJB Specification, for example, center on vendor neutrality. The Servlet Specification, the JSP Specification, JDBC, JMS—all explicitly mention the ability to take a compiled application and run it under any compliant vendor's container without modification as a design goal.

The question is, do you care?

Certainly, J2EE applications intended for resale as third-party components or standalone applications will want to embrace portability and vendor neutrality as much as possible, in order to maximize the potential client market. There's no sense in restricting an application to using the Oracle database, for example, if the application can be made database-neutral by avoiding Oracle-specific extensions and using only SQL-92 syntax. Doing so means clients who aren't currently using Oracle don't have to be convinced to buy it when you pitch them your application.

The fact remains, however, that far more often the J2EE application is an in-house system developed exclusively for use by a single company and/or subsidiaries and maybe a few business partners. The target platform—the hardware, the operating system, the database, and so on—is usually decided well in advance of the first line of code. As a result, there is usually little *need* for the system to be portable across platforms/containers/databases.

More importantly, standards exist as a baseline of functionality to be expected on any platform. If that were the only consideration, what point would there be to multiple vendors selling the exact same product? You could throw a dart at a dartboard to pick your vendor. The fact is, however, that vendors would prefer that your money go into their pockets rather than their competitors' and so will try to come up with reasons you should purchase their product instead of the other guys'. In the business world, this is called *value-add*, and it plays a key role in this question of portability because vendor value-add is what Sun is banking on to keep J2EE alive in the face of that Large Software Company in the Pacific Northwest.

The idea is this: you write your system to the specifications, and then, at the time of deployment, you pick which vendor you wish to use based on price, scalability, clustering capabilities, and so forth. Each vendor will add a host of features that justify the additional cost. You pick the vendor product that best fits what you want to do, and everybody lives happily ever after—because you write code to the specification, the vendor can work its magic under the hood to make your system faster/better/cheaper.

But vendors don't stop with just optimizations under the hood. For example, consider Item 17: when a transaction involving an EJB entity bean is begun from within an EJB container against the data store, data must be synchronized between the EJB container holding the bean instance and the data store holding the bean's persisted state on disk. This is necessary because, by default, the specification assumes that the container cannot have exclusive access to the actual data storage layer (the database). Therefore, it's necessary to "refresh" the container's view of the data at the start of the transaction via a call to `ejbLoad` on the entity bean. Whether this results in an actual trip to the database or not is entirely up to the bean—a CMP bean will, whereas a BMP bean's behavior depends, as always, on how the implementation is written.

Most EJB container vendors, however, see an opportunity here to provide some value-added flavor to their implementation and offer some kind of "exclusivity" flag that programmers can flip on when there are no other systems accessing the database concurrently. This allows the EJB container to assume that it is the only gateway to the database and therefore make all kinds of caching optimizations, such as not forcing the refresh on an entity bean at the start of a transaction. Because of the improved performance this brings, many programmers use that flag.

Doing so, however, immediately renders the bean nonportable—not so much because the bean won't compile or run in another container but because the executional semantics surrounding the bean have changed. The rules of the environment in which the bean is coded, developed, and tested shape the ultimate direction the bean's implementation takes, and if those rules are suddenly changed, redundant code is executed or, worse, bugs are introduced.

For many developers, the argument for portability hinges on the idea that "management can always change its mind at a moment's notice" and that the tools and/or platform used at the start of the project can suddenly shift underneath you. This could happen for a variety of causes: merger, buyout, a change in strategic partnerships, or a nice game of golf courtesy of the vendor's sales rep. The actual reason itself is irrelevant—you're suddenly stuck with an entirely different platform, and if you coded to that platform's specific features, you're facing a major rewrite.

Other developers argue that this is a red herring, that such shifts in direction can never be planned for and never completely accounted for within a given system. Just as the company may decide to change its strategic partnership from Oracle to IBM, the company could just as easily make its choice to go from Oracle to Microsoft, implying a shift from Java to .NET. This is a situation that no J2EE container or specification can accommodate, so writing specification-compliant servlets and EJBs has zero effect.

There's more to a shift in platform than just recoding the system. Truth be told, rewriting the code is often one of the *smaller* tasks compared with everything else that needs to be done: porting the database schema, porting the database data, retraining the support staff, integrating the new platform into the overall support structure, and so on. For existing applications, particularly if the system has been in use for some time, these noncoding costs can run well into the millions of dollars, not even considering the cost of purchasing the new platform or hardware (if shifting hardware/operating systems).

And if historical precedent teaches us anything, it's that standards ultimately won't matter as much in the future as they do now, for the simple reason that the market will tend to centralize behind three or four major vendors, each of which will claim conformance, present their own slight "quirks" in that conformance, and provide a host of value-added features that will slowly come to be recognized as a *de facto* part of the standard.

One example that comes to mind is the ANSI SQL standard (SQL-89, SQL-92, and SQL-99). While the standard exists and continues to refine itself, the major database players continue to provide specific extensions to SQL, and relational databases in general, that aren't portable to other vendors' products. Each vendor supports the majority of the SQL standard, but none are 100% compliant with the SQL-92 Specification. Thus far, for the majority of J2EE applications, however, this hasn't presented a problem—the differences between Oracle's variant of SQL and Microsoft's variant are well known and therefore less of a "porting issue" when attempting to adapt schema from one to the other.

In the end, the decision regarding portability versus vendor value-added features is ultimately a value judgment, a personal and cultural choice. Make that choice consciously, not out of habit.

For those systems that need to maximize portability, stay away from any sort of vendor value-added feature until deployment. Make sure to test against multiple vendor containers, as well as the reference implementation, to find any possible scenarios in which you've accidentally made use of a vendor feature without realizing it—for example, one vendor may do different remote stub generation than the specification calls for, allowing you to get away with a simple cast in your client code instead of the specification-required form using `PortableRemoteObject.narrow`.

For the rest of us, however, portability quite often takes a back seat to two other concerns, performance and scalability. Decide on your container vendor as early as possible, and take every vendor value-added feature offered to you. Flip on that exclusivity flag. Use the vendor's distribution protocol instead of RMI/IIOP. Run the container inside the database, where entity beans can set and retrieve data directly against the table without having to make a SQL call. Or, if the vendor offers it, write entity beans against stored procedures instead of allowing the container to generate the SQL. (This provides you with another hook point to optimize the data-retrieval layer of your system.) Set whatever configuration options the container requires to use local transactions against the database instead of distributed ones. In short, take every single optimization the vendor can give you.

Item 12:   Build in monitoring support

So, now that the project's been deployed to production, how do you know it's still working?

Of course, I know, your code has no bugs, your code would never stop working, you've handled every possible exception, you've covered every possible error condition, and you've written code that's so robust that not even a power outage could keep it from working. Your SQL queries are triply redundant, so that an unexpected database schema change or upgrade will be flawlessly handled and gracefully accounted for. Your EJB calls are always wrapped in `try/catch` blocks, with code in place to gently deal with network outages. You've read Item 7 and memorized it, and your code reacts gracefully and recoverably to every possible error scenario. There's absolutely *no way* your code could break.

Unfortunately, you didn't write the whole thing yourself, and the college intern over there doesn't pay quite as much attention to code quality as you do.

Most of the time, the only way we know something's busted in production is when we get the phone call, either from the users themselves (assuming the application is an intranet one) or from upper management, who got the call from the support staff, who got the call from the user who was in the middle of placing the million-dollar order when suddenly they got a "404" from the browser and now can't get anything to work. This means that regardless of how quickly we move on the information, or how quickly we can move to fix whatever's broken, we're completely in a reactive mode. In this situation, we're always at the disadvantage; it's not like we can fix something that's not broken.

Once something goes wrong, however, it can be devilishly difficult to figure out exactly what part of the system is busted. Unless it's something horrendously obvious, like the entire EJB container has crashed, we're more or less reduced to examining whatever stack traces show up on the user screen to determine where the exception is coming from and why. Thankfully, Java exception traces tend to be pretty informative, but all it takes is one line of code somewhere in your application, like the following one:

```
try
{
   // Do work here
}
catch (Throwable t)
{ /* FIX LATER */ }
```

and suddenly, you don't even have a stack trace anymore—or worse yet, you have the *wrong* stack trace because now the exception is coming later in that method, because something else went wrong thanks to the first unhandled exception. (Of course, we both know that you would never write code like this, as Item 7 points out, but remember, that intern over in the corner hasn't learned his lessons the hard way yet.)

Rather than always starting the scenario at the disadvantage, instead, put some investment in at the beginning so that we can keep track of what's going on inside the system. Rather than having to rely on end users and management to tell us when something's wrong, build some hooks and switches into the application so that we can start to get an idea of what the system is doing and hopefully know before anyone else when something goes wrong.

For starters, take a page from the TCP/IP folks and *come up with a simple test to make sure that everything's running the way it's supposed to, above and beyond any sort of business processing.* In the TCP/IP world, of course, this utility is known as ping, and it is a lifesaver when diagnosing network problems because ping will tell you two things: (1) whether the target server is up (presumably, if it's not responding, it's down), and (2) how long it takes to get from your machine to the server and back (which gives you an idea whether perhaps some kind of intermittent network outage is occurring).

In enterprise systems, this ping, what's sometimes called the "happy bit," usually takes the form of a JSP page or servlet that, when hit with a request, simply checks to see whether all the expected servers and other paraphernalia are up and running. The Axis open-source Web Services package calls this JSP page `happyaxis.jsp`, and all it does is make sure that the Axis plumbing is installed and capable of executing correctly—it tries to load a few classes, and so on. This way, when a problem develops with an Axis-based Web Service endpoint, the first step can be to test `happyaxis.jsp`, to make sure that at least the Axis bits are "happy" and in place.

Within your own system, put in the necessary "happy bits" at every level feasible. Create a `happysystem.jsp` page (or equivalent) that will simply verify that necessary libraries can be loaded; do a `Class.forName` on a few to make sure everything's there. Build a "`PingBean`," a stateless session bean that offers up a single method, `ping()`, and in your `happysystem.jsp` page, do a JNDI lookup and method call on the `PingBean` to know that the link between the servlet container and the EJB container is alive and well. Put a single-row table, called `PING_TBL` (or whatever your database naming conventions demand that it be called), that contains exactly one row with well-known, expected data, as in the string `"PONG"`,[6] so that your `PingBean` and your `happysystem.jsp` endpoints can both try accessing the database to make sure everything there is OK—and so on.

---

6. The classic response to a `"PING"` request is to send back `"PONG"`.

The point here is that when a problem occurs, you now have a tool in your toolchest that you can use to start eliminating potential problems. If, for example, the `happysystem.jsp` page doesn't come up at all, you know the problem at least starts with the servlet container or earlier—perhaps the server it's on is down, or the network between the server and the rest of the world is on the fritz, both of which will be discoverable via a `ping` request, and so on. If `happysystem.jsp` comes up but indicates that it can't execute the "happy table" SQL query, then it's time to look at the database. If everything on `happysystem.jsp` indicates success, it's time to start taking a hard look at your code.

Unfortunately, the "happy bit" test is still a reactive one: it waits for you to test it to see if everything is up but won't notify you in the event something goes down—you have to ping it. I suppose we could make the system administrators try to test the "happy bit" every 15 minutes or so to make sure the system is still up, but this has two problems: (1) your error-detection window is now 15 minutes wide, which means you could have an outage of 14 minutes and 59 seconds before you know a problem is up, and (2) you're really going to make your system administrators angry at you if you force them to check the system every 15 minutes. (Try it: doing anything, no matter how trivial, every 15 minutes is hideously hard, particularly if you're wrapped up in something else in the meantime.)

But this kind of repetitive work is ideal for the computer itself, so put the computer to work doing the notification for you. Set up a simple process that issues an HTTP request to the `happysystem.jsp` page every five minutes or so, or whatever your "acceptable outage" time window is, and uses some kind of HTML screen-scraping API to examine the results and make sure everything's up and running. (The open-source HttpUnit project turns out to be a really good tool for doing this.) In the event that this automated "heartbeat" discovers a problem, it can take one of several actions to notify somebody that something's "not happy": send an e-mail to a mailing list, send an e-mail to an alphanumeric pager, open an IRC or MSM or AIM or Jabber connection to a system administrator and/or developer, post an event to the Win32 Event Log or UNIX syslog, trigger an SNMP fault, and so on. Just as long as it's a channel where we have reasonable guarantee that somebody's listening, anything works.

So far, so good. We've got a tool that will tell us whether there are problems with the underlying plumbing, and we've managed to turn it into an alarm when things fail. We're just getting warmed up here, though. Not only do we want to know *before* things fail, but *we'd also like to have some kind of window "inside" our code so that when things start to go bad, we can take a look at some reasonable guesses about why that might be.*

The first part of getting that "window" into your code requires some effort, although not too much: we need to establish some kind of diagnostic log to which we can write debug and diagnostic messages. While the Servlet Specification provides a log associated with the `ServletContext`, it's alone among the J2EE Specifications in doing so—most notably, the EJB container lacks any such facility, despite the fact it's probably in the largest need of one. It's possible to use the servlet log to log servlet messages and some other mechanism to log EJB messages, but then we lose any sort of continuity in our messages that go from servlet to EJB and back again.[7]

A number of different logging implementations are available (the JDK 1.4 `java.util.logging` API and the Log4j open-source project are probably the two most popular); whichever you choose is really more a matter of personal choice than any technical rationale. Both offer the ability to "categorize" output messages, both in terms of verbosity level and what "subsystems" you're logging from or about. The upshot here, however, is that within your code, you make use of the log to track events occurring within the system:

```
// Using JDK 1.4 logging, just by way of example
//
public class LoginServlet extends HttpServlet
{
  static Logger logger =
    Logger.getLogger(LoginServlet.class.getName());

  public void doPost(HttpServletRequest req,
                     HttpServletResponse resp)
    throws IOException
  {
```

---

7. We'll only get this continuity in containers that are both servlet and EJB containers in one process, but since that's a large percentage of the installed J2EE container base, that's a safe assumption. Nevertheless, it bears saying that if the servlet and EJB containers are running in separate processes, it's (almost) impossible to get a single diagnostic log that logs messages from both environments without being hideously time-expensive.

```
   // Note that we've entered doPost()
   //
   logger.entering("LoginServlet", "doPost");

   // Check our input data
   //
   if (request.getParameter("username") == null ||
       request.getParameter("username").equals(""))
   {
     logger.fatal("Cannot log in without username");
     throw new ServletException("Login failed");
   }

   // and so on

   logger.exiting("LoginServlet", "doPost");
  }
}
```

The granularity of the log messages can be as coarse or as fine as you like, but as a general rule of thumb, put as much into the log as you'd need to debug the servlet or EJB (or whatever) without a debugger running.

At first blush, that may seem excessive—after all, it's not like these logging calls are free—but the reason for having all that information there becomes apparent the first time you have to debug a problem on the production server that you cannot replicate on your machine, the development server, or the QA server. Having that information in the log suddenly makes it a lot easier to figure out what's going wrong than taking guesses (usually incorrect ones) based on a terse sentence or two.

If you're concerned about the performance of your system when writing out all these log messages (which, to be honest, you should be), there are a few things to remember.

- *Don't do a lot of string concatenation.* Most of the logging implementations are pretty quick about determining whether the message even needs to be written to the log (based on some configuration properties), but they can't do anything about the string concatenation that takes place before the logging method gets called. Remember that, like most programming languages, in Java parameters must be evaluated before the method call can take place, and keep the parameters to your log messages simple; if all else fails, if you absolutely have to string a whole slew of information together into a single log message, test to see whether the log is turned on at that level (via the `isLoggable` method in the JDK 1.4 API, for example). For this reason, if you use `toString` to display the contents of an object's state, make sure that it doesn't go off and start a thousand-method-long call chain to walk through every owned field; either write `toString` to be logger-friendly, or else create a new method (e.g., `toLog String`) that is.

- *Log to someplace that's fast.* Most of the time, diagnostic logs write out to the filesystem or the process console STDOUT or STDERR stream by default. Both the JDK 1.4 logging implementation and the Log4J implementation are extremely flexible, however, and allow for custom "log sinks" to be plugged in, so if the standard file logger implementations are spending too much time writing to disk for your taste, write a custom implementation that takes the message and hands it off to a separate thread to do the actual write. (If you do this, make sure you realize that you'll potentially lose log messages if the JVM process abnormally terminates for some reason.) One favorite trick is to write a handler that listens for socket connections on a well-known port number, and write log messages to any connected clients as they come in and throw away log messages when no clients are connected. (Log4J calls this the `TelnetAppender`, for example.)

- *Log to files for archival purposes.* Even when you're not tracking down a problem, log messages to files so that in case something does suddenly go bad, you can go back to the files and look over what was logged in an attempt to figure out why. Again, if the file-writing code isn't as fast as you'd like, you can write your own custom handler doing file writes on a separate thread (with the caveat above). Alternatively, you can turn off logging to the file until a problem arises, but be aware that half the time, the problems are sporadic and impossible to predict in any meaningful way, which is why having the files capture all the logs is so useful in the first place.

- *Make the logging level a hot-configured data item.* In other words, don't force a restart of the system to notice a change in the logging level; otherwise, turning up and turning down the logging level becomes more trouble than it's worth when trying to track down a problem, and the chances of it actually being used as a diagnostic utility decrease dramatically. See Item 13 for details on hot-configurable configuration data.

- *Keep the logging verbosity level low except when tracking down problems.* Logging implementations use verbosity levels to allow you to mark certain log messages as higher priority than others; for example, in the earlier servlet code, the fact that `username` wasn't passed into the servlet when it was expected and required is a fatal error because the servlet can't continue processing without it. The fact that we entered (and later exited) the method is of much less importance by comparison. Normally, a production system will want to keep diagnostic logs turned up only high enough to capture errors (and sometimes warnings), in order to save both processing time and disk space if these logs are being stored to disk. Turn those levels back up to more verbose levels only when a problem occurs, and then turn them back down as soon as the problem has been corrected or eliminated.

Now, when the problem arises, you can check the logs for what might have gone wrong and have a leg up on finding and fixing the problem. (This also means that, as mentioned in Item 7, the bare minimum any exception catch handler should do is log the exception to a diagnostic log, even if no other error-handling heuristic comes to mind.)

The other half of our ideal monitoring situation is to keep track of how the system is performing, not only so that we can become aware of potential failures before they occur but also so that we can get a better idea of where the system might be bogging down due to a performance bottleneck or other constraint. While building such hooks is pretty much beyond the scope of this book, fortunately, the Java Community Process comes to the rescue once again with another specification, this time the JMX, a set of APIs for use by objects that wish to be managed by an external management tool. Several vendors, including several open-source projects like JBoss and Tomcat, already have built-in support for JMX, and the "J2EE Management" JSR brings JMX formally into the J2EE 1.4 environment. (For more details on JMX, see *Java and JMX* [Kreger/Harold/Williamson].)

All JMX technical details aside, the JMX APIs allow you to define managed objects, called *MBeans*, which can keep track of counters and also issue notifications in the event an MBean sees a performance statistic start to climb out of an acceptable range. For example, a servlet may use a "concurrent access" MBean to keep track of the number of concurrent requests executing within its `doPost` method, and when that number exceeds a reasonable number (5, 10, 20, whatever), issue a notification, since the calls aren't executing as quickly through the servlet as they should: it's possible that the servlet's calls to the database are taking far longer than they should, which probably indicates problems at the database (the disk is about to fill up, the database CPU is maxed out, and so on).

One of the best parts of JMX is that, thanks to the JMX vendors' GUIs, it allows system administrators not only to keep an eye on statistics and performance inside your code but also to gather statistics that are useful and important to upper management; for example, it would be trivial to create an MBean that tracked the number of successful transactions through the system against the number of failed transactions, partially completed transactions, and incorrectly formed transactions. (Managers just live on this stuff.) Another useful thing to track, keeping an eye on Item 58, is the number of failed logins; you can then issue an event notification when there are more failed login attempts than is reasonable, whether for a single user or across the system as a whole.

By the way, for the sanity of both you and your system administrators, make sure that these monitoring tools you use (the "happy bit" test, the "happy heartbeat" process, the diagnostic logs, and the JMX integration) are accessible remotely, so that an individual, namely you or your friendly system administrator, doesn't have to be standing over the machine to watch it. Most JMX providers are already hard at work providing remote access to the monitored resources; the "happy bit" tests are typically done from within the system, which already has remote capabilities built within it (HTTP, if nothing else); and the diagnostic logs can write either to a socket or to a file, both of which already have some decent remote support. So, in general, making these tools accessible remotely isn't a big deal. The key here is to avoid having your diagnostic logs write to `System.out` and/or `System.err`, since those are not exactly easy to access from a remote location.

If you're despairing over all the work implied in this discussion, remember that it isn't just about making managers happy with statistics or making system administrators happy by making it easier for them to determine when there's a problem in production, although those are noble goals and worth the work. Having all of the above in place will make your life easier, as well, since now you'll have a collection of tools you can use to help detect and diagnose a problem once it occurs.

This actually has greater implications than you might believe at first, but stop and think about it for a moment: If the database behind your system suddenly goes down or starts behaving unpredictably for some reason, who's going to get the blame when the Web site in front of the users suddenly starts throwing exceptions everywhere? Unless you have tools in place to help diagnose the root cause of a problem within your system, you'll be the one "under the gun," so to speak, until you can prove otherwise. And if you can make those tools available to system administrators, so that they can do the diagnosis instead of you, that's one less interrupted night on your part. And that, my friends, is more than enough justification for all of the work required to put those tools into your toolchest.

Item 13: Build in administration support

One common facet of enterprise applications is that, unlike most "shrink wrap" commercial off-the-shelf software, enterprise applications typically require some kind of administrative control over their behavior and/or functionality. For example, it's not uncommon for administrators to need to perform a variety of tasks, ranging from the ubiquitous "add or remove users from the list of users authorized to use the system," to system-specific tasks like "find the expense report in a particular user's workflow inbox and redistribute it to somebody else," to simple system configuration like "what image should show up in the upper-left corner?"

All of these problems have potential solutions already: system administrators can wade directly into the database to make changes there, or we can simply replace the existing image file with another file and keep the names identical. The problem is, system administrators having to do administration this way need both an intimate knowledge of the application's architecture and the skill to make those modifications as necessary—they need to know enough SQL to be able to replace or modify the data in the tables, for example. And we're assuming that they're perfect while doing this and will never make a mistake with the raw, live data.

The fact of the matter is, *if this application is going to live in a production environment for any length of time, we need to provide administrators with some kind of administrative "console" to enable them to make those updates as necessary without having to enter them directly into the data storage layer itself.* Specifically, we need to consider giving administrators some kind of high-level console for two areas: configuration and control.

Configuration here refers to the various "we don't want that value hard-coded" values that show up periodically within your application. A classic example is the e-mail address of the person or persons who should be e-mailed in the event of a system failure of some kind (see Item 7). Normally, we don't want that data hard-coded inside of the application; even if you establish an e-mail alias (e.g., systempanic@yourcompany.com), what happens when your company is acquired and that domain name suddenly changes? Configuration data could be thought of as data that changes infrequently in response to stimuli entirely outside of the application domain itself. (The distinction is necessary to differentiate it from data that's modified due to user action; without that, there would be very little to differentiate configuration data from any other sort of data in the system.)

Unfortunately, Java has traditionally not had a very strong configuration story. Starting with JDK 1.0, configuration of Java applications has traditionally come in a variety of different flavors, all of which have their strengths, but also some serious disadvantages as well.

The first mechanism is the ubiquitous "Properties file," a text file containing name-value pairs that are read in by your Java code, typically using the `java.util.Properties` class. This mechanism has the positive benefits of being absurdly easy to understand from a programmer's position, and since the "data storage" format here is nothing more complex than a text file, it's also absurdly easy to modify the data. Properties suffer from some severe drawbacks, however, most notably that text data is also absurdly easy to get wrong, most often due to typos. In addition, because the data is stored as a file on the filesystem, your code requires access to the filesystem to get that data (which is denied you in EJB). Attackers might be able to sniff out additional useful information if they can figure out how to look at that file via a file-path canonicalization bug or if the file is somehow visible via HTTP request. And some helpful "power user" may come along and "fix" what are "obviously" errors in that file if he or she can get to it. Couple this with several facts—that only strings can be used as either key or value in the configuration data, that remote access to a file on a production server may not be as easy as you might think, that there's no notification mechanism so the application can reread the values when they change, and that the keys are a simple flat namespace requiring work on your part (concatenating or parsing) if you want to hierarchically arrange them—and you suddenly have a mechanism that isn't nearly "good enough" for production J2EE use. Oh, I'll admit, we can get by, but we can do so much better than this.

A second option in widespread use is to put all that data into the database. We solve a number of the problems with the properties mechanism, but we're back to a fundamental bootstrapping problem: Where do we put the database configuration data, like JDBC URL and/or user ID and password, to use to connect to the database? (Ideally, you shouldn't always connect to the database via a single user ID anyway, but it's such a common idiom that pretending otherwise is foolish.) We could put everything but the database configuration data into the database and put the database configuration data itself in a Properties file, but now we're looking at two different locations to store configuration data, which gives us additional issues. Plus, even when storing configuration data in the database, we're still faced with problems, like that of the hierarchical arrangement of keys (difficult to do in a relational model) and that of updating the configuration data (difficult if your system administrators aren't comfortable with SQL, or you're not comfortable with them wandering around in there, which I wouldn't be).

Along the same lines as using the relational database, we could use a JNDI-accessible layer to store the data, most notably an LDAP server. LDAP, certainly, solves the problem of storing keys in a hierarchical arrangement, but once again we have the bootstrapping issue with the relational database—JNDI requires some initial configuration parameters to know where the LDAP server is, and this itself is data that we don't want to hard-code, so we're back to the same story in that we still need some way to bootstrap the JNDI access into place.

The various J2EE specifications have also offered up their own variations on this story, using XML in the form of the deployment descriptor to store configuration options, which will be made available to the developer via various APIs of one form or another. For example, the Servlet Specification allows for `init-param` tags in the `web.xml` file, which can be obtained via calls to `getInitParameter` on both a per-servlet and per-`ServletContext` basis. Once deployed, many servlet containers then offer some kind of administrative GUI to change those values in the running Web application. Unfortunately, this mechanism carries its own share of problems. Redeploying a new version of the application will reset the existing configuration data to whatever's specified in the deployment descriptor, effectively forcing the system administrator to go back and reset everything by hand to the desired values. Plus, we still have the problems of hierarchical arrangement of keys and the fact that only strings can be stored in the deployment descriptor.

In following the XML theme, we could use an XML file instead of a Properties file to store our configuration data. While still suffering from some of the problems of a Properties file, XML does solve a good number of problems. Because XML is hierarchical in nature, the problem of hierarchical key arrangement becomes moot. XPath makes an awesome way to get at data without having to navigate the tree by hand. Unfortunately, it's still not perfect. We still face all of the problems that otherwise plague Properties files: we need a file on the filesystem and access to the filesystem, system administrators will need to edit the XML file itself to make changes (thus introducing the possibility that they could introduce a typo that makes the file ill-formed), and so on. But we're getting closer.

Starting with JDK 1.4, Sun has introduced a new API that could offer a long-term solution to this configuration dilemma: the `java.util.prefs.Preferences` (and related) classes. Although not formally part of the J2EE Specification,[8] the `Preferences` API offers a number of the advantages found in the other mechanisms, as well as a few new ones.

Using the `Preferences` API in its simplest form is straightforward:

```
// all Preferences classes come from java.util.prefs
//


// Read a configuration value
//
Preferences prefs =
  Preferences.systemNodeForPackage(this.getClass());
String url = prefs.get("databaseURL", "");
```

A couple of things are happening here. First, the `Preferences` API differentiates between system data and user data—system configuration data is

---

8. Some will point out that J2EE implies dependence on, and therefore acceptance of, Java 2 Standard Edition (J2SE) and all of its associated APIs, such as the `Preferences` API. Unfortunately, the problem is that the `Preferences` API requires a particular security permission, a `RuntimePermission`, to be granted in order to access `Preferences` data, and that permission is not listed as part of the J2EE 1.3 Specification.

machine-wide, while user configuration data is held specific for each user and varies depending on which user is currently executing the code. For most enterprise applications running on a server, we'll want to use the system data, since our servlet and/or EJB code isn't typically associated with a single user. Second, preferences are arranged into hierarchical nodes, just as XML Infoset elements are. By arranging nodes in package-named hierarchies, configuration elements can be partitioned into manageable chunks for easier administration. To make things even simpler, the `Preferences` API has utility methods (like the one just shown) that navigate the `Preferences` tree to find the `Preferences` node that matches the package name of this class. Once we've found the right `Preferences` node, we can ask it for the value associated with the key "`databaseURL`"; in the event that no such key is found, the default value, passed as the second parameter to the call, is returned.

At this point, it's fair to ask what data storage mechanism the `Preferences` API is using under the hood—after all, that's going to be important when considering what we need to do to deploy the application. The short answer is, "It depends." Specifically, the `Preferences` API allows for different storage layers, called *backing stores,* to hold the raw data. The default backing store for a `Preferences` node depends on the system on which you're running the code; in the case of the Sun Win32 JVM, for example, the default backing store is the Windows Registry. (Don't automatically turn down the idea of using the Windows Registry to hold important configuration data. Having heard the horror stories of the Registry over the years, I can say with all seriousness that most of those stories came from COM programmers, who horribly abused the Registry in any number of ways. Used as it was intended—to provide a central repository for configuration information—it performs quite admirably.) In the case of a UNIX system, most JVMs make use of text files again, stored in either the user's home directory or the machine-wide `/etc` or `/usr/etc` directories, depending on the JVM and UNIX filesystem conventions for that system.

In addition to storing strings, the `Preferences` API can store byte arrays, which are convenient for storing Serializable objects (see Item 71 for more on Java Object Serialization), as well as several of the primitive types (Booleans, ints, longs, doubles, and floats). More importantly, the `Preferences` API also allows us to register event-callback instances (classes that implement the `PreferencesChangeListener` interface) that will be called in the event of a modification to the data stored in a

Preferences backing store. This means that if the system administrator modifies the data, we can catch that and rescan the configuration data for the new values. This in turn means that changing a configuration value doesn't require a restart cycle of the server to pick up configuration data—in short, giving us the ability to "hot configure" an application.

Because the Preferences API uses different backing stores, if you really don't like storing data in the Windows Registry or the local filesystem (for the reasons mentioned), you can always write your own Preferences class that extends AbstractPreferences to store data in whatever storage medium you wish, including a relational database or LDAP server.

In the event that you really want to view your configuration data in a portable data format, the Preferences API can export preferences data to an XML format (whose document type definition is given in the Preferences documentation), as well as import preferences data from an XML format of similar structure. This makes transmitting preferences data from one machine to another quite simple.

The Preferences API has one major disadvantage, however, and that's because it is an API, with no non-programmatic interface (i.e., some kind of system administrator front end) defined for it. There's no way a system administrator can access that data without using tools to get back at the raw data, something we've already decided is less than optimal in most situations. This is where you as the developer for the project come in: you have to build that user interface.

At first blush, this sounds like it's adding more work to your already overloaded schedule, and that's not a particularly good thing. A couple of advantages come out of doing this, however. First, it eliminates the necessity for administrators to go wandering through the raw data to make configuration changes, and this can help eliminate a few of those latenight phone calls, since now it's not possible for system administrators to accidentally delete crucial data. (Hey, they're just as human as the rest of us.) More importantly, however, providing a user interface gives us the opportunity to do some kind of sanity-checking on the configuration data being passed in—for example, when fed a JDBC URL, we can actually try to open a connection to that URL to make sure the URL works before accepting it. We can screen out obviously invalid conditions (such as a blank e-mail address for system panic notifications), and even put some kind of help into the user interface so that we don't have to field phone calls from administrators who have forgotten what "pool size min-imum" means.

If this still sounds like a lot of work, bear in mind that (1) you're still going to have to write an administrative user interface for control opera-tions, discussed next, which can probably be combined with the configu-ration user interface, (2) there's usually not much configuration data that needs to be established (and the more there is, the greater the need for a clear and comprehensive user interface anyway), and (3) if this system is really going to "run forever," like many enterprise systems are supposed to, a little additional work up front will ultimately pay for itself many times over the system's lifetime.

As mentioned earlier, the other half of administrative needs, besides con-figuration, is *control* of the application and/or system as a whole. For example, in a canonical online e-commerce sales application, it's not uncommon for orders to "get lost" within the system. Typically, when this happens, the data will still be there, it just won't be in the state users expect or need to call up the order. Whether this happens due to a bug in the code, a flaw in the requirements, a missed step in the design, or modi-fications to the system at the eleventh hour is irrelevant—the fact is, the system administrator has a user or customer service rep screaming on the phone because "the system ate the order." Guess who's next on the phone call?

The system administrators, the ones who will be taking care of this partic-ular system (who may in turn be different from those responsible for the servers, the network, and so on), will need some kind of ability to "reach in" to the system and manipulate the data in ways that may violate the standard business practices. Ideally, this power gets used only to help identify bugs, correct accidentally corrupted data, and so on, but we can't ignore the fact that it can also be used sometimes for business purposes, to violate business rules because "the CEO says we need to do it, just this once."

Again, while other approaches—usually those that involve going directly into the database or other data and making changes to the raw data set itself—are possible, they fall into the same traps and disadvantages as configuration. More importantly, however, when working with "live" data, we need to take additional precautions against manipulating the "raw" data because a system administrator may not be as careful with doing so as we would be from code. Think about this for a moment. When was the last time you opened up SQL*Plus (the Oracle database console), the MySQL terminal, iSQL, or any other database console to do your wandering through the system and did all your work under a transaction? Complete with BEGIN TRANSACTION at the start and COMMIT or ROLLBACK at the end? While it's a great trick to know, few database administrators, system administrators, or developers use it when navigating and "fixing" things in the raw tables. So now, if our system administrator suddenly finds that we have three SQL statements that need to be run to fix the latest problem, what are the chances that they will be done under a transaction, isolated from the hundreds or possibly thousands of other transactions going on simultaneously? In a high-load system, direct table navigation and manipulation is a really quick way to really corrupt data, which most people consider to be a Bad Thing, even if it is "just" preferences/configuration information.

Which brings us back to the same conclusion as for configuration options: we need to think about what sort of administrative control features the system administrators will need and provide them via some kind of user interface console (properly protected by well-guarded authorization checks, of course—see Item 63). This console doesn't have to be a marvel of modern user interface design; keep it as simple as necessary, and don't spend a whole lot of time making it user-friendly. In fact, some would argue that because we don't want the average user to be able to use it should they accidentally wander into it, maybe it shouldn't be easy to use at all. It does need to provide system administrators with enough control that they can correct for any foreseeable problem, bug, or system flaw that arises.

Unfortunately, unlike configuration data, identifying the control options a system administrator needs is much more difficult than applying a simple heuristic. One facet that almost all systems have to at least some degree is user management—administrators need some way to add users, remove users, and change user options (passwords, roles, and so on) as well as any role management that goes along with a role-based authorization system (as discussed in Item 63). We could create a simple SQL data console that allows system administrators to execute SQL statements against the database(s) used by the system, but that essentially just grants them another back door into the raw table structure of the database, something we've already decided isn't a great idea. Instead, however, we can build a higher-level model, where we can pull items out of the tables, manipulate them, and put them back under a strictly controlled user interface (so as to preserve appropriate transaction boundaries). This way, administrators can make the necessary data modifications to the live data without transactional "leakage" to worry about.

Another common item that typically falls under administrative control is that of running reports on the database behind the system—unless end users are required to execute one or more reports as part of their business process, the act of running a weeks-end or months-end report typically falls on the shoulders of the operations staff. Some reports are canned, meaning we can hard-code the SQL for the report directly into the code, but most of the time, a report needs some kind of dynamic data variable or criteria selection. You have two choices: let administrators write their own ad hoc SQL queries to get the data back that they want, or bury the SQL behind a rich-enough user interface so that administrators don't need to know SQL to run the report. (Frequently, as it turns out, you'll want both choices, since no matter how rich you make the user interface, there will always be somebody who asks how to run a report based on criteria that's not part of your user interface.)

By the way, in case you were wondering whether you could get away with not providing this sort of functionality or user interface, keep something in mind: if you don't have this user interface, and fixing an application-domain problem, like removing the user credentials and configuration for a terminated employee, requires going into the raw data, chances are likely that you're the one who's going to be doing it, not the system administrators. Barring that, you're going to have to write something to provide that user interface shortly after the system ships, anyway, so you might as well do it up front and get it over with, and maybe earn a few "oohs" and "aahs" from your operations staff (and, dare we say it, upper management?) in the process.

Remember, like deployment and monitoring, careful attention to detail here can not only improve your relationship with your system administrators but also spare you some unwanted late-night interruptions.

Item 14:   Make deployment as simple as possible

At some point in the project's lifetime, you have to ship.

It seems trite to say it, yet large numbers of enterprise software project teams, both Java and otherwise, never actually think about the process of putting the software into a production environment. If anybody actually spends any time on this, it's usually to the tune of "Oh, we'll just copy the files up to the server and restart the server, and that should about do it."

J2EE projects, like most enterprise software projects, are a lot more complicated than that. At a minimum, not only do you have to deploy the software bits you've written into their respective containers (servlet and/or EJB) but you also have a database schema to think about. It gets even more interesting if the database already exists in some format but you've had to make a few schema changes—additions and not alterations or deletions, hopefully—that have to get pushed into the production environment at the same time the code goes into production. Things get even more interesting if you have to install any additional software on the production machines, such as the servlet or EJB containers themselves, punch holes in the firewall to allow communication against those machines, reconfigure firewalls on the inside of the DMZ to allow traffic on new ports from the HTTP server to the database on the other side, and so on.

Guess who has to do all this?

In most large corporate environments, it's *not* the development staff; in fact, in most large data centers developers are frequently not even allowed near the production servers, much less allowed to install software or make changes to the environment there. But before you breathe that huge sigh of relief at not having to deal with all the complexity and mess installing your software will require, take a second to think about who will be: system administrators.

Think about the implications for just a moment. You, as a vetted and J2EE-savvy Java developer, know and understand what J2EE containers are for, why they're necessary, and more importantly, what that bewildering array of installation and configuration options means to your application. System administrators, however, typically have had no such training (or interest, for that matter) and won't have a real clue as to what "stateless session bean object pool maximum size" or "database connection pool starting size" are, much less what values they're set to. Unless you're very, very lucky, do you think they're even going to pay much attention? Most likely, they're just going to take the defaults offered to them (thereby potentially leaving in security holes; see Item 60 for details), and move on to the next item, so as to get this done as quickly as possible.[9]

My point here is simple: unless you really want either (a) an application that doesn't work at all, and/or (b) an application that performs poorly due to the settings configured for it, and/or (c) an administrative staff that's not very happy with you because they had to go through twelve hours and hundreds of pages of documentation to get everything installed correctly, *you need to start thinking about how the system will be deployed much, much sooner than a week before it's supposed to ship.*

Unfortunately, there's not a lot of help here from the J2EE Specification; deployment is one of those tasks that's left as a vendor point of customization, where vendors can compete against one another for developer mindshare and money. As a result, aside from standardizing the ready-to-deploy file format in which Web applications and enterprise applications are expected to be stored, the Servlet and EJB Specifications (and others) don't talk about how deployment takes place. For example, the Tomcat open-source servlet container has at least three different methods of deploying Web applications: (1) you can manually unpack the contents into the webapps directory (or any other directory if you configure Tomcat's master configuration file to point to that other directory), (2) you can simply put the .war file in the webapps directory itself and Tomcat will unpack and install the application itself the next time it starts up, or (3) you can go through Tomcat's HTML-based "manager" Web application, which provides a GUI. The J2EE reference implementation EJB container supports two methods, a command-line utility, and a GUI utility. The Orion application server uses just one method, but it's a very convenient one: it establishes a "deployment directory," and any .war or .ear file copied into that directory is immediately deployed into the container, without requiring a server restart.

---

9. This is absolutely not intended to suggest that system administrators are somehow lazy and/or careless in their actions—far from it, in fact. Most system administrators are hardworking, underpaid staff who have far too much to do and not enough time (or resources) to do it. Sort of like developers, come to think of it. . . .

Stop and think for a moment about the act of deploying the components into the container itself. To be more precise, particularly with respect to EJB deployments, think about the huge array of choices typically presented to the deployer during the deployment step. There's a reason why the J2EE Specification creates two roles for production-related activities, the Application Deployer and the System Administrator—deployment of a J2EE application is unfortunately a nontrivial task—but unfortunately for the rest of the world, not every company has a J2EE Application Deployer on staff, so that role gets relegated back to the system administrators. (Or, worse yet, back to the development team.)

Just to compound an already bad day, take careful note that the deployment activities required by J2EE cover only those parts of the environment covered by J2EE itself—the J2EE Specification makes no effort to cover deployment activities as they relate to the database, for example, or configuring JMS Administered Objects (`Queues`, `Topics`, and `Connection Factories`, for example), or configuring JDBC `DataSource` instances in the servlet and/or EJB containers, and so on. These activities are left entirely to the deployment/administrative staff.

Couple all this with the fact that the system administrator's job is to keep the production servers up and running as long as possible, with little to no downtime, and you start getting a Real Bad Feeling about all this. (To make that feeling worse, imagine that you're the poor sysadmin expected to take care of all this as the developers head out the door to celebrate.)

To save your application from failure right out of the gate and your relationship with the system administrators from an immediate sour downturn, once your application has reached a level where you can start thinking about testing it, start working on a *deployment script* to automate the task of pushing the application—and any associated support requirements—out to a production server. The script can either be the developers' notion of a script, as in a sequence of commands carried out by a software process (Ant works extremely well for this), or, failing that, a piece of paper with the exact sequence of instructions the system administrators need to carry out to install everything as you require it on the production servers.

While we're at it, in keeping with Item 7, think about the possibility of failure during deployment—what happens if the deployment process fails halfway through? Or worse yet, after deploying, you come to realize that there's a huge bug that somehow slipped through your department and QA.[10] What then?

In many ways, we can think of deployment as its own form of transaction (see Chapter 4 for more on transactions). In this case, rather than a transaction done exclusively within the database, it's a transaction against the J2EE container and associated systems (like the database). It fits all the desired characteristics of an ACID transaction: we want the deployment to be atomic, consistent, and durable, and isolation in this case means (ideally) that nobody would see the changes to the application until we "bought off" on the deployment, by committing it.

Unfortunately, since vendors don't yet support JTA for their deployment API, we can't just treat the deployment of a J2EE application as a standard JTA transaction. That means, then, that we can't rely on a transaction manager to handle rollback for us; instead, as Item 28 points out, we have to be ready and willing to run *compensating transactions*—in other words, another transaction or in this case, another deployment—to undo what was just done and to bring things back to the state they were in when we started. In other words, for each deployment script, there should be an "undo" deployment script that brings things back to their original state.

If you're thinking that this sounds like a lot of work, you're right. But before you start procrastinating on this, bear in mind that your application is going to go through a whole series of deployments long before it reaches the production servers. I'm speaking, of course, of the need to deploy the application to the QA servers so the QA testers can test the application before it sees a production server—you can use the various QA releases you'll hand to the test team as practice for your deployment script. You're going to want to automate that process anyway, because if you don't, both the QA team and the system administrators supporting the QA team are going to get tired of going through that deployment step on each release candidate. Anything you can do to automate the deployment process for the system administrators is going to pay off, not only in hours of saved effort for both you and the QA team but also in a much better relationship with the system administrator group.

---

10. Never blame on the QA team the fact that a bug escapes to production—it's just as much your fault as it is theirs.

3 | Communication

> *Whenever someone tells me that adopting their beliefs*
> *could give me the same type of life they have,*
> *I tell them that that's exactly what I'm afraid of.*
>
> —H. W. Kenton

Interprocess communication (IPC) is a fundamental part of any enterprise system. We've long since moved beyond the day when everything—user interface, processing, and data storage—can be stored on a single machine and still be effective. Code needs to be able to communicate with processes running on other machines. IPC is what makes a distributed system, well, distributed.

Lots of different technologies could be lumped under the global category of communications. For example, database access to a remote database requires a communications layer over which to send SQL commands and receive the results. Coordinating with a distributed transaction controller (such as the EJB container or other JTA-compliant software process) requires network communication. Even simple HTTP itself is a form of communication between two endpoints. For purposes of this chapter, however, *communications* is the layer of software that lets my client code call into your server code for some kind of arbitrary processing authored by one or the other of us—ordering a book, checking the status of an order, filling out a corporate expense report form, and so on.

Item 15: Understand all your communications options

Java communications APIs can be classified along three axes of interest: transport, format, and communication patterns.

Every communications API must move across some sort of communications layer, what we call the *transport layer*. While virtually all of them end up traveling across TCP/IP (or, less frequently, its connectionless partner, UDP/IP), many of them take advantage of higher-level protocols that build on top of TCP/IP; one such example is everybody's favorite transport, HTTP. Every transport channel has its own unique aspects, however, so it's still worthwhile to differentiate between a communications API using raw TCP/IP as its transport and one that makes use of HTTP—for example, firewall products that can scan HTTP traffic will be happier working with a communications API that uses HTTP as its transport than one that uses raw TCP/IP.

If necessary, Java can be extended to make use of other transport layers via JNI or the `java.nio` "New I/O" channels. For example, it's sometimes faster to make use of other operating system–specific IPC APIs, such as pipes, named pipes, and shared memory, than to go through TCP/IP. Some channels provide additional behavior, such as encryption, over traditional channels—for example, HTTP over SSL provides a "secure" HTTP channel, what we of course call HTTPS. The ability to move across a different channel is often exposed as a hook point (see Item 6) at the API level of the communication library.

In order to pass data across a transport, the data needs to be in some wire-friendly format. Typically this means we need to either make sure only primitive types are passed across the wire (which are easy to turn into a wire-friendly format) or else turn what we see as fully formed objects in a nice spider web of object references into some kind of flat array of bytes that can be reconstituted into the spider web of object references on the other side. This is known as *marshaling,* and it's typically (although not always) the responsibility of the communications plumbing to do the data marshaling for you. The data, once marshaled, is often referred to as the *payload,* and it usually consists of both the data the programmer passes and additional information needed by the communications plumbing (which is sometimes referred to as the *framing data*).

Two popular marshaling formats in Java are Java Object Serialization and XML. Serialization is popular since it provides all the behavior necessary to turn an arbitrary Serializable object into an `ObjectStream` without modification to the object in any way—all you need to do is implement the `Serializable` interface, and off you go. More importantly, Serialization is a completely lossless process. Doing the complete round-trip from object to serialized format back to object guarantees no loss of data. When marshaling into XML, a variety of formats are possible, but more and more XML marshaling is being done via the Simple Object Access Protocol (SOAP), or more recently, XML Schema, using schema types to define what the marshaled data should look like. Other marshaling formats are in use throughout the industry, such as CORBA's Internet Inter-Orb Protocol (IIOP) or the RELAX/NG XML Specification, and some formats remain entirely proprietary and closed.

At the TCP level, all data sent over a socket is broken down into packets of data that are sent over the IP network and reassembled at the destination to be turned back into the original stream of data. Over time, however, we've come to rely on several abstractions—patterns of network communication—that help shield us programmers from the ugly realities of network communication.

Two basic approaches to network communications have emerged. One is the now-familiar *Remote Procedure Call* (RPC) model, in which a programmer makes what looks like a local method or procedure call, leaving it up to the communications plumbing to marshal the parameters, send them over the transport, block until a response is received, unmarshal the response, and return the unmarshaled data (or throw the unmarshaled exception, if that was the result) to the caller. (This is why most RPC-style toolkits require a postcompilation step, such as RMI's rmic, which generates the local classes—often called *proxies* or *stubs*—that do all this work.) More generally known as *request-response communication*, RPC has found much favor with the programming community due to its conceptual familiarity: "I just call this method, and the rest is all magic until it gets to that method implementation over on the server."

Fundamentally, however, the RPC request-response model is just one of several lower-level communications patterns built on the notion of "sending a message": in the request-response model, a sender sends a message to the recipient (the request, consisting of the marshaled parameters) and blocks until the recipient sends the expected message back (the response, consisting of the marshaled return value or fault code). Other (non-RPC) forms of request-response include the HTTP protocol itself, SQL, and even Telnet.

When viewed this way, however, it becomes apparent that communication has more possibilities than just "send a message, block, receive a message." For example, I could send a message without blocking, send a message and expect zero to many messages back, send zero to many messages without expecting a response, and so on. In essence, we're just describing different ways to send a message.

This concept of sending a message and the inherent flexibility that comes with it are what *messaging communications APIs* provide. While typically a bit more difficult to work with, in that more supporting code on your part is often required, messaging offers a number of capabilities an RPC-based request-response model cannot. Three such additional "patterns" of communication include *solicit-notify*, in which one party asks another party to send notifications (such as how electronic mailing lists work); *fire-and-forget*, also known as *one-way* or *asynchronous calls*, in which one party sends a message without waiting for a response; and *asynchronous response*, in which one party sends a request message expecting a reply but doesn't block waiting for the response, which comes in later. Some messaging systems also support the idea of *broadcast messages*, in which one message is flung out to multiple recipients.

While messaging itself is a fundamental low-level networking concept, the idea of messaging and its commensurate flexibility has proven powerful enough to merit moving this approach to network communications up to the same level of abstraction as RPC. As a result, we can talk about *messaging systems*, or *message-oriented middleware*, which provides this same kind of functionality but at a higher level of abstraction—the Java Message Service, for example, is a specification that defines a standard Java API for working with such systems and defines how to send a message whose payload is a Serializable Java object, simple byte array, a `String`, a Java `Map`-implementing object, and so on.

Having defined these two basic approaches to communications (RPC and messaging), we can go one level higher and begin classifying different architectural styles of network communications. A *client/server architecture*, for example, has one process—designated the server—that will be available to process requests on behalf of a process that initiates communication with it—the client. In a *peer-to-peer architecture*, however, generally there is no designated server, and processes communicate with one another freely, either side initiating the communication as desired. (See Item 16 for more on peer-to-peer architecture and discovery.) Note that neither client/server nor peer-to-peer architectures are inherently RPC-based or messaging-based; either one can make use of either approach just as easily.

To show how the communications APIs supported by Java break down along the three axes of interest—transport, format, and communication patterns—let's examine each API in turn.

- *Remote Method Invocation (RMI):* Following an RPC approach, RMI uses the Java Object Serialization layer for marshaling the data and, by default, sends the data over a raw TCP/IP socket. Later, however, a variant of RMI was introduced as part of JDK 1.2, called RMI/IIOP (pronounced "RMI-over-IIOP"), designed to provide interoperability with CORBA servers, which use IIOP as their marshaling layer. Essentially, it's just RMI, with the marshaling layer using IIOP (a CORBA-specific binary format) instead of Java Object Serialization. As part of later revisions, RMI opened up its transport layer, allowing programmers to write custom socket factories, essentially allowing RMI programmers to provide their own custom transport layers if desired. The most typical use of this functionality is to create an SSL transport for RMI, thus giving RMI a measure of confidentiality that it otherwise lacks. Communicating with an EJB 2.0 or earlier system is almost always done using RMI, specifically RMI/IIOP; some vendors offer their own form of RMI (BEA offers its T3 protocol-based version of RMI, for example), but using this is outside the boundaries of the J2EE Specification and won't be understood by other vendors' systems. (Note that as of the EJB 2.1 draft specification, however, there is no vendor-neutral way to do any kind of SSL-encrypted form of RMI against an EJB server, so you may have to fall back to vendor-proprietary extensions if security inside the firewall is a concern.)
- *Common Object Request Broker Architecture (CORBA):* CORBA was the "other" technology staring down Microsoft's Distributed COM architecture in the late 1990s, and Sun made CORBA support ubiquitous within the Java community with the release of JDK 1.2, by bundling a CORBA Object Request Broker (ORB) as part of it. CORBA, like RMI, is an RPC approach, using IIOP as its marshaling layer and TCP/IP as the transport. CORBA supports other marshaling-plus-transport combinations, but none have gained any predominance since IIOP was introduced.
- *Servlets:* Servlets are built around a request-response communication pattern, of which HTTP is the most popular (and arguably only) protocol. Unlike most of the other communications systems we'll be talking about in this chapter, servlets require that programmers do the marshaling of the data by hand, by writing the request data to the

body of an HTTP request, and writing the response data via the `println` methods of `HttpServletResponse`. Of course, coupling servlets with an XML payload format takes you squarely into the realm of Web Services.

- *Java Message Service (JMS):* The JMS API is fairly obvious to classify in our three-tuple taxonomy: it's all about messaging, usually using TCP/IP as the transport and the Java Object Serialization format as the marshaling layer, although several JMS vendors now offer the ability to use other transports and/or marshaling layers. Once again, coupling JMS with XML message payloads takes you squarely into Web Services.

- *Jini:* Although not part of the J2EE family, Jini offers some powerful and enticing capabilities to enterprise Java projects, most notably the idea of self-healing networks and service discovery, both of which are more fully discussed in Item 16. Modulo the discovery-based lookup capabilities, Jini is really just an exercise in binary-marshaled RPC communications over straight TCP/IP. (A lot of interesting services, such as JavaSpaces, were built on top of Jini, but that was mostly an implementation detail—for example, IBM's TSpaces is another spaces-based toolkit, as JavaSpaces is, and TSpaces doesn't require Jini in any way.)

- *JXTA:* Also not a part of the J2EE family, Project JXTA focuses on providing cross-platform peer-to-peer capabilities by operating over TCP/IP and/or HTTP channels and using XML as the wire format. Each peer can send messages to any other peer it discovers in the collection of visible peers—no request-response format is assumed. Later versions of JXTA have created a socket-like abstraction on top of the JXTA plumbing.

- *Java API for XML RPC (JAX-RPC):* The JAX-RPC classification is also fairly obvious: RPC communications using XML marshaling, typically over an HTTP transport. Note that the Web Services bindings introduced as part of the EJB 2.1 Specification pretty much fall directly into this category, since both JAX-RPC and the EJB bindings use Web Services Description Language (WSDL) documents to describe their endpoints, just as CORBA uses its own Interface Description Language (IDL) to describe an object's interface and RMI uses Java interfaces.

- *Java API for XML Messaging (JAXM):* Built more or less directly over SOAP, JAXM is a message-based approach, using XML for its marshaling layer and typically using HTTP as the transport. Both the

SOAP and JAXM Specifications talk openly about using Simple Mail Transport Protocol (SMTP) as another transport, however, which would provide non-request-response (i.e., asynchronous) options. (By the way, JAXM seems to be on its last legs as a specification—several notable voices from Sun have commented via public forums and newsgroups that JAXM doesn't seem to serve any real purpose and, more importantly, despite its presence in early drafts, JAXM is not part of the J2EE 1.4 Specification.)

As you can see, the Java enterprise programmer (that's you) has a widespread set of choices for slinging data around between computers in a network. Which, of course, raises a question: How on earth are you supposed to decide?

After all, any of them will ultimately get the job done—moving data from machine A to machine B—so obviously the decision has to be rooted in something other than just "will it work?" *Any* of these would work. The larger question is, "Which of these will work well for what I/we need to do?"

Much of the decision-making process lies in identifying, to yourself, the particular context in which your communication needs to take place. Consider the following questions.

- *Do you need to communicate across firewalls?* Before you answer this definitively, bear in mind that this doesn't imply going outside of the corporate network—many companies are starting to segregate their internal networks, practicing a "defense in depth" strategy, and putting up firewalls between. Firewalls tend to favor HTTP as the main transport channel, since HTTP is a well-known format the firewall can inspect and scrub. Firewalls also really screw up any sort of client-driven RPC back against the server (which many Observer-style [GOF, 293] callback notification schemes tend to rely on) because they won't allow incoming traffic on arbitrary TCP/IP ports, toward which both RMI and CORBA tend.
- *Do you need to communicate synchronously?* If most of your communication patterns are of a request-response style, RPC certainly stands out as a preferred communication pattern choice—the messaging-based style permits greater flexibility but generally requires much more work on your part.
- *Do you need to be able to communicate to any platform, including those you don't know about yet?* Web Services (i.e., XML-based payloads

over standardized channels like HTTP) create a "middle ground" between all platforms, thanks to XML's ubiquity. But, as described in Item 43, XML comes with its own costs, which may be more than you're really willing to incur for interoperability between just two platforms (.NET and Java). More importantly, you need to make sure that you're taking *all* those other platforms into account when you build your communications stack in a Web Services–based model (as described in Item 22).

Certainly, there are other questions we could ask. We could even create a giant decision-making flowchart of communications technologies, but doing so starts to encroach on the value judgments that each architect and system designer will want to make differently. The point, simply, is to consider your communication needs carefully before committing to anything. (And remember, assuming you've used components in your system well, per Item 1, you can usually change and/or add new communications strategies without too much hassle.)

Item 16:   Consider your lookup carefully

Quiz time: What, precisely, does the term *location transparency* mean in its original context?

In the early days of networks, it was a rare scenario when your program had to go off-machine in order to make use of some resource, assuming you were even part of a network. In fact, if your organization even had more than one computer, more often than not it was more cost-effective to just set up the traditional SneakerNet system rather than try to wade through all the techno-details to set up a more formal network.

But as computers became more ubiquitous and networks became more prevalent, network and operating systems vendors began to realize that the notion of some kind of *transparency* was necessary—in other words, we as users want the system to hide the fact that certain processes and resources are physically distributed across multiple computers. In essence, transparency was a desire to add a layer of abstraction on top of the network; whereas before it was acceptable to force users to know that the file they wanted was on the machine named FILESERVER in the sharepoint titled PUBSRV03, now users just want to know that "it's on the M: drive," where the M: drive in a Windows-based network is "mapped" to the file server's sharepoint just mentioned. UNIX Network File System (NFS) goes even further, extending the single-rooted name-space across the network in such a way that most users can't even tell what machine the file `/usr/home/~neward/book.pdf` lives on—or at least, they won't be able to tell what machine it's on until that machine stops working, anyway. (A popular alternative definition of a distributed system, attributed to Leslie Lamport, is "You know you have one when the crash of a computer you've never heard of stops you from getting any work done" [Tanenbaum, 7].)

There are several forms of transparency in a distributed system; Andrew S. Tanenbaum, for example, describes eight different forms of transparency: access (hiding differences in data representation and how a resource is accessed), location (hiding where a resource is located), migration (hiding that a resource may move to another location), reloca-tion (hiding that a resource may move to another location while in use), replication (hiding that a resource is replicated), concurrency (hiding that a resource may be shared by several competitive users), failure (hid-ing the failure and recovery of a resource), and persistence (hiding whether a software resource is in memory or on disk) [Tanenbaum]. Within the J2EE space, all of these are hidden behind a single API intended to pro-vide the necessary layer of indirection required to pull off this degree of transparency: JNDI.

When first approaching J2EE, it's not uncommon for a novice Java pro-grammer to question the necessity of JNDI in the first place—it's the boil-erplate that you "just always do" to get hold of something you want to work with. For most J2EE practitioners, that's where JNDI ends, too: once the boilerplate code is out of the way, you just toss it aside and move on to the good stuff, calling methods on the returned `DataSource`, `EJBHome`, or whatever.

Stop.

JNDI exists in J2EE for a very real and highly underrated purpose, and to simply ignore it this way runs a very real risk of running into serious problems later.

Consider, for a moment, what happens when we write the following line of code:

```
URL u = new URL("http://www.neward.net/ted/weblog");
u.openConnection();
```

When we open the connection to the URL, the Java networking libraries do a Domain Name System (DNS) lookup to find the IP address of my home server, then open a standard TCP/IP connection across the Internet to that IP address on port 80.

Question: Why not just embed the IP address directly in the URL? Why take the hit of doing this lookup (even if it is cached somewhere on the local machine or even the process) if we don't have to? Why not just hit http://168.150.253.23/ted/weblog (or whatever my IP address is by the time this book ships) directly?

Arguably, you don't care what the IP address is, you care only about its human-readable representation. While this argument holds water when talking about your average "clueless user," for distributed systems where presumably clueless users aren't the ones writing the calls across machines, it's less effective. No, the main reason we accept the overhead of doing the DNS lookup on each and every TCP/IP connection like this is a combination of several transparency concepts.

- *Location transparency:* You don't particularly care what machine the resource lives on. Think about it—you just want to get to my blog, you don't particularly care whether my blog lives on the machine running out of my house or a rack-mounted machine in some ISP somewhere. I care about honoring your requests for my blog, however, so I want to make sure that you can always find it regardless of what machine it's running on. This leads us to the next point.
- *Migration and relocation transparency:* URLs serve as an important layer of abstraction; if I decide tomorrow that too many people are hitting my poor home-based server and I need to "move up" to a faster machine or fatter pipe, I can do so simply by changing the DNS entries for my domain to point to a different machine running in a different part of the country, and you would never know it. In fact, if the load becomes too great, say, because I suddenly get Slashdotted (positively, of course!) several times a day, I can try the next idea. . . .
- *Replication transparency:* I can pull a common trick and use the DNS entry as a "front" to one of several machines, rather than tying it to one physical machine as might be expected. (You didn't *really* think there's just one machine behind Google.com or Yahoo.com, did you?) Again, the layer of indirection provided by DNS and, in this case, by certain router hardware and software, gives the impression that it's a single machine when in fact it may be two, three, or dozens more.

Think what would happen if you cached off the IP address to my server, and then I decided to upgrade (or downgrade—maybe Slashdot decided they don't like me anymore and it's not cost-effective to maintain the expensive clustered Web farm at the ISP anymore); suddenly, your code starts failing left and right, and you have to make a code change to accommodate the change.

JNDI serves an important piece of the middleware puzzle, that of lookup: *in order to avoid being accidentally broken by changes in resource configuration and/or replication, we put a layer of abstraction between users and the resource itself.*

The classic scenario is that of the database. Prior to the JNDI days, developers had to establish JDBC `Connection` objects by knowing, *a priori*, the database URL they wished to connect to, passing that into the `Driver Manager` to construct a `Connection` object. Of course, this means that we have to pass the URL into the `DriverManager.getConnection` call, which leads to the uncomfortable and unacceptable hard-coded scenario that we all loathe—as soon as our code needs to connect to a different database (doing a deployment into the QA environment and needing to connect to the QA database instead of the development database, for example), we have to go back and change the code. So, using JNDI, we create a programmer-friendly JNDI name ("`jdbc/MyDataSource`") to act as the indirection link and let system administrators change the JDBC URL as they wish or need through the application server's administrative interface. In fact, if for some reason the database administrator needs to take the production database down for a while and wants to redirect all database traffic to a different database instance, the administrator can just change the URL on the other side of the JNDI name, and our code will happily start sending requests to that backup database instead of the production database.

Lo and behold, we have just taken an important step toward yielding better uptime statistics. But this layer of abstraction works only when you play by the rules and continue to go through that layer of abstraction to find the resources in question. Numerous J2EE books have been written suggesting that you cache off your JNDI lookups in order to avoid a remote round-trip across the network to the resource's home machine (the EJB server in the case of looking up an EJB, for example). Understand something very important here: if you cache these lookup results, you can't "switch over" without at least restarting the server. Remember how failover was supposed to be a large part of why we adopted J2EE in the first place? Think very hard about whether the inability to silently deal with a switchover like this is worth the cost savings of a potential round-trip across the network, particularly since in many cases the application server can do some smart caching of its own and avoid the need for the round-trip after all.

By the way, bear in mind that the traditional client/server style of lookup enshrined in the JNDI API isn't the only form of lookup available to us: the first half of the 2000 decade was all abuzz about a new form of resource sharing named "peer-to-peer" or "P2P" for short. Napster, Kazaa, and GNUtella all proclaimed revolutionary ways of sharing (and stealing, if you want to get right down to it) resources like MP3s and videos.

But if you crack open the code for these sorts of systems and take a look underneath, you discover something interesting: in almost all cases, the "peer-to-peer" nature of the system is purely in the lookup aspects. In other words, all Napster really did was tell you who near you was available, and from there your client engaged in traditional client/server interactions with the other party (acting as the server) to discover what songs they had, and you in turn acted as a server to them for the same purposes. All Napster really did was tell the two of you that you were around and that you might want to talk to each other. In short, Napster allowed two otherwise unaware processes to *discover* one another: it's just lookup by a different name.

(Interestingly enough, a JNDI provider for this kind of dynamic discovery isn't all that difficult to write, since the JNDI API provides for JavaBean event-style notifications; using that, a potential client could ask its local JNDI provider implementation for a callback when something else entered the naming context—presumably in response to a broadcast announcement of a new server—thus making JNDI a dynamic peer-to-peer system as well. But as of yet no vendor has taken JNDI to the point of supporting this.)

There's a lot of room within enterprise applications for discovery as a lookup mechanism; consider the idea, for example, of a client being able to "register" with a discovery service for notifications when a server of interest to that client becomes available. Two existing technologies from Sun (among others) provide this kind of capability: Jini, which uses an RMI-friendly model, and JXTA, which builds an entirely new API for doing so based on XML data exchange (thus providing for a more access-transparent mode of interacting with non-Java resources). Unfortunately, not much has been made of either of these technologies, or the concept of discovery itself for that matter, at the J2EE level, so making use of discovery may require stepping outside the J2EE API for a bit.

One of the easiest ways of doing discovery, for example, is to use UDP/IP, the connectionless peer to TCP/IP. A "client" can do a broadcast UDP/IP request to a LAN, and any machines on the LAN that are listening on the given UDP/IP port will respond to the packet, typically sending back enough information about themselves to give the client the ability to connect back over traditional TCP/IP. (This is how Jini's DiscoveryService works, by the way.)

So one cheap way to get a certain amount of clustering is to set up the application servers on two or more machines, then set up UDP/IP listeners on each. When it comes time for the middleware layer to find a server to execute some processing, issue the UDP/IP broadcast and take the first server that responds. Taking the first one to respond also provides a certain amount of load balancing, since a server that's being hammered will most likely take longer to respond anyway.

One interesting aspect that emerges from this idea of discovery as a lookup mechanism is the idea of self-healing networks. For years, we've struggled with the problem that networks are not always reliable— routers go down, power goes out, network trunks get cut by street construction workers,[1] and other disasters occur. Normally, when a client can't communicate to the server, it just gives up and terminates because most client applications can't perform any processing without the server. In fact, most client applications check to see whether the server is up just once, at the start of the application, and never bother to check again, just assuming the server will always be there.

In a self-healing network environment, however, the client is written explicitly to deal with the idea that the server could "go away" for whatever reason. So, for example, in a rich-client application (see Item 51), when a server appears to go "offline" for whatever reason, the client can display some kind of "disconnected" icon, informing the user that things aren't well. If the application is written to use a local database (see Item 44), the client can simply use discovery to determine when the server comes back up (either by polling periodically, as JXTA does, or else registering with a

---

1. True story—a few years ago, a San Jose street construction crew accidentally sheared a major cable line, cutting Internet access to most of the Silicon Valley for roughly half a day.

discovery service, as Jini does) and resume connected operations at that point. Voilà: the application "repaired" or "self-healed" a network outage that would kill other applications. The user saw nothing but successful operation (to a point, anyway).

Whether or not you choose to explore discovery as a lookup mechanism, don't just treat the lookup portions of your middleware coding as something you just have to get out of the way to get to the good stuff. Lookup is fundamental to the success of any middleware system because it enables location transparency. By the way, note very carefully that location transparency only wants to hide *where* the resource is located, not the fact that the resource is located remotely—sometimes location transparency is cited in situations (such as the common fallacy that "I don't care where objects are") where it's not the right kind of transparency to use; see Item 18 for details.

Item 17: Recognize the cost of network access

Although this usually doesn't come as much of a surprise to developers when they stop to think about it, it costs a great deal of time and effort (measured in CPU cycles) to move data across the network. What they don't often realize is *how much* more expensive, usually about three orders of magnitude (i.e., 1,000 times) more expensive, if not more.

Prove it to yourself. Let's say we design a simple API interface that will be implemented in three ways, once inline (i.e., putting the code directly in the caller, rather than making a function call, to test the JVM's efficiency in making method calls), once as a standard in-memory object, and once as an RMI-exported object. We'll host the registry in the same process to keep things simple and even run it all on the same machine to reduce wire transmit time to zero—in other words, the optimal situation we can create for remote objects.

The driver behind this test is listed here; `IApi` is our simple interface, `ApiImpl` is our RMI-exported implementation, and `Driver` is, as its name implies, the driver behind the test.

```
// IApi interface
//
public interface IApi extends java.rmi.Remote {
  public int function(int k, int i)
```

```
        throws java.rmi.RemoteException;
}


//
// ApiImpl not shown here for brevity
//

// Driver code
//
public class Driver
{
    public static final int J_LOOP = 7;
    public static final int I_LOOP = 5000000;

    public static void main(String[] args)
    {
        init();
        noFunctionCall();
        functionCall();
        noFunctionCall();
        functionCall();
        rmiCallOnLocalHost();
        System.exit(0);
    }

    private static void init()
    {
        int k = 0;

        // Warm everything up (ClassLoading, JIT, etc.)
        //
        System.currentTimeMillis();
        for (int i = 0; i < I_LOOP / 1000; ++i)
        {
            for (int j = 0; j < J_LOOP; ++j)
            {
                // Do something to avoid removal
                if (j < i)
                {
                    ++k;
```

```
                }
                else
                {
                    --k;
                }
            }
        }
        System.currentTimeMillis();
        ApiImpl.startServer();

        try
        {
            IApi api = (IApi) java.rmi.Naming.lookup("API");
            for (int i = 0; i < I_LOOP / 100000; ++i)
            {
                api.function(k, i);
            }
        }
        catch (Exception e)
        {
            e.printStackTrace();
            System.exit(1);
        }
    }

    public static void noFunctionCall()
    {
        int k = 0;
        // Now do real timings. This is used to remove all
        // computing time from other tests
        long start = System.currentTimeMillis();
        for (int i = 0; i < I_LOOP; ++i)
        {
            for (int j = 0; j < J_LOOP; ++j)
            {
                // Do something to avoid removal
                if (j < i)
                {
                    ++k;
                }
```

```
                else
                {
                    --k;
                }
            }
        }
        long end = System.currentTimeMillis();
        displayResults("No Function Call", k, start, end);
}

private static void rmiCallOnLocalHost()
{
    int k = 0;

    try
    {
        IApi api = (IApi) java.rmi.Naming.lookup("API");

        long start = System.currentTimeMillis();
        for (int i = 0; i < I_LOOP; ++i)
        {
            k = api.function(k, i);
        }
        long end = System.currentTimeMillis();
        displayResults("API Call", k, start, end);
    }
    catch (Exception e)
    {
        e.printStackTrace();
        System.exit(1);
    }
}

public static void functionCall()
{
    int k = 0;

    long start = System.currentTimeMillis();
    for (int i = 0; i < I_LOOP; ++i)
    {
```

```
            k = function(k, i);
    }
    long end = System.currentTimeMillis();
    displayResults("Function Call", k, start, end);


}


private static int function(int k, int i)
{
    for (int j = 0; j < J_LOOP; ++j)
    {
        // Do something to avoid removal
        if (j < i)
        {
            ++k;
        }
        else
        {
            --k;
        }
    }

    return k;
}


private static void displayResults(String desc, int k,
                                   long start, long end)
{
    System.out.println("k = " + k + ", " + desc + ": " +
                       (end - start) + "ms");
}
}
```

When executed on my laptop, this code returned the following results.

```
C:\Prg\Projects\Publications\Books\EEJ\code>java Driver
k = 34999944, No Function Call: 340ms
k = 34999944, Function Call: 271ms
k = 34999944, No Function Call: 190ms
k = 34999944, Function Call: 351ms
k = 34999944, API Call: 437559ms
```

As you can see, that's some significant difference between the No Function Call and the Function Call times compared against the remote API Call time. And worse, this experiment doesn't even involve the wire in any way. We're just measuring the cost of marshaling and moving it down to the loopback adapter in the TCP/IP stack.

(Ironically, note that it took longer to do the Function Call times the second time around, whereas the inline No Function Call times got better, probably due to JIT hot-spot inlining. I can't honestly explain why the Function Call times got worse; perhaps JIT compilation of the function call code actually hurt more than it helped, possibly due to interpreted-to-native transition boundaries. Fortunately, we're talking a difference of .08 seconds over 35 million calls, so it's probably not something to worry about.)

To put this into perspective, imagine for a moment that you're hungry: you want a sandwich. You go to the refrigerator, and you discover that you're completely out of everything you need to make a sandwich—no bread, no mustard, no ham, no lettuce, no tomato, nothing. So you figure you'll head down to the grocery store (which just happens to be our baseline "local method call") and get the stuff. It takes you twenty minutes to get your keys, grab some cash, drive to the store, park the car, go inside, shop, go back outside, unlock the car, drive home, go inside, unpack the stuff, and spread it out on the table, ready to go.

Now imagine that instead of going to the grocery store down the block, you hear of a really good deli your buddy uses (the "remote method call"). If it takes you twenty minutes to go to the local deli, and a remote call takes three orders of magnitude (or more) longer to execute, you're spending roughly the same amount of time in transit as it takes you to travel to Pluto. (That had better be a really, *really* good deli.) And Heaven help us if the deli wants to sell us only one item at a time or we forget our list of ingredients and have to keep going back for each item, one at a time (see Item 18).

Where does all the cost come from? A variety of things, as it turns out—marshaling the parameters into wire-friendly format from their in-memory representation (which is pretty minimal, in this case, since all we're really passing across the boundary is isomorphic types like int, which require no work to transmit), as well as passing the marshaled data down the TCP/IP stack to the localhost loopback part of the TCP/IP adapter (which then turns around and immediately passes it back up the stack), and vice versa for the response on the other side. Where the exact time loss comes from is not significant—it's the fact that, in the aggregate, it's hideously time-expensive to move data across the network.

This, along with the "identity breeds contention" problem (see Item 5), is what kills most distributed object systems: good object-oriented design encourages small, atomic objects that focus on doing one thing well and defer all other requests to other objects via method calls, which in distributed object systems usually means network access. Imagine, for a moment, what happens to your performance if you combine the Visitor pattern [GOF, 331] with remote method calls—with each method call between the objects traveling across the wire, and each traversal requiring at least two or more method calls, you're looking at a significant amount of time spent just going back and forth between remote objects. Ouch.

This isn't just an RPC thing, by the way—any technology that involves moving data across machines (or even just across process boundaries) has to go through the same kinds of gyrations that the RPC toolkits do. JDBC, JMS, HTTP, all of them spend a certain amount of time turning objects into 1s and 0s, and all of them are still limited by the speed (or lack thereof) of the underlying wire. For these reasons, make each trip to Pluto count. Make sure you pass data in bulk when you can (see Item 23), consider moving data closer to the processors or vice versa (see Item 4), and even think about taking the time to write smarter RPC proxies (see Item 24). Anything you can do to minimize the amount of time spent on the wire, as long as it doesn't interfere with the overall goals of middleware in general, will pay off in better performance.

Item 18:   Prefer context-complete communication styles

Context-complete communication offers a number of advantages that context-incomplete calls don't. The notion of context turns out to be a major component in distributed design as a whole, so it makes sense to first examine the notion of context in communications.

Imagine for a moment a conversation between yourself and a friend over the phone.[2]

---

2. This example was inspired by a similar example in *Loosely Coupled: The Missing Pieces of Web Services* [Kaye, 119–120].

Stu: Hey, you wanna grab lunch today?

Justin: Sure. When?

Stu: How about noon?

Justin: Doesn't work for me. 11 OK?

Stu: Sure. Where at?

Justin: How about the pizza place downtown?

Stu: Gotcha. See you there.

When viewed this way, the conversation is easy to follow because the context of the conversation is easily visible and understood.

But think about what would happen if you wandered into the middle of this conversation, at about the fifth line. You know they're meeting at the pizza place downtown, but not what time or what day. You might have a vague idea that this is a lunch or dinner meeting, but they could be choosing the location as a simple gathering point for a convoy trip to a distant state. In short, the context of the conversation establishes important elements about the outcome that aren't visible unless you were there from the beginning. Worse, in the case of two friends who have been to lunch together on a regular basis (as Stu and Justin have), the conversation could have been far more cryptic:

Stu: Hey, you wanna grab lunch today?

Justin: Sure. When?

Stu: How about the usual?

Justin: Doesn't work for me. 11 OK?

Stu: Sure. Where at?

Justin: Same place as yesterday?

Stu: Gotcha. See you there.

Now the context stretches across a much longer chronological window, and unless you happen to know their eating habits, there's absolutely *no* way to follow this conversation.

Many distributed object designs take this same approach, often without meaning to:

```
Context rootContext = new InitialContext();
CartoonCharacter cc =
    (CartoonCharacter)rootContext.lookup(PATH);
```

```
cc.setFirstName("Fred");
cc.setLastName("Flintstone");
cc.setHometown("Bedrock");
String catchphrase = cc.utterCatchPhrase();
   // Returns this character's catch phrase as a string
```

By the time we get to the `utterCatchPhrase` call, the context has already been established by the series of calls prior to it, implicitly establishing the context of the call by setting state on the object instance itself.

But what would happen if that context were lost? Or confused?

Many distributed system architects make the major mistake of not accounting for the various ways that remote objects can fail, even in a short period of time. Let's spin out a simple scenario: the call to `setLast Name` throws a `RemoteException`, and we catch it. What now? Is the entire object itself no longer good? Is that call the only thing that failed? Can we call `setLastName` again and continue?

Worse yet, consider the code written by the college intern over in the corner; we all know that you'd never do this, but what's to stop him from writing something like:

```
Context rootContext = new InitialContext();
CartoonCharacter cc =
   (CartoonCharacter)rootContext.lookup(PATH);
try { cc.setFirstName("Fred"); } catch (Exception x) { }
try { cc.setLastName("Flintstone"); } catch (Exception x) { }
try { cc.setHometown("Bedrock"); } catch (Exception x) { }
String catchphrase = cc.utterCatchPhrase();
   // Returns this character's catch phrase as a string
```

I know, it just makes you weep to think that somebody might actually write something like this and turn it loose in a production system, but it happens, and the author of `CartoonCharacter`'s implementation needs to code defensively in order to be robust in the face of failure (see Item 7).

This, then, implies that the `utterCatchPhrase` method should probably check to make sure its internal state is good before continuing forward:

```
public class CartoonCharacterImpl extends UnicastRemoteObject
   implements CartoonCharacter
{
```

```
private String firstName = null;
private String lastName = null;
private String hometown = null;
private boolean goodness = false;

public String utterCatchPhrase()
{
  if (this.goodness)
  {
    // Do database lookup to get character's catch phrase;
    // only do this if we have good firstName, lastName,
    // and hometown values
    //
  }
  else
    throw new IllegalArgumentException(
      "Invalid arguments!");
}
}
```

Now we get into an interesting conundrum: How do we set, or unset, the goodness flag?

Clearly the easiest thing to test is that all three of the private values aren't null; that is, put a test into the end of each mutator method that looks something like this:

```
if (firstName != null && lastName != null &&
    hometown != null)
  goodness = true;
else
  goodness = false;
```

Note that the else clause is a necessary part of the test; without it, simple code like the following would easily confuse the goodness bit:

```
cc.setFirstName("Fred");
cc.setLastName("Flintstone");
cc.setHometown("Bedrock");
  // At this point, goodness turns 'true'
cc.setFirstName(null);
  // Without else clause, goodness remains 'true'
```

In fact, things are even more insidious than this, even with that `else` clause—what happens when the following code runs?

```
cc.setFirstName("Fred");
cc.setLastName("Flintstone");
cc.setHometown("Bedrock");
   // Goodness turns 'true'
cc.setFirstName("Thundarr");
   // Is it still good?
```

What should take place now when we call `utterCatchPhrase`? Obviously, `"Thundarr Flintstone"` isn't exactly a valid combination, but because initialization has taken place in a piecemeal fashion, there's no way for the language to catch and enforce this.

Things can also get really hairy when only parts of the state are necessary and the rest remains optional. Those old enough to remember the cartoon series will remember that unlike the Flintstones, Thundarr didn't have a last name, nor did he have a hometown. Still, his first name was enough to identify him, so the following code should be sufficient:

```
cc.setFirstName("Thundarr");
String catchphrase = cc.utterCatchPhrase();
```

Meanwhile, He-Man didn't have a last name, but he did have a hometown (his home planet of Eternia—hey, it's a stretch, but so is an enterprise Java system built around cartoon characters, so bear with me):

```
cc.setFirstName("He-Man");
cc.setHometown("Eternia");
String catchphrase = cc.utterCatchPhrase();
```

Consider how you might set the `goodness` bit based on these requirements, then think about what happens in the event of this chronological scenario:

```
cc.setFirstName("Fred");
cc.setLastName("Flintstone");
cc.setHometown("Bedrock");
String catchphrase1 = cc.utterCatchPhrase();
cc.setFirstName("He-Man");
cc.setHometown("Eternia");
String catchphrase2 = cc.utterCatchPhrase();
```

```
cc.setFirstName("Thundarr");
String catchphrase3 = cc.utterCatchPhrase();
```

By the time of the third call, we've got leftover initialization data from the previous two calls because the programmer didn't clear out the old data by doing a complete initialization all over again—a fairly easy mistake to make, particularly if the `CartoonCharacter` class used to just require `firstName`, with `lastName` and `hometown` being added later.

In formal terms, two steps need to take place for every object created: *instantiation,* in which the object itself is spun out of nothingness, and *initialization,* in which the object is given the initial state required in order to begin carrying out meaningful work. Normally, this is done via the constructor by defining constructors that require certain parameters and not providing a default constructor. If the parameters passed in aren't valid, we can throw an exception and effectively invalidate the object itself. In the case of a remote object, however, instantiation is often done in an entirely different timeline than initialization, so we lose the opportunity during instantiation to validate initialization parameters.

In classic object-orientation, we never want to use an object that's not ready for use (i.e., an object that hasn't been initialized properly), so languages go to great lengths to make sure initialization occurs at the same time as instantiation, usually via constructors. If the parameters are invalid, the constructor can throw an exception and effectively kill the object. If the necessary parameters aren't passed in at all, the compiler will complain. In short, we have linguistic support to make sure that an object is given what it needs in order to perform its job.

Remote objects have a tendency to screw this up, however. Because the instantiation of a remote object usually has to happen before the client can pass initialization in, the remote object has to separate initialization from instantiation, which is where we start to get into trouble. In keeping with classic Java design patterns, we tend to make such initialization calls individual to the property level, leading us to need multiple calls to establish context (state) within the object in order to carry out some kind of useful behavior. Which brings us full circle to the problem established earlier: What happens if one of those context-establishing method calls fails? There's no linguistic way to handle this gracefully.

Let's take context out of the picture, or perhaps more accurately, let's remove the possibility of context getting lost by including it as part of all communications back and forth, starting with our lunchtime conversation again:

Stu: Hey, you want to go grab some lunch?

Justin: Sure, lunch sounds good. When?

Stu: Let's go for lunch at the usual time, noon.

Justin: Lunch at noon isn't good for me. 11?

Stu: Sure, lunch at 11 is fine. Where?

Justin: Let's do lunch at 11 at the pizza place downtown.

Stu: Great, I'll meet you at the pizza place downtown at 11 for lunch.

Nobody ever talks this way. It's awkward, it's redundant, and it's entirely unnecessary between two people who have any sort of short-term memory whatsoever. But bear in mind, that's exactly the point: we don't *want* the two conversationalists, objects in this case, to have to remember anything—that's what will enable the system to scale better, because now any object at any time can participate in this conversation: each back-and-forth exchange between the two principals is *context-complete*.

Putting this idea into code means that instead of establishing context as part of an API that's removed from the call, we include it as part of each "do something" call:

```
CartoonCharacter cc =
  (CartoonCharacter)rootContext.lookup(...);
String catchphrase =
  cc.utterCatchPhrase("Fred", "Flintstone", "Bedrock");
```

In this case, instead of passing the context via three separate API calls before being allowed to call utterCatchPhrase, we're doing it as part of the call itself. This also makes it easier for the utterCatchPhrase method to ignore any state from previous calls:

```
CartoonCharacter cc =
  (CartoonCharacter)rootContext.lookup(...);
String catchPhrase1 =
  cc.utterCatchPhrase("Fred", "Flintstone", "Bedrock");
String catchPhrase2 =
  cc.utterCatchPhrase("He-Man", null, "Eternia");
```

```
String catchPhrase3 =
  cc.utterCatchPhrase("Thundarr", null, null);
```

This works because usually the context is stored in local variables and/or method parameters:

```
public class CartoonCharacterImpl extends UnicastRemoteObject
  implements CartoonCharacter
{
  public String utterCatchPhrase(String first,
                                 String last, String ht)
  {
    // Do our lookup here
  }
}
```

In fact, this looks a lot like what the stateless session bean does for us: because the stateless session bean can hold no state across method calls, it implicitly requires context-complete communications. And this is partly why context-complete communications are preferable: because any object in the cluster can answer the request. There's no implicit identity due to the context established on any particular object (which is the case with both stateful session beans and entity beans).

One other useful benefit arises out of context-complete calls, in that you have everything you need to recreate the call later if it cannot be carried out at this time. This is useful in the event of a failure in the call's processing: shunt the context off into some kind of intermediate storage, and pull it back later to try again. In fact, if that intermediate storage is a messaging layer, we can obtain asynchronicity for free when we need it, since now we can take the context, push it into a Message, and put the Message onto a Queue for later processing, presumably when load decreases or the outage is recovered.

Transactional considerations factor into this discussion as well—under the context-complete approach, it becomes pretty clear when and where the transaction should begin and end. In the getter/setter approach, it's much less clear. Do we begin with the first call to set and end the transaction only when the utterCatchPhrase call is invoked? That leaves transactions open between method calls, a clear violation of Item 30. If we want to avoid leaving the transaction open, each call needs to operate under its own transaction, which then leaves us open to semantic corruption, in that other clients could conceivably call other `set` methods on this same object, interleaved with the sequence above. It just gets uglier from there.

Interestingly enough, this model fits in well with the Web Services notion of document-literal communications (as opposed to rpc-encoded), since document-literal communications require the complete set of parameters to be present as part of the packet. Servlets, too, can benefit from this; it becomes easier for forms to be reused through the Web application (or even across Web applications) if there aren't any implicit dependencies on context stored in `HttpSession`.

Avoid context as much as you can, and you'll build better scalable systems. In doing so, almost by accident, you'll tend to build remote APIs that require fewer trips across the network (thus obeying Item 17), since no "initialization methods" need be invoked to set context into place before the call itself.

Item 19: Prefer data-driven communication over behavior-driven communication

Over the years, IPC has steadily evolved from the idea of "shipping data from one process to another" to "making a function (or method) call in another process." While we can explain away the difference as one merely of detail and encapsulation ("Oh, making a remote procedure call is just sending a request message and waiting for a response message, it's no different"), the fact remains that the *intent* of the communication style drives two very different kinds of communication interaction, one *behavior-driven*, the other *data-driven*. In general, you'll want to prefer data-driven communications, particularly when navigating across component boundaries. And, although this mostly applies to Web Services, known there as *document-oriented style*, it's also desirable in straight Java-centric communications layers.

For most developers, the concept of behavior-driven and data-driven communications is new ground. The difference effectively lies in what you, the developer, intend when you make the network communication take place. In standard object-RPC toolkits like RMI and CORBA, you're invoking a method—that is, you're ordering an object instance to execute a particular method and return. You pass parameters, wait for execution on the remote machine to complete, then harvest the result sent back to you. Pretty straightforward, no?

In a data-driven approach, however, you never "invoke a method" per se but instead simply send a packet of data to a remote resource to do what it will with it. There is no implicit assumption that a response will return—in fact, in many respects, it would be much better all around if there wasn't one, since that frees you to continue processing locally without having to wait for the data to come back across the wire (see Item 20).

To put this into more concrete terms, consider the idea of an online order-processing system, much as Amazon.com might use. The user has already filled out the shopping cart and moved to the checkout page, indicating the order is ready. It's now your responsibility to take this order and its contents and do the usual things to it: verify the credit card number, charge the card, and so on.

One approach is to build a collection of remote objects, invokable from the client tier (in this case, a servlet, but an EJB session bean would look almost identical), and invoke them one at a time as the order dictates:

```
public void doPost(HttpServletRequest req,
                   HttpServletResponse resp)
  throws ServletException, IOException
{
  // . . . Put in verification and input-validity-checking
  // code here; see Item 61 for details
  //

  HttpSession session = req.getSession(false);
  OrderModel order =
    (OrderModel)session.getAttribute("order");

  Context ctx = new InitialContext();
    // Always do lookup, in order to permit failover;
    // see Item 16

  // Verify credit card
  //
  CreditCardProcessor ccp =
    (CreditCardProcessor)ctx.lookup(...);
  if (ccp.verify(order.getCreditCard().getName(),
```

```
                    order.getCreditCard().getNumber(),
                    order.getCreditCard().getExpirationDate()))
  {
    if (ccp.charge(order.getCreditCard().getNumber(),
                   order.getAmount()))
    {
      for (OrderItem oi : order.getItems())
      {
        // Process each item, take it out of stock, whatever
      }
    }
  }
}
```

Again, whether this code occurs in a servlet, a session bean, or something in between is really irrelevant—the point here is that each step is carefully measured via behavioral actions against beans (whether remote or local) that carry out each step in modular fashion.

In a data-driven approach, however, the sender of the data makes no assumptions about what needs to happen; in fact, the client revels in its relative ignorance. Rather than making any behavioral demands, the client simply packages the data and sends it to a neutral party (usually some kind of storage layer), from which other interested parties retrieve the data for processing. The classic way to do this is via JMS:

```
public void doPost(HttpServletRequest req,
                   HttpServletResponse resp)
  throws ServletException, IOException
{
  // . . . Put in verification and input-validity-checking
  // code here; see Item 61 for details
  //

  HttpSession session = req.getSession(false);
  OrderModel order =
    (OrderModel)session.getAttribute("order");

  Context ctx = new InitialContext();
    // Always do lookup, in order to permit failover;
    // see Item 16
```

```
// Remain ignorant, just send it on for further processing
//
Connection conn = ...; // Where we get this isn't important
                       // now
try
{
  Session session =
    conn.createSession(false, Session.AUTO_ACKNOWLEDGE);
  Destination dest = ctx.lookup("jms/NewOrders");
    // Note that there's no hint of what will happen in
    // the queue name
  MessageProducer producer = session.createProducer(dest);
  ObjectMessage msg = session.createObjectMessage();
  msg.setObject(order);
    // JMS ObjectMessage requires Serializable objects; if
    // OrderModel is a JavaBean, it must be Serializable
    //
  producer.send(msg);
}
finally
{
  session.close(); // Aggressively release resources;
                   // see Item 67
}

// And we're out, happy and carefree; generate some kind of
// "Thank you" response page back to the user, probably by
// forwarding to a JSP
//
}
```

Note that in the data-driven example, the client code gives absolutely no hint of what will happen to this order—we're simply letting somebody (we don't even know who) know that a new order has been received. What happens to it from there is not our concern.

It might be tempting to simply classify the two approaches as RPC and messaging, respectively, since behavior-driven systems are most easily modeled using RPC-based toolkits like RMI and CORBA, while data-driven systems fit messaging-oriented systems (such as JMS) like a glove. If it helps, then feel free to use this classification, but keep in mind that it is an oversimplification—it's always possible to build a behavior-driven system using JMS or a data-driven system using RMI, with all the commensurate benefits and drawbacks. It's the style of approach, not the technology on which it's built, that makes the difference.

Given all that, so what? The behavior-driven approach is much easier for developers to understand and build, particularly since it fits in pretty easily with the standard way J2EE applications are built—why on earth should anybody look to avoid this, particularly in favor of something that won't gel as quickly with the way we traditionally think?

Three reasons: evolution, intermediaries, and recoverable operations.

It's a fact that an enterprise system has a "reach" that stretches beyond the team that builds it and the group they built it for—remember the 10 fallacies of enterprise systems discussed in Chapter 1, in particular Fallacy 9: "The system is monolithic." Change is inevitable, and once an API has been published to the world, it can never change. Or, to be more accurate, it can only change when all consumers of that API agree that it can change, which is more or less saying the same thing—getting business partners, departments, and system administrators to all agree on rolling out a new change is about as likely as getting conservative and liberal politicians to agree on . . . well, anything.

Unfortunately, change must happen, and dealing with it becomes much easier in the data-driven approach than in the behavior-driven approach. For example, credit card charges in the 21st century often require not only the standard 16-digit credit card number but a 3-digit "verification code" printed on the back of the card in small print. Unfortunately, the API designed in our `CreditCardProcessor` class doesn't expect a 19-digit number, only a 16-digit one, so we'll need to change the class API to allow for a fourth parameter, the verification code.

Under EJB, or any other method-call-based distributed toolkit for that matter, this means changing the interface and regenerating the remote stubs shipped to the client. Fortunately, a certain amount of change can be handled silently—for example, a method to the interface can often be silently added to the remote implementation without breaking previous stubs (RMI supports this)—but it doesn't take much to quickly exhaust the forgiveness of the remoting toolkit. Deleting a parameter, for example, or deleting a method entirely will break existing clients faster than you can say "D'oh!"

If all I'm sending, however, is a data structure with no implicit behavior behind it, adding that extra bit of data is as simple as adding the additional field to the `CreditCard` class whose instance is stored inside `Order`. If this is a Serializable object, I can use the facilities of Serialization (see Item 71) to handle the evolution of the data structure as necessary when those breaking changes come.

Or, in fact, I can simply create a new data structure, maybe calling it `Order2`, or `OrderEx`, or one of an infinite variety of uninspired names, and the message processors (the programs that pull the message and handle it) can examine the actual type at runtime to figure out what to do next. In fact, nobody ever said that the process pulling these messages out of the JMS `Queue` has to work alone. While it's convenient sometimes to have just one processor handle these new orders, in the case of a fundamental change (perhaps now certain orders need to be encrypted where before it wasn't necessary), it can sometimes be easier to simply create an all-new processor, even while we leave the old one in place to handle the previous collection of messages, which clients may still be sending us. JMS doesn't care—all it sees, at its heart, is a byte array.

If you don't want to deal with Serialization versioning, you can always choose a more loosely typed approach by not sending actual objects but just `Collection` objects that in turn contain primitive types. The `Map` interface works well for this because each key/value pair in the `Map` can correspond roughly to a field in a traditional class. Yes, you're sacrificing compile-time safety for flexibility, so code defensively and test relentlessly to avoid any production deployment embarrassments.

Last but not least, of course, we have to consider the ultimate flexible data format, XML. Sending the message in an XML-based format permits a great deal of data evolutionary flexibility, both with or without the use of XML Schema. What's more, the use of XML in your data-driven designs allows for a future degree of interoperability that wouldn't be present in the JMS-based approach, although it's not difficult to factor in. (Make sure your XML doesn't make undue assumptions about the platform that will be receiving the XML, however. That means no automatic object-to-XML conversion APIs except in very simple doses; see Items 43 and 22 for details.)

Evolution isn't the only reason for preferring data-driven designs, though it is a definite plus. A data-driven channel can include a number of intermediaries, software or hardware processors that act in some useful and typically invisible manner on behalf of the entire communications process, layering in useful crosscutting concerns like using different transport mechanisms (e.g., SMTP/POP3 or even an instant messenger protocol like Jabber).

In fact, the notion of intermediaries could conceivably be generalized in a larger sense, that of the flexibility gained when the client remains ignorant of the ultimate recipient of the information. For starters, in a message-driven environment, the messaging layer holds the message even while the ultimate recipient is offline. In other words, the client never has to deal with an outage of the code processing the messages—as long as the messaging layer remains active, we can evolve and modify the code behind the Queue as often as we wish without impacting the clients (the order-taking Web site, in this case), since messages will simply accumulate until we're ready to bring the processor back online. (This, of course, assumes that the client isn't blocking while waiting for some kind of response, which may imply that you're using JMS in a behavior-driven manner.)

More importantly, again because of the disconnect between sender and ultimate recipient, we can do a lot of interesting things to this message that wouldn't otherwise be feasible with behavior-driven communications. Hohpe and Woolf [EAI] document a number of useful patterns, such as Message Router ("decoupling individual processing steps so that messages can be passed to different filters depending on a set of conditions," 78), Content-Based Router ("handle a situation in which the implementation of a single logical function is spread across multiple physical systems," 230), and one already alluded to earlier, Normalizer ("process messages that are semantically equivalent but arrive in a different format," 352). In essence, we're creating all kinds of opportunities for hook points (see Item 6) in the system.

But wait—act now, and we'll throw in context-completeness (see Item 18) and a tendency to avoid excessive "chattiness" across the network (see Item 17) for free! Because the data-driven approach tends to prefer simple and complete data sets, rather than Domain Model [Fowler, 116] objects, there's less tendency toward building a system that will create numerous accidental round-trips across the network. (The easiest way to make sure of this, of course, is to ensure that nothing that gets passed across the wire inherits from `java.rmi.Remote`.)

Unfortunately, data-driven communication is a subtle science; it's a slippery slope at best, an impenetrable pedantic nit at worst. For example, go back to the e-commerce Web site for just a moment. The semantic difference between posting an "Order" message and an "Add Order" message is a very small one. The key difference here is what happens when an existing order gets changed or modified. In the case of the data-driven architecture, the order simply gets placed back into the same queue, and it's assumed that the back-end processors will handle it appropriately, whereas in the behavior-driven case, we'll have to create new methods and code to handle the idea of "modifying" an order, as opposed to placing a new one.

The real payoff in using a data-driven design comes when you need to move to an open-integration model, where clients could be coming in from entirely different platforms. Because your API is now defined in terms of simplistic data structures, rather than complex object models, it makes it easier to move to a doc/literal Web Service model and in turn easier for clients in non-object-oriented languages to adapt.

By the way, just in case you were about ready to chuck the whole idea and go back to your favorite behavior-driven design approach, keep in mind that if you follow J2EE conventional wisdom and use Data Transfer Objects [Fowler, 401] to keep from having to bang on entity beans directly from the client layer, you're effectively using a data-driven communications approach (depending on how your session beans are implemented, of course). It's not that radical of an approach, despite how it may seem on the surface: for example, no law written states that the DTO has to mirror *exactly* the entity bean it fronts. This gives you the opportunity to decouple the DTO from the entity (or entities, perhaps), gaining some of the advantages discussed earlier.

Using DTOs is a relatively easy way to get started working with data-driven communications, but regardless of whether you take an XML-based approach, a collection-based approach, or one that uses DTOs, the key is to focus on the data you wish to exchange, not on the behaviors you want executed. In a loosely coupled component architecture (see Items 1 and 2), this allows each component to evolve independently of the others without triggering massive recompilation or, worse, massive failure reports the minute the new code goes live.

Item 20:   Avoid waiting for remote service requests to respond

One of the drawbacks of the request-response communications model is embedded in its very intent: we have to wait for the response. It seems pretty silly to have to say this, but waiting for the response turns out to be a major hurdle in communications.

This notion of response time has a nasty tendency to stack up across the system. Look at it from the end user's perspective. The user clicks a button on the Web form in the browser. The browser sends the HTTP request to the HTTP server (going through whatever other infrastructure lies between the two: proxy servers, gateways, whatever). The HTTP server hands the request to the internal processing agent—probably a servlet of some form, which then does some processing on the POSTed data (hopefully validating the input in addition to script on the page that does the same thing—see Items 61 and 56, respectively), then makes a call to the database to store the data. This, of course, means we effectively have to put the servlet on pause until the database request is parsed, planned, and executed and the data returned. Or perhaps we make a request out to an EJB layer, which then carries out some processing before again heading out to the database to retrieve some data. Based on that data retrieved, we execute a few more processing steps, then execute another database call to update the data, and return back to the servlet, which then forwards the request off to a JSP page. . . .

Meanwhile, our poor user has died of old age.

In many cases, the long latency of an HTTP-based system isn't necessarily due to any particular component of the system. It's not the fault of RMI, HTTP, or the native wire protocol of whatever database you happen to be using. The system isn't held up by any particular hardware element or the speed of the network. Certainly, any one of these can create a bottleneck, but their absence doesn't guarantee low latency. Instead, the long pause times are attributable to the summation of a little bit of latency involved in each step of the process, combined with the fact that we have to wait for each one to finish before we can move on.

Consider, for example, the canonical e-commerce Web site again. We know already that the front-end servlet/JSP layer is going to need to communicate with several back-end agents, such as the database, in order to display certain parts of the site. (Hopefully the book catalog itself is pretty static, thereby leading us to make the pregenerated content optimization, as described in Item 55.) We know that a good part of this will need to be done before we can continue with carrying out user requests and directives, but exactly how much of this needs to be done in *direct* response to user actions?

Think about the final checkout stage, for example: we know that we'll want to process the user's credit card number, but does this need to happen as part of the processing before the "Thank you for your order" response shows up? Credit card services can take a *long* time to execute—remember standing there at the register last time you were at the mall?—and are sensitive to load on the rest of the system. Is this really something you want to subject your users to, just to display "Thank you for your order," particularly since users have this nasty tendency to click the button a second time if they think nothing's happening?

Whenever possible, look for ways to break this synchronous model into asynchronous communication steps, in order to avoid having to force the client to wait. Note that I take particular care here to say "the client" rather than "the user" since your client could very well be another program.

In the case of the checkout stage of the e-commerce site, for example, we don't need to process the credit card as part of the final processing stage. Oh, don't get me wrong, I'm not suggesting that we don't need to process the credit card payment, I'm just suggesting it doesn't need to be done while the user is waiting.

This may come as a surprise to you: What do you do if the user's credit card fails? We can't just "eat" the order and not do any further processing on it, leaving the user to think that the transaction completed successfully. So what happens when it fails?

First, consider the likelihood of this actually happening. Depending on your clientele, it's far more likely that the credit card transaction will go through successfully than it is that the transaction will fail. Most people know when their credit card is full, after all, and don't bother using it if they know it will fail. (Some credit counseling representatives may disagree with this assessment, but anecdotal evidence suggests otherwise.) So, picking a number out of the air, even if 25% of all credit card transactions fail, that means that 75% of the time your user is being forced to wait for something that will never happen—the "Your credit card failed" message. Three out of four users are being forced to endure unnecessary delays.

Second, we're making a critical assumption here—that all the services on which the front end depends are actually up and running. Remember, "stuff happens," and we can't assume that it's a perfect world. It's entirely possible that the credit card processing service is down, for reasons ranging from something benign (perhaps we haven't paid our monthly dues to the agent that handles credit card processing for us, if we don't do it directly) to something catastrophic (God forbid it should happen, but earthquakes, floods, and tornados aren't uncommon, and 9/11 put terrorist actions on the list of risk assessments we have to consider, too). If the processing is done in an asynchronous fashion, in many cases the user perception remains entirely unaware of the outage. If the processing is done synchronously, for as long as the outage is in place, our system is entirely down.

This has larger implications than you might think. If we make use of five synchronous remote services, and each one is down only one day a year (which is a pretty good failure record, when you look at it, around 0.33% downtime per year), our entire system is down five days a year, plus whatever time we're down due to our own software upgrades, maintenance, bugs, and whatever else takes the system down. In essence, our downtime becomes a factor not only of our bad habits but the bad habits of each and every service we depend on.

Third, it's not like we don't have mechanisms to asynchronously notify the user in the event something goes wrong—this is where the most popular Internet technology, electronic mail, comes into play. (E-mail has been quoted in numerous places as being more widely used than HTTP and the Web itself.) If HTTP is the king of request-response protocols across the Internet, then SMTP and POP3 or IMAP4 are the kings of messaging protocols across the Internet. Use them. If the credit card fails to go through successfully, send the user an e-mail and let him or her respond as they will—some users may not even bother to respond, thus reducing the load on the system entirely.

Finally, however, going asynchronous can help to avoid the "Slashdot effect." I use this term to describe the effect on servers when the highly trafficked geek Web site, Slashdot, posts a message regarding something interesting on the Internet. Thousands of requests per second start to flood in, and a site that was quite happily handling its usual traffic load suddenly groans under the additional weight. If you have any scalability weaknesses, you'll find them the first time this happens to you—of course, it also will typically result in your site collapsing under the strain, creating a rather ugly public-relations situation.

If our e-commerce front end chooses to do as much processing as possible in an asynchronous manner, and our back-end services can't keep up with the sudden load, we're still safe: the back-end processes will process messages as quickly as they can, even as the messages pile up. Presumably, at some point the spike will start to wear off, and the game of catch-up can begin. Over time, the extraneous messages will be processed, the queues will have cleared out, and the system will have weathered a scalability nightmare scenario. Or, in the worst case, the processors can't keep up with the messages coming in, and system administrators (who are, of course, keeping a close eye on the situation via the monitoring support you built into the system, as described in Item 12) can fire up another instance or two of the back-end processing element on another machine until the queues start to clear out.

Asynchronous processing can take place in a variety of ways. One way is to go with a completely asynchronous model, as suggested above, by using messaging and message-oriented technologies like JMS or e-mail (via JavaMail, most likely). EJB Message-Driven Beans (MDBs) make this trivial to accomplish—in the e-commerce scenario, at the conclusion of the user's shopping experience, rather than making a collection of calls out to EJBs and other remote services, we simply drop a JMS message into a Queue or Topic and return immediately. MDBs listening on that Queue or Topic will see the message, wake up, process it, and carry out any processing required. If there's a problem, such as the credit card not going through, we send an e-mail to the end user asking him or her to contact a customer service representative to resolve the failure.

Another way is to execute remote requests on a separate thread, thereby allowing the "main" thread to continue processing while we wait for the remote service to respond. This is less preferable than MDBs (or some other messaging solution), for two reasons: (1) we're still limited to the fact that we expect some kind of response and therefore can't complete our response until all our remote service requests return, and (2) it leaves our service open to a denial-of-service attack—an attacker could flood the HTTP layer with a collection of HTTP requests, and each one of those could spin off five threads to various parts of the back end behind the HTTP layer. . . .

At a certain level, we can't eliminate request-response communication entirely—it's simply too useful and too necessary to give up completely. Authentication requests, for example, usually can't be optimized away with an asynchronous communication approach because we can't know what to show the user until we've ascertained the user's identity. In some cases, however, we might be able to play certain kinds of tricks, by putting the authentication-required user interface elements into a separate HTML frame, thereby allowing the rest of the page to render and display itself, giving the user something to look at while we finish the authentication action itself. Remember, in many respects, it's not the *actual* latency but the *perceived* latency that differentiates a "fast, usable" site from a "slow-as-a-dog" one.

Item 21: Consider partitioning components to avoid excessive load on any one machine

Almost from the very beginning, *clustering* and *failover* and other such words have been a part of the J2EE programmer's lexicon. In fact, they've been so much a part of J2EE since its inception that they've almost lost all meaning whatsoever. To many J2EE developers, *clustering, failover, partitioning,* and *distribution* have been shouted so loudly by vendors and J2EE evangelists that the advantages—and disadvantages—of each become lost in the noise.

Enterprise systems, owing to their multiuser nature, are almost always distributed in some fashion. It's a necessary evil. Distribution makes it easier for data to be shared across multiple users and/or applications (by centralizing the data), but distribution can also lead to better operation, by ensuring that the system as a whole can remain alive even if parts of it are currently down due to an outage, whether planned or unplanned. On top of all that, a properly distributed system can offer a number of optimizations, mostly in the area of avoiding network traffic (see Item 17) by keeping necessary data local to the machine.

Before you mutter to yourself, "Duh, clustering, everybody's got it" and move on, take a deep breath and hang in there with me. Clustering is only one of several ways to distribute the system, and from several angles, it's not even the most efficient way to take advantage of the partitioning of components and load across multiple machines. Let's step back for a second and consider the situation from a higher level.

By their nature, middleware systems tend toward centralization—after all, part of the whole point of middleware in general was to bring disparate systems together into some kind of unified whole. Part of making that possible comes by creating "glue" that welds the systems together, and for maintenance reasons, if nothing else, it's best if a given component exists only once on the network.

But centralization has its problems, most notably that when we exhaust the available capacity of a given machine—that is, when we run into a situation when more users and/or resources need to be supported than the centralized server can provide—simply adding a new machine into the mix suddenly creates a whole host of issues. Concurrency concerns, in particular, rear their ugly head, but bottlenecks and other scalability issues crop up, too.

One method of partitioning is to distribute the system. In essence, we'll take a given component, split it into smaller, "subatomic" pieces, and strategically scatter those pieces across the system.

Consider, for a moment, the DNS. If there is one service on which the entirety of the Internet is built, DNS is it. Think about it—without DNS, www.neward.net is a meaningless collection of ASCII characters, and you'd have to remember the actual IP address, a meaningless quartet of numbers to most people. As if that's not enough, however, remember that DNS provides a measure of location independence, as described in Item 16, that would be impossible (or at least very difficult to build) without it.

But consider how DNS works. Every time you open a socket to some remote server anywhere on the LAN or WAN, you do a DNS lookup to obtain the IP address of the human-readable domain name. Multiply that by every person on the Internet doing the same, and you suddenly realize that if there was ever a system that needed to be scalable and reliable, DNS is it. Now imagine if all of those requests were headed directly at *your* server—how long do you think it would last before it would simply melt through the floor?

The fact is, DNS isn't implemented as a centralized service or data repository for a very good reason: no machine on the planet is powerful enough to handle the millions upon millions of concurrent requests that a centralized DNS server would have to endure. Instead, DNS is distributed across the Internet in a highly partitioned manner, in a large hierarchy divided into nonoverlapping zones. When resolving a DNS name, it's like walking a collection of servers directly within the domain name itself. For example, simplistically speaking, in the domain name *www.neward.net*, we start with the top-level domain, *net*, under which we will (eventually) find the second-level domain name *neward*, which will in turn forward off to my server, which in turn recognizes the third-level name *www*. Should I choose to create another domain name that resolves to a different server within my intranet, I publish it to my DNS server, but nothing else on the Internet needs to know about the change—*ftp.neward.net* follows exactly the same path, and my DNS server acknowledges the new *ftp* prefix just as it did *www* for previous requests. (One problem with this scheme, however, is that it requires clients to make several network hops before the domain name is fully resolved, and as a result DNS has evolved to include client-side caching of domain names. We'll examine the ramifications of this in just a second.)

> As an interesting side note, Date makes a clear distinction between distributed databases and what he calls "remote data access systems": "In a remote data access system, the user might be able to operate on data at a remote site, or even on data at several remote sites simultaneously, but 'the seams show'; that is, the user is definitely aware, to a greater or lesser extent, that the data is remote and has to behave accordingly. In a true distributed database system, the seams are hidden" [Date, 652]. The distinction isn't as necessary for our purposes, since J2EE's whole point is to make those seams disappear again, but it's useful to see how perspective defines terminology.

Database professionals have known about this kind of partitioning for some time. The eighth edition of *Introduction to Database Systems* [Date] discusses it at length in Chapter 21, speaking specifically about distributed databases. In it, Date defines *data fragmentation* as the ability to divide data into pieces or fragments for physical storage purposes; for example, we might fragment an EMPLOYEE table into two tables, one for the New York branch of the company and one for the London branch:

```
FRAGMENT EMPLOYEE AS
  N_EMP AT SITE 'New York' WHERE dept="Sales" OR
    dept="Admin",
  L_EMP AT SITE 'London' WHERE dept="TechSupport";
```

In other words, any data in the EMPLOYEE table that satisfies the first predicate (i.e., the employee works for either the Sales or Admin departments) will be stored physically in a table called N_EMP at the New York server, and any data that fits the second predicate will be stored in London. In a truly distributed database system, "the seams don't show"; queries such as "SELECT * FROM employee WHERE last_name='Date'" should operate against both the London and the New York databases.

In fact, we can talk about two different kinds of data fragmentation: *horizontal partitioning,* in which we segregate the data according to elements in the data itself (as we do above), and *vertical partitioning,* where we fragment "down the middle" of the table, perhaps putting the employee's FIRST_NAME, LAST_NAME, and EMPLOYEE_ID columns onto the New York database, and the DEPT and SALARY columns onto the London site. (For what it's worth, DNS chooses a horizontal fragmentation scheme; in fact, it's a recursive horizontal fragmentation scheme, since servers are nested inside of other servers' partitioned space.)

We can apply much the same principle to J2EE systems, at both a code level and a data level. We can partition data horizontally across the database, putting location-aware data into database servers geographically centralized (such as putting data related to human resources into a database that's local to that department, for example), or we can partition data vertically, and "split" tables and/or parts of tables across multiple servers, all depending on how the system will want to use it. In a similar vein, we can partition code in the same way—put the code that works most closely with the human resources tables on a server close by those tables, and so on. While code is less likely to partition horizontally, it's still feasible. For example, you may distribute near-identical session beans across two servers, the difference between them being expected input or output—"expense reports totaling more than $1,000 go to server A, less than $1,000 to server B."

Another way to distribute the system occurs when we scatter the JMS Topic and Queue instances across a network, ensuring that the processors that consume those messages are running on the same machine that hosts the `Topic` or `Queue`. Each `Topic` and `Queue` can itself obey a certain amount of distribution, as well—if it turns out that a given `Queue` is being overloaded with work (and thus is turning into a bottleneck), we can simply horizontally split the `Queue` into two separate ones, for example, the first `Queue` for last names A–M and the second for N–Z.

The key problem with horizontal partitioning is that somewhere, the "rules" regarding the horizontal partitioning must be kept, and, more importantly, kept up-to-date. For example, if we partition an employee database horizontally along the employee's last name ("Data for all employees with last names beginning with A–M is stored on server1, and N–Z on server2"), we need some kind of rule somewhere that reflects this—and if this is hard-coded into code, repartitioning to three servers requires recoding. Ditto for vertical partitioning.

A second method of partitioning is to replicate the system. This is the universal "clustering" that many, if not all, J2EE systems offer, whereby we take copies of the system and put those copies on multiple nodes, on the grounds that if one of them fails, any other node can take up the request just as easily as the first. Replication offers a couple of advantages. If the data is replicated locally, it means less network traffic to carry out whatever requests are needed, as well as a better availability factor—if any node (server) in the collection fails, no outage is recorded, since any node is capable of responding to the request, unlike the distributed case discussed earlier. If the DNS server for www.neward.net goes down, nobody else can logically take its place, thus denying DNS service for that domain until the server comes back up.

We discuss replication again in Item 37, but a couple of communication-specific issues deserve some words here.

As described in Item 37, the problem with replication is simple: *update propagation.* Assume for a moment that we store the data on three different database instances across the enterprise. As long as all we do is read from these three databases, we can read without concerns—each has an exact copy of the data, so any of the three can answer our request with confidence. As soon as we try to make an update to one, however, things get truly sticky—we now have multiple copies of that data, so modifying one means we're inconsistent with the others until they can be updated accordingly. And if two should happen to be updated simultaneously. . . .

We see this problem with DNS, for example; because clients replicate DNS entries in local storage (they cache them off), it often takes on the order of days before a DNS change manages to percolate across the entire Internet. In the meantime, however, if the "old" server is down or offline for some reason, clients are effectively left with an outage that isn't—the server is up, it's just not the server the client thinks it is. This kind of latency might work in DNS, where updates to domain-name/IP-address relationships don't happen very often, but in a system where updates could be coming every second, much less every subsecond, that's not going to fly well for long. (Ironically, we see this kind of latency all the time with credit cards—for some reason, it takes *forever* for your payment to go through, even though charges seem to materialize on the card even before you've finished signing the receipt.)

At this point, it may be tempting to fall back to some kind of global syn-chronization scheme, such as a Remote Singleton that acts as an update manager; but if you want your system to scale, don't do this. As described in Item 5, you're effectively introducing a bottleneck, since updates to your databases will now be throttled by how fast your update manager can handle requests. You're also requiring a remote service to respond before you can proceed, getting you into trouble with Item 20. Of course, you could always partition your update manager, but now you're back to the problems of distribution or replication again. You might think you can use timestamps, per the discussion of optimistic concurrency (see Item 33), but you'll quickly run into a problem that has plagued com-puter science for years: it's almost impossible to get two computers' clocks to agree on the time, particularly at the millisecond-level resolution you'd need for a high-scale system.

Simply updating all the copies as part of the update operation may sound like the best way to go; unfortunately, this is a naïve suggestion at best. Remember, we can't assume that all parts of the system will always be available (see Item 7), and if an update operation has to block waiting for a server to finish rebooting, just one machine having to reboot or restart will hold up the *entire system,* since no update can complete until that server comes back online. Ouch.

It gets worse with respect to transactions—taking out a lock on one data item in one server should, logically, take out that same lock on other servers, in order to avoid the accidental possibility of the same data item being updated to different values in different locations. But here we run into the very real problem of two concurrent updates each asking for a lock on the same data item, and due to the latency involved in transmitting the request over the wire, finding it already locked—who should give up the lock first? (Of such questions, by the way, are doctoral theses written. This is *not* an easy problem to solve.)

If you've already read Item 5, you may suddenly be realizing that replicating data brings up many of the same identity issues discussed there—you're right. And, unfortunately, there's no real silver bullet solution that solves the identity problem here, either. If you can accept a certain latency in update propagation across the data, it's not nearly as difficult, but unfortunately for some systems and/or tables, inconsistency is absolutely *verboten;* for such systems or tables, replication is not a great avenue to pursue.

Note that caching data returned from a database (or any other data, for that matter, but most caches deal with database data, it seems) is just a subset of replication, with the interesting distinction that the client chose to replicate the data, rather than the server. Commensurately, we have the same consistency and update propagation problems that go with replication, which means that if you plan to cache data, you'd best have some kind of answer in mind to the question of what should happen when somebody updates the database through a channel that's *not* one you expect—remember, you don't own the database, as discussed in Item 45.

Note also that we can substitute the word "data" in the discussions above for "state" in a discussion of stateful session beans and/or entity beans—replicating state (or caching it) across multiple machines in a cluster turns out to be painfully difficult to accomplish. Particularly in the case of stateful session beans, ask your vendor how they implement state caching—if they defer the state to a "state server" (as several do), then effectively whatever gain you get from it being cached is more than likely lost due to the cost of retrieving it from the state server (see Item 17), and unless the state server is somehow replicated, you're back to the single point of failure (the state server) that clustering was supposed to solve for you.

Ultimately, no partitioning scheme solves all problems. If you distribute, you evenly spread the load across the system (as evenly as your horizontal or vertical rules allow, anyway), but you lose the redundancy that a replication scheme offers. Of course, if you replicate, you run into update propagation problems that aren't easily solved. Some combination of the two can sometimes serve as the best policy, distributing the data that can afford no inconsistency and replicating the data that can.

Item 22:   Consider using Web Services for open integration

Enterprise systems tend to be heterogeneous in nature. They may not start that way, but in the fast-changing dynamic environment of the IT shop, much less the corporate world surrounding it, heterogeneity becomes an eventual reality. Even if your boss is completely sympathetic to the idea of remaining an all-Java environment, his or her boss may not be. Or the company you just acquired wasn't a Java shop, and now it's up to you to integrate the two. Or a new business partner is demanding access to a system you wrote, but the partner uses .NET. The fact is, it's the rare enterprise that is completely platform-aligned.

We can approach a foreign technology in three ways: *portability, migration,* and *integration.*

If the technology is portable, we can just take it as is and run it within our environment. In the J2EE case, that means the foreign technology has to be a J2EE-compliant component that can be dropped into our container and simply reused. While possible, such as situations where Python code can be run under the Jython Python-on-Java environment, it definitely doesn't cover the cases of .NET code.

Where we can't port the code, we might migrate it—that is, rewrite it completely in the technology of our current environment. While attractive in some ways, it's pretty impractical to expect business partners to be willing to rewrite their perfectly functioning .NET code in Java; in fact, they might in turn ask *you* to do the migrating instead of the other way around.

Which means we're left with integration: trying to make the two components work together, as is, with little to no modification in implementation. Hey, how hard can it be? After all, we've managed to get Windows systems to talk HTTP flawlessly to UNIX machines and vice versa for years now, right?

As it turns out, getting interoperability between any two platforms—Java, .NET, COM/DCOM, Perl, Python, Ruby, C/C++, whatever—isn't actually all that difficult. Numerous Java-to-.NET binary RPC interoperability tool-kits are on the market. For example, Jython takes care of Java-Python, JRuby handles Java-Ruby, and several open-source toolkits offer Java-COM or Java-C++ integration fairly easily.

It's when we need to interoperate against them *all* that things get hairy.

To make interoperability across all of these platforms easier, we need a *lingua franca,* a common language that each one speaks in a (more or less) native way. Web Services step in here, using XML's and HTTP's ubiquity to address that need for a common format that each can understand, so that instead of having to worry about an exponential number of connectors to each platform, we worry about connecting to just one (XML/Web Services), and let each platform itself worry solely about getting data into XML and back out of it.

What's more, the Web Services community, led by standards organizations like the World Wide Web Consortium, OASIS, and the newly-formed WS-Interoperability group, are building a set of protocols and standards on top of XML to make building and consuming Web Services easier. On top of that, J2EE 1.4 has taken steps to make integration with Web Services easier for the Java developer, integrating JAX-RPC as part of EJB, for example, and incorporating the other JAX* specifications as part of the J2EE Collective. In short, from a distance it looks like your interoperability needs are already taken care of.

As with many efforts of this nature, however, things below the surface aren't quite as placid as they seem from up top. For starters, we have the basic problem of the object-hierarchical impedance mismatch between objects and XML Infoset representations, as described more fully in Item 43, that will make it awkward to transform objects into XML documents and back again. To complicate matters, J2EE 1.4 assumes that the Web Services endpoints exported from a J2EE container should be "rpc-encoded"-style services, whereas .NET, the major candidate for Web Service integration, assumes "doc-literal" style out of the box. While not an unassailable obstacle, it still requires more knowledge of the Web Services stack, most importantly WSDL, than most developers probably prefer.

The far greater danger, unfortunately, lies in the basic premise that all of the Web Service vendors are offering, that you can start with your platform-specific code, flip a magic switch, and suddenly have a Web Service all served up, ready to eat. Consider the following session bean interface:

```
public interface TellerBean extends EJBObject
{
  public void
    generateBouncedCheckMessages(Set checks, Account acct)
    throws RemoteException
}
```

Clearly, from the first parameter, the bean is expecting a collection that contains only unique items—if the same check somehow is inserted twice into the collection, it should generate an exception. Here's the problem: What exactly should the WSDL definition for this method be?

The second parameter we can handle pretty easily, since Account is (hopefully) just a simple wrapper around an account number, but Set creates some problems. .NET has no Set-equivalent type, and even if it does, remember that Set is just an interface whose implementation varies—it could be a java.util.TreeSet, it could be a HashSet, it could be your own custom Set implementation tuned in ways expressed only via behavior, not via interface. The code looking to generate a WSDL document will probably turn that Set parameter into a simple collection, thus losing an important *implicit* part of the API, that of uniqueness in the collection. .NET clients will have no chance to avoid accidentally passing the bean duplicates, and if the bean is written to assume that no duplicates are present, we could be in for a *very* long night of debugging.

For best interoperability, Web Services should be context-complete, data-driven communications endpoints (see Items 18 and 19, respectively), yet most EJB Session Bean interfaces aren't designed that way. Even worse, Java programmers looking to pass data in bulk (see Item 23) to a Session Façade [Alur/Crupi/Malks, 341] will chose either a Data Transfer Object [Fowler, 401] or a collection, like a Map or List. The Data Transfer Object will suffer from the limitations of object-hierarchical data mappings, and the Map or List will have no good equivalent in XML, much less the things contained in them.

In short, you can't afford to make platform-centric assumptions about your communications endpoints if you're planning to make your code available via a Web Services endpoint. Instead, you'll need to start from something platform-agnostic—usually XML Schema definitions for data types and WSDL documents for endpoint definitions, both of which should be written *before* the first line of Java code is generated—just as CORBA objects required you to design the IDL first, or as EJB requires the business/remote interfaces to be defined before the implementation can be written. It also means that once published, those interfaces can never change—even more than in the J2EE environment, Web Services are intended for public consumption, and you can't assume that if you change the URLs or the definitions of the message types expected at those URLs, that clients will be able to keep up with the change.

In many ways, Web Services are the pinnacle of middleware software. Remember, middleware is supposed to be the "glue" that binds systems that were designed independently of one another, and that fits the definition of Web Services. All of the specifications emerging for higher-order Web Service protocols are middleware-focused: WS-ReliableMessaging, WS-Transaction, WS-Security, and WS-Addressing reflect functionality provided by most middleware toolkits over the last twenty years. We're just adding angle brackets (< and >) around them.

Like most other things in the enterprise, Web Services offer some powerful capabilities, in this case the ability to interoperate with foreign platforms, but you don't get those benefits for free. If you're thinking about using Web Services, make sure they're worth the work—they were designed and intended for open interoperability, that is, interoperability against any number of platforms simultaneously. If you're not looking to provide interoperability against any and all platforms, it may turn out to be easier to choose something that's targeted to your specific platform.

Item 23:   Pass data in bulk

Consider, if you will, your run-of-the-mill entity bean (either container-managed or bean-managed, it makes no real difference) representing some detail about a person, perhaps from a U.S.-localized address book application. When used from the client, the entity bean looks something like this:

```
Person p = personHome.create(new SSNPK("555-12-9876"));
String fullName = p.getFirstName() + " " + p.getLastName();
String streetAddr = p.getStreet() + "\n" +
    p.getCity() + " " + p.getState() + " " + p.getZip();

. . . // Get some user input
```

```
p.setFirstName(firstName);
p.setLastName(lastName);
p.setStreet(street);
p.setCity(city);
p.setState(state);
p.setZip(zip);
```

Many readers familiar with EJB see a huge flaw with this code—it's too "chatty," making multiple method calls on the entity bean to set the necessary data on the bean instance. Each of these calls is a remote call, which in turn means you're making a round-trip per get and/or set call, thus violating Item 17 in a big, big way. Not only is this introducing latency into the application, it's also tanking scalability because this entity bean is being asked to do lots of "little" operations that don't justify the cost of making a round-trip.

The cost of this field-by-field approach isn't just in the networking layers; conceptually, the six set calls are all taking place as part of a single business operation and should probably be protected from modification between set calls by a transaction. In fact, however, all calls to entity beans are protected individually by their own distributed transaction, so instead of doing all six calls in a single transaction, each set call creates a transaction, enlists the database resource on the transaction, sets the data, runs through the two-phase commit protocol to commit the transaction, and tears it back down again. Six times we have to run through this non-trivial exercise.

Worse, we're still not protected completely from data corruption; because the transactions managed by the container are on a per-method basis, there are five windows, one between each of the set calls, where another client can come in and change the data on the bean. As a result, it's not difficult to imagine a scenario something like this:

```
Client 1 wants to set bean to:
Ted Neward, 1 Artesia Way, Davis, CA 95616
Client 2 wants to set bean to:
Ted Neward, 1 Microsoft Way, Redmond, WA, 55512

Client 1 calls setStreet()
Client 2 calls setStreet()
Client 2 calls setCity()
```

```
Client 1 calls setCity()
Client 1 calls setState()
Client 2 calls setState()
Client 2 calls setZip()
Client 1 calls setZip()


Bean is now set to:
Ted Neward, 1 Microsoft Way, Davis, WA, 95616
```

This is obviously not a great state of affairs. Even though transactions were used, even though full synchronization was used, we still got *semantic data corruption*—data that's syntactically legal yet still incorrect. Even if there *is* a city named "Davis" in Washington, it won't have the zip code of 95616—that's reserved for the city named Davis in the state of California. Moreover, I can guarantee there's no such address as "1 Microsoft Way" in Davis.

Faced with this, your first reaction might be to solve the problem by taking out the transaction on the client side, but as Item 29 shows you, client-side transactions are a slippery-slope decision that can quickly turn into an evil thing that no self-respecting J2EE programmer would ever claim to have authored. We want to execute all six `set` calls where we can take out a transaction without the commensurate cost.

The generalized solution, then, is to pass data in chunks large enough to justify the overhead of the remote call. In short, don't pass data one element at a time, but pass it in bulk: either in whole-object chunks, or even in sets of objects. (This is the basic idea behind the IBM/BEA proposal for Service Data Objects and is arguably just one step shy of a procedural-first persistence layer, as described in Item 42.) For those of you familiar with marshaling terminology, we want to pass-by-value, instead of the default pass-by-reference approach used by entity beans and/or other distributed object technologies.

One approach is to create Data Transfer Objects [Fowler, 401], objects whose data representations are exactly those of the entity beans or persistent objects they represent, or at least something close to them:

```
public class PersonDO
  implements java.io.Serializable
{
  public String firstName;
```

```
    public String lastName;
    public String street;
    public String city;
    public String state;
    public String zip;
}


public interface PersonTransferBean implements SessionBean
{
    // mandatory EJB methods left out for simplicity

    public PersonDO getData();
    public void setData(PersonDO data);
}
```

Notice how `PersonDO` implements the `Serializable` interface—this ensures that when `PersonDO` is sent across the wire, it is marshaled by value instead of by reference. This means rather than sending a kind of pointer (stub) to the recipient, we send a complete copy of the object, so that all of the data will remain local in the target JVM. Now, when it's time to update data on the `PersonBean` instance, we can pass all the data at once, instead of dribbling it over a small piece at a time. We lose some of the "object-orientedness" of the system because now we have to abandon the traditional get/set property idiom that has been a part of Java since its early beginnings, but at least this way we're avoiding massive performance issues. What's better, we can put the `setData` call under a transaction, thereby ensuring that all six calls will follow ACID transactional semantics.

If you're not keen on writing a Serializable version of each entity bean class (and I can't say that I would blame you if you're not), remember the goal here is simply to pass all the data across in one bulk network call, not to partition the data in any sort of meaningful way. So any sort of bulk data pass-by-value approach would work, including either passing data in Java collection class implementations, which are all Serializable, such as `HashMap` or `ArrayList`, or both—an `ArrayList` of `HashMap` objects is not an uncommon approach

A drawback to passing data this way is the lack of type safety in doing so. With a transfer object class per entity bean approach, where each of the fields is strongly typed (as in any Java object definition), the compiler can catch when a typo creeps in and warn you if you try to access the `lsat-Name` field instead of `lastName`. If the field name is a key to a `Map` value, on the other hand, the compiler won't validate your code (to avoid typos), and you won't notice the problem until runtime (hopefully as part of unit tests to verify the code is good, or during the QA process).

Alternatively, you can use a `RowSet` to pass data across, since `RowSet` objects are Serializable objects themselves. One of the interesting properties of `RowSet` implementations is that they typically operate in a *disconnected* manner. Unlike a `ResultSet`, the `RowSet` doesn't hold an active JDBC `Connection` back to the database to retrieve data in chunks; instead, all the data in the `ResultSet` is copied to the `RowSet` and held locally, within the `RowSet`, so that when the `RowSet` is serialized, all the data is serialized with it. What's more, JSR 114 and J2SE 1.5 are defining a set of standardized `RowSet` implementations with a variety of interesting features, including the ability to hold more than one set of tuples (result sets) as part of the `RowSet`.

It's fair to ask at this point whether there's anything special about the Serializable format, and of course, the answer is "not really"—it's just a well-known binary format. Thus, as mentioned in Item 15, another acceptable Serialization format is that of XML, since other platforms, most notably .NET, can consume XML much more easily than they can a binary format not intrinsically known to them. Toward this end, Sun created the `WebRowSet`. Although not formally part of J2EE, it has been available from the Java Developer Connection in beta form since 2000 and is now in the process of being ratified under JSR 114, along with several other `RowSet` implementations. The `WebRowSet` is an implementation of `RowSet` that extends `CachedRowSet` but adds two new methods—`toXml` and `fromXml`—each of which does exactly as its name implies: converts a `RowSet` to an XML Infoset instance and back again, respectively. It's a proprietary XML format, to be certain, but at least it's in XML, which is still better than a proprietary binary format when interoperating with other platforms (see Item 22 for more on interoperability).

Be aware, by the way, that when using entity bean CMP implementations, it's still entirely possible that multiple round-trips are being executed between the container and the database—for example, depending on how the transactional affinity is marked on the session bean "fronting" the entity bean, you could be making separate trips due to the container's need to start and end transactions on each call (see Item 31). In some cases, the EJB container has no choice but to generate some truly brain-dead code for CMP-marked entity beans, such as a standalone SELECT on each entity bean get call and UPDATE on each set call, due to the lack of any standard hints to the container about this bean, such as a read-only flag or a dirty bit that can be manually inspected and used. Vendors frequently offer such optimizations, but taking advantage of them renders your code vendor-specific (see Item 11). For this reason, running a "spy" JDBC driver or using your database's monitoring tools to look at the SQL (see Item 10) is crucial to understanding exactly how many round-trips that CMP entity is generating.

Passing data in bulk has its limitations, too—passing large amounts of data across the network repetitively is no better than making multiple round-trips, since now you're soaking up network bandwidth and forcing the communications layer to expend significant effort to marshal, transmit, receive, and unmarshal that data. Exercise your own judgment in whether a particular large data item is better sent across by reference or by value, based on how clients will (or won't) use it; pay particular attention to collections and Serializable objects, since thanks to rules of Serialization it's not uncommon for just one reference to bring along a whole slew of other objects you never would have thought should be serialized (see Item 71). Remember, the goal is to avoid spending excessive time on the network, not to be dogmatic about one approach or another.

Item 24:   Consider rolling your own communication proxies

Recall, for a moment, that one of the benefits of an RPC-based communication system like RMI is that it's easy for developers to work with—it looks like a local object, smells like a local object, and acts like a local object. All the ugly communications stuff is buried under the hood of the local object, a Proxy [GOF, 207] to the remote object. This model is so tempting that despite all the problems associated with remote objects (see Items 5 and 17 for details), it's still widely used.

So why give it up?

Once we recognize that the temptation of the model lies in the local object proxy, it's easy to realize that nothing stops us from rolling our own proxies, giving us the opportunity to provide whatever optimizations and/or different implementations we desire. Want to use HTTP as the communications backbone? Write a proxy that serializes the parameters and ships that as the body of an HTTP request to a servlet that unpacks it and executes the call. Want to avoid some of the problems with objects-first persistence schemes? Write a proxy that eager-loads data, lazy-loads data, or even eager-loads parts of the data and lazy-loads the rest.

For example, as discussed in Item 23, one suggested solution to the problem of chatty distributed persistent objects (namely, entity beans) is to pass data in bulk, so that all updates to the underlying data store happen all at once, thus justifying the cost of the remote call. The problem with passing data in bulk is that it tends to bleed away the "object-ness" of the system, meaning clients have to logically navigate the difference between a Data Transfer Object [Fowler, 401] and the API used to persist and/or restore it. If you want a more "objects-first" approach to preserve a bit more of the object-ness of the system domain model, one choice is to use a Half-Object Plus Protocol [AJP, 189] and create "smart data proxies" that cache the data locally until the client is ready to commit the data all at once.

It's fair to ask why this kind of optimization isn't already in place, particularly with respect to EJB entity beans—if the entity bean is just an objects-first way to model data (see Item 40), it seems to be an obvious understatement that the entity bean stub should somehow optimize the transfer of data to the server. Again, the problem here is the wording of the EJB Specification—because access to each attribute of an entity bean must be done under the auspices of a transaction, the data must be pushed through to the underlying data store. (Remember, changes to an entity bean have to be preserved in the event of a server crash.) Because the current EJB Specification doesn't allow for this notion of "local caching," any EJB container providing such an optimization would be officially incompatible. That's not to say that it wouldn't be a useful optimization—just make sure to read Item 11 and decide whether vendor neutrality is important to you before using it. (Note that if you write the entity bean as bean-managed, you can put this optimization in place, but now you're basically writing the proxy all over again.)

In fact, many vendors and open-source projects are starting to do this; for example, many JDO vendors can now return "parts" of an object returned by a JDO call, thus eliminating one of the principal criticisms I leveled at objects-first persistence layers (see Item 40). This is a welcome and overdue development because it means that you won't have to create these smart data proxies by hand, as suggested here. If your particular vendor and/or toolkit doesn't do what you want, however, this is your fallback.

Data access is only one possibility.

Most EJB containers make use of RMI for their communications link between EJB clients and the EJB container itself. RMI is a useful object-RPC system, but the reference implementation shipped by Sun has one particularly nasty flaw in it that works contrary to our purposes in a J2EE environment: the RMI stub returned by the RMI server is implicitly "pinned" against a particular server. In other words, the stub you get only knows how to talk to the server it was returned from, and if that server should for some reason stop accepting incoming RMI calls (perhaps the server crashed), your stub is now worthless. Even in the event that the container is distributed against two or more machines in a cluster, the RMI stub you've received can't talk to the other machines in the cluster; you'll have to renegotiate a new stub by asking for a new client from the Home object. So wrap it up in a proxy.

Other possible situations that suggest the use of a smart proxy include the idea of creating a Home that always does a JNDI lookup to preserve location independence, or caches the results of a JNDI Home lookup to avoid network round-trips back to the container, or times out a cached JNDI lookup after 24 hours.

You won't want to do this for all possible proxy situations that come up within your system, obviously—this would represent a tremendous amount of work. Use smart proxies only in situations where the default behavior of the stub or proxy handed back to you isn't what you want, and the cost of creating the smart proxy is justified in the amount of saved network traffic, better failover behavior, or some other tangible, measurable benefit.

4 | Processing

*You must lay aside all prejudice on both sides, and neither believe
nor reject anything, because any other persons, or descriptions
of persons, have rejected or believed it. Your own reason is the
only oracle given you by heaven, and you are answerable,
not for the rightness, but the uprightness of the decision.*

—Thomas Jefferson

*Go not to the Elves for counsel,
for they will say both no and yes.*

—Gandalf to Frodo, *Lord of the Rings*

Processing is the part of the enterprise system that the middleware can't
handle for you, the "meat" of your applications. It goes by many names:
business rules, business logic, domain logic, application code, *ad infini-
tum*. At its essence, processing is what the business is paying for in the first
place: to do things with the data that aren't being handled elsewhere.

A large part of processing in an enterprise system deals with concurrency—
for maximum throughput, we need to assume that two things can happen
at the same time. No matter how fast the hardware, trying to run a system
where everything happens just one step at a time for all users in the system is going to bog down pretty quickly. So as programmers, we need to
deal with the fact that multiple threads of execution, whether logical or
physical, are a reality. Unfortunately, this is easier said than done.

In an enterprise Java system, concurrency touches on two subjects simultaneously: Java's native object monitor-based synchronization system and
the transaction-based synchronization mechanism built into most enterprise resource managers. While it would be nice if we could simply ignore

one in favor of the other, at this time that's not possible—the Java language (and/or virtual machine) hasn't got transactional capabilities built into it, and trying to "hide" the transactional nature of resources has proven over and over again to create bottlenecks. As a result, we need to be aware of both aspects of concurrency.

For more details on Java's object monitor-based concurrency mechanism, I highly recommend *Concurrent Programming in Java* [Lea]. In addition, I assume that you've already read Items 48 through 53 of *Effective Java* [Bloch]; for example, you will never want to mark a servlet `doGet` or `doPost` method as synchronized for the reasons described in Bloch's Item 49 ("Avoid excessive synchronization").

You'll note pretty quickly that many of the items in this chapter deal with transactional processing; any others (like rules-based processing or workflow) take a definite back seat. While this may seem a bit heavy-handed, the majority of enterprise IT systems are, implicitly or explicitly, transaction-processing systems of one form or another, and as such many of these items are directly relevant to your daily life as an enterprise Java developer. Even if you're not currently using EJB, keep reading—not only is it likely that you will in the future (your system, if successful, is quite likely to have to talk to multiple databases simultaneously, thus creating a situation ripe for EJB, per Item 9), but the same concepts apply whether you access the enterprise resources through an enterprise bean or directly, through a `Connector` or vendor-proprietary API.

Item 25:   Keep it simple

KISS (Keep It Simple, Stupid). Do the Simplest Thing That Could Possibly Work. The Rule of Simplicity. It goes by several names, but they all come back to the same idea: prefer simplicity to complexity in your code.

This item really shouldn't have to be here, but it's amazing how often architects and technical leads get carried away with their own cleverness (yours truly included, I'm ashamed to admit). "All we have to do is pass the data through this complex series of processing objects, and they'll all combine to produce the results we're looking for. It's just so cool. It's the classic Blackboard pattern combined with Visitor and Observer, with some Composite and Transaction Script thrown in for good measure. . . ." Unfortunately, what they forget is that complexity kills more than anything else. A friend of mine once said, "Every project has a complexity budget: once you've spent all the complexity in your budget, that's it. If you try to go over that, the project will die. Stay within it, the project will be a success." Remember, some of that complexity will need to be applied to the domain problem itself, so if you spend it all on complex technology that doesn't address the bottom line, the project is going to fall apart. I have more than one project in my history that I now realize failed for precisely that reason, and I suspect anybody who has ever architected or led more than one project can say the same; certainly everybody I know in the same position has said as much.

If you can't explain what a given "piece" of processing code does in a single sentence, at most two, it's probably too complicated.

The problems with complex solutions are myriad but basically boil down to several simple tenets.

- *Complex solutions are hard to modularize and, therefore, reuse.* A complex solution typically tries to solve everything within its own borders, leaving no room for combining this code with other portions of the code. In other words, making effective use of the hook points (if any; see Item 6) built into the code is much more difficult when a complex order of evaluation must be considered.
- *Complex solutions are hard to debug.* This is a known principle, dating back to the very early days of C and UNIX: "Rule 3. Fancy algorithms are buggier than simple ones, and they're much harder to implement. Use simple algorithms as well as simple data structures" [Raymond, 12, quoting Rob Pike's *Notes on Programming in C*]. If nothing else, the complex solution presents more lines of code to consider, more classes to understand, and a lot more interaction between objects to keep straight in your head. As a general rule, human beings are good at keeping between three and seven things clear—go beyond that, and we start to lose track of the details.
- *Complex solutions are hard to optimize.* While you should never optimize without profiling first (see Item 10), once you've ascertained that the bottleneck is somewhere inside that complex tangle of method calls, object creation, and double-dispatch logic, you have to figure out how to optimize it. For simple algorithms and/or classes, it's fairly easy to spot where the optimization should go, or whether it's even possible to optimize. Unfortunately, in the name of optimization the simple often becomes complex, so make sure the gains are worth the costs.

- *Complex solutions are hard to maintain.* We've all been there—there's a bug in that one class or module, and when it comes time to assign an engineer to fix it, everybody groans and waves it off. "No way do I want to go in *there,* that stuff's a mess." Nine times out of ten, the code that most desperately needs refactoring is code that's too complex.

Other reasons certainly leap to mind; these are simply those most often cited in the popular literature.

Problems of complexity most frequently arise in the processing, the code that we write that's most domain-centric. It's tempting to get tricky with the J2EE specifications—for example, having discovered the `Request Dispatcher` functionality of the 2.2 servlet container, it's tempting to consider using the `forward` method multiple times or calling `include` on other servlets multiple times, with each "subservlet" doing a small part of the processing involved in the whole. Resist. You introduce a huge swath of complexity into the system when doing so, such as failure handling and/or output generation.

For example, complexity tends to rear its ugly head in the area of "special-case" logic that occurs within processing—"if our customer has more than 100 outstanding orders, make sure this gets run through a supervisor before letting the order continue," "make sure the credit card charge goes through before committing this row to the orders table, since we don't ever want to ship items that haven't been paid for," or even such simple situations as "if the customer isn't in the database, go ahead and use a 'default' customer entry since we don't require customers to be in our database in order to purchase something."

It's tempting to suggest that we can handle these situations directly within code. Fowler documents the idea of using a subclass of a particular class as the Special Case pattern [Fowler, 496], but the examples there, of a `Customer` class and special-case subclasses `MissingCustomer` and `UnknownCustomer`, are both domain-specific and fairly simple; the subclass approach doesn't work well in the processing-centric examples mentioned previously.

For our example of a customer with 100 outstanding orders, a rules-based engine can simplify your processing by taking you out of the imperative programming model and letting you work in a more declarative fashion (see Item 26 for details). In addition, the first example also implies that more than one party (human or otherwise) may need a shot at processing this particular request—in the enterprise world this is frequently known as *workflow,* and while both expensive and open-source workflow engines are available, often you can just as easily handle workflow by adopting a messaging-based processing model. For the example of charging a credit card before committing the order, look into using transactional processing as a way to ensure that failure scenarios get handled in an atomic and fairly transparent way; see Item 27 for more details. For the final example of using a "default" customer, a variation of Special Case [Fowler, 496] might work, where the `Customer` returned is an actual `Customer` in the database, no different from any other `Customer` except that the data stored is nonsensical or acts as a sort of database-driven Null Object [PLOPD3, 5].

Notice that in all of those situations, the words "roll it yourself in the code" never showed up. Implementing special-case code directly in your processing logic is the best way to create a complex situation; it may seem counterintuitive, but the best line of code is the line you don't have to write.

As a rule, enterprise projects tend to favor the complex rather than the simple: it's a perverse idea that somehow a complex system is more "macho" than a simple one. Perhaps it's some kind of unconscious desire to build a little job security into the system, or maybe it's the architect's suppressed need to assert him- or herself as the Big Geek on the Block. Whatever the reason, it's worth repeating over and over again: Keep It Simple. Let the tools (in this case, J2EE and its related specifications) do as much of the work as possible.

Item 26: Prefer rules engines for complex state evaluation and execution

Frequently, business or domain logic reaches degrees of complexity that are difficult, if not outright impossible, to express in imperative languages like Java. Purists will no doubt scoff at the idea that there's anything that the Almighty Object can't do, but the basic fact is, business rules don't always fit neatly into object-oriented categories, and we end up creating Blobs [Malveau, 73] with "validate" or "process" methods that encompass these rules—in essence, falling back on procedural habits for lack of something better.

Consider for a moment the computer on your desk and all the possible variations of hardware combinations that the manufacturer offers for that one model—memory, hard drive, monitor, not to mention all the peripherals—and the inevitable incompatibilities encompassed therein. ("If they order the DVD, then we need to make sure they didn't get the KorSplatt 5900 video card, because it won't work with this DVD model, unless of course they want the combo CD-RW/DVD instead. Oh, and the KorSplatt 5900 won't run in a machine that has less than 512MB of RAM, unless it's SuperReallyFastRAM. . . .") Factor in all the possible promotionals that the company will want to run on top of the basic incompatibility restrictions, plus the fact that all this stuff changes on a monthly (if not weekly!) basis, and suddenly the idea of trying to create a "Computer Configurator" for an online PC manufacturer makes the most hardened IT veteran consider retirement.

The problem here is that this kind of complex evaluation is hard to do in an imperative language like Java, where the language focuses on step after step for the CPU to carry out. In essence, we're telling the machine *how* to do its job, and that means we have to be very explicit about the conditions that need to be evaluated and the order in which they need to be considered. It leads to complex and hard-to-maintain code like this:

```
if (currentPC.drives().contains("DVD"))
{
  if (currentPC.videoCard().equals("KorSplatt 5900") &&
      !(currentPC.drives().get("DVD").equals("CD-RW/DVD")))
  {
    warn("DVD incompatible with KorSplatt 5900");
  }
}
else if (currentPC.videoCard().equals("KorSplatt 5900") &&
         currentPC.memory() < 512)
{
  // . . .
}
```

We can talk about trying to abstract out higher-order incompatibilities and refactor them into more generic base-class-oriented code, but the truth remains that in many cases, businesses create product-targeted rules that make no sense to engineers but help drive business up 5% for the quarter.

This kind of processing is a specific form of programming, called *rules-based programming*, and fortunately there are *rules engines*, software that can examine a set of data, look at the list of rules declared within the engine, and infer what rules need to fire in response to the current state of the data. More importantly, the rules engine can then reapply the rules as necessary as the data changes, until the data reaches a stable state that triggers no further rules.

Rules-oriented implementations have been around for years and are becoming more popular in consumer use. The ubiquitous sendmail program for handling e-mail uses a cryptic set of rules to decide how to forward mail based on the contents of each message. Spam filters use rules to evaluate whether an incoming mail message is from your mother wishing you a happy birthday or an anonymous e-mail address trying to sell you love potions.

By the way, lest you think this is a spurious application, one of the first and most famous rules-based applications was Digital Equipment Corporation's XCON system, which did exactly this: it helped DEC sales consultants configure DEC mainframe computer orders, to ensure the order had all the necessary components and accessories.[1] By 1989, XCON included over 17,000 rules and knew about 31,000 hardware requirements, saving DEC an estimated $40 *million* annually due to increased accuracy, reduced testing costs, and higher customer satisfaction. And on the off chance you're not in the business of selling computers, rules-based systems are useful for a wide variety of other domain-oriented tasks, including "customer recommendations" based on previous purchasing history, something that marketing departments everywhere are starting to ask for in public-facing purchasing systems. In fact, with a little bit of analysis, it's hard to find an IT system in place that *doesn't* have some kind of rules-based processing in it.

Rules engines typically serve two purposes: (1) to capture business rules in a first-class fashion, and (2) to allow those rules to be modified without requiring recoding of the Java code itself. The first is typically the biggest gain, since trying to track down business rules within a pile of if/then/else statements is not only difficult but also error-prone. If your users are sophisticated enough, however, teaching them the "rules

---

1. This discussion of the DEC XCON system is based on information from *Jess in Action* [Friedman-Hill, 10].

language" the rules engine understands has the added benefit of giving them the ability to modify a substantial part of the business logic of the application, effectively taking the programmer out of the loop on business logic changes that would otherwise require a complete development cycle (development, testing, QA, release, deployment, and so on).

Several different implementations are available: one, an open-source implementation called drools, is available from http://www.codehaus.org; BEA includes one as part of its WebLogic platform, and ILOG sells a third-party engine for integration with other servers. JSR 94 defines a standard API (in the package `javax.rules`) for interfacing with rules engines; its reference implementation, called the Java Expert System Shell (JESS), is freely available for noncommercial use. Explaining the complete JESS language and API is far beyond the scope of what we can cover here; for more details, consult *JESS in Action* [Friedman-Hill].

Using a JSR-94-compliant rules engine follows the same basic principles as any other J2EE resource, in that you start by obtaining an instance of a `RuleServiceProvider` through a JNDI lookup. Initializing the rules engine requires creating a `RuleExecutionSet`, a loaded set of rules ready to be executed. Register the `RuleExecutionSet` with a `RuleAdministrator` instance, and you're ready to go:

```
RuleServiceProvider provider = // . . .
  // Either use a JNDI lookup, or else use
  // RuleServiceProviderManager, similar in concept
  // to the JDBC DriverManager
RuleAdministrator admin = provider.getRuleAdministrator();
RuleExecutionSet ruleSet = null;

// Load the rules from a local file using
// LocalRuleExecutionSetProvider
//
FileReader reader = new FileReader("rules.xml");
try
{
  HashMap props = new HashMap();
  props.put("name", "Configuration Rules");
  props.put("description",
            "Rulebase for company PC configuration");
```

```
LocalRuleExecutionSetProvider lresp =
    admin.getLocalRuleExecutionSetProvider(props);
  ruleSet = lresp.createRuleExecutionSet(reader, props);
}
finally
{
  reader.close();
}


admin.registerRuleExecutionSet("rules", ruleSet, props);
```

The `rules.xml` file, as its name implies, contains the rules in an XML-oriented format. The JSR-94 Specification makes no mandate as to the rules language itself; the XML format is entirely specific to the reference implementation, based on JESS. Other rules engines may also offer an XML-like format or use something else entirely.

Once the engine is initialized, using it at runtime is a fairly straight-forward exercise. JSR-94 defines two kinds of `RuleSession` types, stateful and stateless, roughly corresponding to the difference between stateful and stateless session beans in EJB: a stateful `RuleSession` has its working memory preserved across calls, whereas a stateless one doesn't. This means that objects that are added to working memory (for the rules to evaluate against) are lost in the stateless `RuleSession` after the rules are evaluated:

```
//Create the RuleSession instance
//
RuleRuntime runtime = rep.getRuleRuntime();
StatefulRuleSession srs =
  (StatefulRuleSession)runtime.createRuleSession("rules",
      props,
      RuleRuntime.STATEFUL_SESSION_TYPE);


// Populate the RuleSession's working memory with the data
// to evaluate against
//
srs.addObject(new Integer(12));
srs.addObject("Hello, world");
srs.addObject(new CustomDataObject());
```

```
// Execute the rules
//
srs.executeRules();

// Examine the entire contents of the working
// memory-objects may have been modified by
// executing rules
//
List results = srs.getObjects();

// Release the RuleSession
//
srs.release();
```

Depending on the contents of the rules themselves, the results `List` will contain modified objects that were created/modified by the body of the rules in the `rules.xml` file.

Rules engines, when used appropriately, can be a powerful way to express business logic in such a way that doesn't require piles of `if/then/else` statements; it is, however, yet another language to learn, and in the situations where your business analysts or end users either can't or won't learn the language, that task then falls on your shoulders. Much like SQL and XSLT, most rule languages are declarative in nature, meaning you don't bother specifying *how* so much as *when* and *what*—that is, you specify some kind of predicate condition that triggers the rule and the action to take when the rule is triggered. For example, in a completely fabricated XML-like rule language, a rule for the PC Configurator might look like the code shown here, where the condition element is some form of XPath-like query syntax and the action element is some kind of script language.

```
<rule>
  <condition>(drives[@type="DVD" and @type!="CD-RW/DVD"] > 1) and
             (video[@mfr="KorSplatt"] and
              video[@version="5900"])
  </condition>
  <action>
    put("KorSplatt 5900 is incompatible with regular DVD")
  </action>
</rule>
```

While it won't necessarily replace objects as the principal general-purpose language we use to build enterprise systems, a rules engine can certainly make your life a lot easier when working with complicated conditional logic. Although JSR-94 isn't a formal part of the J2EE Specification collection, it was designed primarily for J2EE applications, and many of the existing rules vendors were part of the Expert Group. At the very least, it's something to keep your eyes on.

Item 27: Prefer transactional processing for implicitly nonatomic failure scenarios

As programmers, we are used to a model where operations carried out by the languages we use are implicitly atomic: that is, a function called will either return the correct value or send back some kind of error code or exception. More importantly, we assume that it will return either a completely finished result or nothing at all—there's no such thing as a "partial" answer from the `Math.sqrt` method, for example. Either it's a good square root value or it throws some kind of exception (if we ask it for the square root of −1, for example).

Unfortunately, this view of atomic operation is an entirely fictitious one. Almost nothing at the high level at which we program is truly atomic. For example, when we call the `Math.sqrt` method, the thread of execution we're using in turn starts to execute the code within `Math.sqrt`'s definition, which in turn breaks down into individual CPU instructions, which in turn are executed serially on a CPU that must interrupt periodically to ask the bus to fetch some additional data from RAM, and so on. Instead, a great deal of work is done "under the hood" to present the vision of this atomicity—in fact, that's a large part of the job of a language and/or compiler, to hide much of this complexity so that it doesn't "get in the way" of what we really want to do, which in this case is find the square root of something.

Fortunately, presenting this degree of atomicity is a fairly simple operation, as long as everything we do is read-only; if anything goes wrong, we can just throw an exception and forget about the entire idea. If, however, the executed method does something to change the internal state of the object (or class, in the case of statics) against which it is called, now things aren't so simple. Should we return the state of the object/class back to its original values in the face of an error? (Probably.) What about methods we call in turn? Will they do so, as well?

Consider Item 46 in *Effective Java* [Bloch]: "Strive for failure atomicity." What holds for simple Java programming holds doubly for Java enterprise programming. In fact, it's even more difficult to achieve atomicity in enterprise programming because now there's more than just Java code to consider—we have to consider resources outside the JVM (such as database tables, message queues, files on the filesystem, and so on) as well.

Enter transactional processing.

The basic model of a transaction, from the programmer's perspective, is a simple one: you create a transaction against a *resource manager,* something that you want to do some work against. The traditional resource manager, of course, is the relational database, but other resource managers are certainly possible, including but not limited to the JMS message broker, a legacy mainframe or other Connector-accessed system, and possibly even the underlying filesystem, if the filesystem supports it. In some cases, ambitious and failure-conscious programmers can even write their objects to implement the resource manager portions of the Java Transaction API, thus making the objects you work with transactional in nature.

Once the transaction is open, you write what work you want done as part of that transaction. This is the resource-specific work, such as executing a SQL statement, retrieving a message, issuing a request to the legacy system, or whatever. When all work is complete, you can choose to *commit* the transaction, thereby "making permanent" the changes you've suggested, or *rollback* the transaction, effectively throwing away any and all changes against the resource since the transaction started. (It turns out that, if supported, you can choose to throw away only parts of the work done—see Item 36 for details.)

In other words, either all of your changes succeed or they all fail. You don't have to deal with "partial failure" or "partial success." No need to write code to explicitly undo the actions of earlier work in the method if the third or fourth step suddenly fails for some reason—either everything works or nothing does. And no additional work on your part is necessary to make this atomic failure scenario a reality; it's all part of the transaction-processing model.

To put this into practical perspective, consider the following code:

```
public class Person
{ . . . }


public class Minister
{
  public void marryPeople(Person spouse1, Person spouse2)
  {
    System.out.println("Do you, " + spouse1.getName() +
                       " take " + spouse2.getName() +
                       " to be your spouse?");
    if (spouse1.isOKToMarry(spouse2))
    {
      System.out.println("How about you, " +
                         spouse2.getName());
      if (spouse2.isOKToMarry(spouse1))
      {
        System.out.println("If any here know why these two " +
                           "should not be married, " +
                           "let them speak now " +
                           "or forever hold their peace.");
        if (Crowd.isOKWithMarriage(spouse1, spouse2))
        {
          System.out.println("Kiss, " + spouse1.getName() +
                             " and " +
                             spouse2.getName() +
                             ", I now pronounce you
                             married.");
          spouse1.setSpouse(spouse2);
          spouse2.setSpouse(spouse1);

          System.out.println("Let's party!");
        }
      }
    }
  }
}
```

On the surface, it's a pretty simplified version of the traditional American wedding ceremony for two Person objects in the system. We do the usual "ask if everybody's OK with this marriage" ritual, asking first the one person, then the other, if they take so-and-so to be their lawfully wedded whatever, then turning to the crowd as a whole. If everybody agrees, we pronounce the pair married, party the night away, and send the happy couple off to Hawaii, or Bermuda, or Disney World, wherever the honeymoon will be.

(In fact, the traditional wedding is a prime example of the *distributed two-phase commit protocol* used in distributed transaction management: Phase 1 is the "vote" phase where all the resources involved in the transaction—the couple-to-be, as well as the audience—are asked to commit to the transaction, and Phase 2, where the results of the vote are announced. If any resource in the group votes "no," the deal's off; otherwise the happy couple heads to Bermuda. More on this in Item 32.)

How many possible failure scenarios are here? Think about it for a moment before continuing.

Ready? Offhand, I count several.

- We have a concurrency concern between the interrogation of the two spouses and "flipping the married bit" later in the code. If, for example, the same spouse is being used in another ceremony, it's entirely possible that the questions could come right after one another, since threads tend to run side-by-side. This is a simple Java concurrency problem, but it's not easily solved—we can't just mark the method itself synchronized because that will synchronize only this `Minister` object and won't lock the `Person` objects being used directly. And synchronizing methods on the `Person` class won't solve the problem, either, since it's the interleaving of the calls that's the problem, not the same object having two methods called simultaneously.
- What happens if, thanks to the concurrency problem above, an `AlreadyMarriedException` is thrown out of `spouse2.setSpouse`? We never actually reset `spouse1` to be single or remove `spouse2` as `spouse1`'s spouse, leaving poor `spouse1` married to somebody who doesn't consider him- or herself to be married in turn. Such situations might be great fodder for writing soap operas and human drama, but they're generally considered bad for computer systems.
- A slight variation: What happens if an `OutOfMemoryError` (or other `Error` or `RuntimeException`) is thrown from the same place? Again, one or the other of the two spouses aren't reset back to their original state.

- And, of course, we haven't even considered what should happen with respect to paying the DJ, the florist, the church, or the minister for their efforts even if the ceremony itself fails—after all, despite the fact that the groom or bride suddenly backs out of the wedding, these people still expect to get renumerated for their efforts. We need to handle the situations where one spouse, both spouses, or even the crowd prevents the wedding from taking place by returning `false` out of the `isOK . . .` methods. Although it's not an issue in this case, in theory we have a half-dozen failure scenario possibilities (think of all the permutations of `spouse1`, `spouse2`, and `crowd` decisions).

I'm sure there are more possibilities here—a little imagination takes you a long way.

Now consider how we might write this in some kind of transactional system. (I'm taking some liberties here because Java doesn't support transactional processing out of the box, but the basic idea turns out about the same.)

```java
public class Person { . . . }
public class Minister
{
  public void marryPeople(Person spouse1, Person spouse2)
  {
    Transaction txn = TransactionManager.getTransaction();
    txn.begin();

    // Enlist all the players who get a say in the results
    //
    txn.enlistResource(spouse1);
    txn.enlistResource(spouse2);
    txn.enlistResource(Crowd.getCrowd());

    try
    {
      if (spouse1.isOKToMarry(spouse2) &&
          spouse2.isOKToMarry(spouse1)&&
          Crowd.isOKWithMarriage(spouse1, spouse2))
      {
        spouse1.setSpouse(spouse2);
        spouse2.setSpouse(spouse1);
```

```
        goOnHoneymoon(spouse1, spouse2);

      // Pay for the wedding services
    }
  }
  catch (Exception x)
  {
    // Nothing to do here—spouse1 and spouse2 are returned
    // back to their original state automatically
  }
 }
}
```

Note that no additional work is necessary to restore the system to its original state in the event of a failure—any kind of failure—because the objects, being transactionally aware, can reset themselves. (If you're not ready to accept the idea of objects being transactionally aware, then imagine this is a stored procedure instead of Java code—the end result is the same.)

When viewed this way, it's hard not to get excited about writing transactional code, particularly for code that's more complicated than the scenario above. When you think about it, it's the Java equivalent of never having to say "I'm sorry": the Resource Manager somehow magically restores the state of the system to where it was when you started, for anything and everything touched as part of this processing.

Unfortunately, transactional processing gets something of a bum rap. On the one hand, it's considered "old-fashioned" because it's the core principle behind many of the older mainframe systems ("Transactional Processing" is the "TP" in the terms "TP Monitors" and "TP Systems"). On the other hand, it's considered to be either something that only database administrators deal with on a regular basis or a "head-hurting" world filled with arcane specifications and indecipherable implementations. Truth is, most of that complexity is intended to be buried behind the transactional veneer—for most programmers, transactional systems are far, far simpler to work with than the alternative (coding it by hand) would ever be.

Things do get awkward if you need to work against other resources as part of this unit of work—for example, you need to not only make a change to a user's account but also reflect the change made as part of an audit log in a separate database. This is where *distributed transactions* come into play, and while they make it possible for you to treat operations against multiple resource managers (i.e., more than one database) to still succeed or fail atomically, they carry their own costs, as described in Item 32.

Before you run off and immediately start looking for ways to make your objects intrinsically transactional, as is assumed in the Java examples presented earlier, bear in mind that nothing ever comes for free, and transactional processing definitely carries its share of costs. First of all, transactional processing isn't just looking for atomic failure, it's also a concurrency model, meaning that any time a transaction is started against a resource, a lock must be taken out against that resource to ensure that other players in the system can't make updates simultaneously against it. In fact, a transactional system is generally said to provide ACID properties. These locks, if not properly managed (see Items 29 and 30), will yield a system that could only be described as a scalability disaster.

In the long run, however, once the scalability concerns are addressed, transactional processing offers a powerful mechanism for writing code that automatically handles the failure scenarios in a simplified, consistent, and coherent way. And in the end, that's a powerful tool for keeping it simple (see Item 25).

Item 28: Differentiate user transactions from system transactions

A user is working with an online banking system. She wants to do a simple balance transfer from her savings account to her checking account (probably to cover the large check she just wrote earlier today). She selects the Balance Transfer option from the menu, selects her checking account from the list of accounts presented, types in the amount she wishes to transfer, selects her savings account from the second list of accounts presented, and clicks Go.

Exactly how many transactions are used here?

The question isn't as simple as it might seem. To the user, and any student of accounting, this will seem like one transaction, but to the system, it could be two database transactions, particularly if we're talking about working with multiple databases or other resources: for example, in order to help avoid keeping database locks open for a long period of time (see

Item 29), we might first issue a query against the source account to make sure our user hasn't elected to transfer more money than is actually in the account, another query to make sure the target account still exists (the bank may have elected to close it because of some excessive insufficient funds problems, for example), and finally an update to take the money out of the source account and put it into the target account.

In some cases, we may even break the update statement into multiple steps, particularly in scenarios where the user's actions depend on the state of the data in the database at the time she begins. For example, our user may decide from which account to transfer money based on which one has more money at the moment, as shown in the list of her accounts.

Let's look at another situation, perhaps easier to recognize, in which the simple transaction model more or less fails. Assume we're speaking of a travel agency application. I want to travel from Sacramento, California, to Munich, Germany.[2] Since there are (at last look) no direct flights from Sacramento to Munich, I have to take at least two flights to get there—one to an airline's central "hub" and the second to Munich. As a matter of fact, it's entirely possible that I'll travel on three flights—Sacramento to the U.S. hub to the European hub to Munich. Being a seasoned traveler, however, I have some preferences about how I travel. Specifically, I want to minimize the number of "hops," and I don't mind staying overnight between hops, as long as I don't have to take a train or taxi as part of the trip, and so on.

The travel agent, using a transacted system built to give him access to the travel systems of the major airlines, is going to take all this information and plug it against their databases to try to come up with a reasonable travel itinerary. He plugs my departure point into his system, which presents him with a list of possible destinations. He's more or less guessing about where to go next, so let's assume he starts by booking a flight from Sacramento to Chicago's O'Hare airport, since O'Hare is a major international airport and is likely to have a better choice of successive hops than, say, Rochester. He books that flight, then finds from there a flight to Heathrow in London. Unfortunately, at this point, there's no direct flight from Heathrow to Munich, but he can get me to Frankfurt and a taxi from Frankfurt to Munich, which I don't want, because I hate taxis. Time to start over.

---

2. This example comes from *Transaction Processing* [Gray/Reuter, Section 4.2.4].

So, again, how many transactions are we looking at?

Remember that the goal of a scalable system is to minimize locks (see Item 29), and the airlines are certainly interested in building the most scalable system possible. So let's consider the two possible ways the travel agent could use his system to try booking this flight.

1. He could use a distributed two-phase commit transaction that begins by enlisting the first airline's database as part of the transaction. He books the flight from Sacramento to Chicago. Then he moves on to another airline's database (enlisting that database as part of the transaction as well) and books the second leg. Now, however, when it comes time to book the third leg, he finds that the trip overall will be unacceptable to me. So, he simply issues a ROLLBACK to the entire distributed transaction, and everything's back the way it was before.

2. He could do each of these as individual transactions: one transaction against the first airline's database, the second leg again as its own transaction, and when the third leg comes around, simply abort that third leg (or never even try to place it).

While many programmers choose the first model, because in many respects it's the "cleanest" of the two, the first approach has some inherent problems.

Rolling back the distributed transaction essentially forces the travel agent to start over from scratch. Even if the Sacramento to Chicago leg is perfectly acceptable and has more options to explore, rolling back the entire thing forces the travel agent to rebook that leg. This, of course, assumes that the leg is still available—it's entirely possible that some other traveler, seeking to go from Sacramento to Chicago, has taken that window of opportunity between the completion of the rollback and the start of the second transaction to book that last remaining seat, leaving our travel agent with less to work with than he thought.

More importantly, however, the airlines are not going to allow the travel agent to hold locks against open seats for that length of time, for exactly the same reason: some other traveler may be interested in a seat that you're still "thinking about," and a "sure" sale is being denied in favor of a "possible" sale. This is not the way to keep revenues high. Instead, the airlines usually run with an optimistic concurrency model (see Item 33) that checks to see if the seat is still there only when I actually want to purchase it—yes, it's possible that a seat I had my eye on will suddenly disappear out from under me, but they're betting that the chances of that happening are far fewer than the number of seats that might not get sold if they allow people to "lock" seats without paying for them.

So, from an overall system perspective, the second approach is often better, despite the additional work it lays on the programmer. Astute readers will have already spotted a major flaw in this analysis: What happens if we need to roll back one of those earlier, completed transactions? If we've already committed to that Sacramento to Chicago flight, and we need to back out of it, it's not like we can just issue a ROLLBACK and undo the committed work—that would violate the durability part of the ACID transaction.

This is where the transactional community talks about a *compensating transaction,* a transaction that knows how to undo the effects of an earlier, committed transaction. In our trip planner example, then, the code has to know how to undo the committed transaction for both the Sacramento–Chicago and Chicago–Frankfurt legs, in order to allow the travel agent to undo the work done earlier. (Presumably the airlines are OK with travel agents being able to back out committed transactions in exchange for the locks against the database being held open for shorter periods of time, and in fact, this generally holds true for systems that have high scalability requirements.) Not to mention, any other travel agencies looking to book a flight from Sacramento to Chicago won't realize that the seat I was originally going to have is now free until that compensating transaction runs—in other words, we're also violating the atomicity aspect of the transaction.

Worse, you may start looking at the practical realities of writing compensating transactions. That's about when the blood starts to drain from your face: consider all the work that a system based on compensating transactions will require. "But it's so much *simpler* to just use the distributed transaction!" will be the rallying cry, and I, for one, won't disagree. But, as with many things, what's simpler for the programmer is not always better for the user. In this case, the tradeoff here is pretty straightforward: simplicity of the programming model against greater scalability of the system against multiple data sources.

Before you return this book to the bookstore in protest, let me add a couple of caveats, hopefully to assuage your sense of apprehension and keep the book in your hands.

First and foremost, this scenario only really applies when working against *multiple* databases. Yes, although we'll periodically want to control the lock granularity for transactions against a single database, there are other ways to do that, including trusting the underlying database plumbing to keep the locks as fine-grained as is reasonably possible. Database vendors spend a significant amount of their development lifecycle looking for ways to maximize the throughput of transactions conducted against their systems, far more time than you or I would (or even could), so at a certain level it doesn't make sense to try to second-guess their efforts. There are a few ways we can help, however, and much of the rest of this chapter discusses those.

Second, this compensating transaction model assumes that the actions performed against both databases must remain essentially atomic, but it willingly sacrifices isolation in exchange for scalability. This is much the same choice we make when deciding to turn down isolation levels on transactions (see Item 35), except here it's done at a multidatabase level. If this lowered isolation is unacceptable, we can't make use of the compensating transaction model, period. As with many things, this decision has to be made in conjunction with the users (and/or their business analyst representatives) and developers.

Finally, however, we already have an established pattern by which we can make this work much simpler from a programmatic standpoint: the Command pattern [GOF, 233], used to encapsulate "commands" to be carried out by wrapping the code in objects executed from a common interface. In Java, this interface is frequently the `Runnable` interface (which has the side benefit of making it easy to plug the `Command` object into a separate `Thread` of execution). One of the less-realized benefits of Command, however, is that it's also possible to bundle the "undo" operation of the Command right alongside the "do" operation:

```
public interface DatabaseCommand extends Runnable
{
  // We inherit public void run(); from Runnable
  //

  public void undo();
}

public class DatabaseWorker
```

```
{
  ArrayList commandList = new ArrayList();

  public void execute(DatabaseCommand dc)
  {
    commandList.add(dc);
    dc.run();
  }

  public void rollback()
  {
    ListIterator li =
      commandList.listIterator(commandList.size() + 1);
    while (li.hasPrevious())
      li.undo();
  }
}
```

Now it becomes trivial to create DatabaseCommand objects that implement not only the committed work but also the rollback work, and hand them one by one into the DatabaseWorker instance that is, in essence, now representing our user transaction.

And there we finally come to the crux of the situation: we need to keep the user's view of a transaction entirely separate from the system's view of a transaction, for the reasons cited earlier. In many cases, particularly when working with a single database, the two will align quite easily and naturally, and when that happens, feel free to simply fall back on the standard transaction mechanism without hesitation. Just be aware of transactional locks, and be willing to surrender the ease of the transactional model when necessary to achieve better scalability.

Item 29:   Minimize lock windows

Readers of *Effective Java* [Bloch] will undoubtedly remember this advice from Item 49: "As a rule, you should do as little work as possible inside synchronized regions." This same principle holds true for enterprise systems, where locks in shared resources create contention, restricting the ultimate scalability of the system.

To start with, even in the absence of any kind of contention, the act of acquiring an object monitor and later releasing it is not trivial. In fact, given the performance improvements in recent JVMs regarding object creation, where we used to say that "the most expensive thing you can do in Java is to create an object" (leading to all sorts of pooling mechanisms that are now largely unnecessary—see Item 72), it's now fair to say that "the most expensive thing you can do in Java is to acquire an object monitor."

Consider this trivialized example, in which one thread calls a nonsynchronized method 35 million times and after that an exactly equivalent synchronized method another 35 million times, then compares the resultant timings. We're going to write three different versions of this trivial bit of code—one that uses no synchronization at all, one that uses a synchronized modifier on the method call itself, and one that uses a more coarse-grained synchronization approach. Execution will be in two parts—the first part will execute a method 35 million times from a single thread, then we'll spin off a command-line number of threads and let them each execute 35 million times as well. First, the unsynchronized version:

```java
// Driver.java
//
// UnsyncDriver: just let 'em rip
//
public class UnsyncDriver
{
  private static int callCount = 0;

  public static void call()
  {
    // Do something to avoid dead code removal optimizations
    //
    callCount++;
  }

  static class CallRunner implements Runnable
  {
    public void run()
    {
      long start = System.currentTimeMillis();
      for (int i=0; i<35000000; i++)
        call();
```

```
      long end = System.currentTimeMillis();
      System.out.println(Thread.currentThread().getName() +
        " Call() Start: " + start + "ms " +
        "End: " + end + "ms Diff = " +
        (end - start) + "ms");
    }
  }

  public static void main(String[] args)
  {
    // Warm up the JIT
    for (int i=0; i<100000; i++)
    {
      call();
    }

    long start = System.currentTimeMillis();
    for (int i=0; i<35000000; i++)
      call();
    long end = System.currentTimeMillis();
    System.out.println("Call() Start: " + start + "ms " +
                       "End: " + end + " ms " +
                       "Diff = " + (end - start) + " ms");

    if (args.length > 0)
    {
      int threads = Integer.parseInt(args[0]);
      System.out.println("----------- Executing " + threads +
                         " threads. -----------");

      Thread[] threadArray = new Thread[threads];
      for (int i=0; i<threads; i++)
        threadArray[i] =
          new Thread(new CallRunner(), "Thread " + i);

      for (int i=0; i<threads; i++)
        threadArray[i].start();
    }
  }
}
```

The synchronized version is almost identical except that the `call` method is decorated with the `synchronized` keyword, and the coarse-grained version uses a private `Object` lock to lock against in the body of the method itself:

```
// FineSyncDriver.java
//
// Just like UnsyncDriver, except for the following
public class FineSyncDriver
{
  public static synchronized void syncCall()
  {
    // Do something to avoid dead code removal optimizations
    //
    syncCallCount++;
  }
}
```

```
// CoarseSyncDriver.java
//
// Just like UnsyncDriver, except for the following
public class CoarseSyncDriver
{
 private static int callCount = 0;
 private static Object lock = new Object();
 public static void call()
 {
  // Do something so as to avoid dead code removal
  // optimizations
  //
  syncronized(lock)
  {
   callCount++;
  }
 }
}
```

Running the three versions with 10 threads yields some interesting insights, as shown in the following output:

```
C:\Projects\EEJ\code> java UnsyncDriver 10
Call() Start: 1076330441441ms End: 1076330441651 ms
                           Diff = 210 ms
```

```
public class CoarseSyncDriver
{
----------- Executing 10 threads. -----------
Thread 1 Call() Start: 1076330441721ms
                End: 1076330442402ms Diff = 681ms
Thread 3 Call() Start: 1076330441841ms
                End: 1076330442512ms Diff = 671ms
Thread 0 Call() Start: 1076330441661ms
                End: 1076330442572ms Diff = 911ms
Thread 2 Call() Start: 1076330441781ms
                End: 1076330442572ms Diff = 791ms
Thread 4 Call() Start: 1076330442142ms
                End: 1076330443043ms Diff = 901ms
Thread 5 Call() Start: 1076330442202ms
                End: 1076330443343ms Diff = 1141ms
Thread 7 Call() Start: 1076330442803ms
                End: 1076330443403ms Diff = 600ms
Thread 8 Call() Start: 1076330442753ms
                End: 1076330443403ms Diff = 650ms
Thread 9 Call() Start: 1076330442702ms
                End: 1076330443413ms Diff = 711ms
Thread 6 Call() Start: 1076330442262ms
                End: 1076330443413ms Diff = 1151ms


C:\Projects\EEJ\code> java FineSyncDriver 10
FineCall() Start: 1076330565970ms
           End: 1076330566731 ms Diff = 761 ms
------------ Executing 10 threads. ------------
Thread 0 FineSyncCall() Start: 1076330566731ms
                        End: 1076331238256ms Diff = 671525ms
Thread 8 FineSyncCall() Start: 1076330566791ms
                        End: 1076331310000ms Diff = 743209ms
Thread 4 FineSyncCall() Start: 1076330566791ms
                        End: 1076331310010ms Diff = 743219ms
Thread 9 FineSyncCall() Start: 1076330566791ms
                        End: 1076331310010ms Diff = 743219ms
Thread 2 FineSyncCall() Start: 1076330566791ms
                        End: 1076331310010ms Diff = 743219ms
```

```
Thread 7 FineSyncCall() Start: 1076330566791ms
                        End: 1076331310010ms Diff = 743219ms
Thread 1 FineSyncCall() Start: 1076330566791ms
                        End: 1076331310010ms Diff = 743219ms
Thread 3 FineSyncCall() Start: 1076330566791ms
                        End: 1076331310010ms Diff = 743219ms
Thread 6 FineSyncCall() Start: 1076330566791ms
                        End: 1076331310010ms Diff = 743219ms
Thread 5 FineSyncCall() Start: 1076330566791ms
                        End: 1076331310010ms Diff = 743219ms


C:\Projects\EEJ\code> java CoarseSyncDriver 10
CoarseCall() Start: 1076331255291ms
             End: 1076331255361 ms Diff = 70 ms
------------ Executing 10 threads. ------------
Thread 0 Call() Start: 1076331255371ms
                End: 1076331255641ms Diff = 270ms
Thread 1 Call() Start: 1076331255431ms
                End: 1076331255942ms Diff = 511ms
Thread 2 Call() Start: 1076331255431ms
                End: 1076331256252ms Diff = 821ms
Thread 3 Call() Start: 1076331255431ms
                End: 1076331256553ms Diff = 1122ms
Thread 4 Call() Start: 1076331255431ms
                End: 1076331256863ms Diff = 1432ms
Thread 5 Call() Start: 1076331255431ms
                End: 1076331257164ms Diff = 1733ms
Thread 6 Call() Start: 1076331255431ms
                End: 1076331257474ms Diff = 2043ms
Thread 7 Call() Start: 1076331255431ms
                End: 1076331257774ms Diff = 2343ms
Thread 8 Call() Start: 1076331255431ms
                End: 1076331258075ms Diff = 2644ms
Thread 9 Call() Start: 1076331255491ms
                End: 1076331258265ms Diff = 2774ms


C:\Projects\EEJ\code>
```

First, we can clearly see that the unsynchronized version is the fastest, taking anywhere from 600 to 1200 milliseconds to execute; the differences are probably due to the thread scheduler and which threads happen to get launched first (and therefore get the longest run before having to yield the CPU). By the way, take careful note that the 10 threads executing the unsynchronized method could easily be corrupting its value entirely, something I'm completely ignoring at the moment. You don't have that luxury, so don't expect that you can improve the performance and scalability of your systems simply by removing synchronized blocks. Your code might run faster, but the late nights debugging the production server just aren't worth it.

Second, we can also clearly see that the coarse-grained synchronization version takes a lot less time than the fine-grained synchronization version, but a curious thing kicks in: it's as if the time spent executing is linear in proportion to when the thread was kicked off. In fact, this is precisely what's happening—the first thread scheduled grabs the lock and holds it for the entire 35-million-iteration loop, never yielding it, so the other threads have to wait until that lock gets released before they can contend for it. By the time the last thread gets the lock, that thread has been waiting a while.

Third, the fine-grained mechanism, where the monitor is acquired and released on each and every call, yields the most even numbers, yet the worst: roughly 740 seconds, or a full 12 minutes before execution completes for each thread. And this is just for 10 threads; imagine what 20 or 50 or 100 threads will require.

Don't draw too much from a single run, but clearly synchronization has its costs, long before we consider the amount of time spent *inside* the synchronized region.

To put it in simple one-sentence terms, *contention is the enemy of scalability*. The more contention in the system, the more time we spend waiting, which in turn bloats the latency of the system as a whole. We can't scale a system that suffers from contention problems because, remember, the point of scalability is to be able to add users to the system simply by throwing more hardware at the problem—all the hardware in the world won't help us if the latency is caused by everyone having to wait to share a single lock.

Toward that end, keep two remedies in mind. First, avoid taking locks when you can help it—even if nobody else ends up contesting you for the lock, it still takes up precious time just to acquire the monitor and yield it back again. This means don't synchronize the entire `doGet` or `doPost` method of a servlet "just to be safe." Instead, spend the time analyzing the code to determine where the possible hot spots are and synchronize *only* those hot spots.

Second, keep the time spent inside the synchronized region as small as possible; I'll leave it as an exercise to the unconvinced reader to put a `Thread.sleep` call in the `call` method to simulate holding the lock for some length of time, experimenting with varying numbers of threads. Suffice it to say, the longer the call window, and the higher the number of threads, the worse (exponentially so) the times become. (Do yourself a favor, though, if you plan to run the tests yourself: cut the number of iterations down from 35 million to something a bit more reasonable, or you'll spend a *lot* of time waiting for the tests to complete.)

Of course, other remedies exist, too. One approach is to prefer to work with immutable resources (objects, data, whatever) that need no synchronization because they can't change, as described in Item 38. Another is to offload the resource processing into a queue (per Item 20) where it can be handled in asynchronous-yet-serialized fashion, much as a batch process does. The point is still the same: lock as little as possible for as short a time as possible.

Item 30:   Never cede control outside your component while holding locks

Readers of *Effective Java* [Bloch] will undoubtedly remember this item's title as advice from Item 49, phrased in almost exactly the same way. Fortunately, deadlock isn't quite as much of a concern in J2EE systems thanks to some of the built-in safeguards established by the EJB Specification as well as some of the transactional deadlock avoidance code built in to most modern relational databases. Despite that, for reasons that partially relate back to keeping lock windows small (see Item 29), it's still a bad idea to call out to "alien" components while holding locks open.

As a quick reminder, what *exactly* happens here?

```
public class Example
{
  private Object lock = new Object();
  public void doSomething()
  {
```

```
  synchronized(lock)
  {
    // Do something interesting
  }
 }
}
```

To be precise, the thread executing the doSomething method attempts to acquire ownership of the object monitor for the object instance referenced by lock. Assuming no other thread owns that monitor, this thread will acquire it.

Take it one step further: What will happen when a thread calls recursively into a synchronized region?

```
public class Example
{
  private Object lock = new Object();
  public void methodA()
  {
    synchronized(lock)
    {
      methodB();
    }
  }
  public void methodB()
  {
    synchronized(lock)
    {
      // Do something interesting
    }
  }
}
```

The JVM remembers that the thread that called methodA owns the monitor for object lock, so it breezes right through the synchronized region in methodB; it's impossible for a thread to deadlock itself in Java.

This is Remedial Java 101; why bring it up here? Take this into a different dimension for a moment and put some RMI semantics behind it. In particular, remember that the RMI Specification states that a remote method call on an exported object (i.e., a method call from outside the JVM via the RMI stack) can come on any arbitrary thread. Because the JVM remembers only the *local* thread that owns a monitor, it becomes possible for a thread to deadlock itself by calling outside the JVM and back in again:

```
// Deadlock.java
//
import java.rmi.*;
import java.rmi.server.*;

public class Deadlock
{
  public static interface RemoteFoo extends Remote {
    public void doTheCall() throws RemoteException;
  }

  public static class RemoteFooImpl
    extends UnicastRemoteObject
    implements RemoteFoo
  {
    public RemoteFooImpl() throws RemoteException { super(); }

    private Object lock = new Object();
    public void doTheCall() throws RemoteException
    {
      try {
        System.out.println("Entered doTheCall()");
        synchronized(lock) {
          System.out.println("Entered synchronized region");
          RemoteFoo rf = (RemoteFoo)
            Naming.lookup("rmi://localhost/RemoteFoo");
          rf.doTheCall();
        }
      }
      catch (NotBoundException nbex) {
        System.out.println("Not bound?"); }
      catch (java.net.MalformedURLException malEx) {
        System.out.println("Malformed URL"); }
    }
  }

  public static void main(String[] args) throws Exception
  {
    RemoteFooImpl rfi = new RemoteFooImpl();
```

```
      Naming.bind("RemoteFoo", rfi);

      RemoteFoo rf =
        (RemoteFoo)Naming.lookup("rmi://localhost/RemoteFoo");
      rf.doTheCall();
    }
  }
```

The output from this program sends chills down the spine of any distributed systems programmer:

```
C:\Projects\EEJ\code\RMIdeadlock>java Deadlock
Entered doTheCall()
Entered synchronized region
Entered doTheCall()
  Window hangs
```

And sure enough, if we do the Ctrl-Break trick in the Windows JVM to get a complete thread dump, we can see the deadlock:

```
Full thread dump Java HotSpot(TM) Client VM (. . .)

other thread dumps removed for clarity

"RMI TCP Connection(3)-192.168.1.102" daemon prio=5
        tid=0x02edaf30 nid=0x7d8
        waiting for monitor entry [32cf000..32cfd8c]
        at Deadlock$RemoteFooImpl.doTheCall(Deadlock.java:29)
        - waiting to lock <0x1050d3d8> (a java.lang.Object)
        at sun.reflect.NativeMethodAccessorImpl.invoke0(
            Native Method)
        at sun.reflect.NativeMethodAccessorImpl.invoke(
            NativeMethodAccessorImpl.java:39)
        at sun.reflect.DelegatingMethodAccessorImpl.invoke(
            DelegatingMethodAccessorImpl.java:25)
        at java.lang.reflect.Method.invoke(Method.java:324)
        at sun.rmi.server.UnicastServerRef.dispatch(
            UnicastServerRef.java:261)
        at sun.rmi.transport.Transport$1.run(
            Transport.java:148)
        at java.security.AccessController.doPrivileged(
            Native Method)
        at sun.rmi.transport.Transport.serviceCall(
```

```
                        Transport.java:144)
        at sun.rmi.transport.tcp.TCPTransport.handleMessages(
                TCPTransport.java:460)
        at
sun.rmi.transport.tcp.TCPTransport$ConnectionHandler.run(
                TCPTransport.java:701)
        at java.lang.Thread.run(Thread.java:534)

"RMI TCP Connection(2)-192.168.1.102" daemon prio=5
        tid=0x02ed9238 nid=0x91c
        runnable [324f000..324fd8c]
        at java.net.SocketInputStream.socketRead0(Native
          Method)
        at java.net.SocketInputStream.read(
                SocketInputStream.java:129)
        at java.io.BufferedInputStream.fill(
                BufferedInputStream.java:183)
        at java.io.BufferedInputStream.read(
                BufferedInputStream.java:201)
        - locked <0x1006a110> (a java.io.BufferedInputStream)
        at java.io.DataInputStream.readByte(
                DataInputStream.java:331)
        at sun.rmi.transport.StreamRemoteCall.executeCall(
                StreamRemoteCall.java:189)
        at sun.rmi.server.UnicastRef.invoke(
                UnicastRef.java:133)
        at Deadlock$RemoteFooImpl_Stub.doTheCall(
                Unknown Source)
        at Deadlock$RemoteFooImpl.doTheCall(Deadlock.java:31)
        - locked <0x1050d3d8> (a java.lang.Object)
        at sun.reflect.NativeMethodAccessorImpl.invoke0(
                Native Method)
        at sun.reflect.NativeMethodAccessorImpl.invoke(
                NativeMethodAccessorImpl.java:39)
        at sun.reflect.DelegatingMethodAccessorImpl.invoke(
                DelegatingMethodAccessorImpl.java:25)
        at java.lang.reflect.Method.invoke(Method.java:324)
        at sun.rmi.server.UnicastServerRef.dispatch(
                UnicastServerRef.java:261)
        at sun.rmi.transport.Transport$1.run(
                Transport.java:148)
```

```
    at java.security.AccessController.doPrivileged(
        Native Method)
    at sun.rmi.transport.Transport.serviceCall(
        Transport.java:144)
    at sun.rmi.transport.tcp.TCPTransport.handleMessages(
        TCPTransport.java:460)
    at sun.rmi.transport.tcp.TCPTransport$Connection
        Handler.run(TCPTransport.java:701)
    at java.lang.Thread.run(Thread.java:534)
```

As you can see, the two threads—the one caller, the other the thread dispatched by RMI to answer the incoming request—are deadlocked because the caller is blocked waiting for the callee to return, and the callee is waiting to lock on the object locked by the caller.

This is a nasty turn of affairs; it means that the RMI Specification has no capacity to detect a logical call sequence that leaves the JVM yet circles back into the same JVM as part of that process, what *Transactional COM+* [Ewald] refers to as a *causality* and the EJB Specification refers to as a *loopback*. Without this, there's no way to detect a logical self-creating deadlock, much less a deadlock created by two clients. If there's any possibility for a circular call like this, it's up to you to handle it.

Note that EJB doesn't exactly help out a whole lot here—in the event that a concurrent callback like this occurs on a stateful session bean, the container throws an exception (`RemoteException` if it's a remote call, `EJBException` if it's a local call), thereby effectively rolling back the entire chain of work. This behavior is deliberately designed, as stated clearly in the specification (Section 7.12.10): "One implication of this rule is that an application cannot make loopback calls to a session bean instance." It avoids deadlock but invalidates work, and only at runtime, to boot.

If this were the only concern, we could probably ignore it—after all, the most likely possibility for this kind of situation is a designer trying to build some sort of notification mechanism on a stateful session bean using the Observer pattern [GOF, 217], as is commonly done for Java event handling, and now that we've identified a problem with this approach, we just fall back to messaging-based approaches to avoid the problem. Given the relative rarity in which this problem arises, it wouldn't be worth discussing.

No, the larger problem comes from the fact that when you call out of your component while holding a lock, you're effectively including whatever effort the "alien" code wishes to undertake as part of your lock window (see Item 29). This means that it's entirely possible that the "alien" code, code by definition not under your control, could be doing such brain-dead things as calculating pi to the 100th decimal place, making remote service calls, or even worse behavior, all while you hold locks.

The implications of this are more than you might think at first. For starters, you need to be excruciatingly careful when choosing transactional affinity on EJBs, particularly for EJBs operating under container-managed transactions, because the window of a CMT transaction is the entire body of the method call, thereby giving you no opportunity to do nontransactional processing before opening the transaction and possibly taking out locks. Only if the EJB is entirely atomic in nature (i.e., it makes no calls to other components, beyond the database whose processing is—hopefully—well understood) is CMT a viable option.

You also need to be aware of the fact that a JMS consumer invoked asynchronously via a `MessageListener` (which includes the Message-Driven Bean) is invoked on any arbitrary thread, meaning that we're back to the danger of holding an object monitor needed by a different thread. In particular, when using messaging to break the request-response cycle (see Item 20), be aware that the delivery of the message could kick the asynchronous processing off immediately, and any locks that you're holding at the time you deliver the message could create contention or, in the worst-case scenario, a deadlock, as the message processor takes out a lock on something you want before trying to acquire the locks your thread is currently holding. And because it's so timing-dependent, it will happen only under severe load or during a demo to a potential million-dollar client.

Do yourself a favor and make sure the locks are all released before performing any communications outside of the component; you'll be a much happier and carefree programmer for doing so.

Item 31:   Understand EJB transactional affinity

It's one of those aspects of the EJB Specification that many EJB programmers either never think about or, if they do, they sort of shunt it off to the side until later. It doesn't really have anything to do with programming, per se, since it never really shows up in code. Instead, most programmers just rely on the tools or IDE they're using to pick whatever values "feel right" and leave it at that. Unfortunately, the choice of transactional affinity on your EJB beans has as great an effect on the ultimate performance and scalability of your beans as anything else, perhaps more so.

Consider the classic Session Façade [Alur/Crupi/Malks, 341]—as an optimization to network trips, wrap all access to an entity bean via a session bean, thus forcing clients to access the entity bean in bulk rather than in individual method calls. So, for example, given an entity bean that has five attributes, rather than individually setting each attribute on the entity bean from the client, pass all five attributes via a single method call to the session bean. The session bean then does the set calls against the entity bean, thus cutting out a leg of the round-trips against the entity bean. Pretty straightforward, right?

Enter transactional affinity.

By this point, I assume that you're more or less familiar with the six different container-managed transactional affinity settings in EJB: Mandatory, Requires, RequiresNew, Supports, NotSupported, and Never. But what may not be familiar to you is the interaction of these affinity settings—how the container will react when a call comes from one bean into another. For example, when a bean currently executing under a transaction calls another bean marked with Requires, the transaction from the first bean is propagated to the second, so both calls now operate under a single transaction. Table 4–1 details the complete set of interactions, both for container-managed and bean-managed transactions.

Table 4–1 | Transactional affinity setting effects

	In transaction scope?	Root of transaction scope?	Shares caller's scope?
CMT: NotSupported	Never	Never	Never
CMT: Never	Never	Never	Never
CMT: Supports	If caller is	Never	If caller has one
CMT: Requires	Always	Only if caller has none	If caller has one
CMT: RequiresNew	Always	Always	Never
CMT: Mandatory	Always	Never	Always
BMT: User begins	Always	Always	Never
BMT: None started	Never	Never	Never

The key thing to recognize in this table is that transactional affinity interaction between beans will define a large part of how the bean will perform.

Assume, for the moment, that the entity bean's `set` methods, for whatever reason, are all marked with transactional affinity `RequiresNew`. This means that each `set` call must run under its own transaction, which in turn means that the entire state of the bean must be loaded at the start of the transaction and stored back to the database at the end of the call. Not only will this mandate an additional round-trip to the database for each call, but it also will go out with full two-phase distributed transaction semantics for it (unless your container supports the use of local transactions, in which case you should see Item 32).

In reality, rarely will an entity bean set transactional affinity on attribute methods to `RequiresNew`. It's far more likely that these methods will be set to `Requires`, indicating that it will borrow the transaction of its caller; this makes the bean most flexible for Session Façade usage. But if the Session Façade [Alur/Crupi/Malks, 341] session bean fronting it is set to `Supports`, `NotSupported`, or `Never`, we're back to the same situation described earlier—each call to a method on the entity bean will result in a new transaction against the database, meaning multiple round-trips.

Consider, for a moment, the average EJB container running without any special exclusive access to the database (which would not be portable across containers anyway; see Item 11 for details). Entity beans hold data inside the container also held in the database. Because these two processes frequently don't run on the same machine, much less inside the same process space, it's entirely possible that the EJB container holds data in memory that has been changed on the database.

Now picture that same entity bean being ordered to change an attribute value to some new value (whether from a Session Façade [Alur/Crupi/Malks, 341] or directly from a client, it really doesn't matter). Any entity bean access must be done under a container-managed transactional semantic (Section 17.6.1 in the EJB 2.1 Specification), so a transaction is started. However, because it's possible that the data in the database was modified through a process outside the EJB container's awareness, the EJB container must reload the bean entirely before allowing the call to proceed. The set can then take place, the transaction can commit, and the data is flushed back to the database.

What this implies, then, is that *any* access against the entity bean (again, without using vendor value-added exclusivity capabilities) means that the EJB container must make at least two round-trips from the EJB container to the database: one to fetch the data in, the other to flush the modified data out. Fortunately this only needs to be done at transactional boundaries, so an entity bean being modified through a properly marked transactionally aware Session Façade [Alur/Crupi/Malks, 341] won't do this except at transaction begin and transaction commit.

It's fair to point out, however, that this additional pair of round-trips is only necessary because the data is being held in two places simultaneously—in the relational database and in the EJB container. If entity beans are bypassed entirely in favor of direct SQL access against the relational database (see Item 41 for details), the data resides solely within the relational database and no additional fetch-flush cycles are needed.

It's not enough to recognize the impact of a given choice of transactional affinity for a given method. In addition, in order to maximize the use of a transaction (to avoid taking out more transactions than necessary) but minimize its lifetime (see Item 29), the union of transactional affinity on methods called within the EJB container also has to be considered because you're effectively calling out of your component, as described in Item 30. This implies, then, that for any given bean, call it bean x, defined within your EJB container, you must consider not only the transactional affinity of every method on x, but also the affinity of any bean calling x as well as the affinity of any bean called in turn by x. Failure to do so may result in longer transactions than absolutely necessary.

Item 32: Prefer local transactions to distributed ones

Creating a transaction against a given resource is typically a technology-specific action—for example, in a relational database, a transaction is created by using the SQL statement BEGIN TRANSACTION. After this point, all work is done in some kind of temporary space where the effects of the executed instructions (SQL) aren't felt until the transaction itself is either completed (using the SQL COMMIT syntax) or abandoned (using SQL ROLLBACK).

Nevertheless, problems still arise—most notably, what happens when we have two resources we need to operate against as part of a single transaction?

The canonical scenario is that of operating against two different databases,[3] but under J2EE this can also be a database and a JMS provider, or a `Connector` provider. Ordinarily, when just one resource is in use, we can rely on the provider to deal with the problem of guaranteeing transaction inviolability. If we span vendors, however, things get more complicated.

To deal with this problem directly (which predates J2EE by quite a long time), a number of database players came together to define a *distributed transaction protocol*, called the *two-phase commit (TPC) protocol*. In the TPC protocol, we formally define three parties that are part of every transaction: the client; the Resource Manager (RM), which provides the shared resource we're trying to share access to; and the Transaction Manager (TM), which takes care of creating distributed transactions and handling the interaction between the clients and the RMs.

The TPC protocol, pared down to its essentials, looks something like the following sequence.

1. The client acquires a distributed transaction from the TM.
2. The client enlists the desired RMs as part of the transaction. It does so by presenting the transaction to the RMs, so that the RMs are aware of the distributed transaction and know to expect the remainder of the protocol.
3. The client does work against the enlisted RMs as usual. The RMs, aware that this is part of a distributed transaction, ensure that the work isn't committed or rolled back until the TM is heard from. (It is the RMs' responsibility to keep this data around, for reasons that will become clear later.)
4. When the client is ready to finish, the client signals the TM to commit. The TM takes over at this point.
5. Phase 1: The TM first signals each RM on the transaction, asking it, in essence, "Are you prepared to commit?" This is the RM's only chance to back out of the transaction, for any reason whatsoever—low disk space, relational integrity constraints, and so on. As a result, the RM usually writes the data to "almost committed" state; it knows the data but keeps it hidden from other transactions on the system.

---

3. Usually from two different vendors—for two different database instances of the same vendor type (Oracle and Oracle, for example), the vendor provides hooks to keep everything straight. It's when we're going against Oracle and DB/2, or DB/2 and Sybase, for example, that problems creep up.

If any RM on the transaction indicates some kind of failure, the entire transaction must be rolled back, and the TM immediately orders all RMs on the transaction to abort, even if they previously indicated they were willing to commit.

6. Phase 2: If all parties (RMs) on the transaction signaled a willingness to commit, the TM then sends around a signal again, essentially telling them, "Go ahead and commit." There is no vote here—the RMs must commit the data, and there can be no backing out, no excuses for failure. If all RMs signal successful commits, the TM then signals a successful commit back to the client, and the transaction is finished.

As you can see, the TPC protocol is a relatively complex piece of machinery. Fortunately, it's also a very reliable one, having successfully powered database access for several decades now with exceedingly high consistency rates. In fact, most relational databases use a localized version of TPC for local transactions to offer the same kind of consistency and reliability—in these situations, the TM and the RM are the same process, so it becomes a much simpler process.

Nothing comes for free, however, and TPC carries its own share of costs. In particular, because TPC requires distributed communication, the amount of time spent executing a distributed transaction is orders of magnitude higher than a local one. Even in the scenario where a single RM is enlisted against the transaction, the interaction between the TM and RM requires interprocess (if not intermachine) communication, and as Item 17 describes, this is nontrivial latency. This means that locks held inside the RM to provide the necessary ACID properties for this distributed transaction are held longer, which is an undesirable quality (as described in Item 29).

Where does this leave you? Well, for obvious reasons, you want to avoid distributed transactions unless you absolutely *must* have them, which means you must have ACID properties against multiple resources (databases, JMS providers, JCA Connector providers, and so on). Take careful note of how that's phrased: you want distributed transactions only if you have multiple data sources *and* you must have transactional semantics when working with those multiple resources—when a message to a JMS Queue must go out if and only if the database INSERT succeeds, for example.

While it may seem that this requirement comes up frequently, it turns out to be less prevalent than you might think. For many systems, for example, even though other databases may be the ultimate recipients for data gathered by this system, rather than access those databases directly, developers work against their own databases, and back-end processes pull the desired data and ship it around to those other databases. Or, your system may require real-time read access against another database but won't make any updates, so no transaction is necessary against that other database (see Item 35 for reasons).

The worst part of this story, however, comes next: by default, all transactions taken out by your favorite EJB container will be distributed TPC transactions, even if only one resource manager is ever in use. The EJB Specification (Section 17.1.1) contains an informative paragraph (set off by italic font) that states:

> *Many applications will consist of one or several enterprise beans that all use a single resource manager (typically a relational database management system). The EJB Container can make use of resource manager local transactions as an optimization technique for enterprise beans for which distributed transactions are not needed. . . . The container's use of local transactions as an optimization technique for enterprise beans with either container-managed transaction demarcation or bean-managed transaction demarcation is not visible to enterprise beans.*

Or, in other words, you can't guarantee that your container will choose to use local transactions, nor can you somehow indicate to the container that your enterprise beans *should* use local transactions. This is one area where the EJB Specification clearly takes the attitude that "the less you as a programmer know, the better." And if the container decides that your access to the database and the JMS Queue must take place under a distributed transaction, you're now running under a distributed transaction, whether you wanted to or not. And, thanks to the wonders of auto-enlistment—that magic within the EJB container that automatically enlists a resource, like a database, as part of the transaction as soon as it is retrieved from the JNDI Context—simply referencing a JMS Queue and a DataSource in the same method puts those two in the same transaction, even if you don't want them to be. (This is true once the transaction is open, regardless of whether container-managed transactions or bean-managed transactions are used. Thus your only hope of avoiding this situation—if you want or need to avoid it—is to write bean-managed transactions and not open the transaction until after you've acquired the resources that shouldn't be in this EJB transaction. Ugly.)

Net result? If you want to keep your transaction windows as short as possible (see Item 29), due to the increased communication requirements of the TPC protocol, you really want to use local transactions wherever possible. Doing so may require other approaches to doing your enterprise logic because EJB doesn't allow you to enforce the use of local transactions and prefers instead to run distributed ones regardless of your opinion on the matter. Combined with EJB's concurrency model (described in Item 31), this in turn reinforces the notions that (a) EJB is really for transactional processing only, and (b) in particular, EJB is really for *distributed* transactional processing, as described in Item 9.

Item 33: Consider using optimistic concurrency for better scalability

Consider the canonical problem of two users trying to work with the same data: each takes out a working copy of the data in the database and makes updates to it (thus creating *transient state* for each, as described in the introduction to Chapter 5). Now each looks to preserve the changes back to the data store. Several mechanisms are available to us—in one case, we might rely on the underlying database's concurrency facilities by starting a transaction when the first user reads the data, thus taking out a lock on the data and ensuring that nobody else can tamper with the data until our first user commits the changes made. Unfortunately, this approach creates a huge lock window (violating the advice of Item 29) by explicitly ceding control back to the user while holding a transaction open (see Item 30). As scalability goes, you can't do much worse than this.

So the next approach might be to make the read be one transaction and the updates a separate transaction. The problem we encounter here is plain to see when we run through the full scenario—our two users do their reads, then when the time comes to do their updates, the two updates are done one right after the other, the second one blithely overwriting the first. Worse yet, the underlying resource manager, the database, in this case, doesn't offer any hint or signal that data has just been overwritten.

An alternative might be to turn down the isolation level on each transaction (see Item 35 for details), thus allowing simultaneous reads to occur. The net effect will be the same, however: data is lost because each user will update without realizing that he or she is overwriting another user's changes.

Optimistic concurrency models, also known as Optimistic Offline Locks [Fowler, 416] or Optimistic Locks [Nock, 395], offer a way to have your cake and eat it too—for a small bit of additional work on your part, you can keep the number of actual locks taken out to a minimum. In essence, you're tacking on some kind of "data-modification marker" to each set of data retrieved from the data store, and when doing an update, checking that marker held in transient state against what's in the database, and if they're different, taking appropriate action to resolve the difference. "Appropriate action" varies from one system to the next, but some possibilities include trying to automatically merge the changes, presenting the user with the changed data and allowing him or her the opportunity to do the merge, simply overwriting (the problem we tried to get away from in the first place is sometimes still the right thing to do), or presenting "hey, somebody modified your data, what should I do next?" messages to the user.

Actual optimistic concurrency implementations can take a variety of forms; Version Number [Marinescu, 70] is one such approach, in which each table contains an additional column for a version number; other approaches prefer to use a timestamp of last modification. Using a version number gives you an indication of how many times the data has been modified since you last looked at the data (if you're holding version 1, and the current version is 20, the data has had a lot of changes, and you might prefer to just throw it away and start over), which isn't present with a simple timestamp approach. On the other hand, a timestamp approach takes you halfway to having a temporal element to your database, which can be extremely useful for auditing purposes, something we'll discuss in a bit.

Regardless of which approach you choose, the basic code for accessing data under an optimistic concurrency model looks something like this:

```
SELECT primary_key, data elements of interest, last_modified
  FROM Table
  WHERE primary_key=?


Cache off last_modified; when it comes time to update, do:


UPDATE Table SET (data elements of interest = new values,
             last_modified = system-generated timestamp)
  WHERE primary_key=? AND last_modified=old last_modified value
```

Keeping an eye on the row count of the UPDATE statement is crucial; if it returns 0 rows, it means that the update's predicate (the WHERE clause) failed. Unless you have a data corruption problem, that means the row identified by the primary key doesn't have a last_modified column matching the last_modified data you thought it should have—that's a sign that the last_modified timestamp of the row in question has changed, which tells you the whole row has possibly changed.

At this point, what happens next is entirely up to you. In particular, the question on the table is what to do with the data that's now out of sync with what's stored in the database.

- *Abort:* Simply throw away the changes and start over with the recently modified data. In some situations, this is the best approach, particularly if the changes are significant or if the user doesn't really have the capacity to decide which values should be merged. It goes without saying that you need to tell the user what you just did, however—aborting without telling the user is pretty unfriendly.
- *Overwrite:* Sometimes the best approach is to simply let the last one in win. If this is the case, however, there's really no need for optimistic locking in the first place—a blind UPDATE would have worked just as well.
- *Merge:* Take this user's data, compare it against the old data, and merge in the changes. This is a tricky approach, however, since you've got some hard decisions to make about how the merge should take place. How do you tell which data was changed from the original data set, in order to know which columns your user modified, and in the event that both this user's data and the current data disagree from the original, which one wins? In some cases, the best bet might be to ask the user about some or all of the merge.
- *Ask:* This is the confirmation dialog that tells the user, "The data changed, do you want to abort, overwrite, or merge?" As already stated, however, merging can be a difficult prospect at best, so typically the "ask" approach simply seeks to reload the data with the new current values and let the user edit what needs to change again, sort of a hybrid abort/ask approach.

Not one approach will fit all systems—in many cases, you'll use more than one resolution approach even within the same module or section of code. It all really depends on the business and the domain logic needs.

In some cases, you may even want to add a temporal axis to your data; by including both start and end timestamp columns, representing the "live" period this data was active, and then creating a composite primary key consisting of the original primary key column(s) and the `start` and `end` columns, you create a historical record of every row in that table:

```
CREATE TABLE person
  ( primary_key INTEGER,
    first_name VARCHAR(120),
    last_name VARCHAR(120),
    other interesting data elements,
    start TIMESTAMP,
    end TIMESTAMP ),
  PRIMARY KEY (primary_key, start, end);
```

Retrieving the "most current" row for a given `primary_key`[4] simply means querying for the record where the `end` column is set to either 0, `NULL` (if your database supports `NULL` values in primary keys), or some nonsensical value:

```
SELECT first_name, last_name, ... FROM person
  WHERE primary_key=? AND end=0
```

Updates to the table are deceptively simple, in that you only UPDATE the existing row to close off the record's lifetime by filling in the `end` column, and INSERT a new row (with the new data) with a `NULL` end column:

```
Date now = new java.util.Date();
String sql = "UPDATE person SET (end=?) " +
    "WHERE primary_key=? AND end=NULL";

PreparedStatement ps = conn.prepareStatement(sql);
ps.setTimestamp(1, now);
ps.setInteger(2, primaryKeyValue);

int rows = ps.executeUpdate();
if (rows != 1)
  throw new InconsistentDatabaseException(
    "Something's rotten...");

sql =
```

---

4. Remember, since the `start` and `end` columns are now part of the primary key, we can have multiple rows consisting of the same data in the `primary_key` column. This is deliberate—we want to have multiple versions of each "logical" row in the table.

```
        "INSERT INTO person(" +
        "primary_key, first_name, last_name,..., start)" +
        "VALUES (?, ?, ?, ..., ?)";
ps = conn.prepareStatement(sql);
ps.setInteger(1, primaryKeyValue);
ps.setString(2, firstName);
ps.setString(3, lastName);
// ... Fill in any other data for the person table as well
ps.setTimestamp(10, new java.util.Date(now.getTime()+1));
    // In other words, 1 millisecond after the
    // end of the previous record

rows = ps.executeUpdate();
if (rows != 1)
    throw new InconsistentDatabaseException(
        "Something's rotten...");
```

Bear in mind that both of these statements should really be done as part of a transaction, to eliminate the race condition between the UPDATE and the INSERT statements. Deletions are similarly simple: you just UPDATE the row to fill in the end column, and don't insert a new record with a given start and an empty end column.

While it means that data is never actually erased from the database, it also means that by including timestamps on each of your audit log statements, you can recreate the exact state of the database at any given moment of time—a powerful auditing tool. It also helps to simplify some of your programming logic, since you never actually UPDATE an existing row to modify data (although you will have to UPDATE to fill in the end column at some point). Instead, you just INSERT a new row with the current timestamp in the start column and the new data. In fact, the only time you need to do any special-case logic is the moment the first logical row is entered (in other words, when a new primary-key-identified row is inserted), since there will be no corresponding UPDATE to fill in the "previous" version's end column.

Bringing this discussion back around to optimistic concurrency, clients working with data sets they've read from the database can verify the continued authenticity of the data they hold by checking to see whether the start column of their data matches the most recent row's start column. If the two don't match, obviously somebody modified the data, and we go back to the four-point decision raised earlier: abort, overwrite, merge, or ask.

Optimistic concurrency offers a couple of benefits, the first and foremost of which is the lack of any native database locks taken out during the modification of data read earlier; in other words, client code reading data doesn't have to decide "up front" whether it wants to take out a lock. Instead, simply read the optimistic marker (version number or time-stamp) as part of the data, and only later, when you want to update the data back to the database, do you check to see whether the data was modified. Only then, during the actual modification (the UPDATE statement), do you need any kind of transactional lock, and that's usually handled for you by the database and/or the JDBC driver (if it's in auto-commit mode).

A side benefit to the optimistic concurrency approach is its improved diagnostic capability. In the event that another user modified the data, your code has an opportunity to inform your user of what's happened, as well as what to do about it. Had native database locking been used, no information about why a SQLException was thrown would be available unless the database itself chose to present it. As Nock points out, "You can tailor this notification to include whatever diagnostic information will suit clients best. For example, it may be helpful to inform users who updated the data last and when it changed. This type of information can encourage users to be more aware of concurrency issues and remind them to refresh working copies after returning from extended breaks" [Nock, 398–399].

Unfortunately, all is not perfect with the optimistic concurrency model. In particular, you're relying on application code to keep the concurrency model straight, meaning that if some other program decides to access your database (see Item 45), you're at the mercy of that code and its programmers to get the concurrency model right. For that matter, you're even at the mercy of the other programmers on your team to get the model right, which makes a good case for hiding the details of the concurrency model behind some kind of encapsulation layer (see Item 42).

Also, you may find that the optimistic concurrency model doesn't give you quite as much control as you'd like over how everything works together. For example, you may want to create "read-intent" locks or "write-intent" locks within the system, where a user indicates the desire to have exclusive access to a row or collection of rows for a period of time.

Yet you're still reluctant to fall back to native database locks, both for scalability reasons and because you want to control the locking a bit more finely than the database itself will allow. In such situations, you should consider building a pessimistic concurrency model (see Item 34), which can coexist quite peacefully with an optimistic concurrency model, as long as you don't try to use both for the same data.

Many object-relational data access toolkits (JDO implementations and the like) may provide optimistic concurrency mechanisms "out of the box" for you. If the one you use provides such a mechanism, unless you have solid reasons not to (see Item 11), take advantage of it, particularly since it usually costs you nothing more than a line in a configuration file or persistence descriptor.

In general, the optimistic concurrency model is intended purely as a scalability measure, designed to minimize lock windows (see Item 29) by reducing the actual number of native database locks taken out and the length of time they're held. In general, for most enterprise Java systems, the optimistic concurrency model should probably be the default concurrency model—relying on the underlying database to provide all concurrency might work for a short while but ultimately will create contention as you scale up the system.

Item 34: Consider using pessimistic concurrency for explicit concurrency control

Consider once again the problem of two users and one set of data, as introduced in Item 33. Each user reads the set of data, makes local changes, then seeks to update those changes back to the data store. Without some kind of control mechanism, we have a "last one wins" scenario—the last user to write his or her changes to the data store effectively overwrites any previous changes made by any other users. For most applications, losing one or more updates this way is generally considered by most users to be a Really Bad Idea.

Optimistic locking (see Item 33) partially solves this problem by tagging each set of data with some kind of "marker" that will indicate when data has been updated by some other party, so that when the data is updated we get some awareness of the change. Unfortunately, optimistic locking assumes that receiving that notification at the time of update is acceptable—that is, we won't know about the change to the underlying data until we try to actually commit our transient state back. For some situations, like the ubiquitous e-commerce shopping cart, where abandonment of transient state is common, this is acceptable—a lot of users' shopping carts never actually turn into viable orders, so the update against the database never occurs.

In other situations, however, the optimistic concurrency model's failure to notify until an update attempt creates a problem. Consider a Web application that requires a user to go through a complicated twelve-screen process in order to update a given order. If you come back with an error message along the lines of "We're sorry, somebody already updated this order" and force the user to start over from the first page, you're going to be looking for a new job pretty quickly. It gets more subtle than this, though—sometimes a system has to allow updates against the database even though another user has already "locked" the data. Some users may be "superusers," system administrators or supervisors who have to be able to indicate that certain customers are no longer able to purchase items from the e-commerce site (perhaps due to bad credit ratings or too many bounced checks). Or, perhaps, we need to run a global price change against all the items in the database (it's a 50% off sale starting December 26th), and that change needs to take effect regardless of how many users have open shopping carts.

In such situations, both the optimistic concurrency model and the native locking model of the underlying resource manager fail us, and there's no other recourse but to handle it ourselves. This technique is called a pessimistic concurrency model (also known as the Pessimistic Offline Lock [Fowler, 426] or the Pessimistic Lock [Nock, 405] in some quarters), and while it has several drawbacks, it offers the overall benefit of giving you, the programmer, more control over what's going on. (It's called "pessimistic" because it assumes that other parties will attempt to update the same data you're currently using—we're "pessimistic" that naïve concurrency control will work.) In this model, the application programmer assumes full control over all concurrency semantics.

Implementing a pessimistic concurrency scheme is pretty straightforward: before obtaining any data, your code checks a common "lock" table to see if that row is free:

```
SELECT userid, lock_start, comment FROM lock_tbl
  WHERE lock_table=? AND lock_pk=?
```

Here, the first parameter is the table you're wanting to fetch from, and the second parameter is the primary key value of the row you're wanting to fetch. If the result set returns empty, no lock exists for that row, and you first create a lock by running an INSERT command into the lock table before fetching the data you're interested in. Make sure to run DELETE on that row when you're done with the data, by the way, or the data will remain forever locked and thus inaccessible to the rest of the system.

In some cases, you can embed the lock information in each row, appending a lock_user and/or lock_timestamp column to the table definition to contain the user ID and/or timestamp that indicates who locked this row and when. The first approach is less intrusive, the second one simpler.

If the lock query returns a nonzero set of rows, the data is locked and you can either display a message to the user that the data is currently in use (e.g., "User 'FRED' is currently working with the data you've requested—please contact that user if you require access to this data") and abandon the request, or silently wait for some specified period of time and try again.

At first glance, this seems like a lot of work. It is, no argument about it. What's worse, much of the work required isn't immediately obvious. For example, in order to avoid race conditions where two clients consult the lock table, find the lock isn't currently out, and simultaneously take out a lock against the same row (thus effectively overwriting one client's lock with the second client's lock), the lock-query/obtain-lock-update must be done under native transactional semantics. So the revised algorithm has to look something like this:

```
BEGIN TRANSACTION

SELECT userid, lock_start, comment FROM lock_tbl
  WHERE lock_table=? AND lock_pk=?

(assuming no rows returned, continue with:)

INSERT INTO lock_tbl (lock_table, lock_pk, userid,
                      lock_start, comment)
  VALUES (?, ?, ?, ?, ?)

COMMIT
```

```
(having locked the data, now you can continue with:)

SELECT * FROM table WHERE . . .
```

You've also got to be careful that in the event of a failure, you release the lock; this implies some kind of exception handling in your processing code that will delete the lock from the lock table if a Java exception is thrown or some other failure occurs. This is a lot of work to do for each and every SQL statement you want to run, and it's best when tucked away behind a procedural-first persistence scheme (see Item 42).

The payoff from a pessimistic model comes in the fact that you have much, much greater control over the concurrency that takes place; for example, to "bypass" a pessimistic lock, just don't bother with checking the lock table in the first place, relying instead on the underlying database transactional scheme to prevent any data corruption. Generally speaking, this would be done only under the most stringent circumstances, with the knowledge that clients could end up in some very odd situations if the circumstances handled correctly—for example, a user filling out a shopping cart could suddenly find that the total charged to his or her credit card was different from the total displayed on the previous screen because the price-change update came through right after that "Are you sure you want to place this order?" message was displayed.

Alternatively, you might want situations where a superuser can "break" a lock on a given row or chunk of data. Perhaps the system has gotten itself into some kind of deadlock, or perhaps the superuser needs to reassign the data to a different user. ("Joe? Fred went on vacation, and he left a few items unfinished. Can you assign them to George so we can finally process those outstanding orders Fred started?")

In fact, you can get as subtle and as tricky in your concurrency model as you wish. Perhaps it's possible for two users to simultaneously hold a lock against a given row, as long as they work on the same team, implicitly assuming that they can resolve any data concurrency problems between them in one of those infamous cubicle hallway conversations. Or perhaps certain users get read-only access to all data despite the presence of a lock but can't do updates. There are many possibilities.

Diagnostics are also much simpler, as well as more informative, with a pessimistic locking scheme than in relying on native concurrency. When a user requests data already in use by another user, the diagnostic message can indicate who holds the lock and for how long, and with an always-online system, you can even go so far as to pop up some kind of message to the user holding the lock, asking if he or she can release it yet. You might also write some kind of daemon process that periodically scans the lock table, looking for locks that are older than x seconds/minutes/hours/days/months/years/whatever, releasing them automatically (with appropriate notifications to the users holding the locks) on the grounds that it's probably a deadlock or application failure.

In some cases, pessimistic concurrency is the only form of concurrency available to you. For example, when working with files on the filesystem, because most filesystems don't yet provide any sort of X/Open transactional interface (see Item 32), in order to ensure that you're exclusively accessing a particular file, you'll often need to have some form of "external" concurrency model in place. This can again be the lock table discussed earlier, or many older systems use the concept of *lock files,* files that serve the same purpose as the lock table: create the lock file (usually by doing an "open" operating system API call of some form that fails if the file already exists), do the work, then delete the file when the work is complete. Note that you can use the lock file itself to hold the data normally stored in the lock table—user ID, comment, that sort of thing—and the file's creation timestamp can serve as the actual time of lock acquisition. This approach also holds the advantage that releasing the locks is particularly simple: just delete the lock files. (Skeptical that this whole approach works? If you're using CVS as your source control system, you've been using lock files the entire time—CVS uses them to ensure exclusivity of access when you're committing source files to the repository.)

If you're particularly ambitious, you can even try to build a JTA-compliant resource manager around a pessimistic concurrency scheme, but this is usually a lot more work than most programmers are willing to undertake. It has the distinct advantage of providing pessimistic concurrency models while keeping the programmatic simplicity of the transaction processing model (see Item 27), which is particularly useful if you want pessimistic concurrency against one resource while working with multiple resource managers simultaneously.

Pessimistic concurrency schemes provide you with a tremendous amount of power over the concurrency capabilities of your system; remember, however, as the comic book hero learned the hard way, "With great power comes great responsibility." Pessimistic concurrency gives you great flexibility, but it's up to you to make sure the concurrency decisions you make are solid ones; otherwise, corruption is the result.

Item 35: Consider lower isolation levels for better transactional throughput

Consider for a moment the Isolation property of an ACID transaction. It puts up artificial "walls" between transactions, screening out any changes made to the data set until the transaction either completes or rolls back. It does so for good reason: imagine, if you will, a world in which transactions weren't isolated and could "leak" their effects to other transactions currently executing. Two parties, let's call them Bob and Jane, both access the database at the same time; let's assume they're a married couple, each trying to do some work against their bank account from different locations. Based on what each is trying to do and when, several kinds of results can take place.

- *Lost update:* Bob reads their checking account row from the checking account table at the bank. As soon as Bob's read completes, Jane then also reads the same row. Jane's next action, an update of $100 to the account (a deposit) is added to the total she holds and written back to the database. Then Bob gets to go, adding $100 to the total he holds, writing that back to the database. Each then commits. Note that Jane's deposit is now effectively lost—if there was $500 in the account to begin with, it now reads $600.
- *Dirty read:* Bob reads their checking account row from the checking account table. He then adds $100 to the total and writes it back. Jane then reads the row (perhaps she simply wants an account balance update). Unfortunately, Bob made a mistake and now rolls back his work. Jane is left believing the account has $100 more than it actually does since she got to see the uncommitted work.
- *Nonrepeatable read:* Jane reads the account balance. Bob reads the account balance. Jane then writes a data change—again, the $100 deposit—to the account balance row. Bob decides to play it safe and reread the data that, to him, he just read a few seconds ago, and suddenly he gets a different value than before.
- *Phantom read:* This one is harder to understand from the perspective of Bob and Jane, since we're now dealing with multiple rows. In

essence, assume Bob looks at not just the checking account but the complete assets for the two of them. Jane, immediately after Bob's request completes, decides to open a new retirement account with the bank. When Bob decides to do a refresh of that exact same view, he suddenly sees the retirement account that wasn't there just a second ago.

The absence of any of these effects, the default scenario when transactions are "fully enabled," is called *serializable access* and essentially mimics the environment a given transaction would see if it were the only open transaction in the entire database—as if each and every transaction were lined up (serialized) and allowed to execute one right after the other. This is the safest mode to execute in but also requires the most locks and thus represents the highest contention.

Normally, most developers look at the list or possible problems and wonder precisely why I bring any of this up—after all, even the suggestion that a given database query might not return "correct" data is usually enough to drive most developers away from the idea. Don't be too quick to toss it entirely, though.

Imagine that I have a database of all the people currently living in Sacramento, California, a city of over a quarter of a million people—this is a fairly sizable database. I want to run a query that finds the average age of those who list their occupation as computer programmer. This query will not be fast, and during that time, the data will be changing—people getting hired, people getting fired, and so forth. Assume that I hold off updating the data until the query finishes—is the query still any good once the query returns? It's not likely that the average age will change much with the new changes to the data; in fact, it's entirely likely that nobody would even notice the difference. This is what the statisticians call the "margin of error" within a given set of data.

Now consider the cost of having held locks on the data during the query: everybody accessing that data was locked out during the query's execution, effectively increasing the latency and reducing the scalability of our application. Was it worth it for a query that's going to be off by a few fractions of a percentage point as soon as the query completes?

Certainly, not all data transactions will fit this looser model: for example, financial information systems involving debits, credits, and transfers will not be successful for very long if a debit from one account isn't carefully balanced by a credit to a different account. These, certainly, justify the cost of a lock. But a large category of situations comes up during application development where a given system can afford to be a bit out of sync with the data, particularly if it means that we reduce contention of the system overall.

As a result, most database systems support the idea of reducing transaction isolation, either through a straight SQL call or through the call-level interface, which in Java's case is JDBC. The following standard isolation levels, and the effects that can happen as a result, are available in standard SQL.

- SERIALIZABLE: None of the effects described above occur.
- REPEATABLE READ: This isolation level guarantees to maintain the same view of the database to the client—what data is there will remain there. It protects against dirty reads and nonrepeatable reads but allows phantom reads to take place.
- READ COMMITTED: This level allows transactions for this client to see the actions of other committed transactions and so protects against dirty reads, allowing nonrepeatable reads and phantom reads.
- READ UNCOMMITTED: This level protects against chaos, but that's it. It permits this user to see actions taken by other transactions that haven't committed (or possibly won't commit). It allows dirty reads, nonrepeatable reads, and phantom reads; in short, it allows pretty much anything short of outright corruption.

Note that the other three properties of transactions are still fully in force: a READ UNCOMMITTED isolation-level transaction is still atomic, still consistent, and still durable—it will either all succeed or all fail, it will always have the same effects on the database, and its actions will be stored when the transaction is complete. The only thing that has changed here is the transactions' visibility to the rest of the system and vice versa.

Remember that the benefit here is the reduced contention that lowered isolation levels permit. When executing update logic against the database directly, we will likely want that update to run in SERIALIZABLE isolation—that way, the update is sure that it works with the "right" set of data and can't be accidentally co-opted by a change to the underlying data. However, for queries, pick lists, and the like, turning down to just REPEATABLE READ isolation can help reduce locks against the system. For processes that need to pull vast quantities of data from the database at a predetermined time (batch processes that pull from this database to push into a different one, perhaps a data warehouse), running at READ COM-MITTED keeps contention much lower, allowing users to continue to work against the database even as the batch is running. For the one-page executive summary report ("How much money did we make this quarter?") that involves a lot of database work but not a high degree of precision, use READ UNCOMMITTED. In fact, most reports can run at READ UNCOMMITTED without notice. (Try it—run one without it and one with, and see if you can spot the changes.)

Setting isolation levels at the SQL level involves using the SQL syntax:

```
SET TRANSACTION ISOLATION LEVEL <level>

<level> ::=
   READ UNCOMMITTED |
   READ COMMITTED |
   REPEATABLE READ |
   SERIALIZABLE
```

Be careful to do this outside of a transaction however (i.e., before executing the BEGIN TRANSACTION statement), as most database vendors promise "undefined behavior" if you do, a euphemism for "it'll blow in a big way, probably right in front of your boss during the big demo."

To do the same at the JDBC level, use the Connection method setTransactionIsolation, like this:

```
import java.sql.*;

public void run(Connection conn)
   throws SQLException
{
  conn.setTransactionIsolation(
    Connection.TRANSACTION_READ_UNCOMMITTED);
  // or TRANSACTION_READ_COMMITTED,
  // or TRANSACTION_REPEATABLE_READ,
  // or the default, TRANSACTION_SERIALIZABLE

  Statement stmt = conn.createStatement();

  // This statement will run at the isolation level
  // established in the lines above
}
```

Note that the transaction isolation is a `Connection`-level property, meaning that this is the setting for the entire database `Connection`, not just a `Statement`. And, as with the SQL syntax above, calling `setTransaction Isolation` in the middle of a transaction is "implementation defined," to quote the JDBC documentation, which again is a euphemism for "is almost guaranteed to embarrass you and/or your company at the big demo."

Unfortunately, having now just convinced you of the wonders of reduced transaction isolation, we come to the bad news: the EJB Specification, for the most part, punts entirely on the whole idea of supporting transaction isolation within the EJB container. Section 17.3.2 of the EJB 2.1 Specification states that:

> The API for managing an isolation level is resource-manager specific. (Therefore, the EJB architecture does not define an API for managing isolation level.) . . .

> For session beans and message-driven beans with bean-managed transaction demarcation, the Bean Provider can specify the desirable transaction isolation level programmatically in the enterprise bean's methods, using the resource-manager specific API.

> For entity beans with container-managed persistence, transaction isolation is managed by the data access classes that are generated by the container provider's tools. The tools must ensure that the management of the isolation levels performed by the data access classes will not result in conflicting isolation level requests for a resource manager within a transaction.

Loosely translated, this boils down to a couple of simple points.

First, if you want to take advantage of the scalability benefits of lowered isolation levels, you're stuck with bean-managed transactions. This also means that you cannot use transaction isolation on entity beans, period, because the EJB Specification very clearly states that entity beans, regardless of whether you're using container-managed or bean-managed persistence, always run under container-managed transactions (Section 17.3.1). If your container doesn't provide for the local transaction optimization (see Item 32), then you're looking at a full, two-phase commit on each and every single entity bean access. You might try to work around this by setting your entity bean's transactional declaration to `NotSupport`, `Supports`, or `Never`; doing so, however, immediately renders your bean nonportable. Section 17.4.1, with emphasis added, states, "Containers may *optionally* support the user of the `NotSupported`, `Supports`, and `Never` transaction attributes for the methods of entity beans with container-managed persistence. However, entity beans with container-managed persistence that use these transaction attributes will not be portable." Ouch. Yet another reason to decide whether portability is important to you (see Item 11).

Second, if you want to take advantage of lowered isolation levels, you need to go to the resource manager's API to do so; for relational databases, this means you have to get at the JDBC `Connection` object and call `setIsolationLevel` on the `Connection` itself to turn it down. This isn't a real hardship; however, make sure you do this before you open the bean-managed transaction because, as we've already noted, changing isolation levels within a transaction is a fast way to a long debugging session.

Finally, however, be very, very careful if you do start turning down isolation levels in your bean-managed transaction beans because that last sentence in the specification is a killer—in essence, the container must make sure that differing isolation levels don't show up within a single transaction. However, the specification offers no hints as to how this rule should be enforced, so what happens if a bean-managed transaction session bean with lowered isolation level calls into an entity bean? There's no way to know without trying it for your particular container. The danger is that your container could lull you into thinking that you're safe because your container is silently handling the issue. Another container might not, and, of course, it's not until you port the application to that other container that the exceptions start to fly.

Item 36: Use savepoints to keep partial work in the face of rollback

Unfortunately, transaction atomicity isn't always a wonderful thing.

In particular, one of the problems that can arise with an atomic transaction is that when something goes wrong within the transaction's workspace, *everything* goes wrong. Once a database statement has failed within the transaction, every bit of the work conducted as part of that transaction is also invalid now and therefore must be aborted.

Normally, we regard this behavior as a positive thing. After all, the reason we want atomic transactions is so that we don't have to write the rollback or compensating transaction code (see Item 28) to undo what has been done in the event of a failure. But even though this is the behavior we want most of the time, sometimes it works against us.

As we saw in the trip planning scenario (again, see Item 28), it's not always the case that we want to abort the entire scope of work executed so far. In simple scenarios, this all-or-nothing failure model works well, but certain actions build up more context along the way, not all of which is invalidated in the event of a failure—just because we couldn't book that final leg from Frankfurt to Munich doesn't mean the first two legs of the trip need to be thrown away.

To put this into a more systemic, concrete light, imagine for a moment a banking system calculating interest on all of its savings accounts. One way to do this is to set up a message-driven bean inside an EJB container and set up the new EJB Timer Service to fire a message at a specific time. When this message is received, the `InterestCalculatingBean` executes a pretty straightforward SQL UPDATE statement to increase the balance of all savings accounts by whatever the current interest rate is. Naturally, we want to make sure this calculation is completed; to be more accurate, we need to make sure *all* of our account holders' accounts are updated, so we put this into a single transaction to make sure the action is atomic.

Unfortunately, there are well over ten million accounts at our bank, and it takes a while to run through an UPDATE statement on ten million rows (particularly if the SQL statement is at all complex, such as only updating those savings accounts with a minimum balance plus those accounts held by VIPs and those accounts opened by members between the dates of February 15 and April 15—you get the idea). Even on heavy iron, this could easily take several hours, perhaps all night, to run successfully.

On the 9,947,831st row, we hit a snag, the UPDATE fails, and the entire transaction must be aborted. Guess we'll just have to try again next month, right? After all, the interest probably doesn't amount to all *that* much money. . . .

This is one case where the standard transaction semantics don't serve us well—it's not really necessary to abandon all the work done before the failure because all we really need to do is mark the failed row and continue onward.

For this reason the JDBC 3.0 Specification introduced a new concept into the API, called the *savepoint*. The idea here is fairly simple: it effectively plants a stake in the ground, telling the database that through "this point in time" (the time at which the savepoint was created), everything looks good and could be committed safely. Note the very careful wording of that statement: "*could* be committed," not "go ahead and commit"—we can still roll back work marked with a savepoint, if necessary.

The benefit of savepoints comes when a failure occurs. If part of the transaction suddenly fails, we can roll back the transaction to the most recent savepoint, thereby abandoning only the work done since the last savepoint was demarcated, and start over again; in essence, the savepoint mechanism allows our hapless travel agent to abort the third leg of the flight and keep the first two as part of the established transaction.

Using a JDBC `Savepoint` is straightforward. While using a `Connection`, at any point during the transaction, call `setSavepoint` either with a `String` to name the `Savepoint` or with no arguments to let the system choose a name for you, and a `Savepoint` object will be returned:

```
Connection conn = ...; // Get this from someplace
Statement stmt = conn.createStatement();
stmt.executeUpdate(someSQLHere);
Savepoint svpt = conn.setSavepoint();
stmt.executeUpdate(someOtherSQL);
Savepoint svpt2 = conn.setSavepoint();
ResultSet rs = stmt.executeQuery(SQLToTestWorkSoFar);
if (rs.next())
{
  // Whoops! There's not supposed to be anything in here yet!
  // Time to abort part of the work
  //

  conn.rollback(svpt);
    // Note that we can roll back to any Savepoint, not just
    // the last one marked

  stmt.executeUpdate(someCorrectiveSQL);
}
stmt.executeUpdate(someMoreSQL);
conn.commit();
```

Savepoints offer the opportunity to preserve the work that has been done already within a transaction, so that we can choose whether our transacted work should be atomic or not. That's the good news; the bad news is that the savepoint model is brand-new to the JDBC 3.0 Specification, and as of this writing few database drivers actually support it. If you know the JDBC driver you're working with, make sure to find out whether it supports savepoints (see Item 49 for details, and use `DatabaseMetaData.supportsSavepoints` to find out).

Item 37:   Replicate resources when possible to avoid lock regions

Imagine, for just a moment, that you are a kindergarten teacher. Twenty kids, all five years old or so, are under your care for what feels like forever but in fact is just four hours a day. It comes time for recess, and you take them out to the playground to burn off some energy. Little Johnny grabs the jump rope and starts skipping. Naturally, children being what they are, nineteen other voices cry "No fair!" and all want to start using the lone jump rope, all at the same time. Your first inclination is to tell each of them to take turns. After all, that's what you're supposed to do as a teacher: teach children to be well-behaved citizens of the world, starting with lessons on how to share.

Whoever suggested this idea has obviously never had to try to keep nineteen five-year-olds in a single line for anything longer than two minutes.

Here's the problem: assume that each child gets to jump rope for one minute, then has to hand the jump rope over to the next child in line and get back to the end of the line. This means that for nineteen minutes (assuming each one is perfectly willing to surrender the rope at the end of his or her turn, not likely with five-year-olds), each child is doing absolutely nothing. This translates into one minute of activity for every twenty minutes, and that doesn't translate into much energy being burned off.

Solutions? One approach would be to force each child to jump faster, restricting each one to thirty seconds per turn, but all this does is speed up the churn in the line—it's still a ratio of one minute of activity per twenty-minute segment. You might instead choose to count the child's turn by the number of jumps, but this penalizes the fast jumpers, since the slow jumpers thus get more time with the rope and create even more inactivity for the fast jumpers.

Ask any kindergarten teacher how to solve this problem, and they'll tell you: *buy more jump ropes.*

The central problem with the single resource is that frequently these resources create points of contention that have to be managed using synchronization constructs (either Java object monitors or database locks or whatever). A single point of contention creates a system that won't scale because additional hardware will just introduce additional clients that are competing for that single point of contention; in other words, the lone jump rope situation only gets worse when we try to scale the kindergarten classroom up from twenty students to two hundred or two thousand.

So, remembering Item 21, we start looking for ways to partition the resource up, this time to reduce load on the system by removing the point of contention.

In the simplest cases, this is just a matter of choosing to create duplicate Java objects, rather than trying to force all processing through a single one; for example, imagine a servlet/JSP that has to do some date formatting. It might be tempting to pool your object (which is itself an Inherently Bad Idea, as described in Item 72) and create just one `Simple` `DateFormat` instance used by all callers against the servlet, but you'll quickly discover that `SimpleDateFormat` isn't thread-safe and must be synchronized externally.

Stop right here and take a step back. In this case, the cost of having a single resource—the `SimpleDateFormat` instance—will be far outstripped by the cost of having to acquire and release an object monitor. Replicating this, by creating a `SimpleDateFormat` on each incoming HTTP request, will allow you to eliminate the point of contention and let this thread continue onward at its own pace. In particular, this is an easy win, since the `SimpleDateFormat` itself has no identity (see Item 5), per se, just the state given to it at construction to indicate what format it should have.

We start running into complications with replicated resources when we start thinking about replicating identity-bound resources, most notably the database (or extensions thereof, like entity beans or persistent data objects as in JDO). Once again we run into the problem of *update propagation*, introduced in Item 21—if we update the copy of the `Person` record held on machine A, we need to make sure that every copy of that same `Person` record gets updated on every other machine in the cluster, or else clients reading this same `Person` record could conceivably get different results, thus ruining consistency. We have the problem that synchronizing this update propagation effectively requires not only all of the threads running in this JVM but also all of the threads running in any JVM on any machine, since this lock will have to be cluster-wide. It will be as if there's just one jump rope for the entire school, not just one per classroom.

Returning to prior art for a moment, consider again the problem of DNS. We don't want to have to go back to a single server for every DNS record we need to look up, so DNS clients routinely cache local copies of the DNS settings they've retrieved. These are obviously identity-bound elements—if I change the IP address of neward.net, there's exactly one "real" record that holds the original fact, namely, my DNS server. If clients cache off the record, how will they know when to retrieve the new data?

In this particular case, DNS effectively states that it can afford a certain latency and assigns each DNS record with a *time-to-live (TTL) value*. This value indicates how long the data described in the DNS record is guaranteed to be good, and it's the clients' collective responsibility to keep track of this value and "go back to the source" when this time is up to ensure they're working with the latest-and-greatest values. In this situation, the latency is acceptable—I can probably keep the old server running in parallel to the new server (presumably keeping the two servers identical in content and functionality) until I know the DNS records have propagated throughout the world's collection of DNS caches.

Ironically, given our concern here with synchronization and lock windows, since DNS data is typically read-only or read-mostly, we probably could treat it as immutable for all intents and purposes (see Item 38), which again helps facilitate its replication. In fact, there's almost no reason why read-only and read-mostly data of all sorts can't be replicated across the network because if there's no need for updates, there's no update propagation problem and therefore no reason not to replicate.

We can extend the DNS approach to a more generalized idea of *leasing* data from the centralized database. In essence, we'll "borrow" data from the central database by taking a TTL value along with the data itself and storing this value with the data when we copy it off into a localized copy of the schema. Then, when working with the data, if a comparison of the TTL value and the current time indicates the data has expired, we go back to the centralized database for a refresh. Again, it's not as useful for absolutely-must-be-accurate data like bank account balances and such, but within many systems it turns out that a fair amount of data can afford this degree of latency.

In fact, in some cases, you can combine the local database with optimistic concurrency (see Item 33) to run your application entirely off of the local database, only pushing data to and from the centralized database at well-known synchronization points (nightly, hourly, whenever the network is detected, and so on). Again, however, you need to make sure that the application can handle the inevitability of a concurrency problem, such as the price of an item having been changed in the central database on Monday, yet the order was placed on Tuesday with Sunday's prices because we hadn't yet synchronized. (What happens in this case is a business decision, by the way, not a technical one—don't make any assumptions about what should happen, or you'll likely end up with some very unhappy users and/or customers.)

Replication isn't going to solve every one of your scalability problems, but when carefully applied, it can release a great deal of tension against a single resource. The key to successful replication, in the end, is to make sure that the resources you replicate are identity-less because as soon as unique objects are replicated, we get into consistency issues that have no good all-purpose solutions.

Item 38: Favor the immutable, for it needs no locks

After reading through this chapter, you may begin to despair—after all, if Java, transactions, or even the EJB Specification can't keep you from having to worry about synchronization concerns (or rather, if the solution yields such unimpressive results that you *have* to start worrying about them on your own), blissful ignorance no longer remains. You have to start thinking about synchronized blocks, race conditions, deadlock, livelock, and all those other things.

One approach that saves you from having to worry about synchronization is to avoid it entirely, by creating objects whose state can never change—by virtue of the fact that an immutable object cannot change its state, synchronization is entirely unnecessary. This avoids the need for synchronized blocks, locks, and thus, contention.

Taking this approach brings with it a couple of constraints. First, immutable objects are not easy to build—it's harder than it looks to build an object that doesn't make back doors to its data available to its clients. Second, we often require immutable objects to change state, that is, we want a new immutable object with slightly different state. This requires the construction of an entirely new object, rather than simply teasing the fields in the existing object to come around to the state we're interested in.

Building an immutable object is a bit harder than it first appears; see *Effective Java* [Bloch, Item 12], for some of the details involved. As an additional example, consider our canonical class representing a carbon-based life form on planet Earth:

```
public class Person
{
  public Person(String firstName, String lastName, int age,
               Address homeAddress, Person spouse)
  {
    // Do what you'd expect here-copy parameters to fields
  }

  public String getFirstName() { return this.firstName; }
  public String getLastName() { return this.lastName; }
  public int getAge() { return age; }
  public Address getHomeAddress() { return this.homeAddress; }
  public Person getSpouse() { return spouse; }
}
```

At a casual glance, the `Person` class appears to be entirely immutable—there are no setter methods anywhere in the class API, so it's impossible to modify the class's members, right?

Quick question: What happens if we do this?

```
Person p = new Person("Michael", "Neward", 10,
                      new Address(...), null);
p.getAddress().setStreet("100 White House Way");
```

Although it's not immediately obvious, the `Person` class "leaks" a handle to the `Address` object referenced by the `homeAddress` field inside of `Person`. This offers clients the ability to "reach around" the referencing object (`Person`, in this case) and directly modify the object within. This violates `Person`'s immutability and leaves it vulnerable to synchronization concerns in that `Address` object.

But when we do want to modify a `Person`'s state, instead we must create an entirely new `Person` instance in which to do this. The simplest approach is to just reuse the constructor, as defined above, like so:

```
Person p = new Person("Michael", "Neward", 10,
            new Address(...), null);
// Michael just had a birthday: increment his age
p = new Person(p.getFirstName(), p.getLastName(),
            p.getAge()+1, p.getAddress(), p.getSpouse());
```

The problem with this approach is that while keeping synchronization out of the picture, it forces the allocation of lots of objects, making more work for the garbage collector, at least in theory. Fortunately, as explained in Item 72, many garbage collectors work well with lots of short-lived temporary objects, so it's not a big deal.

If you follow some of the EJB "best practices" books that recommend the use of Data Transfer Objects [Fowler, 401] as the means by which to pass data between an EJB client and the entity that needs to set that data into the database, making the Data Transfer Object an immutable object makes a lot of sense. Similarly, if you decide to pass all data by value between the various layers in your system (see Item 23), making these objects immutable not only ensures that synchronization scenarios can't sneak up on you but also ensures that the by-value object can't be accidentally modified, either.

5 | State Management

A large part of the work of an enterprise system involves handling data. In fact, arguably, that's the only thing an enterprise system really does.

Although this was never really apparent during the era of the two-tier client/server system, the enterprise programmer needs to take care of two kinds of state: *transient state,* which is not yet a formal part of the enterprise data footprint, and *durable state,* which needs to be tracked regardless of what happens.

Transient state is data that the enterprise cares little about—in the event of a crash, nothing truly crucial has been lost, so no tears will be shed. The classic example of transient state is the e-commerce shopping cart. Granted, we don't ever want the system to crash, but let's put the objectivity glasses on for a moment: if the server crashes in the middle of a customer's shopping experience, losing the contents of the shopping cart, nothing is really lost (except for the time the customer spent building it up). Yes, the customer will be annoyed, but there are no implications to the business beyond that.

In a thick-client or rich-client application, transient state is pretty easy to handle: it's just the data stored in local variables in the client-side process that hasn't been preserved to the durable storage layer yet. Nothing particularly fancy needs be done to handle the lifecycle around it—when the client-side process shuts down, the transient state goes away with it.

In a thin-client, HTML-browser-based application, on the other hand, transient state takes on a whole new dimension. Because HTTP itself is a stateless protocol, with no intrinsic way to store per-client state, we've been forced to implement transient state mechanisms on top of the underlying plumbing. To most developers, this is exposed via the `HttpSession` mechanism that is part of the Servlet 2.x specifications. Unfortunately, nothing in life comes for free, and `HttpSession` definitely carries its share of costs, most notably to scalability of the entire system as a whole. Judicious use of per-client session state is crucial to a system that wants to scale to more than five concurrent users.

Durable state, on the other hand, is that which we normally think of when somebody starts to ask about "persistent data"—it's the data that has to be kept around for long periods of time. Officially, we'll define durable state as state that absolutely must be kept around even in the event of a JVM termination or crash, but since we could conceivably come up with situations where we'll want transient state to be stored in a database, it's more convenient to simply say that durable state is state that we care about.

Commonly, durable state has implicit legal and/or financial stakes—if, for example, you write a system that loses the items in a book order after the customer's credit card has been charged, you're exposing the company to a lawsuit, at the very least. Or, to flip it around, if you lose the fact that the customer hasn't been charged when the books ship, you're directly costing the company money and will likely find yourself filling out a new résumé pretty soon.

The distinction between the two is crucial when discussing state management because mechanisms that are useful for keeping transient state around won't necessarily be suitable for tracking durable state and vice versa. In some situations, we see some overlap, where we may want to track users' session state in a relational database in order to avoid any sort of situation where a user might lose that transient state. Perhaps it's not a commerce site at all but a human resources process that requires a long-running collection of forms to fill out, or a test that we don't want students to be able to "throw away" and start over just by closing the browser. In such situations, the distinction between transient and durable state may start to blur, but intuitively, it's usually pretty easy to spot the one from the other. Or, arguably, durable state *is* what we perceive at first to be transient state, as in the case of the students' test or the human resources forms. Either way, drawing this distinction in your mind and designs will help keep straight which mechanisms should be used for state management in your systems.

Item 39: Use **HttpSession** sparingly

In order to maintain transient state on behalf of clients in an HTML/HTTP-based application, servlet containers provide a facility called *session space*, represented by the `HttpSession` interface. The idea itself is simple and straightforward: a servlet programmer can put any Serializable object (see Item 71) into session space, and the next time that same user issues a request to any part of the same Web application, the servlet container will ensure that the same objects will be in the `HttpSession` object when requested. This allows the servlet developer to maintain per-client state information on behalf of a Web application on the server across HTTP requests.

Unfortunately, this mechanism doesn't come entirely for free. In the first place, storing data on the server on behalf of every client reduces the resources available on that server, meaning the maximum load capability of the server goes down proportionally. It's a pretty simple equation: the more data stored into session space, the fewer sessions that machine can handle. So, it follows that in order to support as many clients as possible on a given machine, keep session storage to a minimum. In fact, for truly scalable systems, whenever possible, avoid using sessions whatsoever. By not incurring any per-client cost on the server, the machine load capacity (theoretically) goes to infinite, able to support however many clients can connect to it.

This suggestion to avoid sessions if possible goes beyond just simple scalability concerns. For servlet containers running within a Web farm, it's a necessity. Sessions are an in-memory construct; because memory is scoped to a particular machine, unless the Web farm has some mechanism by which a given client will always be sent back to the same server for every request, subsequent processing of a request will not find the session-stored objects placed there by an earlier request.

As it turns out, by the way, pinning HTTP requests against the same machine turns out to be frightfully hard to do. If the gateway tries to use the remote address of the client as the indicator of the client request, it will run into issues on a couple of points. Internet service providers that supply IP addresses to dialup consumers, proxy servers, and NATs will offer the same IP address for multiple clients, thus accidentally putting all those clients against the same server. For a small number of clients behind the same proxy, this isn't a big deal, but if the proxy server in question is the one for AOL, this could be an issue.

The Servlet 2.2 Specification provides a potential solution to this session-within-clusters problem, in that if a servlet container supports it, a Web application can be marked with the `<distributable />` element in the deployment descriptor, and the servlet container will automatically ensure that session information is seamlessly moved between the nodes in the cluster as necessary, typically by serializing the session and shipping it over the network. (This is why the Servlet Specification requires objects placed in session to be Serializable.) On the surface, this seems to offer a solution to the problem, but it turns out to be harder than it first appears.

A possible mechanism to provide this support is to designate a single node in the cluster as a session state server, and on each request, whichever node is processing the request asks the session state server for the session state for the client, and this is shipped across the network to the processing node. This mechanism suffers from two side effects, however: (1) every request will incur an additional round-trip to the session state server, which increases the overall latency of the client request, but more importantly, (2) all session state is now being stored in a centralized server, which creates a single point of failure within the cluster. Avoiding single points of failure is frequently the reason we wanted to cluster in the first place, so this obviously isn't ideal.

A second possible mechanism is to take a more peer-to-peer approach. As a request comes into the node, the node issues a cluster-wide broadcast signal asking other nodes in the cluster whether they have the latest session state for this client. The node with the latest state responds, and the state is shipped to the processing node for use. This avoids the problem of a single point of failure, but we're still facing the additional round-trips to shift the session state around the network. Worse yet, as a client slowly makes the rounds through the cluster, a copy of that client's session state is stored on each node in the cluster, meaning now the cluster can support only the maximum number of clients storable on any single node in the cluster—this is obviously less than ideal. If each node in the cluster throws away a client's session state after sending it to another node, how-ever, it means that any possibility of caching the session state in order to avoid the network round-trip shipping the session state back and forth is lost.

The upshot of all this is that trying to build this functionality is not an easy task; few servlet containers have undertaken it. (Several of the EJB containers that are also servlet containers, such as WebLogic and Web-Sphere, support distributable Web applications, but this is typically done by building on top of whatever cluster support they have for stateful ses-sion beans. Needless to say, clustered stateful session bean state has the same issues.) Before trusting a servlet container to handle this, make sure to ask the vendors exactly *how* they do it, in order to understand the costs involved.

In the event that some kind of distributed session state mechanism is needed but the servlet container either doesn't provide it or provides a mechanism that is less than desirable for your particular needs, all is not lost. Thanks to the power of the Servlet 2.3 Specification, and filters, you can create your own distributable session mechanism without too much difficulty. The key lies in the fact that filters can nominate replacements for the HttpServletRequest and HttpServletResponse objects used within the servlet-processing pipeline.

The idea here is simple—create a filter that replaces the default HttpServletRequest with one that overrides the standard getSession method to return a customized HttpSession object instead of the stan-dardized one. Logistically, it would look something like this:

```
import javax.servlet.*;
import javax.servlet.http.*;

public class DistributableSessionFilter
  implements Filter
{
  public void doFilter(ServletRequest request,
                       ServletResponse response,
                       FilterChain chain)
    throws ServletException
  {
    HttpServletRequest oldReq =
      (HttpServletRequest)request;
```

```
    HttpServletRequestWrapper newRequest =
      new HttpServletRequestWrapper(oldReq)
    {
      public HttpSession getSession(boolean create)
      {
        if (create)
          return new DistributedHttpSession(oldReq, response);
        else
        {
          // If user has created a distributed session already,
          // return it; otherwise return null
        }
      }
    };

    chain.doFilter(newRequest, response);
  }
}
```

In this code, `DistributedHttpSession` is a class that implements the `HttpSession` interface and whose `getAttribute/setAttribute` (and other) methods take the passed objects and store them to someplace "safe," such as the RDBMS or the shared session state server, and so on. Note that because the standard `HttpSession` object is no longer being used, it will be up to you, either in this filter or in the `Distributed HttpSession`, to set the session cookie in the HTTP response headers. Normally the servlet container itself handles this, but since we're not using its default session mechanism anymore, we have to pick up the slack. Use large random numbers for session identifiers, to prevent attackers from being able to guess session ID values, and make sure not to use the standard `JSESSIONID` header in order to avoid accidental conflicts with the servlet container itself.

The actual implementation of this fictitious `DistributedHttpSession` class can vary widely. One implementation is to simply store the session data into an RDBMS with hot replication turned on (to avoid a single-point-of-failure scenario); another is to use an external shared session state server; a third is to try the peer-to-peer approach. Whatever the implementation, however, the important thing is that by replacing the standard session system with your own version, you take control over the exact behavior of the system, thus making this tunable across Web applications if necessary. This is a practical application of Item 6 at work.

Another session-related concern to be careful of is the *accidental* use of sessions. This isn't a problem within servlets written by hand by developers—a session isn't created until explicitly asked for via the call to `getSession` on the `HttpServletRequest`. However, this isn't the case with JSP pages. The JSP documentation states, quite clearly, that the directive to "turn on" session for a given JSP page (the `@page` directive with the `session` attribute) is set to `true` by default, meaning that the following JSP page has a session established for it, even though `session` is never used on the page:

```
<%@ page import="java.util.*">

<html>
<body>
Hello, world, I'm a stateless JSP page.
It is now <%= new Date() %>.
</body>
</html>
```

Worse yet, it takes only one JSP page anywhere in the Web application to do this, and the session (and the commensurate overhead associated with it, even if no objects are ever stored in it) will last for the entire time the client uses the Web application. As a result, make sure your JSPs all have session turned off by default, unless it's your desire to use sessions. I wish there were some way to establish `session = false` as the default for a given Web application, but thus far it's not the case.

Lest you believe otherwise, I'm not advocating the complete removal of all session use from your application; in fact, such a suggestion would be ludicrous, given that HTTP offers no reasonable mechanism for providing per-user state. When used carefully, `HttpSession` provides a necessary and powerful mechanism for providing per-user state within a Web application, and this is often a critical and necessary thing. (How else could I ensure that the user has successfully authenticated or track his or her progress through the application?) The danger is in overusing and abusing the mechanism, thereby creating additional strain on the servlet container when it's not necessary. Don't use sessions unless you need to, and when you do use them, make them lean and mean in order to keep the resources consumed on the servlet container machine as light as possible.

Item 40:   Use objects-first persistence to preserve your domain model

You've spent weeks, if not months, designing an elegant object model representing your application's business domain objects, searching for just the right combination of inheritance, composition, aggregation, and other object-modeling techniques to build it. It has taken quite a while, but you're finally there—you have an object model the team can be proud of. Now it's time to preserve that domain data into the database, and you want to keep your object model in place; after all, what good is an object model if you're just going to have to turn around and write a whole bunch of ugly SQL to push the data back out to the database?

In an objects-first approach to persistence, we seek to keep the view of objects during persistence; this means either the objects know how to silently persist themselves without any prompting from us or they provide some kind of object-centric API for doing the persistence and retrieval. Thus, in the ideal world, writing code like the following would automatically create an entry in the database containing the person data for Stu Halloway, age 25:

```
Person p = new Person("Stu", "Halloway", 25);
System.out.println(p);
    // Prints "Stu Halloway, age 25"
```

Writing these next lines of code would automatically update the existing row created in the first snippet to bump Stu's age from 25 to 30:

```
Person p = Person.find("Stu", "Halloway");
System.out.println(p);
    // Prints "Stu Halloway, age 25"
p.setAge(30);
System.out.println(p);
    // Prints "Stu Halloway, age 30"
```

Notice one of the great benefits of the objects-first persistence approach: no ugly SQL, no worries about whether we need to do an INSERT or an UPDATE, and so on. All we see are objects, and we like it that way.

An objects-first approach tends to break down fairly quickly when trying to retrieve objects, however. Generally speaking, an objects-first approach takes one of two possible methods: either we issue queries for objects by creating objects that contain our criteria in pure object-oriented fashion or we use some kind of "query language" specific to object queries.

In a strictly purist objects-first environment, we never want to see anything but objects, so we end up building Query Objects [Fowler, 316[1]] that contain the criteria we're interested in restricting the query around. Unfortunately, building a complex query that executes by using criteria other than the object's primary key (sometimes called an *OID*, short for *object identifier*, in the parlance of OODBMSs is often complicated and/or awkward:

```
QueryObject q = new QueryObject(Person.class);
q.add(Criteria.and(
        Criteria.greaterThan("dependents", 2)),
            Criteria.lessThan("income", 80000)));
q.add(Criteria.and(
        Criteria.greaterThan("dependents", 0)),
            Criteria.lessThan("income", 60000)));
```

Here, we're trying to build the equivalent of the following lines:

```
SELECT * FROM person p
  WHERE ( (p.dependents > 2 AND p.income < 80000)
        OR (p.dependents > 0 AND p.income < 60000) )
```

Which is easier to read? Things get exponentially worse if we start doing deeply nested Boolean logic in the query, such as looking for "people making less than $80,000 with more than 2 dependents who in turn claim them as parents, or people making less than $60,000 with any dependents who in turn claim them as parents." In fact, it's not uncommon to find that an objects-first purist query approach has much stricter restrictions on what can be queried than a general-purpose query language, like SQL.

Which leads us to the second approach, that of creating some kind of "query language" for more concisely expressing queries without having to resort to overly complex code. All of the objects-first technology approaches in Java have ultimately fallen back to this: EJB 2.0 introduced EJBQL, a query language for writing finders for entity beans; JDO introduced JDOQL, which does the same for JDO-enhanced persistent classes; and going way back, OODBMSs used OQL, the Object Query Language. These languages are subtly different from each other, yet all share one defining similarity: they all look a lot like SQL, which is what we were

---

1. By the way, if you use Fowler's implementation of the Query Object found in his book, note that as written, the code could be vulnerable to a SQL injection attack (see Item 61).

trying to get away from in the first place. (JDOQL is technically a language solely for describing a filter, which is essentially just the predicate part of the query—the WHERE clause—while still using a Query Object–style API.) Worse, EJBQL as defined in EJB 2.0 lacks many of the key features of SQL that make it so powerful to use for executing queries. The 2.1 release will address some of this lack, but several features of SQL are still missing from EJBQL.

Another unfortunate side effect of using an objects-first approach is that of invisible round-trips; for example, when using the entity bean below, how many trips to the database are made?

```
PersonHome ph =
  (PersonHome)ctx.lookup("java:comp/env/PersonHome");


// Start counting round-trips from here
//
Collection personCollection = ph.findByLastName("Halloway");
for (Iterator i = personCollection.iterator(); i.hasNext(); )
{
  Person p = (Person)i.hasNext();
  System.out.println("Found " + p.getFirstName() +
                     " " + p.getLastName());
}
```

Although it might seem like just one round-trip to the database (to retrieve each person whose last name is Halloway and to populate the entity beans from the PersonBean pool as necessary), in fact, this is what's called the $N+1$ query problem in EJB literature—the finder call will look only for the primary keys of the rows matching the query criteria, populate the Collection with entity bean stubs that know only the primary key, and lazy-load the data into the entity bean as necessary. Because we immediately turn around and access data on the entity bean, this in turn forces the entity bean to update itself from the database, and since we iterate over each of the items in the Collection, we make one trip for the primary keys plus N more trips, where N equals the number of items in the collection.

Astute developers will quickly point out that a particular EJB entity bean implementation isn't necessarily required to do something like this; for example, it would be possible (if perhaps nonportable—see Item 11) to build an entity bean implementation that, instead of simply pulling back the OIDs/primary keys of the entity as the result of a query, pulls back the entire data set stored within that entity, essentially choosing an eager-loading implementation rather than the more commonly used lazy-loading approach (see Items 47 and 46, respectively). Unfortunately, this would create a problem in the reverse—now we will complain about too much data being pulled across, rather than too little.

The crux of the problem here is that in an objects-first persistence scenario, the atom of data retrieval is the object itself—to pull back something smaller than an object doesn't make sense from an object-oriented perspective, just as it doesn't make sense to pull back something smaller than a row in an SQL query. So when all we want is the `Person`'s first name and last name, we're forced to retrieve the entire `Person` object to get it. Readers familiar with OQL will stand up and protest here, stating (correctly) that OQL, among others, allows for retrieval of "parts" of an object—but this leads to further problems. What exactly is the returned type of such a query? I can write something like the following lines:

```
SELECT p.FirstName, p.LastName
  FROM Person p
  WHERE p.LastName = 'Halloway';
```

But what, exactly, is returned? Normally, the return from an object query is an object of defined type (in the above case, a `Person` instance); what are we getting back here? There is no commonly accepted way to return just "part" of an object, so typically the result is something more akin to a `ResultSet` or Java `Map` (or rather, a `List` of `Map` instances).

Even if we sort out these issues, objects-first queries have another problem buried within them: object-to-object references. In this case, the difficulty occurs not so much because we can't come up with good modeling techniques for managing one-to-many, many-to-many, or many-to-one relationships within a relational database (which isn't trivial, by the way), but because when an object is retrieved, the question arises whether it should pull back all of its associated objects, as well. And how do we resolve the situation where two independent queries pull back two identical objects through this indirect reference?

For example, consider the scenario where we have four `Person` objects in the system: Stu Halloway is married to Joanna Halloway, and they have two children, Hattie Halloway and Harper Halloway. From any good object perspective, this means that a good `Person` model will have a field for spouse, of type Person (or, more accurately, references to Person), as well as a field that is a collection of some type, called children, containing references to Person again.

So now, when we execute the earlier query and retrieve the first object (let's use Stu), should pulling the Stu object across the wire mean pulling Joanna, Hattie, and Harper across, as well? Again, should we eager-load the data—remember, these objects are referenced from fields in the Stu object instance—or lazy-load it? And when we move to the next result in the query, Joanna, which in turn references Stu, will we have one Stu object in the client process space or two? What happens if we do two separate queries, one to pull back Stu alone, and the second to pull back Joanna? This notion of object identity is important because in Java, object identity is established by the this pointer (the object's location), and in the database it's conveyed via the primary key—getting the two of them to match up is a difficult prospect, particularly when we throw transactions into the midst. It's not an impossible problem—an Identity Map [Fowler, 195] is the typical solution—but as an object programmer, you need to be aware of this problem in case your objects-first persistence mechanism doesn't take care of it.

The ultimate upshot here is that if you're choosing to take an objects-first persistence approach, there are consequences beyond "it's easier to work with." In many cases, the power and attractiveness of working solely with objects is enough to offset the pain, and that's saying a lot.

Item 41: Use relational-first persistence to expose the power of the relational model

For years (if not decades), the undisputed king of the data storage tier has been the relational database; despite a valiant run by OODBMSs in the mid-1990s, the relational database remains in firm control of enterprise data, and relational vendors appear unwilling to part with that position any time soon. We developers want to continue to use object-oriented languages, since we've found them to be most convenient for us to solve our problems, but businesses want to continue their investments in relational databases. So it seems natural that we would want to "hide" the messy details of persisting object data to the relational database. Unfortunately, therein lies a problem: objects and relations don't mix well. The difficulty in achieving a good mapping between these two technologies even has its own name, the *object-relational impedance mismatch.*

Part of the problem of working with relational access technologies (like JDBC) from an object-oriented language is simply that the two technology bases view the world in very different ways. An object-oriented language wants to work with *objects*, which have *attributes* (fields) and *behaviors* (methods), whereas a relational technology sees the world as *tuples*, collections of data items grouped into a logical "thing"—what Date referred to as "relations" [Date]. In essence, a relational model deals with collections of relations, which we commonly refer to as *tables*; each relation is a *row*, each item in the tuple is a *column*, and an entire language built around the idea of manipulating data in this relational format provides access.

While a full treatise on the problems inherent in an object-relational mapping layer is well beyond the scope of this book, a brief look at just one of the problems involved may help explain why object-relational mapping is such a common problem in J2EE systems. Consider, for a moment, a simple domain object model:

```
public class Person
{
  private String firstName;
  private String lastName;
  private int age;

  // . . .
}


public class Employee extends Person
{
  private long employeeID;
  private float monthlySalary;
}
```

This is probably the world's simplest domain model, but how should we persist this out to a relational database?

One approach is to create two tables, PERSON and EMPLOYEE, and use a foreign-key relationship to tie rows from one to the other. This requires a join between these two tables every time we want to work with a given

`Employee`, which requires greater work on the part of the database on every query and modification to the data. We could store both `Person` and `Employee` data into a single EMPLOYEE table, but then when we create `Student` (extending `Person`) and want to find all `Person` objects whose last name is Smith, we'll have to search both STUDENT and EMPLOYEE tables, neither of which at a relational level have anything to do with one another. And if this inheritance layer gets any deeper, we're just compounding the problem even further, almost exponentially.

As if this weren't enough, more frequently than not, the enterprise developer doesn't have control over the database schema—it's already in use, either by legacy systems or other J2EE systems, or the schema has been laid down by developers in other groups. So even if we wanted to build a table structure to elegantly match the object model we built, we can't arbitrarily change the schema definitions.

From an entirely different angle, there may be other, far more practical reasons to abandon an objects-first approach. Perhaps no object-relational mapping product on the planet can deal with the relational database schema you inherited as part of your project, or you're simply more comfortable working with the relational model and SQL than an object model (although that would likely imply you started life as a database administrator and later became a Java programmer).

For these reasons and more, frequently it's easier to take a relational view of your data and embrace that fully by not hiding the relational access behind some other kind of encapsulatory wall, be it object-, procedural-, or hierarchical-oriented.

To understand what I mean by the idea of taking a relational-first approach, we need to take a step back for a moment and revisit what exactly the relational approach itself is. According to Chris Date, who along with E. F. Codd is considered to be one of the great fathers of the relational model, "relational systems are based on a formal foundation, or theory, called *the relational model of data*" [Date, 38, emphasis added]. For mathematicians, a relational model is based on set theory and predicate logic; for the rest of us, however, in simple terms, the relational model of data is seen as nothing but tables. Accessing data yields nothing but tables, and the operators (SQL) for manipulating that data produce tables from tables.

While this may seem like a pretty redundant discussion—after all, it takes about thirty seconds of looking at a relational database to figure out that it's all about the tables—it's the "relation" in the relational model that provides much of the power. Because the end product of a relational data access (SQL statement) is a table, which is in turn the source of a relational data operator such as JOIN, SELECT, and so on, relational data access achieves what Date calls *closure*: results of one access can serve as the input to another. This gives us the ability to write nested expressions: expressions in which the operands themselves are represented by general expressions, instead of just by table names. This is where much of the power of SQL comes from, although we tend not to use it that much (typically because we keep trying to go for objects-first persistence approaches, and SQL nested expressions don't fit so well in an object-relational mapping layer).

Why is this such a big deal? Because SQL is a powerful language for accessing data out of a relational database, and thanks to the fact that everything produced by a SQL query is a table, we can have a single API for extracting however much, or however little, data from any particular query we need. We don't have the "smaller than an object" problem raised in Item 40 because everything comes back as a table, even if it's a table one column wide. We do face the problem that the relational model frequently won't match the object model programmers would rather work with, but we can address that in a bit. Let's first look at making the relational access itself easier.

Before you shrink in horror at the thought of being condemned to low-level JDBC access for the rest of your life, take a deep breath—a relational-first approach doesn't mean abandoning anything at a higher level than JDBC. Far from it, in fact. We can use several mechanisms to make relational access much easier from Java than just raw JDBC (which still remains as an option in many cases, despite its relatively low-level nature).

First, there's more to JDBC than just Connection, Statement, and ResultSet objects. RowSet, and in particular Sun's CachedRowSet implementation, frequently makes it much easier to work with JDBC by encapsulating the act of issuing the query and harvesting the results. So, assuming you're without a JDBC DataSource, issuing a query can be as easy as this:

```
RowSet rs = new WebRowSet();
    // Or use another RowSet implementation
```

```
// Provide RowSet with enough information to obtain a
// Connection
rs.setUrl("jdbc:dburl://dbserver/PEOPLE");
rs.setUsername("user");
rs.setPassword("password");

rs.setCommand("SELECT first_name, last_name FROM person " +
              "WHERE last_name=?");
rs.setString(1, "Halloway");

rs.execute();

// rs now holds the results of the query
```

Most of the calls to the RowSet could be hidden behind an object factory interface (see Item 72 for details on object factories), so that client code could be reduced to the following:

```
RowSet rs = MyRowSetFactory.getRowSet();
rs.setCommand(. . .);
rs.setString(1, "Halloway");
rs.execute();
```

If you ask me, that's about as simple as you're going to get for direct SQL-based access. The factory itself is not difficult to imagine:

```
public class MyRowSetFactory
{
  public static getRowSet()
  {
    RowSet rs = new WebRowSet(); // Or some other
                                 // implementation

    // This time, use JNDI DataSource
    // rather than url/username/password
    rs.setDataSourceName("java:comp/env/jdbc/PEOPLE_DS");

    return rs;
  }
}
```

The RowSet API has methods to control the details of how the query will be executed, including the fetch size of the ResultSet (which should be set as high as possible, preferably to the size of the rows returned by the query, to avoid round-trips at the expense of one giant "pull" across the network), and the transaction isolation level (see Item 35) of this call.

However, the RowSet API still requires that you author the SQL query you're interested in every time you want to use it, and it can get awfully tiring to type SELECT blah blah blah FROM table WHERE baz=? every time you want to pull some data back, particularly if you're using PreparedStatement objects in order to avoid falling into the traps of doing simple string concatenation and opening yourself to injection attacks (see Item 61). So you get tempted to either blow off the possibility of the injection attack—bad idea, mate—or you start cheating in other ways, like SELECT * FROM table, which pulls every column in the table across, rather than just the data you're interested in, which means you're wasting bandwidth. That might not be an issue on your development machine or network, but in production that could easily max out the pipe if 1,000 users execute that command simultaneously.[2] If you don't need it, you shouldn't ask for it across the wire. So what are self-respecting programmers, seeking to do the right thing while saving their poor hands from carpal tunnel syndrome, to do? (And if you're thinking this is a pretty frivolous example, take another approach to the problem: What happens if we change the table definitions, which in turn means changing the SQL statements now scattered all over the codebase?)

One approach is to keep a table-oriented view of the database but put a bit more scaffolding between you and the data access technology itself, through a Table Data Gateway [Fowler, 144]. Essentially, each table becomes a class, which in turn serves as the point of access to any rows in that table:

```
public class PersonGateway
{
  private PersonGateway() { /* Singleton-can't create */ }

  public static Person[] findAll()
```

---

2. OK, it would have to be an awfully wide table, but you get the idea.

```
{
  ArrayList al = new ArrayList();

  RowSet rs = MyRowSetFactory.getRowSet();
  rs.setCommand("SELECT first_name,last_name,age "+
                "FROM person");
  rs.execute();
  while (rs.next())
    al.add(new Person(rs.getString(1),
                      rs.getString(2),
                      rs.getInt(3));

  return (Person[])al.toArray(new Person[0]);
}
public static void update(Person p)
{
  // And so on, and so on, and so on
}
}
```

Note that when done this way, a Table Data Gateway looks a lot like a procedural-first approach to persistence (see Item 42); the key difference is that a Table Data Gateway is per-table and focuses exclusively on manipulating that table's data, whereas a procedural-first approach provides a single point of access for all persistence logic in a table-agnostic way (since the underlying data store may not even be relational tables anymore).

"This works for tables," you may be tempted to say, "but I need to do a lot of queries that aren't restricted to a single table—what then?" In fact, thanks to the closure property of relational data access mentioned earlier, the Table Data Gateway can be extended to be a new variant, say, the Query Data Gateway, where instead of wrapping around a single table, we wrap it around a query instead:

```
public class ChildrenGateway
{
  private ChildrenGateway() { }
    // Singleton, can't create
```

```
public static Person[] findKidsForPerson(Person p)
{
  ArrayList al = new ArrayList();

  RowSet rs = MyRowSetFactory.getRowSet();
  rs.setCommand("SELECT first_name,last_name,age "+
               "FROM person p, parent_link pp "+
               "WHERE p.id = pp.child_id "+
                 "AND p.last_name=?");
  rs.setInt(1, p.getPersonID());
  rs.execute();
  while (rs.next())
    al.add(new Person(rs.getString(1),
                      rs.getString(2),
                      rs.getInt(3));

  return (Person[])al.toArray(new Person[0]);
  }
}
```

Ironically, it turns out that this approach was commonly used within the relational world, long before we upstart Java programmers came along, so databases support this intrinsically: it's called a *view*. The database basically pretends that a query looks and acts just like a table:

```
CREATE VIEW children AS
  SELECT first_name, last_name, age
  FROM person p, parent_link pp
  WHERE p.id = pp.child_id
```

This creates a pseudo-table called `children` that contains all `Person` objects that have parents. We then issue queries against `children` by restricting against `last_name`.

What's the advantage here? All we've done is create something that looks like a table that isn't, and won't that create some kind of performance scariness inside the database? For some of the older database products, yes—but that problem was pretty much corrected some years ago. While there are some restrictions on views, such as on updates to a view—some database products don't allow updates at all, others allow updates only to one table if there's a multi-table join in the view, and so on—as a means by which to make queries more readable, and in some cases more efficient, views are a powerful tool.

If none of these approaches seem particularly what you're looking for because they still seem like too much work and are too awkward to work with from within Java, another approach is to make use of the recently standardized SQL/J, or "embedded SQL for Java," Specification recently approved as part of the SQL-99 Specification. As with other embedded SQL technologies, SQL/J allows a programmer to write SQL statements directly within the Java code, which is then preprocessed by a SQL/J pre-processor, turned into regular Java code, and fed to javac as a normal compilation step. The SQL/J preprocessor takes care of any of the call-level interface logic in your Java code—you just focus on writing the SQL when you want to talk to the database and on Java when you want to do anything else.

The easiest way to use SQL/J is to write static SQL statements embedded in the code directly, known as *SQL/J clauses,* as shown here:

```
public static float averageAgeOfFamily(String lastName)
   throws Exception
{
  #sql iterator Ages (int individualAge);

  Ages rs;
  #sql rs =
    { SELECT age FROM person
       WHERE last_name = :lastName };

  int totalAge = 0;
  int numPersons = 0;
  while (rs.next())
  {
    numPersons++;
    totalAge += rs.individualAge();
  }

  return ((float)totalAge) / ((float)numPersons);
}
```

It looks and feels like a standard Java method, with the exception of the #sql blocks, setting off the code that will be handled by the preprocessor, and the `Ages` type introduced by the `#sql iterator` clause early in the method body. This isn't the place to discuss the ins and outs of SQL/J syntax; download the reference implementation and documentation from http://www.sqlj.org.

The thing to recognize here is that SQL/J essentially hides almost all of the data access plumbing from sight, leaving only the barest minimum of scaffolding in place to make it easy to write the SQL itself—in many respects, it's the absolute inverse of an objects-first technology like JDO, which tries so hard to hide the relational access from the programmer's perspective. On top of this "get right to the relational data access" idea, SQL/J also offers a major improvement over any other data access technology to date: if the database schema is available at the time of compilation, a SQL/J preprocessor/translator can actually check, in compile time, the SQL in the Java code against the schema, catching typos and syntax errors without having to rely on runtime `SQLException` instances to find them. This alone is a compelling reason to take a hard look at SQL/J.

One major drawback to SQL/J, however, is its relative lack of support within the J2EE community. Although the J2EE and EJB Specifications do mention it by name as a possible data access technology layer, it receives almost no attention beyond that. Oracle is the only major database vendor to have a SQL/J implementation available as of this writing, and there seems to be little support from the community as a whole, which is a shame because in many respects this is the epitome of a relational-first persistence approach.

As with the objects-first persistence approach, the relational-first approach has its share of strengths and weaknesses. It exposes the power and grace that SQL itself encompasses, but at the expense of having to abandon (to at least a certain degree) the beauty of the object model in obtaining and updating data. It means having to write code that takes data out of the relational API, be that JDBC or SQL/J, and puts it into your object model, but the tradeoff is that you get to control the exact SQL produced, which can be a powerful optimization because not all SQL is created equal (see Item 50).

Item 42: Use procedural-first persistence to create an encapsulation layer

Prior to the object-oriented takeover of the programming language community, prior to the almost universal sweep of data storage options in the late 1970s and early 1980s that made relational databases ubiquitous, another approach quickly made its way through the ranks of IT.

Instead of directly accessing the data storage layer through SQL, middleware products (TP Monitors and the like) provided well-known entry point routines, what we would call *procedures* today. These procedures accepted a set of input (parameters) and guaranteed that they would store the data to the system, returning some kind of result indicating success or failure of the action. The details of the actual storage schema and mechanism were hidden behind these opaque walls of the procedure's entry point—so long as the middleware layer ensured that the data was stored appropriately (and could be retrieved, usually via another procedure), no further knowledge was necessary. Later, these procedures were extended to also provide certain kinds of processing, such as providing transactional semantics as a way to guarantee that the entire procedure could execute with ACID properties in place. Even later this processing was made available directly within the database, via what we now call *stored procedures*.

In the beginning, the goal was to provide an encapsulation layer protecting the raw data from programs manipulating it, which eventually set the stage for transactional processing, and later, the database management system itself. In many respects, SQL was an outgrowth of this idea, providing a declarative language that allowed operators to simply say what data they were interested in, based on a set of constraints expressed as part of the SQL statement. This approach, aside from being extremely powerful in the right hands, also proved difficult for programmers familiar with procedural (and later, object-oriented) languages to understand.

Like other declarative languages (Prolog and the more modern XSLT), SQL requires that users state only what data they're interested in, not how to approach obtaining that data. This fits well with the overall "flow" of the relational model but feels awkward to procedural programmers first learning SQL—they keep wanting to "start with this table over here, then go get this data element over here based on . . . ," and so on. Declarative and procedural languages are two very different beasts (just as objects and relations are). This has prompted relational experts like Joe Celko to state, "The single biggest challenge to learning SQL programming is unlearning procedural programming" [Henderson03, 1].

Rather than adopt one of the other models, then, what works best in some cases is to simply bury the details of persistence behind another layer of software, such that the messy details of doing the persistence can be hidden away from the programmer's view—true encapsulation. Doing this can be as simple as the following code:

```
public class DataManager
{
  private DataManager()
  { /* Prevent accidental creation */ }

  public Person findPersonByLastName(String lastName)
  {
    // Open a Connection, create a Statement, execute
    // SELECT * FROM person p WHERE
    // p.last_name = (lastName)
    // Extract data, put into new Person instance,
    // return that
  }
  public void updatePerson(Person p)
  {
    // Open a Connection, create a Statement, execute
    // UPDATE person p SET . . .
  }
}
```

Note that the DataManager is a Singleton but runs locally in the client's virtual machine; it relies on the database access layer (in this case, JDBC) to protect it from any concurrency concerns in order to avoid being a Remote Singleton (see Item 5).

While this makes the DataManager a relatively large class to work with, it does have a number of advantages that make it an attractive option.

- Data access experts can tune the data access logic (which we'll assume is SQL) as necessary to achieve optimal results.
- If necessary, changing data storage systems means changing this one class. If we want to change from a relational back end to an

OODBMS, client code doesn't have to change to do the persistence work (even if it is potentially unnecessary, depending on the OODBMS in use and its underlying persistence semantics).

- Since we know that all the persistence logic for this request is bracketed within this function, clients don't have to worry about transactional semantics or transactions being held open any longer than necessary; this is important to minimize lock windows (see Item 29).

- We can use whatever data access APIs make the most sense for implementing the methods in this one class without changing any client code. If we start by using JDBC and find that JDBC is too low-level to use effectively (not an uncommon opinion), we can switch to SQL/J for this one class only, and clients are entirely ignorant of the change. If we find that SQL/J is easier to work with but doesn't generate optimal JDBC-based access, we can switch back with impunity.

- We could keep back-end portability by making `DataManager` an interface and creating `DataManager` derivatives that specialize in doing storage to one or more different back-end storage layers—an `OracleDataManager`, an `HSQLDataManager` (for in-process relational data storage), a generic `JDBCDataManager` (for generic nonoptimized JDBC-SQL access), and so on. This allows us to tune for a particular back end without sacrificing overall system portability, but at the expense of a lot of work to build each one, including maintenance when the `DataManager` interface needs to change.

- New access requires modifying the centralized class. This may seem like a disadvantage at first—after all, who wants to go back and modify code once it's "done"?—but the fact that somebody wants a new query or update gives the `DataManager` developer an opportunity to revisit the data access code and/or the actual storage of the data. We can use this to add a few optimizations based on the new usage, such as creating new indexes in the relational model. It also serves as a sanity check to prevent looking up data by invalid criteria ("Well, since everybody knows that only men are programmers, I was going to do the programmer lookup by adding criteria to restrict by `gender=male`; that should speed up the query, right?").

In essence, the `DataManager` class serves as our sole point of coupling between the data storage tier and the Java code that wants to access it.

Procedural access isn't always done at the Java language level, however. Most commercial databases offer the ability to execute procedural code directly within the database itself, a stored procedure in DBMS nomenclature. While all the major database vendors offer vendor-specific languages for writing stored procedures, many are starting to support the idea of writing Java stored procedures (an unfortunate overload of the acronym JSP), meaning Java programmers don't have to learn another language. However, one of the brightest advantages of using the stored-procedure-as-persistence model is that we can pass the implementation of the stored procedure to the database staff, leaving the entire data model in their hands to be designed, implemented, and tuned as necessary. As long as the definitions of the stored procedures don't change (we'll get runtime `SQLException` instances if they do) and the stored procedure implementations do what we expect them to (like store or retrieve the data), we can remain entirely ignorant of the underlying data model—which, if you're as good at relational design and execution as I am (that is to say, not at all), is a good thing.

By the way, if you're thinking that the procedural model is a horrible idea, and you would never consider using anything like it, stop and have another look at the Session Façade [Alur/Crupi/Malks, 341], Domain Store [Alur/Crupi/Malks, 516], and other data access patterns. In order to avoid round-trips to the database, recall that current EJB "best practice" thinking has clients calling session beans, passing either Data Transfer Objects [Fowler, 401] or other data in bulk (see Item 23) as parameters to the session bean method, to be extracted and inserted into the local entity bean for storage in the database. This is no different than the `DataManager` presented earlier, except that now `DataManager` is a session bean. The same will be true of just about any Web service–based data access model.

Item 43: Recognize the object-hierarchical impedance mismatch

XML is everywhere, including in your persistence plans.

Once we'd finally gotten around to realizing that XML was all about data and not a language for doing markup itself as HTML was, industry pundits and writers started talking about XML as the logical way to represent objects in data form. Shortly thereafter, the thought of using XML to marshal data across the network was introduced, and SOAP and its accompanying follow-up Web Service specifications were born.

The problem is that XML is intrinsically a hierarchical way to represent data—look at the XML Infoset Specification, which requires that data be well formed, meaning the elements in an XML document must form a nice tree of elements (each element can have child elements nested within it, each element has a single parent in which it's nested, with the sole exception of the single "root" node that brackets the entire document, and so on). This means that XML is great for representing hierarchical data (hence the title of this item), and assuming your objects form a neat hierarchy, XML is a natural way to represent that data (hence the natural assumption that XML and objects go hand in hand).

But what happens when objects don't form nice, natural trees?

Hierarchical data models are not new; in fact, they're quite old. The relational data model was an attempt to find something easier to work with than the database systems of the day, which were similar in concept, if not form, to the hierarchical model we see in XML today. The problem with the hierarchical model at the time was that attempting to find data within it was difficult. Users had to navigate the elements of the tree manually, leaving users to figure out "how" instead of focusing on "what"—that is, how to get to the data, rather than what data they were interested in.

With the emergence of XML (and the growing interest in "XML databases," despite the inherent ambiguity in that term), it would seem that hierarchical data models are becoming popular once again. While a full discussion of the implications of a hierarchical data model are beyond the scope of this book, it's important to discuss two things here: when we're likely to use a hierarchical data model in J2EE, and what implications that will have for Java programmers.

While the industry currently doesn't recognize it, mapping objects to XML (the most common hierarchical storage model today) is not a simple thing, leading us to wonder whether an *object-hierarchical impedance mismatch*—in other words, a mismatch between the free-form object model we're all used to and the strictly hierarchical model the XML Infoset imposes—is just around the corner.[3] In fact, given that we now have vendors offering libraries to map objects to XML for us, as well as the more recent Java API for XML Binding (JAXB) standard to help

---

3. Let's not even consider the implications of objects stored in relational databases being transformed into XML: the idea of an object-relational-hierarchical impedance mismatch is enough to move the strongest programmer to tears.

unify the various implementations that do so, it may be fair to infer that mapping objects to XML and back again isn't as simple as it seems— granted, simple object models map to XML pretty easily, but then again, simple object models map pretty easily to relational tables, too, and we all know how "easy" it is to do object-relational mapping.

Much of the problem with mapping objects to a hierarchical model is the same problem that occurs when mapping objects to a relational model: preserving object identity. To understand what I mean, let's go back for a moment to the same `Person` object we've used in previous items:

```
public class Person
{
  // Fields public just for simplicity
  //
  public String firstName;
  public String lastName;
  public int age;

  public Person(String fn, String ln, int a)
  { firstName = fn; lastName = ln; age = a; }
}
```

Again, simple and straightforward, and it's not overly difficult to imagine what an XML representation of this object would look like:

```
<person>
  <firstName>Ron</firstName>
  <lastName>Reynolds</lastName>
  <age>30</age>
</person>
```

So far, so good. But now, let's add something that's completely reasonable to expect within an object-oriented model but completely shatters a hierarchical one—cyclic references:

```
public class Person
{
  public String firstName;
  public String lastName;
  public int age;
  public Person spouse;
```

```
    public Person(String fn, String ln, int a)
    { firstName = fn; lastName = ln; age = a; }
}
```

How do you represent the following set of objects?

```
Person ron = new Person("Ron", "Reynolds", 31);
Person lisa = new Person("Lisa", "Reynolds", 25);
ron.spouse = lisa;
lisa.spouse = ron;
```

A not-unreasonable approach to serializing `ron` out to XML could be done by simply traversing the fields, recursively following each object as necessary and traversing its fields in turn, and so on; this is quickly going to run into problems, however, as shown here:

```
<person>
  <firstName>Ron</firstName>
  <lastName>Reynolds</lastName>
  <age>31</age>
  <spouse>
    <person>
      <firstName>Lisa</firstName>
      <lastName>Reynolds</lastName>
      <age>25</age>
      <spouse>
        <person>
          <firstName>Ron</firstName>
          <lastName>Reynolds</lastName>
          <age>31</age>
          <spouse>
            <!-- Uh, oh . . . -->
```

As you can see, an infinite recursion develops here because the two objects are circularly referencing one another. We could fix this problem the same way that Java Object Serialization does (see Item 71), by keeping track of which items have been serialized and which haven't, but then we're into a bigger problem: Even if we keep track of identity within a given XML hierarchy, how do we do so across hierarchies? That is, if we serialize both the `ron` and `lisa` objects into two separate streams (perhaps as part of a JAX-RPC method call), how do we make the deserialization logic aware of the fact that the data referred to in the `spouse` field of `ron` is the same data referred to in the `spouse` field of `lisa`?

```
String param1 = ron.toXML(); // Serialize to XML
String param2 = lisa.toXML(); // Serialize to XML
sendXMLMessage("<parameters>" + param1 + param2 +
               "</parameters>");


/* Produces:
param1 =
<person id="id1">
  <firstName>Ron</firstName>
  <lastName>Reynolds</lastName>
  <age>31</age>
  <spouse>
    <person id="id2">
      <firstName>Lisa</firstName>
      <lastName>Reynolds</lastName>
      <age>25</age>
      <spouse><person href="id1" /></spouse>
    </person>
  </spouse>
</person>
param2 =
<person id="id1">
  <firstName>Lisa</firstName>
  <lastName>Reynolds</lastName>
  <age>25</age>
  <spouse>
    <person id="id2">
      <firstName>Ron</firstName>
      <lastName>Reynolds</lastName>
      <age>25</age>
      <spouse><person href="id1" /></spouse>
    </person>
  </spouse>
</person>
 */


// . . . On recipient's side, how will we get
// the spouses correct again?
```

(By the way, this trick of using id and href to track object identity is not new. It's formally described in Section 5 of the SOAP 1.1 Specification, and as a result, it's commonly called *SOAP Section 5 encoding* or, more simply, *SOAP encoding*.) We're managing to keep the object references straight within each individual stream, but when we collapse the streams into a larger document, the two streams have no awareness of one another, and the whole object-identity scheme fails. So how do we fix this?

The short but brutal answer is, we can't—not without relying on mechanisms outside of the XML Infoset Specification, which means that schema and DTD validation won't pick up any malformed data. In fact, the whole idea of object identity preserved by SOAP Section 5 encoding is entirely outside the Schema and/or DTD validator's capabilities and has been removed in the latest SOAP Specification (1.2). Cyclic references, which are actually much more common in object systems than you might think, will break a hierarchical data format every time.

Some will point out that we can solve the problem by introducing a new construct into the stream that "captures" the two independent objects, as in the following code:

```
<marriage>
  <person>
    <!-- Ron goes here -->
  </person>
  <person>
    <!-- Lisa goes here -->
  </person>
</marriage>
```

But that's missing the point—in doing this, you've essentially introduced a new data element into the mix that doesn't appear anywhere in the object model it was produced from. An automatic object-to-XML serialization tool isn't going to be able to make this kind of decision, and certainly not without some kind of developer assistance.

So what? It's not like we're relying on XML for data storage, for the most part—that's what we have the relational database for, and object-relational mapping layers will take care of all those details for us. Why bother going down this path of object-hierarchical mapping?

If you're going to do Web Services, you're going to be doing object-hierarchical mapping: remember, SOAP Section 5 encoding was created to solve this problem because we want to silently and opaquely transform objects into XML and back again without any work on our part. And the sad truth is, just as object-relational layers will never be able to silently and completely take care of mapping objects to relations, object-hierarchical layers like JAXB or Exolab's Castor will never be able to completely take care of mapping objects to hierarchies.

Don't think that the limitations all go just one way, either. Objects have just as hard a time with XML documents, even schema-valid ones, as XML has with object graphs. Consider the following schema:

```
<xsd:schema xmlns:xsd='http://www.w3.org/2001/XMLSchema'
    xmlns:tns='http://example.org/product'
    targetNamespace='http://example.org/product' >
  <xsd:complexType name='Product' >
    <xsd:sequence>
      <xsd:choice>
        <xsd:element name='produce'
                     type='xsd:string'/>
        <xsd:element name='meat' type='xsd:string' />
      </xsd:choice>
      <xsd:sequence minOccurs='1'
                    maxOccurs='unbounded'>
        <xsd:element name='state'
                     type='xsd:string' />
        <xsd:element name='taxable'
                     type='xsd:boolean'/>
      </xsd:sequence>
    </xsd:sequence>
  </xsd:complexType>
  <xsd:element name='Product' type='tns:Product' />
</xsd:schema>
```

Here is the schema-valid corresponding document:

```
<groceryStore xmlns:p='http://example.org/product'>
  <p:Product>
    <produce>Lettuce</produce>
    <state>CA</state>
    <taxable>true</taxable>
    <state>MA</state>
    <taxable>true</taxable>
```

```
    <state>CO</state>
    <taxable>false</taxable>
  </p:Product>
  <p:Product>
    <meat>Prime rib</meat>
    <state>CA</state>
    <taxable>false</taxable>
    <state>MA</state>
    <taxable>true</taxable>
    <state>CO</state>
    <taxable>false</taxable>
  </p:Product>
</groceryStore>
```

Ask yourself this question: How on earth can Java (or, for that matter, any other traditional object-oriented language, like C++ or C#) represent this repeating sequence of element state/taxable pairs, or the discriminated union of two different element types, produce or meat? The closest approximation would be to create two subtypes, one each for the produce and meat element particles, then create another new type, this time for the state/taxable pairs, and store an array of those in the Product type itself. The schema defined just one type, and we have to define at least four in Java to compensate.

Needless to say, working with this schema-turned-Java type system is going to be difficult at best. And things get even more interesting if we start talking about doing derivation by restriction, occurrence constraints (minOccurs and maxOccurs facets on schema compositors), and so on. JAXB and other Java-to-XML tools can take their best shot, but they're never going to match schema declarations one-for-one, just as schema and XML can't match objects one-for-one. In short, we have an impedance mismatch.

Where does this leave us?

For starters, recognize that XML models hierarchical data well but can't effectively handle arbitrary object graphs. In certain situations, where objects model into a neat hierarchy, the transition will be smooth and seamless, but it takes just one reference to something other than an immediate child object to seriously throw off object-to-XML serializers. Fortunately, strings, dates, and the wrapper classes are usually handled in a pretty transparent manner, despite their formal object status, so that's not an issue, but for anything else, be prepared for some weird and semi-obfuscated results from the schema-to-Java code generator.

Second, take a more realistic view of what XML can do for you. Its ubiquity makes it a tempting format in which to store all your data, but the fact is that relational databases still rule the roost, and we're mostly going to use XML as an interoperability technology for the foreseeable future. Particularly with more and more RDBMS vendors coming to XML as a format with which to describe data, the chances of storing data as XML in an "XML database" are slight. Instead, see XML as a form of "data glue" between Java and other type systems, such as .NET and C++.

A few basic principles come to mind, which I offer here with the huge caveat that some of these, like any good principles, may be sacrificed if the situation calls for it.

- *Use XML Schema to define your data types.* Just as you wouldn't realistically consider doing an enterprise project storing data in a relational database without defining relational constraints on your data model, don't realistically consider doing enterprise projects storing data in XML without defining XML data types. Having said that, however, at times, a more flexible model of XML will be useful, such as when allowing for user extensions to the XML data instances. Be prepared for this by writing your types to have extension points within the type declarations, via judicious use of any-type elements. And, although this should be rare within the enterprise space, in some cases some XML data needs to be entirely free-form in order to be useful, such as Ant scripts. In those situations, be strong enough to recognize that you won't be able to (or want to) have schema types defined and that they will require hand-verification and/or parsing.
- *Prefer a subset of the schema simple types.* XML Schema provides a rich set of simple types (those that most closely model primitive types in Java), such as the `yearMonth` and `MonthDay` types for dates, but Java has no corresponding equivalent—a schema-to-Java toll will most likely model both of those, as well as many others, as a simple integer field. Unfortunately, that means you can store anything you want into that field, thus losing the type definition intended by the schema document in the first place. To avoid this situation, prefer to stick to the types in XSD schema that most closely model what Java (and .NET and any other language you may end up talking to) can handle easily.

- *Use XML Schema validating parsers to verify instances of your schema types when parsing those instances.* The parser will flag schema-invalid objects, essentially acting as a kind of data-scrubbing and input-validating layer for you, without any work on your part. This will in turn help enforce that you're using document-oriented approaches to your XML types, since straying from that model will flag the validator. Be aware, though, that schema-validating parsers are woefully slow compared to their non-schema-validating counterparts. More importantly, schema-validating parsers will only be able to flag schema-invalid objects, and if you're taking an object-based approach to your XML types that uses out-of-band techniques (like SOAP encoding does), schema validators won't pick it up, so you'll know there's a problem only when the parser buys off on the object but your code doesn't. That's a hard scenario to test for.

- *Understand that type definitions are relative.* Your notion of what makes a `Person` is different from my notion of what makes a `Person`, and our corresponding definitions of `Person` (whether in object type definitions, XML Schema, or relational schema) differ accordingly. While some may try to search for the Universal Truth regarding the definition of `Person`, the fact is that there really isn't one—what's important to your organization about `Person` is different from what's important to my organization, and no amount of persuasion on your part is going to change that for me, and vice versa. Instead of going down this dead-end road, simply agree to disagree on this, and model schema accordingly if the documents described by this schema are to be used by both of us. In other words, use schema to verify data being sent from one system to another, rather than trying to use it to define types that everybody agrees on.

- *Avoid HOLDS-A relationships.* As with the `Person` example, instances that hold "references" to other instances create problems. Avoid them when you can. Unfortunately, that's a lot easier said than done. There is no real way to model `Person` in a document-oriented fashion if `Person` needs to refer to the spouse and still preserve object identity. Instead, you're going to have to recognize that the `Person`'s spouse is an "owned" data item—so instead of trying to model it as a standalone `Person`, just capture enough data to uniquely identify that `Person` from some other document (much as a relational table uses a foreign key to refer to a primary key in another table). Unfortunately, again, XML Schema can't reflect this[4] and it will have to be captured in some kind of out-of-band mechanism; no schema constraints can cross documents, at least not as of this writing.

Most importantly, make sure that you understand the hierarchical data model and how it differs from relational and object models. Trying to use XML as an objects-first data repository is simply a recipe for disaster— don't go down that road.

Item 44: Use in-process or local storage to avoid the network

Most often, when J2EE developers begin the design and architectural layout of the project, it's a foregone conclusion that data storage will be done in a relational database running on a machine somewhere in the data center or operations center.

Why?

There's no mystical, magical reason, just simple accessibility. We want the data to be accessible by any of the potential clients that use the system.

In the old days, before *n*-tier architectures became the norm, clients connected directly to servers, so the data needed to be held directly on the server, in order to allow all the clients access to all the data; networks hadn't yet achieved widespread ubiquity, and wireless access technology, which makes networking even simpler, hadn't arrived. Connecting machines to a network was a major chore, and as a result, the basic concepts of peer-to-peer communication were reserved for discussions at the lowest levels of the networking stack (the IP protocol, for example).

In time, we realized that putting all of the data on a central server had the additional advantage of putting major load on the server, thereby taking it off the clients. Since the server was a single machine, it was much more cost-effective (so we believed) to upgrade or replace that single machine, rather than all of the clients that connected to it. So not until well after we

---

4. If this XML document is a collection of Person instances, and the spouse is guaranteed to be within this collection someplace, that's a different story, but that also changes what we're modeling here and becomes a different problem entirely.

had established the idea of the centralized database did we started putting our databases on the heaviest iron we could find, loading them up with maximal RAM footprints and huge gigabyte (and later, terabyte) drive arrays.

The point of this little digression into history is that the centralized, remote database server exists simply to provide a single gathering point for data, not because databases *need* to run on servers that cost well into five, six, or seven digits. We put the data on the server because it was (a) a convenient place to put it, and (b) an easy way to put processing in one central place for all clients to use without having to push updates out (zero deployment), and (c) a way to put the data close to the processing (see Item 4).

Transmitting all this data across the wire isn't cheap, however, nor is it without its own inherent share of problems. It's costly both in terms of scalability and performance (since each byte of bandwidth consumed to transfer data around the network is a byte of bandwidth that can't be used for other purposes), and the time it takes to shuffle that data back and forth is not trivial, as Item 17 describes. So, given that we put data on the centralized database in order to make it available to other clients and that it's not cheap to do the transfer, don't put data on the remote database unless you have to; that is, don't put any data on the remote database unless it's actually going to be shared across clients.

In such cases, running a relational database (or another data storage technology—here we can think about using an object database or even an XML database if we choose to) inside the same process as the client application can not only keep network round-trips to a minimum but also keep the data entirely on the local machine. While running Oracle inside of our servlet container is probably not going to happen any time soon, running an all-Java RDBMS implementation is not so far-fetched; for example, Cloudscape offers this functionality, as do PointBase and HSQLDB (an open-source implementation on Sourceforge), essentially becoming a database masquerading as a JDBC driver. Or, if you prefer an object-based approach, Prevayler, another open-source project, stores any Java object in traditional objects-first persistence fashion. If you'd rather see the data in a hierarchical fashion, Xindice is an open-source XML database from the Apache Group.

One simple in-process data storage technique is the RowSet itself. Because the RowSet is entirely disconnected from the database, we can create one around the results of a query and keep that RowSet for the lifetime of the client process without worrying about the scalability effects on the database. Because the RowSet is Serializable, we can store it as is without modification into any OutputStream, such as a file or a Preferences node; in fact, if the RowSet is wrapped around configuration data, it makes more sense to store it in a Preferences node than in a local file in some ways (see Item 13). It won't scale to thousands of rows, it won't enforce relational integrity, but if you need to store that much data or to put relational constraints around the local data, you probably want a "real" database, like HSQLDB or a commercial product that supports "embedding" in a Java process.

There's another side to this story, however—the blindingly obvious realization that a remote database requires a network to reach it. While this may seem like an unnecessary statement, think about that for a moment, and then consider the ubiquitous sales-order application tied into the inventory database for a large manufacturing company. We release the application onto the salesperson's laptop, and off the salesperson goes to pay a visit to the VP of a client company. After a little wining, dining, and 18 holes on a pretty exclusive golf course, the VP's ready to place that million-dollar order. The salesperson fires up the laptop, goes to place the order, and to his horror, gets an error: "database not found." Sitting in the golf club's posh restaurant, our plucky salesperson suddenly pales, turns to the VP, and says, "Hey, um, can we go back to your office so I can borrow your network?"

Assuming the VP actually lets our intrepid salesperson make use of her network to connect back to the salesperson's home network via VPN, assuming the salesperson knows how to set that up on his laptop, assuming the IT staff at home has opened a VPN in the corporate network, and assuming the application actually works with any speed over the VPN connection, the salesperson's credibility is taking a pretty serious beating here. On top of this, the VP has every reason to refuse the salesperson the network connection entirely—it's something of a security risk, after all, to let foreign machines onto the network behind the firewall. And the IT staff at home has every reason to keep the database as far away from the "outside world" as possible, VPN or no VPN. By the time the salesperson returns to the home office to place the order (scribbled on the napkin from the posh restaurant), the VP may have changed her mind, or the salesperson may have forgotten to get some important detail onto the napkin, and so on. (It's for reasons like these that salespeople are trained to place the order as quickly as possible as soon as the customer approves it.)

In some circles, this is called the *traveling salesman problem* (not to be confused with the problem-solving cheapest-way-to-travel version of the problem commonly discussed in artificial intelligence textbooks). The core of the problem is simple: you can't always assume the network will be available. In many cases, you want to design the application to make sure it can run without access to the network, in a disconnected mode. This isn't the same as offering up a well-formatted, nicely handled SQLException when the router or hub hiccups; this is designing the application to take the salesperson's order on the standalone laptop with no network anywhere in sight anytime soon. When designing for this situation, ask yourself how the application will behave when users are 37,000 feet in the air, trying to sell widgets to somebody they just met on the airplane.

One of the easiest ways to accommodate this scenario is to keep a localized database running, with a complete data dump of the centralized database on the same machine as the client (which, by the way, should probably be a rich-client application since the network won't be there to connect to the HTTP server, either—see Item 51). When the machine is connected via the network to the remote database, it updates itself with the latest-and-greatest data from the centralized database. Not necessarily the complete schema, mind you, but enough to be able to operate without requiring the remote database. For example, in the hypothetical sales application, just the order inventory, detail information, and prices would probably be enough—a complete dump of open sales, their history, and shipping information probably doesn't need to be captured locally. Then, when new orders are placed, the application can update the local tables running on the same machine.

Some of you are undoubtedly cringing at the entire suggestion. "Not connected to the remote database? Inconceivable! How do we avoid data integrity errors? That's why we centralized the database in the first place! After all, if there are only 100 widgets left, and both Susan and Steve sell those last 100 widgets to different clients via their laptop systems, we have an obvious concurrency issue when we sync their data up against the centralized system. Any system architect knows that!"

Take a deep breath. Ask yourself how you're going to handle this scenario anyway, because whether it happens at the time the salesperson places the order or when the order goes into the database, the same problem is still happening. Then go take a look at Item 33 as one way to solve it.

Normally, in a connected system, inventory checking occurs when the salesperson places the order—if the requested number of widgets isn't available on the shelves, we want to key the order with some kind of red flag and either not let the order be placed or somehow force the salesperson to acknowledge that the inventory isn't available at the moment. In the connected version of the application, this red flag often comes via a message box or alert window—how would this be any different from doing it later, when the salesperson is synchronizing the data against the centralized system? In fact, this may be a preferable state of affairs, because that alert window could potentially ruin the sale. If the VP sees the message she may rethink placing the order: "Well, I'll bet your competitor has them in stock, and we need these widgets right now," even if "right now" means "we can use only 50 a week." Instead, when the red flag goes off back at the office, the salesperson can do a little research (difficult, if not impossible, to do sitting in the client VP's office) before calling the customer to tell them the news. ("Well, we had only 50 widgets here in the warehouse, but Dayton has another 50, and I'm having them express-mailed to you, no charge.")

While the remote database has obvious advantages for enterprise systems—after all, part of our working definition of an enterprise system is that it manages access to resources that must be shared, which implies centralization—the remote database doesn't necessarily serve as the best repository for certain kinds of data (like per-user settings, configuration options, or other nonshared data) or for certain kinds of applications, particularly those that desire or need to run in a disconnected fashion.

Item 45:   Never assume you own the data or the database

Remember that one of our fundamental assumptions about enterprise software (from Chapter 1) is that an enterprise software system is one in which some or all of its resources are shared. In fact, the core of the enterprise system—the data—is most frequently the shared resource in question. Most of the time, we assume that the extent of the sharing occurs among the various users of the enterprise system. However, it doesn't stop there—many enterprise databases count other enterprise systems as part of their userbase, and unfortunately those "users" have much more stringent requirements than usual.

Some of these other systems making use of your database aren't strangers; it's not uncommon, for example, to design or purchase a reporting engine to allow end users to create their own reports from the database. This is a good thing; without that, the need to create the logic and nicely formatted output will fall into developers' laps. While constantly changing reports to keep up with user whims is one way to stay employed for the rest of your life, it also means you never get to do anything else on the project, and that's not my idea of an interesting job. Those reporting engines typically work directly against the database schema, and here's where we need to be careful.

If multiple systems or agents share a resource, the format or schema of that resource cannot change at the whim of one of those systems or agents without causing a ripple effect through the rest. Alterations to the schema, excessive database locks, and relocation of the database instance are changes that may seem localized to just your codebase but will in turn create problems and issues with these other systems. In fact, this is what keeps legacy systems alive for so long—it's extremely difficult to track down every client for a given resource or repository within the company (particularly large companies), much less figure out all the data dependencies of a given client against a single system. As a result, it's far easier to just leave the legacy system in place and create adapters, translators, and proxies than to replace the legacy system with something new.

To the J2EE developer, this has some sobering, if not chilling, implications: you do not own your database, nor do you own the data within it. Even if you are building the database entirely from scratch for this project, even if the project seems to be tucked away in a little corner of the business where nobody else will have any interest in it, you don't own that database. It's only a matter of time before somebody else within the company hears about your little system and wants to gain access to that data, so you start setting up back-end data feeds, direct connections, and so on. Or worse, somebody else on your team sets them up without telling you. Before long, you make a schema change, and people you've never even heard of, much less met, are howling into your phone demanding to know why you broke their application.

The conclusion here is clear: your schema, once designed, is in far greater danger of being locked in than your code. This is where having an encapsulation layer between the users and the database (as discussed in Item 42) becomes so critical—by forcing clients (any clients, including your own code) to go through some kind of encapsulatory barrier, such as a stored procedure layer or Web Service endpoint layer, to gain access to the data, you essentially plan for the future and the fact that others will need access to the data even as you modify the underlying schema and data description definitions.

This also means that the database schema shouldn't be optimized for the J2EE case: be careful when building your schema not to tie it too closely to your object model, be extremely careful about storing serialized Java objects in Binary Large Object (BLOB) fields since doing so means that data cannot be used as part of a SQL query (unless your database supports it, in which case the query will perform extremely slowly), and don't store "magic values" in the database. For example, although it might be convenient to store Java `Date` objects as long integers (the underlying value held in a `java.util.Date`, accessible via `getTime`, and the only nondeprecated way to construct a `java.util.Date`), other languages will have little to no idea what to do with a value like that, and converting it into a date value acceptable to them is difficult. Some databases may try to implicitly convert an integer value into a date, for example, but how they convert the value will be entirely different for each database. Despite the greater work in Java, it's far better to store the date in the database in either a string-based format or as an ANSI-standard `DATETIME`.

In fact, because your database is likely to become a shared database fairly quickly, and because J2EE isn't slated to take over the entire world any time soon (the .NET and PHP programmers may have a few words for those who think it will), you'll generally prefer to put whatever constraints you can into the database, rather than relying on J2EE code to enforce restrictions. For example, given the choice between checking to see whether an incoming string is fewer than 40 characters long before storing it to the database, go ahead and simply rely on database integrity constraints on the table to check the length of the string, rather than doing it in J2EE and setting the column's size to be something larger than that. Since the database is going to go through the size-constraint check anyway, why do it twice? Similarly, model any sort of relationship between tables/entities in the database directly within the database, using foreign-key constraints to ensure that both sides of the constraint are in fact present within the database.

It may seem easier, at first blush, to go ahead and encode this sort of logic directly within your object model and/or domain logic—after all, Java is probably your first language, and it's a natural human tendency to want to solve problems using the tools we're most comfortable with. Resist. The database provides a lot of functionality that can't be easily—or as universally—applied in your J2EE code. For example, most database products support the concept of triggers, blocks of database code that can be executed on any sort of row- or table-based access, giving you the ability to apply domain logic after the row has been inserted, updated, deleted, or whatever. Trying to build this into a J2EE application, which would have to be universally applied across all parts of the system, requires either building a complex notification mechanism into your code (keeping in mind the drawbacks of an RPC-based callback mechanism, as described in Item 20) or hand-coding directly into your domain object representations of the database entities themselves, leading you down a scary road of maintenance nightmares over time.

While it may seem convenient and entirely plausible to take shortcuts in the database layer to make it easier for you as a J2EE developer, resist the urge. Ultimately, it's just going to create more problems if you don't—when the inevitable question, "Hey, we noticed you were capturing some data we were interested in, and we want to get at it, so how can we?" comes up, it's going to be up to you to make that happen, and it'll be a lot easier to take care of at the front of the project than at the back.

Item 46:   Lazy-load infrequently used data

Given the cost of a trip across the network to the remote database, it follows that we don't want to actually pull any data across the network unless we need it.

This seems like a simple idea, but it's remarkable how often it gets left behind in systems that try to hide the database from the programmer—for example, naïve object-relational mapping mechanisms often map objects to tables in a one-to-one fashion, so that any request to retrieve a particular object from the database means every column for a particular row gets pulled across to completely fill out the object in question.

In many cases, this is obviously a bad situation: consider the canonical drill-down scenario, where I want to present a list of items to the user from which he or she selects one (or more) for a more complete examination. If a large number of items must be presented to the user in a summary view for selection, say, 10,000 persons that meet the initial search criteria, pulling each one back in its entirety means 10,000 $\times$ N bytes of data must be sent across the network, where N is the complete size of a single row from the table. If the row has foreign-key relations that must in turn be retrieved as part of this object retrieval (the `Person` has `0..*` `Address` instances associated with it, perhaps), that number easily bloats to unmanageable proportions.

For these reasons, many object-relational mechanisms choose not to retrieve all of the data for a particular row as part of a standard fetch operation but instead choose to lazy-load the data, preferring to take the additional round-trip to the database in exchange for keeping this summary request down to manageable levels. In fact, this is such a common scenario that it has been documented in several places already, most notably as the Lazy Load pattern [Fowler, 200].

Take careful note: the key is to lazy-load infrequently used data, not just data that hasn't been used yet.

Here the entity beans portion of EJB tends to fall down in catastrophic fashion, similar to the classic $N+1$ query problem. Many EJB entity bean implementers decided that since we wanted to avoid pulling back any data that wasn't going to be used immediately, when retrieving an entity bean from a `Home`-based finder method, *nothing* was going to be retrieved from the actual data store (relational database), and instead only the primary key for the row would be stored in the entity bean inside the EJB container. Then, when a client accessed a property method (`get` or `set`) for that entity bean, a separate query would be issued to retrieve or update that particular column value for that particular bean.

The dangerous part, of course, occurred if you wrote client-side code that did something like this under the hood of the entity bean:

```
PersonHome personHome = getHomeFromSomewhere();
Person person = personHome.findByPrimaryKey(1234);

String firstName = person.getFirstName();
String lastName = person.getLastName();
int age = person.getAge();
```

With such code, you were making requests like this:

```
SELECT primary_key FROM Person
    WHERE primary_key = 1234;

SELECT first_name FROM Person
    WHERE primary_key = 1234;

SELECT last_name FROM Person
    WHERE primary_key = 1234;

SELECT age FROM Person WHERE primary_key = 1234;
```

In addition to this being a phenomenal waste of CPU cycles (parsing each query, projecting a query plan for each, marshaling the returned column in a relational tuple, and so on), as well as flooding the cache to the point of irrelevancy, you're also taking a huge risk that the data doesn't change between bean method calls—remember, each of those calls represents a separate EJB-driven transaction, thus leaving open the possibility that a different client could change the same row between calls (see Item 31). For these reasons and more, two patterns were born: the Session Façade [Alur/Crupi/Malks, 341] and the Data Transfer Object [Fowler, 401].

The problem, however, isn't necessarily with the idea of lazy-loading; the problem is knowing *what* data to lazy-load. In the case of a container-managed entity bean implementation, where all details of SQL are hidden from the EJB developer, the EJB container has no way to know which data elements are more likely to be used than others, so it makes the more drastic assumption that all of them won't necessarily be used. In retrospect, this is probably a bad decision, one that's only slightly better than the other alternative left to the container implementor, that of assuming that *all* of the columns will be used. The ideal situation would be for the entity bean implementor to allow you to provide some kind of usage hints about which fields should be pulled back as part of pulling the initial bean state across and which ones would be best retrieved lazily, but such things are vendor-dependent and reduce your portability significantly (if you care—see Item 11).

If you're writing your own relational access code, such as writing a BMP entity bean or just writing plain-vanilla JDBC or SQL/J code, the decision of what to pull back falls into your lap once again. Here, as with any SQL access, you should be explicit about precisely what data you want:

nothing more, nothing less. This means avoiding SQL queries that look like this one:

```
SELECT * FROM Person
  WHERE ...
```

Although it may not seem all that important at the time you write this query, you're pulling back every column in the `Person` table when this code gets executed. If, at first, the definition of the `Person` table happens to match the exact list of data you want, it seems so much easier and simpler to use the wildcard * to retrieve all columns, but remember—you don't own the database (see Item 45). Several things can happen to the database definition that will create problems in your code if you use the wildcard.

- *Additional columns may get added.* Hey, updates happen, and unless you want the thankless job of going back through every line of SQL code you've ever written to make sure you're dealing with the additional columns, you're going to be pulling back data you didn't want.
- *Wildcard* SELECT *statements don't specify a column order.* Unfortunately, the order of columns returned in a SELECT * query isn't guaranteed by the SQL standard, and in some cases not even by the database product you're using—this means that your underlying JDBC code, which relies on an implicit order of columns returned, will be treated to a whole host of SQLException instances when trying to retrieve the first_name column as an int. Worse yet, this kind of problem won't show up in your development database because the database administrator isn't tweaking and toying with the database definitions to try to improve performance—it will only show up in production systems, leaving you scratching your head in confusion with little to go on when trying to ascertain precisely what the problem is.
- *The implicit documentation hint is lost.* Let's be honest, it's just clearer to be explicit about what you're retrieving when you list the columns. It also means one less comment in your Java code to maintain; whenever possible, it's better to create situations where code speaks for itself.

Despite the additional typing required, it's almost always preferable to list the columns explicitly. Fortunately, it's also something that's fairly easy to generate via a code-generation tool, should the opportunity arise.

Lazy-loading isn't just restricted to loading columns from the query, however. There are other opportunities to apply the same principle to larger scales. For example, go back to the canonical drill-down scenario. In most thin-client applications, when retrieving search results, we often display only the first 10, 20, maybe 50 results to the user, depending on the size of the results window. We don't want to display to the user the complete set of results—which sometimes stretches into the thousands of items when the user provides particularly vague criteria. Reasons for this are varied but boil down to the idea that the user will typically either find the desired result in the first 10 or 20 items or go back and try the search again, this time with more stringent criteria.

So what happened to the other 990 rows you retrieved as part of that request? Wasted space, wasted CPU cycles, wasted bandwidth.

There are a couple of ways to control how much data gets pulled back as part of the SQL query. One is at the JDBC level, by setting `setFetchSize` to retrieve only a number of items equivalent to the display window you wish to present to the user: if you're showing only the first 10 items retrieved, then use `setFetchSize(10)` on the `ResultSet` before retrieving the first row via `next`. This way, you're certain that only that number of rows is retrieved, and you know that you're making one round-trip to retrieve this data you know you're going to use. Alternatively, you can let the driver try to keep what it believes to be the optimal fetch size for that driver/database combination, and instead choose to limit the absolute number of rows returned from this statement by calling `setMaxRows`; any additional rows beyond the number passed in to `setMaxRows` will be silently dropped and never sent.

Another approach, supported by some databases, is to use the TOP qualifier as part of the request itself, as in `SELECT TOP 5 first_name, last_name FROM Person WHERE`. . . . Only the first five rows that meet the predicate will be returned from the database. Although a nonstandard extension, it's still useful and is supported by a number of the database vendors. TOP is SQL Server syntax; other databases use terms like FIRST (Informix), LIMIT (MySQL), or SAMPLE (Oracle). All work similarly.

Again, the idea is simple: only pull back what data is required at this time, on the grounds that you want to avoid pulling back excessive amounts of data that won't be used. Be careful, however; you're standing on a slippery slope when you start thinking about lazy-loading, and if you're not aware of it, it's easy to find yourself in a situation where you're excessively lazy-loading data elements across the wire, resulting in what Fowler calls "ripple-loading" or as it's more commonly known, the $N+1$ query problem [Fowler, 270]. In those situations, sometimes it's better to eager-load the data (see Item 47) in order to avoid network traffic.

Item 47: Eager-load frequently used data

Eager-loading is the opposite of lazy-loading (see Item 46): rather than taking the additional network round-trip to retrieve data later, when it's needed, we decide to pull extra data across the wire now and just hold it on the database client on the grounds that we'll need it eventually.

This idea has a couple of implications. First, the payoff—actually accessing the extra data—has to justify the cost of marshaling it across the wire from server to client. If the data never gets used, eager-loading it is a waste of network bandwidth and hurts scalability. For a few columns in a single-row retrieval query, this is probably an acceptable loss compared with the cost of making the extra round-trip back to the database for those same columns. For 10,000 rows, each unused column just plain hurts, particularly if more than one client executes this code simultaneously.

Second, we're also implicitly assuming the cost of actually moving the data across the wire isn't all that excessive. For example, if we're talking about pulling a large BLOB column across, make sure that this column will be needed, since most databases aren't particularly optimal about retrieving and sending BLOBs across.

You don't hear much about eager-loading data because to many developers it conjures up some horrific images of early object databases and their propensity to eager-load objects when some "root" object was requested. For example, if a Company holds zero to many Department objects, and each Department holds zero to many Employee objects, and each Employee holds zero to many PerformanceReview objects . . . well, imagine how many objects will be retrieved when asking for a list of all the Company objects currently stored in the database. If all we were interested in is a list of Company names, all the Department, Employee, and PerformanceReview objects are obviously a huge waste of time and energy to send across the wire.

In fact, eager-loading has nothing to do with object databases (despite the fact that they were blamed for it)—I've worked with object-relational layers that did exactly the same thing, with exactly the same kind of results. The problem, although "solved" differently, is the same as that for lazy-loading: the underlying plumbing layer just doesn't know which data to pull back when retrieving object state. So, in the case of the eager-loading system, we err on the side of fewer network round-trips and pull it *all* back.

Despite the obvious bandwidth consumption, eager-loading does have a number of advantages to it that lazy-loading can't match.

First, eager-loading the complete set of data you'll need helps tremendously with concurrency situations. Remember, in the lazy-loaded scenario, it was possible (without Session Façade [Alur/Crupi/Malks, 341] in place) for clients to see semantically corrupt data because each entity bean access resulted in a separate SQL query under separate transactions. This meant that another client could modify that row between transactions, thus effectively invalidating everything that had been retrieved before, without us knowing about it. When eager-loading data, we can pull across a complete dump of the row as part of a single transaction, thus obviating the need for another trip to the database and eliminating the corrupt semantic data possibility—there's no "second query" to return changed data. In essence, eager-loading fosters a pass-by-value dynamic, as opposed to lazy-loading's pass-by-reference approach.

This has some powerful implications for lock windows (see Item 29), too. The container won't have to hold a lock against the row (or page, or table, depending on your database's locking defaults) for the entire duration of the session bean's transaction, if accessed via EJB, or the explicit transaction maintained either through a JTA `Transaction` or JDBC `Connection`. Shorter lock windows mean lower contention, which means better scalability.

Of course, eager-loading all the data also means there's a window of opportunity for other clients to modify the data, since you're no longer holding a transactional lock against it, but this can be solved through a variety of means, including explicit transactional locks, pessimistic concurrency models (see Item 34), and optimistic concurrency models (see Item 33).

Second, as already implied, eager-loading data can drastically reduce the total time spent on the wire retrieving data for a given collection if that data can be safely assumed to be needed. Consider, for example, user preferences: data that individual users can define in order to customize their use of the application in a variety of ways, such as background images for the main window, whether to use the "basic" or "advanced" menus, and so on. This is data that may not be needed immediately at the time the user logs in, but it's a fair bet that all of it will be used at some point or another within the application. We could lazy-load the data, but considering that each data element (configuration item) will probably be needed independently of the others, we're looking at, again, an *N*+1 query problem, in this case retrieving each individual data element rather than individual row. Go ahead and pull the entire set across at once, and just hold it locally for use by the code that needs to consult user preferences when deciding how to render output, windowing decorations, or whatever.

Eager-loading isn't just for pulling back columns in a row, either. As with lazy-loading, you can apply eager-loading principles at scopes larger than just individual rows. For example, we can apply eager-loading principles across tables and dependent data, so that if a user requests a `Person` object, we load all of the associated `Address`, `PerformanceReview`, and other objects associated with this `Person`, even though it might mean multiple queries executed in some kind of single-round-trip batch form (see Item 48).

While we're at it, there's never any reason why a table that holds read-only values shouldn't be eager-loaded. For example, many systems put internationalized text (like days of the week, months of the year, and so on) into tables in the database for easy modification at the client site. Since the likelihood of somebody changing the names of the days of the week is pretty low, go ahead and read the entirety of this table once and hold the results in some kind of in-process collection class or `RowSet` for later consultation. Granted, it might make system startup take a bit longer, but end users will see faster access on each request-response trip. (In many respects, this is just a flavor of Item 4.)

In the end, eager-loading data is just as viable and useful an optimization as lazy-loading data, despite its ugly reputation. In fact, in many cases it's a far more acceptable tradeoff than the lazy-loading scenario, given the relatively cheap cost of additional memory compared with the expensive and slow network access we currently live under. As always, be sure to profile (see Item 10) before doing either lazy- or eager-loading optimizations, but if an eager-load can save you a couple of network accesses, it's generally worth the extra bandwidth on the first trip and the extra memory to hold the eager-loaded data.

Item 48:   Batch SQL work to avoid round-trips

Given the cost of moving across the network, we need to minimize the number of times we travel across the network connection to another machine. Unfortunately, the default behavior of the JDBC driver is to work with a one-statement, one-round-trip model: each time `execute` (or one of its variations, `executeUpdate` or `executeQuery`) runs, the driver marshals up the request and sends it to the database where it is parsed, executed, and returned. This tedious process consumes many CPU cycles in pure overhead on each trip. By batching statements together, we can send several SQL statements in a single round-trip to the database, thus avoiding some of that overhead.

Bear in mind that while this is predominantly a state management issue, trying to improve performance by reducing the number of times we have to hit the network, it also applies to transactional processing. We're likely to be in a situation where we're holding open transactional locks, and therefore we want to minimize the amount of time those locks are held open (see Item 29).

There's another element to this, however; sometimes multiple statements need to be executed in a group in order to carry out a logical request. Normally, you would want to do all this under a single transaction (thus requiring that you `setAutoCommit(false)` on the `Connection` you're using), but that doesn't imply that the driver will do it all as part of a single round-trip. It's entirely plausible that the driver will send each statement over individually, all while holding the transactional lock open. Therefore, since it's all happening under a single transaction, it's far better to execute them as a group. The transaction itself is an all-or-nothing situation anyway.

```
Connection conn = getConnectionFromSomeplace();
conn.setAutoCommit(false);
Statement stmt = conn.createStatement();

// Step 1: insert the person
stmt.addBatch("INSERT INTO person (id, f_name, l_name) " +
  "VALUES (" + id + ", '" + firstName + "', '" +
  lastName + "')");
// Step 2: insert the person's account
stmt.addBatch("INSERT INTO account (personID, type) " +
  "VALUES (" + id + ", 'SAVINGS')");
```

```
// Execute the batch
int[] results = stmt.executeBatch();
// Check the batched results
boolean completeSuccess = true;
for (int i=0; i<results.length; i++)
{
  if (results[i] >= 0 || results[i] ==
    Statement.SUCCESS_NO_INFO)
    /* Do nothing-statement was successful */ ;
  else
  {
    /* Something went wrong; alert user? */
    completeSuccess = false;
  }
}

if (completeSuccess)
  conn.commit();
else
  conn.rollback();
```

In this code, we create a `Statement` and use it to execute two non-SELECT SQL statements against the database. (Batching doesn't work with SELECT statements.) In this case, we're adding a person to the database and adding information about the person's new savings account. Note that the key to executing in batch here is to use the `executeBatch` method on `Statement`; this tells the driver to send the statements over to the database en masse.

The `executeBatch` method returns an array of integers as a way to indicate the success or failure of each of the batched methods. Each element in the array corresponds to one batched statement; a zero or positive number indicates the "update count" result (the number of rows affected by the call), and a value of SUCCESS_NO_INFO indicates the call succeeded but didn't have an update count.

In the event one of the statements fails, JDBC allows the driver to take one of several options. It can throw an exception and halt execution of statements at that point, or it can continue processing statements, in which case the integer in the results array will be set to EXECUTE_FAILED.

Note that executing in batch doesn't imply transactional boundaries—the two statements have executed, but because `AutoCommit` is turned off, they have not yet committed to the database. Therefore, we need to either commit or roll back the work done; in this case, we commit only if all the statements executed successfully, a reasonable policy. If you call `commit` before calling `executeBatch`, the batched statements will be sent over as if you'd called `executeBatch` just prior to `commit`. If you try to batch with `Auto Commit` set to `true`, the results are undefined by the JDBC Specification—which is shorthand for "quite likely to yield some kind of exception."

Using JDBC's `executeBatch` method isn't the only way to batch execution, however. Because many databases support some kind of logical line termination character, thus creating the ability to execute multiple SQL statements as part of one logical line of input, it's possible to write JDBC calls like this:

```
Connection conn = ...; // Obtain from someplace
Statement stmt = conn.createStatement();
stmt.execute("SELECT first_name, last_name FROM Person " +
    "WHERE primary_key = 1234; " +
    "SELECT ci.content, ci.type " +
    "FROM ContactInfo ci, PerConLookup pc " +
    "WHERE ci.primary_key = pc.contactInfo_key " +
    "AND pc.person_key = 1234");
ResultSet personRS = stmt.getResultSet();
    // The first SELECT


if (stmt.getMoreResults())
{
  // The other SELECT
  ResultSet contactInfoRS = stmt.getResultSet();
}
```

Although more awkward to work with,[5] batching statements this way carries the advantage of working for both SELECT statements as well as INSERT, UPDATE, and DELETE statements, all while furthering the basic goal, that of trying to amortize the cost of several SQL queries by running them in a single request-response cycle against the database.

---

5. In production code you should check the Boolean return value from `execute` to make sure the first SELECT statement produced results, rather than ignore it as I have here for clarity.

Item 49: Know your JDBC provider

Despite all the revisions and years behind it, the JDBC Specification still doesn't mandate a large number of particulars—deliberately. For example, when a `ResultSet` is created, typically (although again, this is purely by convention, not a requirement) the `ResultSet` holds only the first *N* rows, where *N* is some number that sounded good to your JDBC vendor. For some of the major vendors, this *N* value is—I'm not kidding you—one. Fortunately, this value is not only discoverable but also configurable via `getFetchSize` and `setFetchSize` on the `ResultSet` API, but the point still remains: Do you know what the default is, and is it acceptable? Be sure to check the Boolean return value from `setFetchSize` to ensure you aren't asking for a fetch size that's larger than what the driver and/or the database supports.

Many features of JDBC aren't available, depending on the capabilities of the driver, and your decision regarding how to build the JDBC code using the driver could be deeply affected based on this information. For example, when retrieving data from the `ResultSet`, there appear to be two entirely equivalent ways to obtain the data: either by ordinal position within the `ResultSet` or by column name. Is there any real difference between them, besides perhaps programmer convenience?

It turns out that there's a very real difference between them, depending entirely on your JDBC driver implementation. The first release of the JDBC Specification (the version that shipped with JDK 1.1) only mandated that JDBC drivers provide *firehose cursor* support—that is, once a row or column has been pulled from the cursor, it can never be obtained again. This has huge implications when retrieving data out of the `ResultSet`, in that if you pull a column's data in anything other than the order in which it was declared in the SQL statement, you'll be skipping past columns that can then never be retrieved:

```
ResultSet rs =
    stmt.executeQuery("SELECT id, first_name, last_name " +
                      "FROM person");
while (rs.next())
{
  String firstName = rs.getString("first_name");
  String lastName = rs.getString("last_name");
  int id = rs.getInt("id");
```

```
    // Error! This will throw a SQLException in a JDBC 1.0
    // driver
}
```

Say you've been working with a JDBC 2.0 or better driver up until this point. If somebody deploys your code to use the JDBC-ODBC driver (which is a bad idea from the beginning, since the JDBC-ODBC driver is an unsupported, bug-ridden 1.0 driver that is incredibly slow and is rumored to leak memory in some ODBC driver configurations), suddenly your code will start tossing SQLException instances for no apparent reason.

Now, if you are truly concerned about writing portable J2EE code, you need to account for the possibility of a 1.0 driver by ensuring that this particular scenario never occurs; therefore, you need to always retrieve data in its exact order, and the easiest way to do this is to use the ordinal form of the methods:

```
ResultSet rs =
    Stmt.executeQuery("SELECT id, first_name, last_name " +
                      "FROM person");
while (rs.next())
{
    int age = rs.getInt(1);
    String firstName = rs.getString(2);
    String lastName = rs.getString(3);
}
```

Although not overly painful to write, this code does have several drawbacks. First, if a programmer (or, potentially worse, a database administrator unfamiliar with this little quirk of the JDBC 1.0 API) ever modifies the SQL statement, the corresponding data-retrieval code in the loop will need to be updated to reflect the change in order of columns, or SQLException instances will start to get thrown left and right. (By the way, it's true that using the ordinal form of the functions is slightly faster than using the column-based form, but changing your code to use the ordinal form purely for performance reasons is a micro-optimization and should be avoided, particularly since you lose the inherent documentation hint that using the column names give. If you find yourself tempted to do so, a large number of other optimizations will likely yield a better return, so bypass this one.)

It's not just a simple matter of keeping track of the order of columns (which, by the way, argues against ever issuing a SQL SELECT statement that uses * instead of the individual column names). You need to know whether your driver supports statement batching (see Item 48) and isolation levels (see Item 35), which scalar functions it might support, and so on. Much of this information is available via the DatabaseMetaData class, an instance of which is obtained from a Connection, or to a lesser degree from the ResultSetMetaData class, obtained from a given ResultSet. *SQL Performance Tuning* [Gulutzan/Pelzer] provides several charts describing the results returned from eight vendor databases (IBM, Informix, Ingres, Inter-Base, Microsoft SQL Server, MySQL, Oracle, and Sybase), but you'll want to run some tests regardless—you can't be certain the chart will be true for your particular database, even if it's one of the vendors listed, because capabilities can change from one release to the next.

Another area of interest to the JDBC programmer is that of thread safety: Is it safe to invoke the driver from multiple threads? Do you need to synchronize on Connection, Statement, or ResultSet objects when accessing them from multiple threads? For example, the JDBC-ODBC driver isn't thread safe, so it's up to you to ensure that the driver is never accessed by more than one thread at a time; otherwise you run the risk of some Seriously Bad Things happening in the ODBC driver underneath your Java code. (Which once again underscores that there's never a good reason to use the JDBC-ODBC driver for production code.)

One of the classic performance- and scalability-driven suggestions made in numerous JDBC and J2EE books is the PreparedStatement-over-Statement idea: that you should always prefer to use a PreparedStatement instead of a regular Statement. The argument is simple: because each call out to the database requires a certain amount of work (parsing the SQL, creating a query plan, and running it all through the optimizer, and so forth), it's better to amortize that overhead by keeping those preparations around from one call to the next, assuming the same call will be made again. A PreparedStatement will "prepare" the SQL call once (minus the parameters you want to pass in, since those aren't known yet, so it can't prepare those) and thus you'll get better performance on subsequent calls.

While using PreparedStatement is a necessity from a security standpoint (see Item 61), from a performance and/or scalability standpoint, it's not quite so clear. For example, the JDBC Specification states that when a

Connection is closed, the corresponding Statement objects associated with that Connection also implicitly close. So when you return a Connection obtained from a connection pool back to the connection pool, does that in turn close the PreparedStatement obtained from that Connection, or will the underlying physical connection remain open, thus leaving the PreparedStatement alive and ready to receive additional requests? What about a CallableStatement, since it inherits from PreparedStatement and therefore should obey the same contract as given for PreparedStatement?

Unfortunately, while I could wave my hands here and state that "obviously, REAL drivers would keep the pooled Statement around, only a simpleton or moron wouldn't do this," the fact remains that sometimes you have to use software written by simpletons and morons, and the only way to know for certain whether your database and/or database driver is in that category is to test and find out.

This discussion of PreparedStatement takes a sharp left turn, by the way, when discussing some database vendors (most notably PostgreSQL) that cause a PreparedStatement to become unprepared when a transaction end (COMMIT) occurs; that is, the following code [Gulutzan/Pelzer, 336] won't work as expected, despite the JDBC Specification's insistence that it should:

```
PreparedStatement pstmt =
    connection.prepareStatement(". . .");
boolean autocommit =
    connection.getAutoCommit(); // Let's assume it's true
pstmt.executeUpdate();
    // COMMIT happens automatically, since autocommit == true
pstmt.executeUpdate();
    // FAILS! PreparedStatement pstmt is no longer prepared
```

If that doesn't convince you that you need to know what your JDBC driver does under the hood, then I wish you the best of luck.

The easiest way, in many respects, to know what your driver does is to fire up your database's query-execution profiler tool and have a look at what actually happens when the JDBC query executes. In some circles, this is known as *exploration testing* and is more extensively documented by Stu Halloway (http://www.relevancellc.com); put simply, write a series of JUnit-based tests that exercise your assumptions regarding what happens when you execute a sequence of calls (such as the `PreparedStatement` code shown earlier), and rerun those tests against a variety of scenarios, such as different JDBC drivers, different vendor databases, or even different versions of the same vendor's database. Far better to be surprised during an exploration test run than to be surprised during deployment into production, at the client site, or in the middle of the night after the database administrators upgrade the database without your knowledge (or consent).

Item 50: Tune your SQL

Quiz time: When are two logically equivalent SQL statements not equivalent? Consider the following pair of logically equal SQL statements:

```
SELECT * FROM Table WHERE column1='A' AND column2='B'
```

```
SELECT * FROM Table WHERE column2='B' AND column1='A'
```

Which would you say executes faster?[6]

Answer: You can't tell, and neither can the optimizer in most databases. But if you happen to know, for your particular database schema, this particular client, and/or this particular query, that the likelihood of `column2` being B is a lot less likely, then the second SQL statement will execute faster than the first, even though the two are logically equivalent. (By the way, never do this for Oracle databases when using the cost-based optimizer—it will do exactly the wrong thing.)

Or, as another example, how about these two statements?

```
SELECT * FROM Table WHERE column1=5 AND
    NOT (column3=7 OR column1=column2)
```

```
SELECT * FROM Table WHERE column1=5 AND column3<>7 AND
    column2<>5
```

Answer: For five of eight popular databases, the second turns out to be faster.[7] Again, these are logically identical statements, so the actual results

---

6. This example appears in *SQL Performance Tuning* [Gulutzan/Pelzer, 24].

7. This example appears in *SQL Performance Tuning* [Gulutzan/Pelzer, 16].

returned will be the same; it's just that the database optimizer treats the second one in a different fashion than the first, thereby yielding a better response time.

Tuning SQL remains the number one optimization you can make when working with a relational database. Despite what JDO and entity bean vendors have been trying to achieve for the last five years, we're still in an era where SQL matters. Yes, vendors have made huge strides in making their objects-first persistence models not suck as badly as they first did, but the fact remains that if the database itself can't tell the difference between the two statements, it's highly unlikely that your object-relational layer will be able to. This is why it's crucial for an object-relational system to offer you, at the least, some kind of hook point (see Item 6) to pass in raw SQL that you can tune and optimize as necessary for those queries executed most often.

By the way, bear in mind that for some databases, these two statements are considered to be entirely different and therefore require reparsing, replanning, and reexecution:

```
SELECT column1*4 FROM Table1 WHERE COLUMN1=COLUMN2 + 7
```

```
SELECT Column1 * 4 FROM Table1  WHERE column1=(column2 + 7)
```

That is to say, even though these statements are precisely identical in what they're doing, because the capitalization and whitespace used within them are different, the database treats them as separate and unrelated statements. With a tool generating your queries, we would hope that they're being generated in a consistent style, but can you be certain? (Ideally, you'd know whether this sort of thing bothers your database before worrying about it too much, but that means you're OK with *a priori* vendor awareness like that; see Item 11.)

In many cases, you need to know what SQL is actually being executed against your database before you can think about trying to tune it. For some object-relational systems this can be a difficult prospect if they don't expose the actual generated or dynamically constructed SQL code to you. Fortunately, an answer is only a short step away.

First, most database products offer some kind of database-based view of queries being executed against a given database instance, so it's usually pretty easy to fire up the database profiler tool and take a look at the actual SQL. (While you're at it, assuming your database provides query analysis as part of that same profiler, take the SQL queries and run them against the profiler to see how the database will attack executing this particular query; see Item 10.) This should tell you how your favorite object-relational tool is generating the SQL queries and thereby give you a good idea whether SQL optimization is in order.

If you're working with a database that doesn't provide such a tool (time to get a new database, in my opinion, but sometimes you have to work with the tools at hand), assuming your object-relational layer is still going through JDBC to talk to the database itself, you can play a small trick on the object-relational layer by handing it a JDBC driver that "leaks" the actual queries being fed through it. It's the P6Spy driver, available from http://www.p6spy.com, and its operation is deceptively simple: it exposes the same JDBC driver interface that every other JDBC driver on the planet provides, but it doesn't do any actual work, instead delegating that to a JDBC driver for which you provide configuration data. Instead, the P6Spy driver simply echoes the SQL queries to multiple sources, including Log4J logging streams.

For those situations where your object-relational layer isn't doing the optimal SQL thing and the object-relational layer doesn't provide some kind of hook point to pass in optimal SQL, you have a few options.

- *Switch tools.* There are plenty of other object-relational tools out there, both commercial and open-source, that you shouldn't feel "stuck" with one that doesn't give you the necessary optimization hook points.
- *Follow the Fast Lane pattern* [Alur/Crupi/Malks, 1st ed.], which advocates the idea of doing direct JDBC access against the database, thereby giving you direct control over the SQL being sent. In the case of EJB-based access, this means either doing direct JDBC calls from your session beans or rewriting your CMP entity beans as BMP beans. Unfortunately, this pattern has a number of direct drawbacks (which is probably why it's not present in the second edition), including the fact that if the object-relational layer is doing any sort of cache management, you'll be bypassing that cache management and any implicit Identity Map [Fowler, 195] that's being maintained. Perhaps you can live with the loss of the caching behavior; however, if the Identity Map [Fowler, 195] is being maintained in order to allow the object-relational layer to hold off sending any uncommitted changes to the data, you'll bypass that and create a nasty little concurrency problem for yourself.

- *Pull a bait-and-switch with your object-relational tool,* taking a cue from the P6Spy driver (a classic Decorator [GOF, 175] if ever there was one). Write a JDBC driver look-alike—that is, a class that implements the JDBC driver interfaces—that listens for particular queries that match the queries you want to optimize, and replace those queries with hand-tuned, optimized SQL before handing the query off to the real JDBC driver you've wrapped around. You do take an extra layer of method calls as a hit to the driver, but assuming you've done your homework (see Item 10), the gains from the tuned SQL will more than offset the cost of the additional method call.

Whichever method you choose, before you start caching off JNDI lookup results as an optimization, take a hard look at the SQL being executing on your behalf—more often than not, optimizations in the SQL can yield a far greater return on your investment in time and energy than anything else you attempt. Even if your CMP entity bean layer is doing some kind of adaptive SQL generation scheme, you'll want to know about it and make sure that your database administrator is doing his or her part not to work against that.

6 | Presentation

It's all just dialogs and data.

—Mike Cohn

Presentation: it seems so simple. Just toss up some dialogs, some buttons, a few list boxes and scroll bars, and it'll be obvious to the user what's going on, right? Take the users' input, scrub it, send it back to the server, and we're done.

For many developers, building the user interface is quite possibly the most fun part of the job. Part of the reason lies in the fact that the user interface, unlike much of the rest of the system, is a visible, tangible, measurable indicator of progress. This morning, I had an empty window—this afternoon, I have a screen that a user can interact with (even though it does nothing under the hood). The user interface is also one of the few parts of the system that users can understand and appreciate. Very few, if any, users will be able to look at your transactional-processing logic and say, "Oooh, ACID transactions. Way cool—you guys rock." But show average users a slick GUI in a progress meeting, show them how we can automatically populate a UI form with data based on a field they've just entered, and watch an entire room melt with love for the programming team. Given the choice between a "ho-hum, whatever" reaction and an expression of undying love and respect, is it any wonder that many programmers prefer to build the user interface?

Unfortunately, perils lie in wait for the naïve UI programmer.

Many developers discover, usually just days before the project is scheduled to ship, that users have a very firm mental model of what the system was supposed to do, and if the user interface doesn't reflect that mental model, the users' appreciation will quickly degenerate into scorn. User interfaces tend to be the most heavily modified part of the application, as developers try to placate the user community with last-second changes that seem to be based on nothing more than whims.

Also, as many users learn over time, programmers are not always the best ones to design the user interface in the first place. Alan Cooper, father of Visual Basic and author of UI books *The Inmates Are Running the Asylum* [Cooper99] and *About Face 2.0* [Cooper03], has made a career out of consulting with companies on customer-oriented UI design. He cites UI research from some of the most heavily user-centric applications (particularly those from a large software company in the Pacific Northwest) in his examples of botched UI design. What seems obvious to us as developers tends to be cryptic and obscure to those who don't write code for a living.

And as if those two traps weren't enough, for Web-based applications things get even worse. While the Web brought millions of casual computer users together into a huge, interconnected community, the principal portal of communication for those users—the Web browser—took user interfaces back by at least a decade, returning us to applications whose fanciest UI idiom was the graphical push button. What's worse, the HTML-based application depends entirely on the server; while this means that no special software is required on the end-user machine to execute the HTML-based application, it also means that everything must be conveyed over the network, adding significantly to the bandwidth consumption requirements. For applications that need to scale out to millions of concurrent users, greater bandwidth consumption is exactly what we need to avoid.

The net result? There's more to building the presentation than just slapping some HTML on a JSP page.

Item 51: Consider rich-client UI technologies

No, this tip doesn't refer to the wealthy customer who wants changes made to the application. Instead, it refers to that form of presentation that offers a richer, more powerful user interface, in contrast to the thin (HTML-browser-based) client.

The HTML-browser-based thin-client application offers a significant advantage over traditional two-tier, fat-client, client/server applications: low to no deployment costs. Because the HTML resides on the server, deploying a new version of the application requires zero client-side installation. As long as the client has a Web browser, he or she is ready to use the system. Since literally every operating system on the planet offers a browser as part of the base installation, clients can start using the application as soon as the upload to the server is complete. Even more importantly, updates to the application can happen as often as necessary because nothing needs updating on the client machine. This Zero Deployment scenario is powerful, particularly for enterprise applications because they have a tendency to evolve more quickly than shrink-wrap software. Users don't even need to know when a new version rolls out—they're always downloading what's on the server anyway.

However, HTML also carries with it a number of disadvantages.

- *Portability:* HTML was designed from its inception to be a cross-platform technology, and as a result, it suffers somewhat from that portability. Form controls are rendered entirely as the host (the browser) wishes, so HTML forms behave differently from platform to platform. This can make designing easy-to-use forms difficult, if not impossible, particularly if the forms are complex.
- *State management:* Because the Web browser can't hold client-side state (aside from cookies, which are extremely limited in scope), an HTML-based thin-client application needs to hold all user state on the server, identified by an opaque token usually stored in a cookie or as part of subsequent requests (also known as *URL rewriting*). Unfortunately, this also increases the load on the server and reduces the server's scalability. An alternative is to make the application entirely stateless and pass all data required between the browser and the server, usually encoded in hidden form fields or embedded inside request URLs. Unfortunately, this isn't a perfect solution either, since now additional bandwidth is consumed to transfer all that state back and forth on every request. There's also a security concern. A well-known (perhaps apocryphal) story tells of a creative consumer who noticed that the price of the computer system he was about to purchase online was stored in a hidden field on the form. He created a local HTML page to mimic the online purchase order form but coded the hidden price field to contain a value of $1. He submitted it, and it was accepted—in essence, he purchased a $5,000 system for exactly $1. (The story goes on to say that the computer manufacturer tried to sue him but the suit was denied because the system behaved

precisely as it should. That online system no longer encodes price in hidden form fields.)

- *Control:* HTML offers little in the way of control over how elements are rendered; in fact, HTML's original approach was to be as high-level as possible, deferring to the host browser on how to render elements of the HTML page so that it would be as close to the norm for that platform as possible. Over time, however, HTML page designers have sought more control over how the presentation elements are rendered in the browser (as all good UI designers do). Cascading Style Sheets (CSS) offers some of that ability, but even so, not all browsers support CSS fully, nor does CSS provide complete control over all presentation elements—for example, page designers must provide a set of fonts to use for a given presentation element, in case the font desired isn't available on that platform.

- *Cross-platform differences:* Despite the best efforts of the World Wide Web Consortium, HTML is one of the least-obeyed standards on the Internet. Both major browsers—Microsoft Internet Explorer and Netscape Navigator (Mozilla)—offer significant extensions, and while both claim to comply entirely with HTML 4.01, each seems to have problems rendering certain facets of legitimate HTML 4.01 markup. The story gets even worse when considering client-side scripting languages: Internet Explorer supports both VBScript and JScript, whereas Navigator uses JavaScript. Each provides its own object model for working with items on the page. And each makes enhancements and adds features to new versions of the browser, meaning that a site must consider not only the browser type but the advertised version of that browser as well. As a result, frequently sites just choose a particular vendor and version number to support ("Best viewed with Internet Explorer 5.5") and code to that browser alone, leaving users outside of that range more or less out of luck.

- *Bandwidth:* HTML is a presentation language, designed for providing hints and commands to the host browser on how to render a user interface. On every action by the user that requires a new interface, the entire interface must be sent to the browser, including both data and presentation elements. This means that additional bandwidth is consumed on each request, increasing load on the network (and the server). Some sites try to reduce this by shipping data back to the browser and using an XSL Transformation in the browser to marry the data to the user interface, but this is supported only in Internet

Explorer (and only in very recent versions at that). Even then, the browser must obtain the XSL script via another HTTP request.

■ *Lack of presentation elements:* The HTML form is extremely simplistic, offering about a half-dozen controls for use: push buttons, radio buttons, check boxes, edit controls (single-line, multiline, and password), and drop-down lists. While you could argue that this "core set" of controls is all any application really needs and that HTML's ability to use clickable images can provide additional behavior, the fact remains that in comparison to the UI elements of the operating system underneath the browser, HTML forms are severely constrained. Menu bars and tool bars can be approximated with Dynamic HTML (DHTML) and/or client-side script programming, but now we're back to the realm of cross-platform support.

It's a testament to the benefits of Zero Deployment that so many application developers are willing to develop workarounds to all these problems. In fact, many applications just assume only HTML 4.0 and as a result produce applications whose user interfaces appear to have stepped directly out of the early 1980s.

The problem here is that developers have forgotten why they adopted the HTML-based interface to begin with—trivial, if not zero-cost, deployment of new versions of the code. While HTML certainly is enough for some applications, it pays to take a look around at other UI approaches to see if some of these problems can be solved while still maintaining the benefits of Zero Deployment. As it turns out, several rich-client technologies offer Zero Deployment and the benefits of a richer client-side footprint.

One principal advantage to a rich client is that of state management: not only can the rich client hold state information locally until it needs to be sent to the server for processing (such as when the user finally clicks the OK or Apply buttons), but the lifetime of the rich client also mirrors that of the user's session. When the user exits the rich client, it can perform the necessary cleanup to release the resources for that given user. Because all state is held on the client, load is removed from the server. Thus we avoid all issues of cookies, server-side session state (which in turn leads to more scalable server-side footprints), session timeouts, and so on. That in itself is usually enough to convince the servlet developers of the world to consider another approach than just HTML.

The following subsections briefly discuss several of the available rich-client technologies.

Dynamic HTML

If we view client-side presentation technologies as a continuum with traditional fat clients to the far right and pure HTML 4.0 (or its successor, XHTML 1.0) at the far left of the picture, DHTML is just a half-step to the right of HTML 4.0. In essence, this is your classic JavaScript/JScript/VBScript code downloaded as part of the HTML from the server and executed as part of the client's browsing experience. Both of the major browsers have extensive DHTML support, and as a result some very interesting effects can be accomplished that plain-vanilla HTML can't do, like mouse flyover effects and such.

The problem with DHTML, unfortunately, is its complete lack of standardization. Despite numerous attempts to do so, each of the browser vendors has introduced specific features into its products as value-added benefits, and as a result it's not uncommon to see little graphic images in the corner of an application's entry page reading, "Best viewed with Internet Explorer" or similar text. In addition, as if that weren't enough, trying to degrade gracefully to an older version of the browser can be a difficult task.

Certainly, lots of server-side support has emerged over the years to make working with DHTML easier. JSP tag libraries are just one of several solutions to make this easier, for example. The real problem is that many users don't like client-side scripting for one reason or another (some organizations really dislike it, fearing security holes), and as a result, many browsers in the World Wide Web have client-side scripting turned off—which essentially shuts down your beautifully crafted DHTML user interface. Oops.

Macromedia Flash

Flash is probably the most popular rich-client technology in use today. Although typically used for passive, animation-based multimedia clips, Flash is capable of issuing HTTP requests and parsing the responses, meaning that a Flash-based client, using HTTP to communicate back to the server (typically to a Java servlet), is not only feasible but also practical. A Flash-based approach does suffer from the drawback that the Flash player browser plug-in must be installed on the user's desktop in order to function, but by this point in its lifecycle Flash is well enough established that we can safely assume this for a large number of users. For those users who don't have the Flash player installed, the Flash site has a self-installing download that requires only a single click to install.

Despite all this goodness, Flash is rumored to be notoriously difficult to program against, and many organizations have reservations about hiring Flash developers on the grounds that because that skill tends to run more in the area of graphic designers than hard-core J2EE programmers, it means forking the team across two languages. Macromedia has been working on Flash to extend it into the enterprise area, by putting better XML support into the environment, and as a result some of the first Flash-to-Web-Service back-end applications have started to appear. In addition, Macromedia is pushing Flex, a more developer-oriented way to build Flash applications; whether it will succeed long-term remains to be seen.

The difficulty of programming Flash is a solvable problem; unfortunately, another problem arises, in the same category as the DHTML problem. Because Flash doesn't come installed in the Web browser out of the box, users have to install the Flash plug-in the first time they navigate to your site (assuming they haven't installed it already), and for some users (think of your grandparents, for example) this is a nontrivial process—and, once again, many large organizations are turning off any installed plug-ins in user browsers due to security concerns. While it's certainly more common to see Flash installed than not, it's still a concern if your goal is to reach as many users across the Internet as possible. In addition, you need to keep a careful eye on the minimum browser requirements for the Flash plug-in itself, to make sure that it stretches back far enough for your particular user base.

Applets

Java applets offer solutions to some of the problems mentioned earlier, but they introduce problems of their own. For starters, applets rely on the JVM in the browser, and neither Microsoft's nor Netscape's record is very good here—neither browser supports beyond JDK 1.1 out of the box, and Java's AWT UI library is too significantly constrained in functionality to seriously consider it for an industrial-strength enterprise application. Sun developed the Java Plug-In as a workaround for both browsers, but in addition to the fact that the Plug-In has a nasty reputation among those projects that relied on it, it leaves other browsers still unsupported. In addition, the applet security model is extremely restrictive, requiring digital signatures in order to do even the simplest thing, such as write to the local filesystem. Even worse, the applet must be downloaded each time the user browses to the page, meaning large UI applications face significant download hits.

Quite possibly the largest problem with applets, however, is that if all the browser has installed is the 1.1 JDK, there is no Swing support, and developing a user interface against AWT 1.1 is truly an exercise for the incredibly sick and twisted. Theoretically, you could extract the Swing classes from `rt.jar` and put them into your applet's `.jar` file, but you're looking at several megabytes worth of compiled code, and again, that's going to be downloaded on every visit to the page. This assumes, of course, that there aren't any dependencies within Swing on JDK 1.2, 1.3, or 1.4 (or 1.5 when it ships). And the further away we get from JDK 1.1, the less likely this is going to be the case.

For the most part, aside from their ubiquity, applets are a dead-end UI solution, and I suggest that you take a look at JNLP and Java Web Start (see the upcoming subsection) before falling back to applets. Applets are dead; let them rest in peace.

The `URLClassLoader` class

On top of all these options, there's always the classic roll-it-yourself approach. The `java.net.URLClassLoader` class allows code to be loaded across an HTTP (or FTP, or any other `URLProtocolHandler`-recognized protocol) link; thus, an end user can install a simple Java shim client that in turn pulls down the "real" application from the server:

```
public class RemoteLauncher
{
  public static void main(String[] args)
    throws Exception
  {
    // Construct the ClassLoader to pull the code across
    //
    URL[] urls = new URL[]
    {
```

```
    new URL("http://intranetserver/DeployedApps/HRApp.jar")
  };
  URLClassLoader urlcl = new URLClassLoader(urls);

  // Pull the main class across and launch it
  //
  Class mainClass =
    Class.forName("com.javageeks.HRApp.Main", true, urlcl);
  Method mainMethod =
    mainClass.getMethod("main",
                        new Class[] { args.getClass() } );
  mainMethod.invoke(null, new Object[] { args } );
  }
}
```

Numerous things could be done to make this launcher more generic— allow the name to be passed in via a command-line parameter, dynamically construct the URLs for the URLClassLoader, and so on—but this demonstrates the basic principle.

While simple, this approach does suffer a major drawback in that every class must be pulled across the network every time the application is executed, meaning this is really suitable only for clients with high-speed, high-bandwidth connections. For the most part, that pretty much means onsite clients behind the corporate firewall.

JNLP and Java Web Start

JNLP is a Java specification for delivering client-side Java code to the user's machine via an HTTP request. In many respects, it's the essence of the URLClassLoader example, but with an added benefit: once delivered, the code is stored on the local hard drive. From that point forward only updates are downloaded across the wire. JNLP provides the ability to download and install versions of the JDK onto the user's machine and supports side-by-side installations—JDK 1.3, 1.3.1, and 1.4 can all coexist without conflict. Sun provides a JNLP implementation as part of the J2SE installation, called Java Web Start. JNLP supports a more fine-grained security model than applets, although in its initial revision it supports only three security modes (in increasing order of capability): applet, J2EE client, and application.

A typical JNLP application is a Swing-based client, with all the richness and power of the Swing API available—tool bars, menu bars, theme support, switchable look-and-feels, and so on. JNLP also provides access to a number of underlying operating system capabilities, such as the clipboard, without requiring digital signatures. JNLP is also being considered as a candidate for future inclusion into J2EE, so it's not as far removed from J2EE as you might think.

Building a JNLP-based application isn't much different from building a standard Java application; create your user interface, typically a Swing-based application, in the usual fashion. Once the Swing user interface is complete, copy the .jar file to an HTTP-exposed location, so that users can reach it via an HTTP request from the browser.

At this point, the real development work is more or less finished; the last step is to create a .jnlp file, an XML file that contains information for Java Web Start about the application: where to find the .jar files that make up the application, what sort of security requirements the application has, and so forth. Although this is hardly the place to go into excruciating detail about the JNLP Specification, a simple JNLP descriptor file appears here:

```
<?xml version="2.0" encoding="utf-8"?>
<jnlp spec="1.0" version = "1.1"
  codebase="http://www.neward.net/ted/samples/"
  href="http://www.neward.net/ted/samples/Hello.jnlp">
  <information>
  <title>Hello World</title>
  <vendor>None</vendor>
  <offline-allowed/>
  </information>
  <resources>
  <j2se version="1.2+"/>
  <jar href="helloworld.jar"/>
  </resources>
  <application-desc main-class="Main">
    <argument>Hello</argument>
    <argument>World</argument>
  </application-desc>
</jnlp>
```

Put the .jnlp file into an HTTP-exposed location so that users can reach the .jnlp file directly from the browser.

Now, when a user wishes to use the application, point the browser to the .jnlp file, and if Web Start is already installed on the user's machine, the Web Start browser plug-in (registered to the x-jnlp MIME type) will kick off, parsing the downloaded .jnlp file and using that as a guide to download the .jar file, the version of the JDK required, any support libraries, and so on.

The JNLP Specification provides a number of APIs for accessing the client machine in a secure and safe manner, such as the clipboard or small amounts of drive storage, without having to digitally sign the .jar file downloaded to the client machine; see the JNLP Specification for more details.

JNLP isn't picture perfect, however. (Sigh. Nothing ever is.) Once again, like Flash, JNLP relies on a client-side installation to be present to make everything kick off correctly; in this case, the Java Web Start client (or equivalent JNLP client) needs to be installed and integrated with the browser, so it can recognize the application/jnlp MIME type and start up the necessary JNLP download magic. Unfortunately, unlike Flash, the Web Start client isn't even close to ubiquitous, and unless Sun somehow pulls a miracle out of its hat and negotiates a deal with Microsoft to include Web Start as part of the standard Windows installation footprint,[1] it's not likely to become ubiquitous any time soon. Again, like Flash, installing the Web Start client isn't a difficult task for those users who are already computer-inclined, but your average user, who's barely aware of the difference between the browser and the Internet as a whole, won't necessarily be comfortable doing so.

Everything's a rich client?

Just to reiterate, however, the point of this item is not to suggest that use of a rich client is necessary for all scenarios but to suggest that for a certain collection of Web-centric applications, it is appropriate. HTML is, in many respects, the "lowest common denominator" UI technology for the Web, and there's no reason that applications, particularly those being deployed to a bound set of users (such as those within an intranet), should have to suffer from its limitations.

---

1. This is a lot more likely now that the two firms have patched up their legal differences, but it would still require a serious round of negotiations.

In the long and short of things, JNLP probably works best in an intranet environment within a company, whereas Flash probably works better for Internet-wide applications. The `URLClassLoader` approach is probably best used "under the covers" for rapidly changing components as part of a larger server-side (potentially clustered) system, not generally something that the average J2EE application will need. Applets are, of course, dead and should be left that way.

In the meantime, however, several commercial products are also exploring this space, and it's worth a look to see if they will fit your particular application needs. Droplets, Thinlets, Curl, Sash, and several others are already available, and more are sure to come as developers wrestle with the idea of exactly where they want to be on the UI continuum. The important thing is to recognize that this isn't a binary thin-client/fat-client decision and to pick your spot on the continuum as appropriate to your project.

Item 52:   Keep HTML minimal

A Web application is different from a standard GUI application in a couple of ways, most notably in the fact that the server sends back everything to the client—not only the data to be displayed but also the actual formatting codes necessary to display it. Like the old mainframe terminal-based applications, the response returned by the HTTP server includes both data conforming to the user's logical request as well as the HTML display elements framing it, along with whatever client-side scripting is used to provide behavior within the browser.

It's an unfortunate fact of the Web that Web pages seem to take forever to download, even in an era of high-speed broadband and cable modem hookups. We've all been there—click on a hyperlink or submit a form, and it just . . . takes . . . *forever* to get any kind of response. In the meantime, the user seriously contemplates whether he or she wants to have anything to do with this Web site or Web application ever again. For an intranet application deployed to users inside the corporation, holding users hostage to a slow-responding Web application is a quick way to earn a nasty reputation within the company. For an Internet application used across the globe, this is an even quicker way to make sure that those users never come back, which usually translates into lower earnings for the company, which in turn usually leads to severed paychecks for the developers.

Remember, UI studies have shown that users will wait, on average, about five seconds before giving up and moving on to something else.

What is it, exactly, that takes an otherwise well-built, well-behaved application and turns it into a snail? A large part of it is the HTML being returned. When an HTML page contains dozens of references to images, large and small, scattered all over the page, the page as a whole seems to drag to a crawl as the browser is forced to go back to the server over and over again to download those images. Does the Web site really *need* mouse-flyover image-switching graphics buttons for a main menu? Or a footer of ivy leaves twined around the copyright statement? Or the company logo in the upper-left corner of every page? I'll be the first to admit that these things make the page look pretty, but after they've been seen once, they just fade into the background in the user's mind. Worse, though, they still need to be displayed, which means they still need to be downloaded every time. (A good browser will cache what it can, but there are limits to what can be cached, particularly if the images themselves are somehow dynamically generated.) Even beyond that, consider the sizes of the images themselves—if they have any decent size and color depth at all, they can measure well into the hundreds of kilobytes, all of which have to move across the network from server to client.

It's worse than just end-user latency, though. All that stuff has to move from server to client, which means the pipeline between the two is being used to send gratuitous fluff. This in turn reduces the available bandwidth for other clients, meaning that the application's overall scalability is reduced. Unfortunately, this is one of the few areas that can't be solved by throwing more server hardware at the problem—the pipeline coming into your building or data center is the bottleneck, and widening that can often be a *very* expensive proposition.

In order to keep poor HTML from crushing your application, keep a couple of good-neighbor HTML tips in mind.

- *Minimize use of "heavy" tags.* APPLET, OBJECT, and IMG are all "heavy" tags in the sense that they don't provide the browser with everything it needs to do its job—another HTTP round-trip back to the server is necessary, meaning the user interface is going to go on "pause" in the meantime. Many browsers continue to parse and process the rest of the page but leave a big ugly empty space where the image/applet/ whatever is supposed to go. That's part of what makes the page "feel" slow to the user.

- *Use frames to help separate portions of the page.* If the Web application has a main menu bar running across the top, put that into its own (borderless) frame so that the menu only needs to be pulled across once. Ditto for the copyright banner across the bottom of the page.

- *Where possible, reuse images on a given page.* Because browsers (and intermediate processing nodes, like proxy servers and firewalls) tend to cache data downloaded from a given site, improve the page's performance by repeating the same images across pages. This allows the browser to use the cached image rather than force an extra download from the source Web site. The image's references have to match precisely, however, so make sure all your images are coming out of a common directory on the server in order to unify the URLs to the images across pages.

- *Use HTML features rather than images.* HTML tags offer a wide spread of functionality and require no additional download to display. For example, instead of creating a graphical "button" by putting an image inside a hyperlink, use standard text with various background colors, foreground colors, and fonts to achieve the same kind of interface. This saves a round-trip (see Item 17) to the server to pull the image.

- *Subject to the guidelines of tasteful and useful user interfaces, avoid excessive page navigation* (or, in other words, avoid round-trips—see Item 17). Wizard-style interfaces done in a Web-based fashion tend to break down fairly quickly when each step in the wizard is separated by a 10-second pause waiting for the server to respond with the next step. Try to combine steps into a single form, or if possible, discard the wizard-style interface altogether.

More suggestions for designing an effective HTML-based application can be found in *The Design of Sites* [Van Duyne/Landay/Hong].

While we're at it, let's get another thing out of the way. Raise your right hand, put your left hand on the cover of this book, and repeat after me:

"I, <your name here>, do solemnly swear on pain of permanent caffeine abstinence that I will ensure that all HTML output returned from my Web applications is XHTML compliant, well formed, and standardized. My tags will be lowercase, my attributes will be complete name-value pairs, values will be quoted, and all tags will either be balanced with both start and end tags or else written in the short form. I will use no element that is not standardized by the XHTML Specification, and I will never, ever consider the use of the BLINK tag to be good form, no matter how appropriate it may seem at 4 A.M. after a long debugging session."

There, that wasn't so hard, was it? XHTML 1.0 is a simple XML codification of the HTML 4.01 standard, essentially assuring that an XHTML-compliant page can be parsed by an XML parser successfully. Why is this so important? Because if the output of your servlet/JSP can be consumed by an XML parser, it can also serve as the input to an XSLT process, which could be used if necessary to render the XHTML back into something less compliant for those users who have older browsers. If your output isn't XHTML (which is to say, if it isn't well-formed XML), this transformation can't be done using XSLT, and you'll be facing the rather scary prospect of having to write this adaptation layer by hand using an HTML parser. I can't think of a worse waste of time.

HTML is wonderful in the sense that it offers a machine-independent way to describe a presentation layer in a relatively concise way, but remember that every page has to be downloaded across the wire to the user. By definition, this is a network round-trip, so make sure each reach back across the network to the server is justifiable and necessary. This means having to take a different approach to designing the user interface, away from traditional GUI approaches in places and favoring a more terminal-based approach instead. Make sure your HTML isn't trying to be a GUI application—that's usually when things start to fall apart for the well-meaning HTML application, a pretty clear sign that you should be thinking about other presentation alternatives (see Item 51).

Item 53:   Separate presentation from processing

Consider the following (simplified) JSP page:

```
<%@ page language="Java" %>
<%@ page import="java.sql.*, javax.sql.*" %>


<html>
<head><title>Product Search Results</title></head>

<%
Connection conn = application.getAttribute("dbconn");
   // Assume JDBC Connection was stored in ServletContext
```

```
String SQL = "SELECT name, sku, stock FROM products " +
             "WHERE name = ? AND stock > 0";
PreparedStatement stmt = conn.prepareStatement(SQL);
stmt.setString(1, request.getParameter("name"));
ResultSet rs = stmt.executeQuery();
ArrayList results = new ArrayList();
while (rs.next())
{
  HashMap hm = new HashMap();

  hm.add("name", rs.getString(1);
  hm.add("sku", rs.getString(2);
  hm.add("stock", rs.getString(3);

  results.add(hm);
}
stmt.close();  // Aggressively release resources; see Item 67
%>

<body>
<h1>Product Search Results</h1>
<%
  if (results.size() == 0)
  {
%>
<b>No items found that match your query; try again?</b>
<%
  }
  else
  {
%>
<table>
  <tr>
    <th>Product Name</th>
    <th>Product SKU</th>
    <th>Stock Count</th>
  </tr>
<%
    for (Iterator iter = results.iterator(); iter.hasNext(); )
    {
```

```
        Map current = (Map)iter.next();
%>
   <tr>
     <td><%= current.get("name") %></td>
     <td><%= current.get("sku") %></td>
     <td><%= current.get("stock") %></td>
   </tr>
<%
     }
%>
</table>
<%
   }
%>
</body>

</html>
```

Spot anything dangerous? If not, don't feel bad—lots of JSP pages are written this way, and this particular style of programming seems to be prevalent, particularly within a lot of articles and books on JSP. In some cases, it's done this way to keep the examples simple, but the danger is that readers won't realize that (or care) when it comes time to get the project shipped, so this style of code gets shoehorned into production.

The danger here is that subtly buried within the JSP page is a business rule—in this case, the idea that only those products that are in stock should be searched as part of the search request. In this case, the rule shows up in the same layer of code used to display the results, a dangerous blending of concerns that should normally be separated.

The first reaction by most J2EE architects and experts, when shown this code, is to suggest that this whole sequence be placed within the business tier, usually by taking the search code and dropping it inside a session bean. Typically, a stateless session bean is the first suggestion, although there is merit in making it a stateful session bean if the search is likely to produce more results than can be seen from a single screen. In that scenario, rather than going back to the database again to retrieve the next set of search results, simply hold the results in the stateful session bean and make only one round-trip (see Item 17) to obtain the rest of the search results.

However, putting this code into a session bean (whether stateful or state-less, it makes no difference) has one serious side effect—by adding a network trip between the JSP code and the actual search code, the latency of the page increases significantly. More importantly, if a stateful session bean is used, we have to store a stateful session bean instance reference in per-user state, meaning we have to use `HttpSession` (see Item 39). This in turn adds load to the server and requires the use of sessions even if the rest of the Web application doesn't need it. In addition, we have to make conscious decisions regarding the transactional affinity of the session bean's SQL execution (see Item 31); typically, since this data isn't being modified frequently, we can run this query at a low isolation level, but remember that EJB doesn't allow for varying the isolation level of its queries—therefore we will probably need to run under a transaction and contention (see Item 29) will result.

In those situations, it's common to want to bypass the EJB tier altogether and execute this query directly against the database, so we can control the isolation level of the transaction. This is known in some quarters as the Fast Lane pattern. Unfortunately, doing so brings us back to the original problem again: this is where code with embedded rules creeps in. As described in Item 3, even though we're trying to bypass the EJB layer to avoid round-trips and minimize contention, we don't necessarily want to put this code directly in the presentation code itself.

It's fair to ask why this is so bad—after all, in many cases, it's not like putting this code in some kind of `Model` or `Bean` class will help simplify the actual SQL being executed, and won't that just add another layer of method calls, thereby hurting the performance of the page as a whole? Some people argue that doing so helps preserve the details of the SQL schema being used behind the page, but let's be real—how often will the database schema itself change over the lifetime of the application?

Frequently, as a matter of fact. As it turns out, it's not uncommon to need database schema changes, particularly as the project rolls from one phase to the next. New requirements often mean at least a partial redesign of the storage schema: extending tables to include new information, splitting tables apart to accommodate better organization and/or normalization (or denormalization, when performance calls for it), and in some cases renaming tables and/or columns to better reflect the data being stored.

More importantly, however, directly embedding these business rules in the presentation code frequently leads to violations of what's called the Once-

and-Only-Once Rule: a particular snippet of code should appear exactly once within the codebase. In this case, the violation would occur anywhere another product search would be conducted—perhaps in conjunction with a customer search—and the business rule "only search for products with stock on hand," represented by the `stock > 0` predicate in the SQL statement, would have to be manually replicated in that search code. Then later, when the business decides to search for products without stock on hand, this SQL clause must be found and removed *in both places*. The same will be true, of course, if the database schema changes and inventory is suddenly stored in a separate table—now all queries that implemented this business rule must be updated to reflect the new schema.

As a result, then, create a layer of code (see Item 3) that keeps the presentation code ignorant of the actual details of doing the product search; when used from a JSP page, frequently this layer can be a tag handler in a tag library, but often a simple Java class using static methods to encapsulate the query itself can work just as well:

```
public class Queries
{
  public static List productSearchQuery(String pname)
  {
    // Same JDBC logic as before
  }
}
```

This makes using it from a JSP page look like so:

```
<% page language="Java" %>

<html>
<head><title>Product Search Results</title></head>

<%
  List results =
    Queries.productSearchQuery(request.getParameter("name");
%>

<body>
<h1>Product Search Results</h1>
<%
  if (results.size() == 0)
```

```
    {
%>
<b>No items found that match your query; try again?</b>
<%
    }
    else
    {
%>
<table>
  <tr>
    <th>Product Name</th>
    <th>Product SKU</th>
    <th>Stock Count</th>
  </tr>
<%
    for (Iterator iter = results.iterator(); iter.hasNext(); )
    {
      Map current = (Map)iter.next();
%>
  <tr>
    <td><%= current.get("name") %></td>
    <td><%= current.get("sku") %></td>
    <td><%= current.get("stock") %></td>
  </tr>
<%
    }
%>
</table>
<%
  }
%>
</body>

</html>
```

A side benefit of keeping presentation and processing logic separate comes from the inherent opportunities for parallel development—by creating this layer and keeping the presentation designer ignorant of the actual details of the query, the presentation designer can use mock objects that hand back faked data to test the presentation layer. This helps decouple the schedule so that the presentation can go before the users as quickly as possible to ensure they understand what they're getting. This also means that, in the case of JSP pages using tag libraries to provide the layering, the presentation designer can be a nonprogrammer versed instead in graphic design and layout, ensuring that your Web application doesn't show up in a rogues gallery of badly designed Web pages.

It's an arguable fact that the second JSP example presented earlier, even with the `Queries` abstraction, still isn't "clean" or well abstracted. There's a host of code on the page, such as the decision block to determine whether any rows were returned, not to mention numerous JSP scriptlet blocks, mostly to handle the looping through the `ResultSet` returned from the query. Also, the query itself is processed within the JSP page, which some will argue shouldn't happen here, since JSPs are principally geared toward allowing nonprogrammers (like page designers and graphic artists familiar with HTML or simple scripting) the ability to write dynamic pages. Instead, the argument goes, the query should be carried out in a servlet that forwards to this JSP to display the results: programmers write the servlets, page designers write the JSPs, and thus we have a well-factored separation of concerns.

This idea has become so prevalent that Sun gave it a name, the Model 2 architecture, as part of the JSP 0.92 Specification. (This rather original name came from the fact that it was the second of three suggested usage patterns for servlets and JSP.) Because Model 2 is somewhat lacking as a descriptive term, this has since been amended to be called the Model-View-Controller architecture and is well documented in other writings. In fact, an entire open-source library, Struts, hosted at the Jakarta Apache Web site (http://jakarta.apache.org), has grown up around formalizing this Model 2 architecture into a framework. Other projects use a custom presentation language based on templates rather than JSP. The core idea, however, is always the same: keep presentation (JSP) separate from processing (servlets) and also from domain-related objects (beans).

Item 54:   Keep style separate from content

At first, this item may seem like a repeat of Item 53. While they share some similar ideas, the items are somewhat different. Whereas in Item 53 we seek to separate presentation logic from processing logic, here we seek to differentiate and separate style from content. Before we can dive too deeply into this, though, we need to define the difference between the two.

Content is the actual data being returned by a particular request. This is the data without any sort of display mechanics or markup associated with it. For example, when conducting a search on a Web site, the content will be the various items returned by the search (or the text "No items found").

Style, on the other hand, relates to the aesthetic elements we put around content to make it visually appealing to end users. Font sizes, background and/or foreground colors, layout, and so on fall under the general heading of style. As a basic rule of thumb, we can remove style from a page without affecting its basic usability; we cannot remove content, however, without fundamentally damaging the response. A plaintext, comma-separated list of search results is still usable; a nicely formatted page that contains no results (not even "No items returned") is pretty useless.

The value of this particular item becomes obvious to anybody who has ever heard those dreaded words right before the Web application is scheduled to ship: "We've decided to change the entire look-and-feel of our Web site, so all your pages are going to have to conform to the new look. That shouldn't take very long, right?" If the style of the page is somehow embedded into the output of the application, every single JSP page in the Web application has to be modified to reflect the new look-and-feel. Once again, I can't think of a bigger waste of my time as a programmer. Fortunately, two technologies come to the rescue here, at least for HTML-based applications.

The first is Cascading Style Sheets, known more popularly by its acronym, CSS. CSS provides the ability to control the style and layout of elements on an HTML page from another file, typically centrally defined for the entire site. Colors, fonts, sizes, even exact locations and layout can all be controlled by CSS elements. CSS also supports hierarchical styles, such that it can define styles for all paragraph (P) elements on a page as well as provide a different style for paragraph elements defined with a `style` attribute by name. CSS also has the benefit of being a World Wide Web Consortium standard, meaning it enjoys widespread support from most HTML browsers.

Unfortunately, the level of CSS support varies across different browser implementations and versions; a site that relies heavily on CSS for style may render correctly in one browser version but look entirely differently in another or older browser version. For enterprise applications deployed within a corporate intranet, where browser versions are typically centrally managed, this can be a manageable problem; for applications deployed to the public Internet, however, where users are still using browsers like Internet Explorer 1.0 and Netscape Navigator 2.0, this can be disastrous.

The logical successor of CSS for XML, XSL:Transformations, or XSLT for short, offers another possible solution. XSLT provides the capability to transform any XML source into just about any kind of output, including HTML. This means that if the output of a given JSP is a well-formed XML Infoset, we can run it through an XSLT to turn it into any kind of HTML imaginable.

The XSLT approach has a number of positive points about it. For starters, thanks to the widely varying HTML support among different browsers, it can be difficult to write HTML output that renders nicely in all browsers. Instead, in front of all JSP pages you can place a filter that examines the User-Agent header of an HTTP request to determine the browser sending the request and uses one of several different XSLT pages to transform the JSP output into HTML specific to that particular browser version. This helps avoid having to encode those differences directly within the JSP page. Plus, the style of the rendered HTML can be captured directly in those XSLT files, thus keeping all stylistic decisions in one logical place.

Regardless of which approach you select, the goal is still the same: keep all stylistic decisions localized to a single place, once again to obey the Once-and-Only-Once Rule (see Item 53). This way, when the VP of Marketing stops by your cubicle to tell you about the corporate-wide change to the look-and-feel of the site, updating the Web application to reflect the new changes takes a matter of days or hours rather than weeks or months. In fact, if the site makes use of CSS itself, you can just reuse the new CSS page directly.

Not only that, but now the actual generated output from the JSP (or servlet) can be kept to a minimum, focusing entirely on serving back only the content and leaving all style to be inserted by either the CSS or XSLT process. This means that now the JSP or servlet generating the response will be simpler, making debugging easier, making modifications to the output easier, and, in the case of CSS (which is rendered on the end-user's browser), keeping the bandwidth consumption required to send back the response smaller, thus not only reducing the concurrent load on the server and the network but also reducing the latency of the page as a whole.

We reap an unexpected benefit out of this as well. By taking stylistic decisions away from the generated JSP/servlet output, we effectively remove the developer from the awkward position of having to decide what looks good on the page. Programmers are, unfortunately, notorious for making some hideous UI decisions[2]—mostly because programmers view the world and how we interact with it in a very different fashion than the average computer user. By removing decisions regarding colors, fonts, backgrounds, and even in some cases layout itself, programmers can focus on generating the data responses and leave the stylistic decisions to those who are better trained for them.

If the stylistic elements of the page are generated from a data-only content response from the servlet or JSP, using XSLT to generate the necessary HTML, another benefit accrues—if and when the application needs to interoperate with other, non-Java systems such as .NET, the transition to making the site support Web Services is suddenly much simpler. Now, instead of having to write two separate servlets, one to generate HTML output and the other to generate SOAP response output, the servlet that generates the generic response can be used, and different XSLT stylesheets invoked to create HTML or SOAP output on demand. This transformation can be done from within a filter, and different URL patterns can be established pointing to the same servlet, thus providing two separate endpoints that call into one servlet. The `web-app` deployment descriptor would look something like it:

```
<web-app>
  <servlet>
    <servlet-name>ProcessRequest</servlet-name>
    <servlet-class>
      com.javageeks.webapp.ProcessRequestServlet
    </servlet-class>
  </servlet>

  <servlet-mapping>
    <servlet-name>ProcessRequest</servlet-name>
    <url-pattern>/ProcessRequest</url-pattern>
  </servlet-mapping>
  <servlet-mapping>
```

---

2. I am, of course, making a generalization here—some programmers do have at least passing awareness of good human interface design. But unless you've been trained in it, it's far better to assume that you're in the category of "hideous UI designer"—simply relying on our intuition here typically generates hideous results. Check out Alan Cooper's *The Inmates Are Running the Asylum* [Cooper99] for more information on the subject if you're not convinced.

```
  <servlet-name>ProcessRequest</servlet-name>
  <url-pattern>/WebService/ProcessRequest</url-pattern>
</servlet-mapping>


 .  .  .


</web-app>
```

Now, any changes to the generated output only need to be made once—if the changes are structural in nature (more or different data needs to be returned), the one servlet can be modified, and if the changes are visual in nature (changing HTML stylistic surroundings or adopting a later version of SOAP), the change can be made to the filter and/or the XSLT file used to run the transformation. In both cases, the relevant code is localized to a single place, making maintenance on both much simpler.

Note that nothing comes for free, however, and the same is true of the XSLT-based approach. In this particular case, we're increasing the latency of the request, since the transformation process requires time to execute. For CPU-strapped sites, it may be more desirable to pregenerate the XSLT-rendered output (see Item 55) into different JSP pages (one per browser version) and select between them when forwarding from the controller servlet. This will greatly bloat the number of JSP pages on the site, however, potentially making it cumbersome to change and/or debug. This would be a last-resort approach used only if the latency is entirely unacceptable and other performance-enhancing techniques fail to address the problem.

Item 55:   Pregenerate content to minimize processing

While some applications need to be entirely dynamic, a large class of applications doesn't need to render its output completely at runtime. For example, consider Amazon.com for a moment—in essence, the entire Web site is a read-mostly environment, where 99% of the users on the site are viewing exactly the same content over and over again for a given item. While we could probably build a single `ViewItem.jsp` page to display the details (publisher, price, advertising copy, sample chapters, and reader reviews) for any arbitrary item in Amazon.com's inventory, this would introduce huge amounts of load onto the server, thus reducing the overall performance *and* scalability of the site.

Despite the huge number of items in Amazon.com's inventory, this is a bound set of data that won't change very often. Granted, prices will change, reader reviews will be added and/or removed, new advertising copy may be inserted, and so on, but these changes will likely be measured by the week rather than the minute or second. Most prospective readers won't really care if the Amazon sales rank is up-to-the-second accurate (although some book authors might).

If the page is entirely dynamically generated, however, every request is going to require at least one trip to the database to fetch the data to dynamically plug into the page (although we would hope to keep the number of trips to a minimum in order to minimize latency—see Item 17). This is not only going to create latency in the page waiting for the data to return but could also conceivably create contention (see Item 29) on the database server if these requests are naïvely transacted. Worse, because the data isn't changing frequently, all the transaction support and database querying is pretty worthless, since 99.9% of the time it's exactly the same as it was last request. Unfortunately, database caching won't be of much use here; the site will likely support thousands of concurrent users at a time, so unless the database is able to cache hundreds of thousands of queries, the likelihood of a cache hit is pretty minimal.

Rather than go through the exercise of pulling the same data back for each request, instead pregenerate a static page that already contains the data fixed in place as constant values. The actual act of pregeneration itself can be buried within the Web application—a servlet can generate a JSP page into the Web application directory, for example, or at worst a generalized JSP page can dynamically `include` an external resource into place. On modification, then, the editing servlet can simply regenerate the JSP or external resource to reflect the new changes. While this will create a large number of pages, you can usually mitigate this by putting the pages under a subdirectory on the site, identified by the primary key of the item (the ISBN, for example, in the case of books on a bookseller's site).

Note that this approach works well only for read-only or read-mostly presentation resources. Portals, for example, fit into this category, since most users select which parts of the portal they want to see and don't change those preferences very often. Thus, creating a per-user pregenerated portal page can save a tremendous amount of processing, particularly since we often want the home page of the portal to be as fast as possible.

In some cases, we can achieve a certain balance of pregeneration and per-request rendering by creating a cache (via a servlet filter that accesses an in-memory buffer or some other temporary storage) that holds generated content to be handed back from the cache, rather than by going through the entire page logic again. This has the desired benefit of not having to make the numerous calls and buffer-appends necessary to create the content, but you do run into some problems, most notably that you must be sure that the cache doesn't bloat the memory footprint of the system as a whole, thus reducing scalability. In general, if you take a caching approach, make sure that the only items cached are those usable by every user on the site; caching items on a per-user basis is a slippery slope that leads to massive memory requirements per user. Also, when caching rendered output, you run into the same update propagation problem described in Item 4, since now your caching filter needs to be made aware of changes to the presentation layer it's caching (or needs to discover those changes, which takes time and could reduce the efficacy of the cache).

Assuming you can figure out a quick and easy way to know when to invalidate the cache, and assuming it's applied judiciously to various elements of the site—there's no point in putting a caching filter in front of a static GIF or JPG image, for example—a caching servlet filter can yield some of the same benefits of pregeneration.

Pregeneration has other benefits, too. If we can pregenerate to HTML (rather than JSP), the resource in question becomes entirely static and all the caching nodes between the end user's browser and the HTTP server can kick in and reduce the latency of the request even further. Although not all pages can render to static HTML, pregenerating the content when you can, particularly for the entry point of the Web application, can make a powerful first impression on users working with the application for the first time: "Wow, that's fast."

Item 56:   Validate early, validate everything

It's a well-understood fact that users won't always give you everything you need; in fact, it's pretty much guaranteed that your average users will forget to provide some crucial piece of information at exactly the worst time. On an e-commerce application, users will forget to fill in credit card numbers. On a portal, users will forget to provide usernames and/or authentication credentials (password or hard-token values). Or worse, they'll provide the data, but it'll be wrong—typos, misinterpretations about what the data should be, or just the classic "Whoops, I selected the wrong thing."

It's a fact of programmers' lives that we have to validate what users tell us—but in an HTML-based application, we don't need to punish users when validation failures trip.

Consider, for a moment, the classic user-registration form typically required before reading white papers, downloading product trials, or accessing specialized content reserved for "premium" members of the company's target audience. When the form is submitted, what needs to happen?

For starters, we'll need to verify that there's actually some kind of data by which we can identify the user for future requests; certain fields within the form are required fields, which cannot be left blank without breaking a fundamental assumption of our system. For example, we're probably going to require a user's full name (first name and last name), as well as a username and password to use for subsequent visits to the site. If the user fails to provide that data, we need to ask him or her to provide it again.

Second, certain fields have some data-validation requirements associated with them; for example, assuming this form is for North American customers only, phone numbers must be in the form NNN-NNN-NNNN, and zip codes for U.S. customers must be in U.S. Postal 5+4 format: NNNNN-NNNN. This kind of *syntactic data validation* ensures that the data provided by the user fits a certain expression pattern and disallows anything other than numbers for the two fields above (zip codes and phone numbers).

We could also require that the zip codes provided must match the city cited in the address, and we could even go so far as to verify that the street address exists within the city's boundaries (although this is certainly further than most sites go). Of course we will want to verify that the credit card number submitted matches the name submitted as part of an e-commerce order, and we'll probably want to take advantage of some of the credit card companies' latest attempts to prevent credit card fraud by asking for the new "validation numbers" that appear printed on the back of the card itself. Or we'll want to verify that the product number the user selected in fact actually exists within the catalog, or that the options the user has selected for this particular product in fact make sense for that product (according to some online PC manufacturer sites, some PCs can't have both a DVD and a motion-capture card, for example). This is *semantic data validation*, and it certainly has just as much importance as syntactic data validation.

Here's the biggest question: When should we validate all this stuff?

Answer: As early as possible and as comprehensively as possible. The simple fact is that the earlier we can catch some of these simple data-entry errors (the syntactic data validation), the earlier we can get the user to correct them.

You've seen—and probably swore to avoid in the future, just as I do—sites that don't actually validate the data until the form has been submitted back to the server. You click the Submit button, wait the necessary 5–10 seconds for the server to receive the data, process the request, and send a response, and are greeted with text, usually in red boldface type, telling you that you forgot to fill in some particular field of the form. If the site is particularly bad about it, the original form is now gone, and hitting the Back button sends you to an empty form, forcing you to type everything all over again. Worse, the original form doesn't tell you which fields are required, leaving you to either (a) fill out every single field on the form, making up answers if necessary, or (b) continue to play "Data Entry Roulette" until you happen across the mystical combination of fields that lets you past the form-validating troglodyte at the gate.

Even worse are those applications that validate field by field on the server, returning as soon as the first data validation error is hit, forcing the user to fix that one error and go through another trip back to the server only to find out that the very next field was also bogus.

These are all acceptable reasons for murder, in the minds of most users.

The main problem is that it's tedious and awkward to do validation correctly, not to mention that it flies in the face of programmers' basic instincts. For example, in a library API, where a method expects to receive several `String` arguments that are neither null nor empty, it's perfectly acceptable to write code this way:

```
public class NiftyLibrary
{
  public static String transmogrifyStrings(String[] source)
  {
```

```
      // Verify that none of the Strings are null
      for (int i=0; i<source.length; i++)
        if (source[i] == null)
          throw new IllegalArgumentException("No nulls!");

      // Verify that none of the Strings are empty
      for (int i=0; i<source.length; i++)
        if (source[i].equals(""))
          throw new IllegalArgumentException("No empties!");

      // Do the rest of the work
    }
}
```

Here, we're supporting the required precondition that none of the parameters can be null or empty by throwing an exception as soon as we've detected the error condition. So why shouldn't we support the same kind of error-handling/failed-validation logic in our user interface?

This sort of thinking fails miserably for user interfaces because at the UI level, particularly for HTML applications, each user action requires a net-work round-trip to carry out the request, whereas in a library function, this is entirely internal to the JVM.[3] Therefore, to follow the advice of Item 17, we need to maximize the benefit from each network round-trip in order to keep the number of round-trips to an absolute minimum.

Assuming we're processing form data in a controller servlet (or filter) or some other MVC-like processing agent, as prescribed by Item 53, then all the form validation is happening in a standard Java class; we'll assume a servlet for simplicity's sake. While it would be tempting to write the servlet's validation code like the library code just shown, we need to vali-date extensively before returning an error condition to the user:

```
public class RegistrationServlet extends HttpServlet
{
    public void doPost(HttpServletRequest req,
                       HttpServletResponse resp)
      throws ServletException
```

---

3. But if this library function is a remote object, we're back to making a network round-trip to invoke the method and we'll probably want to change our tune on the validation logic, for the same reasons—avoiding round-trips.

```
{
  // Capture all validation errors in one place
  //
  List validationErrors = new ArrayList();

  // Verify that required fields are non-null
  //
  if ( (request.getParameter("first_name") == null) ||
       (request.getParameter("first_name").equals("")) )
    validationErrors.add("First Name must not be empty");

  if ( (request.getParameter("last_name") == null) ||
       (request.getParameter("last_name").equals("")) )
    validationErrors.add("Last Name must not be empty");

  // . . . and so on . . .

  // If there were errors, send the user back to the original
  // form to reenter the data
  //
  ServletContext ctx = getServletContext();
  if (validationErrors.size() > 0)
  {
    request.putAttribute("validationErrorsList",
                         validationErrors);
    RequestDispatcher rd =
      ctx.getRequestDispatcher("/registration.jsp");
    rd.forward(request, response);
  }
  // Otherwise, pass them on to the goodies behind
  // the registration page
  //
  else
  {
    RequestDispatcher rd =
      ctx.getRequestDispatcher("/premium/index.jsp");
    rd.forward(request, response);
  }
}
}
```

Notice that we send the user back to the original JSP page containing the form; in that page, we make sure to put the validation errors at the top of the form and make sure to extract any data submitted as part of the request back into the fields the user filled out. (Frequently, the browsers cache that data themselves, but why take chances?)

```
<%@ page language="Java" %˘

<html> <!-- the usual head, title elements -->

<body>

<%
  List validationErrors =
    request.getAttribute("validationErrorsList");
  if (validationErrors != null)
  {
%>

<!-- Note that this is probably not the most human-friendly
     way to put this, depending on your target audience;
     consider getting UI advice before putting this into
     production.
  -->
<h2>There were validation errors; please correct the following
and submit the page again:</h2>

<ul>
<%
    for (Iterator iter = validationErrors.iterator();
         iter.hasNext(); )
    {
%>
<li><font color="red"><%= iter.next().toString()
%></font></li>
<%
    }
%>
</ul>
<%
```

```
  }
%>


<%!--
  Probably should check for nulls in the request parameters,
  just to avoid the possibility of the literal string "null"
  showing up in the field values; this is left as an exercise
  --%>
<form method="POST" action="/servlet/RegistrationServlet">
First Name: <input name="first_name" type="text"
  value="<%= request.getParameter("first_name")%>" /> <br />
Last Name: <input name="last_name" type="text"
  value="<%= request.getParameter("last_name")%>" /> <br />

<!-- and so on -->

<input name="submit" type="submit" />
</form>
</body>


</html>
```

As you can see, providing this is not overly difficult but somewhat
tedious, particularly if the JSP page designer is not a programmer. Fortunately, this is why JSP now supports tag libraries:

```
<%@ page language="Java" %>
<%@ taglib uri="http://www.host.com/HTMLSupportLib"
           prefix="html" %>

<html> <!-- the usual head, title elements -->

<body>

<html:validationErrors>
<h2>There were validation errors; please correct the
following and submit the page again:</h2>
<ul>
<html:validationErrorList>
<li><html:validationErrorText /></li>
```

```
</html:validationErrorList>
</ul>
</html:validationErrors>

<form method="POST" action="/servlet/RegistrationServlet">
First Name: <html:textInput name="first_name" /> <br />
Last Name: <html:textInput name="last_name" /> <br />

<!-- and so on -->

<input name="submit" type="submit" />
</form>
</body>

</html>
```

The `validationErrors`, `validationErrorList`, and `validation ErrorText` are all custom tag handlers that rely on the preceding servlet putting a list of validation errors into the `HttpServletRequest` under the name `validationErrors`, just as before, but they simplify the page logic to make the JSP page author's life easier. In addition, the `textInput` tag handler examines the incoming `HttpServletRequest`, and if it finds an input parameter that matches its `name` attribute, prepopulates the value of the HTML field with that data. Suddenly, it's not so tedious anymore.

But we still suffer from the same problem as before—in order to do any validation of the form fields, we have to go back to the server to do it. As Item 17 explains, we need to keep our time on the wire to a minimum if we want to keep latency low and scalability high. Fortunately, most HTML browsers offer a client-side alternative to doing validation on the server: scripting languages like JavaScript (Netscape's flavor of the standard ECMAScript language) for Netscape browsers and either VBScript or JScript (Microsoft's flavor of ECMAScript) for Internet Explorer. While most semantic data validation is impossible (or in some cases simply difficult) from within the client-side scripting environment, certainly most syntactic data validation is quite within the boundaries of those languages. Again, however, putting that code onto every form-containing page is tedious, and again, this is where the tag libraries can offer help. For example, the `textInput` tag can add some script support to the `<input>` element it will emit to ensure that on submission of the form (or on leaving the field, or on clicking a Validate button, or any of a dozen other possible events), the `first_name` and `last_name` fields aren't empty; if they are, pop a dialog box, stop the submission, and let the user fix the problem before we hit the network wire.

We'll have to code the tag libraries somewhat intelligently to take browser versions into account, but fortunately we'll only have to write this code once. More importantly, as explained in Item 51, we cannot assume that the scripting support will always be available, so we'll still need to do the server-side validation. The client-side script makes users' lives easier; the server-side validation makes programmers' lives easier. Use both liberally wherever possible, particularly if they can be codified within JSP tag libraries. (The Jakarta Taglibs project, at http://jakarta.apache.org/taglibs, has several tag handlers already written that provide this kind of support, and the Struts library, at http://jakarta.apache.org/struts, also provides similar sorts of tag handlers that are more deeply tied into the Struts architecture.)

By the way, don't rely on coding the text red to signify validation errors—remember that many people in the world are red/green color-blind and won't be able to recognize the fact that the text is red. Without some kind of supportive text, they'll be clueless as to why their form submission failed. And while we're talking about error messages, make sure your error messages are actually comprehensible to the nondeveloper crowd—get somebody other than a developer to review the messages and decide whether they make sense.

Ultimately, remember that client-side validation serves one purpose: to make it as gentle as possible on the user entering data into your system. You're not going to give up on server-side validation (not after reading Item 61, anyway), but you want users to be able to catch their mistakes as early as possible so as to avoid the round-trip (see Item 17) between client machine and servlet container on every data-entry error. As awkward as it is to do, build validation systems that validate all the user's input at once, and offer a list of all the items that need correction. Remember, at the end of the day, the system is for their use, not yours, so you'd best make sure it's easy to use. User-friendly validation is a key component of that goal.

7 | Security

The superior man, when resting in safety, does not forget that danger may come. When in a state of security he does not forget the possibility of ruin. When all is orderly, he does not forget that disorder may come. Thus his person is not endangered, and his States and all their clans are preserved.

—Confucius

It's the white elephant in the middle of the room that everybody can see, everybody recognizes, yet everybody tries desperately to ignore and goes to great lengths to work around. I speak of that most notorious of subjects in the programmer's lexicon, *security*.

The casual perception among most Java programmers is that security is deeply mystical, arcane, and incomprehensible. It's equal parts administration, cryptography, and FUD (fear, uncertainty, and doubt). Ask Java developers if their application is secure, and some will confidently and somewhat naïvely pronounce, "Absolutely!" while others will shrug their shoulders, look away uncomfortably, and try to steer the conversation back to safer, more comprehensible topics like brain surgery, object-relational mapping layers, and the joys of object pooling.

Unfortunately, such an attitude is roughly equivalent to that of a three-year-old playing hide-and-seek with his parents, putting his hands over his eyes, and pronouncing, "You can't see me!" Developers of enterprise applications, perhaps more so than in any other software development genre, need to be fully cognizant and aware of the security risks they face and how to mitigate them. Stories abound every day of corporations having credit card numbers stolen from their databases or losing millions to denial-of-service attacks and millions more to direct fraud and other illegal activities.

What makes this entire scenario worse is that most developers have only the most narrow-minded idea of what application security really is;

within the Java community, mention of the word "security" evokes one of two responses: either "Java security—that's something to do with the applet sandbox, right?" or "Well, start with two very large prime numbers. . . ."

Security is a large, rich, and exciting topic that stretches far beyond the Java applet sandbox and simple explanations of asymmetric key encryption. Whole books have spent hundreds of pages focusing on just one aspect of security and still not covered the topic completely, and thanks to the ever-escalating arms race between attackers and security experts, what was true today is legacy tomorrow. There is simply no way that one chapter in a book otherwise devoted to enterprise Java development can cover security in any depth. Instead, my goal is to provide you with a generalized primer on security topics and resources to consult if you wish to follow up with more detailed study. In addition, we'll take a quick look at leveraging the existing security mechanisms within the Java platform to make writing secure Java enterprise applications a little bit easier.

Before we get too deeply into the security discussions, however, in the interest of expediency let's establish up front some terminology unique to security discussions.

- *Authentication:* This is the act of verifying that an entity within the system (a *principal*), whether an individual or some other, more nebulous entity (such as a corporation), is in fact who it claims to be. The act of authentication is simple: the security layer demands ("challenges") the entity to prove its identity, and the entity does so by presenting some form of *credentials* recognized by the security layer. If the credentials are genuine, the principal is successfully authenticated; if not, the security layer reacts accordingly, denying access or notifying another security system. Authentication comes in three basic forms: you can authenticate based on what you *know*, what you *have*, or what you *are*. Seen this way, it's obvious that authentication checks are a common fact of life and occur every day—I authenticate myself to my car every morning by presenting appropriate credentials (the car keys) to the security layer (the car door lock and ignition system). I authenticate myself to the guy taking my credit card to pay for lunch by presenting my credentials (my signature on the credit card slip and sometimes, my driver's license) to the security layer (the guy holding the card). We in American society have even begun to teach our kids the basics of authentication: many children are taught special "code words" that only someone legitimately sent by the children's parents to pick them up would know. A child forces an authentication check when he or she responds to "Your Mom told me to pick you up" by asking what the code word is. If the grownup doesn't know it, the child is told to find a recognizable icon of authority (e.g., a teacher, a policeman) and tell them. It's all the same basic principle.

- *Authorization:* Authorization is the act of establishing what a principal within the system is allowed to do. In many cases, in real-life scenarios, successful authentication implies a certain authorization—for example, if I successfully authenticate myself to my car, I'm authorized to start the engine and drive it. My authorization stops, however, when I try to engage in activities that endanger other drivers on the road—speeding, swerving dangerously, and so on. Not that the car itself will stop me, but the police cruiser hiding behind the billboard will. The police, however, have full authorization to engage in whatever activity is necessary to enforce those same traffic laws, including the right to smash into my car to force it off the road. The authentication models are similar (do you have the keys?), but the authorization granted is very different. Within a software system, authorization determines the actions (*permissions*) granted to the various actors within the system—permission to add an item to the shopping cart, permission to cancel the shopping cart, permission to access the underlying table structure, and so on. Frequently, we'll group these permissions into sets, call them *roles*, and assign users to one or more roles as a means of simplifying administration of the system (see Item 63).

- *Cryptography:* Cryptography is the science of taking a message (called *plaintext*) and producing a form of that message in a way that is unreadable to anyone except those who have the means by which to render the encrypted message (now called *ciphertext*) back into its plaintext form. Since the algorithms used to encrypt the message are often well-known (or easily reversible), most cryptographic algorithms rely on a *key*, a bit of data used as part of the algorithm to help make it more resistant to decryption by unwanted parties. If both sides of the message exchange need the same key to encrypt and decrypt the message, it is called *symmetric key cryptography* or, more colloquially, *secret key cryptography*. If each side can have one-half of a key pair, it is called *asymmetric key cryptography* or *public-key/private-key cryptography*.

- *Cryptanalysis:* The "other half" of cryptography, cryptanalysis is the science of breaking an encrypted message back to its plaintext origins without having to know the key(s) with which the message was encrypted.

- *Steganography:* This is the science of "hiding" a message within something else. For example, where a cryptographer seeks to encrypt the message and broadcast it in the clear, a steganographer instead chooses to broadcast an image file, with the message sprinkled within the image file in a way that leaves most of the image untouched, yet people who know about the image's role as a cover can retrieve the message. (Perhaps every 15th byte will in fact be a byte from the message rather than image data itself.) Steganography and cryptography are sometimes combined to make it that much more difficult to discover the plaintext message, on the theory that if you don't even know the message is there, you can't cryptanalyze it.

- *Alice, Bob, Mallory, Eve, and Trent:* Believe it or not, these names aren't just chosen at random in cryptographic writings. In a security protocol discussion, Alice always initiates the conversation with Bob. Mallory is the malicious individual trying to disrupt, change, or redirect the conversation, while Eve is the passive eavesdropper who just wants to listen in on the conversation. Trent is the third party known and trusted by both Alice and Bob. These names help establish whom we're referring to during a security protocol discussion and are explained in more detail in *Applied Cryptography* [Schneier95].

- *Confidentiality:* When I was in the sixth grade, I had a huge crush on my dream girl, Tracey Latipow. She sat two rows over, three seats up, and I thought she was just the most wonderful thing I had ever seen. Being a society-conscious sixth-grader, however, I couldn't just come out and admit that I liked her, particularly since my fragile ego would be absolutely *crushed* if she didn't like me in turn. But I had to know. So I devised a simple plan (one that has probably been used over and over again throughout history)—I would write a friend of hers a note asking the critical question. (Were I in sixth grade today, I would just text-message her on her cellphone, but such things didn't exist when I was 12.) Problem was, my sixth-grade teacher, Mr. Martin, frowned heavily on passing notes in class, and if he caught such activity, he would execute the ultimate punishment to a note-passing sixth grader: *he would read the note out loud to the class.* So I couldn't write the note in plain English—I needed some way to hide the message so that nobody but the intended recipient could read it. In formal cryptographic terms, this is called *data confidentiality*; because the note was being passed over an untrusted medium (the other kids in class), any one of whom could read the note as they handed it to the next person in the chain, the contents of the message must be made confidential. This is different from *steganography*, which is the act of hiding the message (which I did as well, by trying to keep the act of passing the note as subtle as possible, usually by doing it at recess or while Mr. Martin's back was turned).

- *Integrity:* Going back to sixth grade for a moment, just making sure the data was hidden from incidental readers along the way wasn't enough. Suppose somebody figured out my most excellent code and decided to play a trick on me by pretending to be Tracey's friend and answering the question incorrectly. No end of embarrassment, particularly if the interceptor said "yes," and the real answer was "no"— I could very well end up making a fool of myself by admitting my crush to Tracey! In formal terms, what I was looking for here was *data integrity*, a reassurance that the message did, in fact, come from Tracey's friend and not some practical joker in the middle.

On these basic terms are enterprise security discussions founded.

Item 57: Security is a process, not a product

"If you think technology can solve your security problems, then you don't understand the problems and you don't understand the technology" [Schneier01, xii].

To the casual eye cruising the Internet, the various trade press publications, or the various security vendor Web sites, security would seem a kind of postdevelopment add-in that we can sprinkle all over an application to render it suddenly "secure," immune to attack and safe from harm. Just buy a product, make a few API calls, and *voilà*! Instant secure application, and it took only a few minutes to put it in. What could be better?

Developers look at cryptography in much the same way. All we have to do to make the application secure is encrypt the data somehow, relying on the mathematics of the cryptographic algorithm to prevent the data from being viewed by unfriendly eyes. Bruce Schneier himself even subscribed to this view when he wrote, "It is insufficient to protect ourselves with laws; we need to protect ourselves with mathematics" [Schneier95, xx].

Unfortunately, this attitude is exactly the wrong way to think about security. The various vendor products across the Internet cannot make your application secure. No one security technology will protect your application from all harm, not even Transport Layer Security (TLS), also known as the Secure Sockets Layer (SSL).

The problem is simple: developers wrap themselves in the belief that "cryptography equals security" and that if the crypto key is strong enough, the system will be secure. Unfortunately, it's a horrible fallacy and one that Schneier himself admits to in the Preface to *Secrets and Lies*:

> The error of *Applied Cryptography* is that I didn't talk at all about the context. I talked about cryptography as if it were The Answer. I was pretty naïve.
>
> The result wasn't pretty. Readers believed that cryptography was a kind of magic security dust that they could sprinkle over their software and make it secure. That they could invoke magic spells like "128-bit key" and "public-key infrastructure." A colleague once told me that the world was full of bad security systems designed by people who read *Applied Cryptography* [Schneier01, xii].

This is not a confidence-inspiring editorial. If the one man who arguably knows most about cryptography in the Internet era suddenly feels that cryptography isn't the solution, then how, exactly, are enterprise developers who haven't the time to learn cryptography to the depths that Schneier knows it supposed to make our systems secure?

The problem isn't in the use of cryptography itself; the problem is in the belief that most developers have that cryptography holds the solution to all of our security needs. Consider the canonical e-commerce Internet application: a new company, seeking to peddle its wares across the Internet, creates the online shopping site e-socks.com, the World's Premier Internet Retailer of Soft Fluffy Footwear. As developers, we build the site to provide all the classic e-commerce functions: shopping cart, customer checkout, and so on. And, in typical fashion, to allay customers who fear sending their credit card numbers over the Internet,[1] we take their credit card information over an HTTPS connection. So we're secure, right?

---

1. Ironically, these same customers have no qualms about giving their numbers over the phone to unknown customer service representatives or handing their credit cards, on which the numbers are prominently displayed to any who look, to servers at restaurants to pay for dinner.

Unfortunately, no. While the system may be sending the credit card number in secure format to render it inaccessible to prying eyes, the wily hacker is far from stymied. Any number of ways into the system are possible, some of which are highlighted here.

- *Social engineering attack:* "Social engineering" is the euphemistic name we give to that form of attack traditionally practiced by those whom we used to call "con men"—in short, a charming, swift-talking, charismatic individual convinces someone within the system to surrender information. Kevin Mitnick, in *The Art of Deception* [Mitnick, 45–46], describes a story in which a son was able to win a $50 bet with his father—the challenge was to obtain Dad's credit card number from a video store. It took three phone calls and about ten minutes to do so. How hard would it be to convince a customer service rep to hand out a particular consumer's credit card number? Ask Mitnick—he made a living off the idea (and continues to do so today, although from the other direction).
- *Database attacks:* Many systems store consumer information as part of the users' profile on the company site, as a feature to prevent users from having to enter their credit card numbers on every purchase. Most companies don't bother to encrypt these numbers, and in fact many companies aren't *quite* as tight on security procedures on the database as they are elsewhere. (Most companies don't assume insecurity, as explained in Item 60, for example.)
- *Man-in-the-middle attacks within the corporate firewall:* As long as any part of the company firewall can be compromised, the attacker now has free reign anywhere within it. SSL typically runs only to the proxy server or firewall of the corporate network, since load-balancers and routers need access to the underlying data if they're to do their jobs. So the hacker gets into the demilitarized zone (DMZ), sets up a network sniffer, and watches the packets *after* they've been decrypted by the proxy.

Other attacks are certainly possible, and I'm sure we've not even scratched the surface of possible attack vectors. Note that none of them involved trying to go directly against the SSL layer itself; instead, they attack other parts of the overall security of the system. Why bother going against SSL and its key exchange protocol when it's far easier for the attacker to engage in one of the dozens of other forms of attack, all of which end with the same result (i.e., your credit card number in his highly immoral fist)?

Security is not something that we can simply "turn on" as a feature at some point in the system's implementation lifecycle. Unfortunately, this is exactly the attitude that most development teams and managers take: "Well, sure, the system needs to be secure, but we'll get to that after we get it up and running." While this particular approach and attitude might work for optimizing a system (even then, it's debatable), this will never work when discussing the security of a system as a whole. Concerns about security have to be factored into the analysis, design, implementation, and test phases of every iteration of the system's development, or gaping security holes will result.

For example, consider the e-socks.com e-commerce application again. Assuming this is a classic Model-View-Controller application, where do we need to worry about security? What are the security concerns? A partial list includes the following issues.

- Assuming the site makes use of some kind of per-user session state (e.g., `HttpSession`), we need to ensure somehow that an attacker cannot "guess" a valid in-use `JSESSIONID` value and thus gain access to another user's session state. For e-socks.com, the concern would be that an attacker could use my credit card to ship silk stockings to his shipping address. For a site dealing with financial or medical data, the implications could be far, far worse. Never use a servlet container that doesn't generate some kind of secure random value for the `JSESSIONID` query parameter.

- Each servlet processing input on the page must make sure the input falls within valid ranges. For example, when verifying login credentials for the user against the database (`SELECT * FROM user WHERE . . .`), make sure the username and password aren't hiding a SQL injection attack.

- Each servlet and JSP page must be carefully examined to make sure that out-of-order page requests don't bypass critical data-entry information. For example, it shouldn't be possible to bypass the "select method of payment" page to go directly to the "confirm this order!" page. Ideally, of course, the rest of the back-end processing would verify that the order had, in fact, been paid for before sending it out, but how often do you as a programmer double-check something that "I know has already been processed" further up the chain?

- How do the pages calculate the current running price total of the user's shopping cart? If the value is cached in a hidden field, an attacker can always bypass the browser entirely and hand-submit (via Telnet) an HTTP request that contains thousands of items in the shopping cart and that hidden field containing a value of $0.01. Even if the value is calculated on each request, where does the shopping cart get the prices of the items put into the cart? Again, if it's from an HTML form field, this data can be mocked up pretty easily.

Subsequent items in this chapter cover many of these concerns in further detail, but all of these issues are meant to serve as background material to support the main title of this item, a phrase Schneier uses over and over again: "Security is a process, not a product." You have to consciously think about this at every stage of the system's development if you're to have any hope of building a system that's remotely attacker-resistant. This requires a shift in your mental model: it requires you to briefly put on the attacker's black hat and think about how you might attack the system and then, putting the white hat back on, what you might do to prevent that attack. And not only the architect or technical lead needs to think about this—*everybody*, at all levels of the system's implementation, needs to have security in mind. "Write secure code" should be a driving principle of every programmer, just as "write good code" and "write elegant code" are.

Item 58:   Remember that security is not just prevention

Let's ignore the software world for just a second. If we're looking for good models of how to build secure systems, to at least a certain degree we can go back to "the real world" for examples of what works and what doesn't.

Within the real world, in an era where automated video cameras, electric fences, motion detectors, and zone alarms are the norm, simply *preventing* an attacker's entry into the system is not nearly enough. Consider European history for a moment—in the Middle Ages, the pinnacle of defense was the classic castle: stone walls a yard or two thick, rising thirty or more feet into the air, surrounded by a large body of water that made approaching the base of the walls difficult if not impossible. Given this impregnability, certainly it would seem that the castle (at least until the invention of gunpowder) represented an absolutely unassailable target. So why, then, did every castle keep guards? If the castle itself was so impregnable, why pay men to wander the tops of the walls, doing nothing but watching for any attempts at intrusion? For a modern parallel, think about the car alarm—what makes us believe that a shrieking wail will drive a prospective car burglar away? Is it the fact that the sound is loud enough to cause physical harm?

Of course not. The castle, unmanned, will eventually be taken—somebody will figure out that a ladder is of tremendous help here. The car, shrieking its alarm in the middle of an empty parking lot, will get stolen once the thief realizes that nobody's coming to stop him. Simple *prevention*, trying to keep the attacker from gaining entry, is not enough; physical deterrence will only slow an attacker, not stop him. The other two parts of any secure system are *detection* and *reaction*.

Go back to the castle again. When the invading army shows up, the guards at the top of the castle wall are going to immediately notify the rest of the castle inhabitants that some unfriendly folks have just arrived. The castle lord will immediately call out the rest of his troops, who will take up some rather persuasive means of denying entry: swords, crossbows, boiling oil, that sort of thing.

When the enemy attacks the castle, the guards will react, trying to deny the enemy access to the castle, typically by engaging in some barbaric actions, like pouring the boiling oil on top of the attackers, or firing arrows at them, or pushing over their scaling ladders. The guards are not simply going to stand idly by and watch the bad guys climb the walls and lower the drawbridge—they will react with appropriate force to deny the attackers entrance. That's what they get paid for, at least in theory.

The burglar alarm works the same way. I lock the doors on my house and my car to *prevent* an attacker easy entrance into my house or vehicle, but there are methods to get in without having to go through the doors: windows are one easy way in. (An enterprising house burglar in San Diego found another: use a chainsaw to create your own doorway in an otherwise plain wall.) So I put sensors on the windows; if they are broken, an alarm goes off and alerts not only me and my family but also the alarm company I write a check to every month. Either I or the alarm company, having *detected* the intrusion attempt, will immediately call the police, who will *react* by rushing to the scene and detaining the intruder, potentially using force if necessary. Other homeowners might react differently by making use of legitimately owned firearms kept by the bedside—the effect is the same.

So if simple prevention won't work in real life, what on earth makes us believe it will work in software systems? The firewall will certainly prevent a large number of attacks against it, but what will it do if one happens to get through? How will you know you've been attacked? How will you respond? Unfortunately, again, this is an area where the software security industry falls seriously deficient. To be sure, intrusion detection systems are marketed and sold, but all of them carry a serious disadvantage: the *false positive*. The software packages periodically register benign traffic on the network as an intrusion attempt and start ringing the alarms. It turns out the attempt isn't actually an intrusion attempt; the software is reset and the system administrators go back to their daily grind.

Why is the false positive such a bad thing? Go back to our earlier example of the car alarm: it relies on the idea that when the alarm goes off, somebody will hear it (*detection*) and call the police to stop the would-be burglar (*reaction*). When's the last time you did this when you heard a car alarm? In the early days of the car alarm, it was actually not uncommon for concerned citizens to rush to the source of the alarm when it went off, knowing that the alarm going off meant that somebody was trying to break into somebody else's car. After all, someday it could be *my* car getting burglarized, and I'd want people to stop the burglar then, right?

But the problem was that lots of car alarms were set to be too sensitive to any sort of motion around or on the cars: trains or airplanes in close proximity to a vehicle were known to set off the alarm, as was accidentally bumping your car door into the alarmed vehicle, as was your three-year-old scampering away from you in the parking lot and running into the bumper. We learned, as human beings, that false positives happen far, far more often than true positives. We grew complacent to the idea that the alarm going off meant real trouble, and we eventually reached a point that when an alarm goes off, our reactions are either (a) curse the owner for not coming out to shut the stupid thing off, or (b) ignore it and continue whatever we were doing before it went off.

This isn't a new problem —rebels and guerrillas have known for years that the best way to attack a military base isn't to go charging at the electrified gates, guns blazing. Guards with fancy military hardware drive around in Jeeps with machine guns or Armored Personnel Carriers with bigger guns, and a small rag-tag band of freedom fighters armed with rifles isn't going to last long against that kind of hardware. So instead, the rebels use stealth; they want to lull the guards into a false sense of security.

The rebels find a rabbit or some other small animal, fling it against the fence, and melt away into the shadows. The perimeter alarms go off, and the guards come rushing, find the animal's smoking carcass on the fence, call it a false alarm, and go back to the barracks. The rebels do it again an hour later. The guards come rushing, realize it's just another animal, and head back to the barracks. After three or four more of these, the guards are desensitized to the alarm—they may not even bother sending out a patrol to check the gates. That's when the rebels pull out the cutters, cut a hole in the fence (which is what the alarms were supposed to warn against, but by this time they're either ringing to no effect or the guards have just turned the silly things off), sneak in, and do their deadly deeds.

Think this tactic isn't successful? The *mujahedin* used it time and time again against their Soviet occupiers in Afghanistan in the 1980s. The Kosovars used it against their Serbian occupiers in Yugoslavia in the 1990s. It's probably what let the small outboard rowboat laden with explosives get so close to the *USS Cole* ("Eh, it's just another motorboat, Jack—it's not like it's a real threat"). Think this tactic isn't being used against your company? That all depends on whether the company even has any sort of intrusion detection software in place; many don't. Those that do, however, are flooded with hundreds, if not thousands, of false positive intrusion attempts every day, and system administrators get tired of it, enough to turn the alarms down or altogether off.

What does this mean from a programmer's perspective? It means that your software, in order to be administration-friendly (see Item 13), should have detection and reaction mechanisms laced throughout it wherever possible. The classic tactic, of course, is to allow only a finite number of bad logins before locking the user's account in a way that only an established, trusted system administrator can unlock. If your servlet starts to get malformed input that should have been caught by client-side validation code (JavaScript in the HTML browser, for example), it's possible that an attacker is attempting to find the edges of your system's security; notify an administrator and/or log the source of the communication, the number of attempts, and so on. At every point in your threat model (see Item 59), put code to detect what might be an intrusion attempt, log it, and notify an administrator somehow. Be careful to make the notification intrusive enough to get somebody's attention but not so intrusive that people are tempted to shut it off in the inevitable event of false positives. (E-mail works well for this, or a text message to a cellphone or pager sometimes works.) At the end of the day, software can't just rely on prevention—detection and reaction have to be there too, or we might as well not even bother with prevention in the first place.

Item 59:   Establish a threat model

So you're convinced that you need to take security in your application seriously. Now what? Starting to read through the various security resources available (books, articles, Internet papers, and such) tends to leave developers with a really depressed outlook on the whole idea—no matter the cryptographic angle, no matter the security protocol being discussed, there always seems to be a way through it. Is there nothing we can do that will render the application secure?

First, remember that security is more than just prevention (see Item 58), and many of the attacks against a security protocol or cryptographic algorithm assume an attacker has an infinite amount of time to attack a given system. The security code you put in will never be able to defend against an attacker who has that kind of advantage over you, so don't even think you'll be able to.

Second, however, we need to accept the sobering reality that building the "perfect security system" is like chasing the Holy Grail—it's going to soak up a lot of time that ultimately won't produce much in the way of tangible benefit. As the old saying goes, "Don't spend a million dollars to protect a dime." So now we need to do the cold-hearted analysis to figure out precisely what kind of resources we're willing to commit to securing the application. Ideally, it'll be a reasonable amount of both time and money, but a large part of "how much we need to spend" frequently comes out of "how much will it cost," something we'll get to in just a bit.

Once we've figured out the dollar amount and/or person-hours we're willing to commit to securing the application, we next have to turn our attention to what to secure the application against. An attacker can come at the system in many different ways, and trying to cover them all is likely to be infeasible and to spread our efforts out too thin to be of much effect. Instead, we need to figure out precisely what parts of the system have the greatest exposure and liability and protect those first. There are two ways to go about this.

The first way, the one most developers choose by default, is to simply rely on developer intuition about which parts of the system are the most vulnerable and/or the largest liabilities in the event of a successful attack. As Item 10 points out, however, most developers' intuition sucks and shouldn't be trusted—not for optimization, and not for security.

The second way is to take a measured, planned approach to all this.

We've learned the hard way over decades of software development projects that to simply turn developers loose without some kind of guiding model, a grand vision for the system as a whole, is a Really Bad Idea. This is where we get the "design-first" methodologies like the Rational Unified Process, because as implementers we really need to be able to see the big picture in order to get all the details right the first time—otherwise, we risk huge costs in correcting those details later.

(Note that most agile methodology proponents, who are frequently misquoted as being anti-design, will in fact suggest that some kind of design is still necessary—for example, in Extreme Programming the design comes during the task implementation, and particularly when refactoring is necessary. The Extreme Programming crowds just argue against "design for tomorrow" and instead stress "design for today.")

Similarly, with respect to security, we need some kind of big picture of the security landscape *vis-à-vis* our application. We need to know where the largest vulnerabilities are, and what the damage would be if those vulnerabilities were exposed. This information in turn helps us prioritize which vulnerabilities we need to be concerned with and which ones we can safely ignore. This assessment is commonly called a *threat model*, and as its name implies, it serves much the same purpose as an object design model does.

Numerous security authors have suggested methodologies for developing threat models. Schneier, for example, has "attack trees" that hierarchically map the vulnerabilities into a large, almost UML-like diagram that can be expanded or contracted as necessary [Schneier01, 318–333]. It tends to give a good big-picture view of the various ways into the system, and the hierarchical arrangement allows for some easier estimation of whole categories of attacks.

Other writers have suggested a simpler model, in which developers sit around a conference table, brainstorming about all the different ways an attacker could attack the system. Then, each item on this brainstormed list is given a threat value, which is the product of two things: the financial damage that would occur if the threat were successfully carried out, and the percentage chance of the threat actually occurring. (This model is also used in risk assessment studies; since security is often about managing risk, in this case the risk of an intrusion, many of the same principles apply.) So, for example, if we've determined that an attacker successfully gaining root privileges on the Web server and defacing the site represents two person-hours work to undo the defacement (we keep good backups) and possibly $10,000 in lost revenue due to the defacement, then the *liability* of that vulnerability is roughly (assuming good system administrators make $60K/year, that's roughly $30/hour) $10,000 + 2 hours at $30/hr, or $10,060 total. Now we estimate the chances of this vulnerability actually materializing to be about 10%, since we are very careful to run the Web server in a least-privileged account (thus forcing the attacker to have to engage in some kind of luring attack elsewhere to get those root privileges; see Item 60). This means the total security risk here is roughly $1,006, which is how much we should spend closing this hole—anything more isn't worth it.

Not all security assessments are as easy to calculate as this; some damages are extremely hard to estimate, such as the damage resulting from bad publicity if and when the company is hacked and consumers' personal data is suddenly posted on hacker Web sites. Remember that the values assigned here are purely for threat-modeling purposes and serve only as a guide to estimate which vulnerabilities need to be addressed before others. Calculate the damages in abstract "Badness" units, if that makes the estimation any easier.

The point here is that without some kind of threat model, it's impossible to know how much time and energy should go into fixing one of the innumerable potential security vulnerabilities that a given enterprise system opens up. For example, do you trust your system administrators? Do you trust your users? Do you trust anybody and everybody on the corporate network inside the firewall? If you think the answer is yes to all of these questions, allow me to remind you of risks like disgruntled system administrators, socially engineered users, and Java instructors visiting your company's site to teach classes (or any other visitor, for that matter) who plug into the network "just to get mail" but in fact are being paid by your competition to snoop around on the network to eavesdrop on conversations and generally try to sniff out confidential data. Not that I've ever been approached by a company's competitor to do this, but raising this point in class almost always raises a few eyebrows and makes people start to think, which is, of course, the whole point of suggesting it. Industrial espionage *is* alive and well, folks.

If you suddenly think the answer is no to some or all of those questions, the next step is to figure out what you intend to do about it, and that's precisely what the threat model tries to tell you—which threats do you actively defend against, and which threats do you just shrug your shoulders to and admit there's not much you can do about them? After all, if heavily armed commando teams storm the data center and start physically pulling the hard drives out of the servers, there's not much your software can do to stop them, is there?

Item 60:   Assume insecurity

So you've finally got the big J2EE system done, ready for deployment into the production environment, and everybody's really excited. The CEO has promised major bonuses for all parties concerned, and the VP of Development is about ready to pass out from all the kudos and back-slapping congratulations coming her way. It has been a good trip for everyone so far. The system has gone through quality assurance with flying colors (OK, there were a few bugs, but nothing that should stop the system from being deployed into production), and we're ready to go.

The system administrators, ready to put this puppy into place, begin by installing the database software (if it's not already installed), the J2EE container, as well as any third-party software needed to make the whole thing work. They pop in the CDs, accept the defaults, and a few hours later, everything's ready for deploying your code. They go through the deployment script (see Item 14), run through a quick "happy bit" test to make sure everything's in good shape and turn on the monitoring tools (see Item 12), and announce that everything's in place; the system has officially been deployed into production! The crowd goes wild, everybody heads out to the bar for major celebrations, and the company's stock goes up several points on the good news.

Before you break out that second bottle of champagne, however, beware the huge, dangerous assumption that you (and everybody else) are making as you head out the door. You're assuming that the installation defaults are, in fact, acceptable. Certainly, from a performance and/or correctness perspective, the defaults may work, but more importantly, are you sure that the defaults set up by the vendor leave the system secure?

Consider, for a moment, the Oracle database installation. By default, assuming no other steps are taken to correct this, every Oracle database comes with at least one login that everybody knows about: the `scott` username, `tiger` password account. It's used as the example account in just about every Oracle book on the planet, and a lot of Oracle database administrators and developers are so used to having it there they forget that every other Oracle developer on the planet knows it's there, too. Similarly, SQL Server ships with the administrative account `sa` set to a default password of nothing, as in, "just hit Enter when asked for the password" nothing. Other databases follow suit.

Here's an interesting test for you: go through all your company's Oracle and SQL Server database instances, trying `scott/tiger` and sa/<nothing> and see how many successful logins you get. (Of course, make sure you've notified your system administrators of what you're doing, in case you accidentally trip an intrusion detection system or they happen to catch you wandering through the databases; I'd hate for you to get fired on my advice.) If your company is like many companies, chances are you'll be somewhat shocked and appalled at how many times these default accounts are left turned on.

Worse yet, many times these accounts still have their default permissions turned on, which means that in the case of the standard administrative accounts, you have complete and total access to every database instance installed on that server or cluster. Imagine the chaos you could wreak if you were feeling particularly malicious.[2] Even for those installations where the default logins aren't particularly powerful, what's to stop you from engaging in a denial-of-service attack by filling up the disk with streaming media from some of the Internet's most popular Web sites?

---

2. In no way am I suggesting that you actually use this as a means of "getting back at your boss" or the company for insults or slights, real or imagined. But a certain amount of security preparedness means thinking like an attacker, to understand how they will attack your system.

This is a particularly sticky point of building a secure system: you must assume everything is insecure, including any particular point in the system you're building, until you can establish beyond any sort of reasonable doubt that the system is secure against intrusion and attack. Of course, if you trust your vendor when they tell you it's secure, then by all means, go ahead and assume it's secure, but before you do, stop and think: Do you seriously believe the vendor would tell you if it weren't?

The logical next step is to somehow prove the system is secure. You can probably establish a pretty comprehensive checklist of common attacks to try, particularly when aided by the Open Web Application Security Project (OWASP)[3] Top Ten Web Application Vulnerabilities list and other documents. You can test against known attacks that have been historically successful against that vendor's product, and you can even try a few new ones you've thought up along the way. The unfortunate fact is, all this testing *still* isn't going to prove that the system is secure.

The problem is that proving a system is secure is much like proving somebody was planning to commit treason: it's slippery, nebulous, and subject to change from one moment to the next. For example, even if we can prove that the system is secure today, a new vulnerability in the vendor's software could be discovered by the hacking community tomorrow, and suddenly our system has a vulnerability that we don't even know exists, at least not until it's used successfully on our system.

To summarize, there are two laws of enterprise security.

1. Assume a component is insecure until proven otherwise.
2. A component can never be proven secure.

So where, exactly, does that leave us? The combination of the two seems to lead to a rather impossible situation.

Welcome to the scary world of enterprise security.

Before you think I'm being a bit paranoid and defeatist about the whole thing, I'm not alone in preaching this particular depressing song; Schneier writes, "In all our years of working in [security], we have yet to see an entire system that is secure. That's right. Every system we have analyzed has been broken in one way or another. There are always a few

---

3. An open-source collaborative effort designed to help organizations recognize and understand the details of securing Web applications and Web Services; see http://www.owasp.org.

components that are good, but they invariably get used in insecure ways" [Schneier03, 1].

Where this leaves us is pretty simple: always assume that everything is insecure and that you *will* be attacked successfully at some point. Given the practical realities of the situation facing us in the current decade, you really have no other choice but to accept this. I realize this isn't an easy pill to swallow—take a moment and gather your composure if you need to— but it is a pill you need to take.

As it turns out, this isn't a final pronouncement of doom, much as it may seem like one. If we again go back to the real world for a moment, it turns out that this is a pretty common state of affairs. Most physical security devices are built and designed in such a way that they can be broken eventually. Think about it: If the bank didn't assume that the burglars could get past the locks on the doors, why would they stick the money into a vault deep inside the building? If the government didn't assume that the enemy could get past the barbed wire fence, why put troops in jeeps with machine guns to patrol the perimeter? If automakers didn't assume that car thieves could get past the locks on the doors, why make the engine start only to a particular key?

In essence, each of these real-world security systems is using a *defense-in-depth strategy;* rather than placing all the security eggs into the basket at the perimeter, they assume that at each level, the defense can be broken, so another defense needs to be ready just in case. Again, to go back to the bank scenario, a typical bank has several layers of security established to prevent people from walking out with money stolen from the vault. Assuming the bank thief strikes at night, we have locks on the doors, we have cameras watching the doors and windows (to deter the thieves on the idea that we'll be able to identify them and hunt them down), we have sensors tied to alarms at the local police station on each of the doors and windows, and we have a vault made of yard-thick steel with a really hard-to-break lock on the front door. If the bank thief wants to strike during the day instead, we have a guard in the lobby, who may or may not have a gun (more deterrence), the tellers usually stand behind some kind of physical barricade and have some kind of silent alarm they can trip to alert the police, and the vault door can be closed if the thieves aren't quite quick enough.

How do we translate this defense-in-depth concept into an enterprise system? For starters, we abandon the notion that the firewall will make everything secure or that if we keep up on the latest operating system patches, we'll be fine. Simply dropping the Web server into the DMZ is not enough—it's a step, but we have to carry it further, just as having a firewall or a DMZ is just a step.

Some ideas (but certainly not an exhaustive list) to consider for deploying a defense-in-depth strategy follow.

- Establish a firewall around the core components of the system (HTTP server, database server, and so on).
- Establish a second firewall behind the "forward" parts of the system (those parts the user's client software must communicate with, typically the HTTP server), thus creating a DMZ. Configure the second firewall to accept traffic only from the HTTP server.
- Turn off every system service on both the HTTP server and database server; there is no reason, for example, the HTTP server or the database server needs to answer TCP/IP date or echo requests. Ping may be about the only thing you need here as far as TCP/IP basic services, and even that's a matter of debate. For Win32 operating systems, for example, the HTTP server machine really doesn't need MSMQ, the COM+ system application or event system services, infrared monitor service, and so on. Each of these is a potential vulnerability point, and if they're not being used by the server for anything, why have them turned on? Do a similar checklist for Solaris and/or Linux servers—do you really need X running on those production machines? Granted, it's convenient sometimes, but is it worth the potential security risk? Even Telnet should probably be turned off, assuming the system administrators have access to a physical keyboard and monitor to do machine administration. (Yes, I know it's more convenient to have Telnet turned on, but again, can you prove that the machine's Telnet daemon is secure?)
- Never use the same login credentials within the application as those used to administer the HTTP or database services. In other words, make sure the system administrators and database administrators have different username/password identities than those used within the application; as a corollary, never use those administrative accounts across a remote connection if possible, and never from outside the firewall.
- Make sure *everything* on the security perimeter (i.e., somewhere between the servers that users access and the users themselves) has had every single authentication credential checked—turn off the defaults, make sure the passwords selected aren't weak or easy to

crack (if possible—there's only so much you can do here when users insist on having "password" as their password), and so on. This goes for every piece of equipment, including routers, hubs, firewalls, proxies, and so on.

As you can see, it's pretty easy to start to get into a paranoid mind-set when thinking about security like this. That's probably a good start.

Remember, we can't stop an attacker—prevention by itself will never guarantee a secure system (see Item 58). Instead, the goal is to slow the attacker down, so that a combination of intrusion detection systems and alert system administrators can detect the attack and take the appropriate reactionary steps, including shutting down accounts and/or systems if necessary (depending on the sensitivity of the system being attacked, which is why you build a threat model in the first place—see Item 59).

One corollary to this item is to follow the *principle of least privilege*—that is, don't grant anything more than the absolute minimum set of rights to your code to execute. For code that accesses a relational database, for example, *don't* use a database account that has rights beyond the simple SELECT/INSERT/UPDATE/DELETE actions. As explained in Item 61, if the code somehow gets smashed by a command injection attack, if the account has rights to manipulate the schema itself, you could end up staring at a database instance with absolutely zero tables in it. Similarly, if the code has rights to the file system and the code again is successfully smashed, you could find yourself with a ton of unrecognizable files (all of which start with the three letters XXX, strangely enough) stored on your server's filesystem.

This attitude doesn't stop with your code, by the way. Apply the principle of least privilege at every opportunity, including that point at which Java meets the underlying operating system. If you install a J2EE container to run as a standalone user-agnostic application (a daemon process under UNIX, a service under Win32), make sure the process executes as the least-privileged user possible, even if this means creating a user account specifically for that container.

(Under NT/Win2K/XP, by the way, the account used to run the process is configurable through the Services snap-in—bring it up, find the service in question, and bring up that service's Properties page, typically by right-clicking it and selecting Properties from the menu. One of the tabs in the Properties page is called Log On, and this is where you can configure the account used to execute the process. Generally speaking, for a production system, you won't want to use the `LocalSystem` account, since this account is used for other services, and you'll want to tune the rights assigned to the account to be as minimal as possible. For more information on Win32 security, including all the rights and what they mean, I highly recommend *Programming Windows Security* [Brown].)

Item 61: Always validate user input

The Open Web Application Security Project (http://www.owasp.org), as mentioned in Item 60, is an open-source collaborative effort designed to help organizations (particularly, as of this writing, developers within those organizations) recognize and understand the details of securing Web applications and Web Services. As part of this effort, OWASP has produced a Top Ten Web Application Security Vulnerabilities document, in the same style as the SANS/FBI Top Twenty list.

The number one vulnerability on the OWASP list is Unvalidated Parameters. In fact, three of the ten directly deal with user input in some way: Unvalidated Parameters (#1), Buffer Overflows (#5), and Command Injection Flaws (#6). If we extend the idea of handling user input a bit, we can also include Cross-Site Scripting Flaws (#4) and Error Handling Problems (#7). Clearly, how we deal with user input is critical to building a secure system. And when you stop to think about it for a moment, it's pretty clear why this is the case: anywhere the system accepts user input is an open door for an attacker to try to come through.

When building an HTML-based application, validating user input is an absolutely crucial step in securing the application. Unfortunately, too many developers trust the technology to take care of this for them and leave themselves exposed to sneaky, underhanded tactics by attackers. For example, numerous Web applications, in keeping with Item 56, make heavy use of client-side script to perform most, if not all, validation in the browser. It's fast and it prevents a round-trip; we can manipulate the UI elements directly if we need to change the user interface, rather than having to go back to the server and regenerate a new screen.

As a matter of fact, the client-side validation story seems such a good idea, why bother validating the input again on the server? After all, the browser will execute the script as the user and/or would-be attacker move around on the page, and since we (presumably) made sure the user's browser had scripting support turned on from the entry/login page, why duplicate effort to do all that validation again on the server? It's just going to burn CPU cycles in a redundant effort, and wasting CPU cycles hurts not only performance but scalability as well.

The problem, once you stop to think about it, is that attackers don't play by the rules—they don't limit themselves to attacking your application through the browser. Many attackers have a strong enough knowledge of HTTP that they can mock up the form submission themselves using nothing more sophisticated than Telnet, and since most Telnet clients haven't yet been extended to support JavaScript, all your wonderful client-side validation logic goes right out the window.

The brutal truth is that as a developer, you *have* to assume that the client-side validation logic failed to execute somehow, and on every user input submission, go through a rigorous set of validation checks to ensure the user input has been thoroughly scrubbed for all sorts of nasty kinds of input-based attacks.

Parameter validation errors come in a variety of sizes and shapes. For example, as part of testing your Web application, every time users are asked for input, and even in cases where they're not but incoming data is expected to be there—HTTP headers, cookie values, and so on—try passing in a variety of "bad" data and see how well your Web application reacts. What happens when you pass in:

- Null?
- Characters from a different character set? Unicode characters? Unprintable ASCII characters?
- Zero-length parameters? 1K parameters? 10K parameters?
- Numbers where characters are expected, and vice versa?
- Duplicate data (the same parameter twice in the same form, for example)?

You might consider this to be more in the realm of "QA weirdness" because, of course, no user would ever pass a name where a phone number is expected, but remember, we're not talking about users anymore. We're talking about attackers, and they don't play by the rules.

As an example, let's start with the canonical user login page. In many, if not most, systems, user authentication details are stored in an RDBMS table, typically in a rather simple two-column table consisting of the user's login name (uid, a VARCHAR 20 characters long) and the user's authentication credentials, in this case a password (password, another VARCHAR 20 characters long). Any other user-specific details stored in this table, such as configuration settings, personal data, authorization settings, and so on, are for the moment irrelevant.

In the usual fashion, we'll build a login JSP page, the heart of which will look something like this:

```
<form action="/LoginProcessor" method="POST">
Your Username: <input type="text"
                       name="username"><br />
Your Password: <input type="password"
                       name="password"><br />
<input type="submit" value="Log in">
</form>
```

So far, so good. The LoginProcessor URL is mapped to a servlet, the key parts of which need to issue a SQL statement against the database to see if this uid/password pair exists within the table. Nothing could be simpler, right?

```
Connection conn = getConnectionFromSomewhere();
Statement stmt = conn.createStatement();
String SQL = "SELECT * FROM users " +
   "WHERE uid = '" + request.getParameter("username")+
   "' AND password = '" +
   request.getParameter("password") + "'";
ResultSet rs = stmt.executeQuery(SQL);
if (rs.next())
{
   // User/password pair was there; go ahead
   // and forward to the next JSP in the page flow
}
else
{
   // Whoops! User failed to authenticate safely;
   // keep track of the number of times this user
   // fails to authenticate (see Item 60). After
   // a few more tries, lock out the account in case
   // it's an attacker trying a brute-force attack.
}
```

We're done, right? We check that one off the task list and move on to the next story/task/whatever.

Unfortunately, no, we're *not* done. As it stands, this code is vulnerable in a big way to a *command injection attack* (OWASP Vulnerability #6). A command injection attack occurs when user input can carry executable code that will be executed by some layer of the system when processed; in this way, it's conceptually very similar to a *buffer overrun attack*, which seeks to smash the stack instead.

To see this sort of attack in action, let's switch hats for a moment and take on the perspective of the attacker. One of the first tricks to try is to blindly launch an injection attack and see if it's successful in some way ("success" here is any indication that an attack might work somehow). For example, the attacker may submit a username of `'SELECT'`, that is, a single quote, the word `SELECT`, and another single quote, and see what he gets back. In the earlier code, the single quote in front of the text will turn off the single quote in our SQL statement, thereby leaving the SQL parser to assume that the string is *supposed* to be empty, then it will see the `SELECT` text, which is of course a keyword in SQL, in the wrong place to successfully parse, and it will throw a `SQLException`.

So . . . exactly what did we do with the `SQLException` again?

There are two different scenarios. In the first, ideal, scenario, we catch the `SQLException`, regardless of the error, and display a nicely formatted page that tells the user that something went wrong, and would they please try again? The problem here, unfortunately, is that displaying this message on a failed login is going to confuse the user, so we'll also have a different page that tells them their login failed, and please try again. Thanks to our differentiation between bad user input and a failed SQL call, however, we've given the attacker an important hint. In fact, this differentiation is music to the attackers' ears—he now knows that his single-quote-escaped input somehow screwed up the SQL statement, which means that a SQL command injection attack just might work. So he continues the attack.

In the second scenario, which is the unfortunate default, we just catch the `SQLException` and rethrow it as either a `ServletException` or an `IOException` (since that's what the servlet `doPost` method is declared to throw), figuring that if a `SQLException` ever occurs, it must be a programmer error and we, at least, want to see the stack trace. Which is absolutely awful, because now when the attacker conducts his command injection experiment, he'll see a stack trace that probably reads something like, "Malformed SQL statement: unexpected SELECT" or something similar in the message portion of the exception. To an attacker, this roughly translates into, "Green light! Keep going! You're almost there!"

So our wily attacker chooses his next command injection attack with a bit more care. If our attacker wants to gain access as a particular user, he could submit the login form as:

```
username = boss'; SELECT pwd FROM users WHERE password = 'foo
pwd = foo
```

Plugging this into the SQL statement that's going to be dynamically constructed inside the servlet, we start to get a Really Bad Feeling:

```
SELECT * FROM users
   WHERE username = '

boss';SELECT password FROM users WHERE password='foo

' AND password = '

foo

'
```

Reformatted to be more human-readable, we get:

```
SELECT * FROM users WHERE username = 'boss';
SELECT * FROM users WHERE password = 'foo' AND password =
          'foo'
```

Now, because the semicolon acts as a statement separator in many SQL dialects, where we thought we were executing one SQL statement, thanks to our attacker's rather unorthodox input, we're now executing two of them. How the JDBC driver will react depends, of course, on the actual JDBC driver in use, but most of them will simply support the two `ResultSet` instances as "extra results," meaning to get to the second `ResultSet` we need to call `getMoreResults`. In our servlet code, however, we're just checking to see whether there are any results in the first `ResultSet`, and since the query succeeded (assuming, of course, our attacker got the username correct, which usually isn't a hard thing to do), our attacker is now logged into the system as `bigboss`, which is probably a Bad Thing.

Assume our attacker isn't interested in being so subtle, however:

```
username=boss'; DELETE FROM users WHERE password != '
password = <empty>
```

Again, making this into readable SQL statements, we get a really nasty turn of events:

```
SELECT * FROM users WHERE username = 'boss';
DELETE FROM users WHERE password != '';
```

Suddenly, our system administrators' vigilance in not allowing empty passwords works against us as all the users in the system have their login credentials gleefully erased by the ever-helpful SQL executor in the RDBMS. Suddenly nobody can log in, and you get a phone call at 3 A.M. from the CTO and/or VP demanding to know why your system is suddenly not letting anybody in. This is *not* the kind of attention you want from upper management.

It gets even more interesting; assuming your system has some kind of role-based authorization scheme, and that (as is typical) your "root" account is the first one installed in the users table, an attacker can do this:

```
username = boss' OR 1 = 1 --
password = <irrelevant>
```

Which, again, turning this into human-friendly SQL, yields:

```
SELECT * FROM users WHERE username='boss' OR 1=1 -- AND
    password="
```

Note that the double-dash is an end-of-line comment character in most SQL flavors, thus rendering the check for the password entirely irrelevant. Since 1=1 is an always-true predicate, the entire users table will be returned from this query, and since the ultra-empowered administrator account will be the first row returned, that's what our intrepid attacker will be logged in as at this point. Oopsie.

It's not just the login page that potentially has this vulnerability, either, folks. It's everywhere that servlet code directly takes input from the user and creates a SQL statement out of it. Actually, this vulnerability exists anywhere servlet code takes input from the incoming HTTP request and creates a SQL statement out of it, regardless of whether the user actually was supposed to type something into a form or not. The classic culprit here is to put data into a hidden form and use that as part of the created SQL statement:

```
String SQL = "INSERT INTO order_totals VALUES (" +
  // . . . Other data, like order ID and items,
  // go here . . .
  (totalPrice *
    Float.parseFloat(request.getParameter("discount"))) +
  ")";
```

where `"discount"` is a hidden field set by an earlier page via JavaScript. So our wily attacker does a View Source on the HTML page (or just hits the URL directly with Telnet), sees the hidden `"discount"` field, and suddenly he's buying all sorts of stuff with a 99% discount. (If he did it with a 100% discount, the total would be 0, and that might trip other alarms further down the line. This way he's getting almost the same benefit with lower risk.)

We could go through more examples like this, but they're all variations on the same theme. What's important at this point is to figure out what to *do* about it.

In the specific case of the login and the order-processing servlets, the first step is to stop constructing the SQL statements directly from user input. Our first reaction might be to write validation code that would somehow trap and exclude the SQL code in the input fields (in the case of the login servlet), but this won't help the order-processing servlet, particularly if there's an actual business case that allows certain people to purchase items with a 99% or 100% discount. (CEOs do this all the time, for example.)

Fortunately, another, simpler answer for SQL statements exists: never use a `Statement` to do the SQL based on user input. Doing so forces you to worry about taking care of character escaping, which is why the attacker's single-quote trick works in the first place. Instead, if you make use of a `PreparedStatement`, not only will you get a possible performance boost (see Item 49), but the `PreparedStatement` mechanism has to take care of properly escaping the input passed in as input parameters to the `PreparedStatement`. So now our login servlet reads like this:

```
Connection conn = getConnectionFromSomewhere();
String SQL = "SELECT * FROM users " +
             "WHERE uid = ? and password = ?";
PreparedStatement prep = conn.prepareStatement(SQL);
prep.setString(1, request.getParameter("username"));
prep.setString(2, request.getParameter("password"));
ResultSet rs = prep.executeQuery();
// Rest as before
```

Now, assuming the *driver* isn't written to allow an injection attack (which is a distinct but rapidly shrinking possibility—make sure you've tested your driver against this possibility, among others; see Item 49), a SQL command injection attack attempt will fail with a SQLException.

Not only SQL commands have this vulnerability, however—any time data is being passed to an external system for execution, such as creating a command string to be executed by an external shell, you're back to worrying about validating user input. Fortunately, JDK 1.4 introduces support for regular expressions on strings, which makes this kind of validation simpler. It turns out to be much easier to use a regular expression to verify that a given string doesn't contain the kind of escape characters that make an injection attack possible.

By the way, if your site allows users to post comments on the page using HTML, you're vulnerable to a *cross-site scripting attack* (OWASP Vulnerability #4), meaning an attacker can put malicious HTML input onto *your* site that engages in an attack against the user's browser when the user views your site. This is not the way to build good customer relations. (*Writing Secure Code* gives an example of using a regexp to validate against a cross-site scripting attack [Howard/LeBlanc, 430].)

In some ways, it would be nice if Java supported the idea of a "tainted" string (i.e., one that comes in from outside the JVM), as Perl does, but neither Sun nor the Java Community Process is showing any signs of adding this to the language, so we'll have to live without it for now. If your developers are a disciplined lot, you could create a TaintedString class like the one shown here that does all sorts of validation on the data, and use that to wrap any end-user input:

```
public class TaintedString
{
```

```java
private final String endUserData;
private boolean validated = false;

public TaintedString(String input)
{
  endUserData = input;
}

public void validateForXSS()
{
  validate(new XSSTaintValidator());
}
public void validateForSQL()
{
  validate(new SQLTaintValidator());
}
public void validate(TaintValidator v)
{
  try
  {
    v.validate(endUserData);
    validated = true;
  }
  catch (SecurityException secEx)
  {
    validated = false;
  }
}

public String getString()
{
  if (validated)
    return endUserData;
  else
    return null; // Or throw an Exception,
                 // whichever you prefer
}

public interface TaintValidator
{
```

```
      public void validate(String data);
   }

   public static class XSSTaintValidator
      implements TaintValidator
   {
      public void validate(String data)
      {
         // Run through validation scenarios to
         // make sure data doesn't contain an XSS
         // attack; if it does,
         // throw a SecurityException
      }
   }

   public static class SQLTaintValidator
      implements TaintValidator
   {
      public void validate(String data)
      {
         // Run through validation scenarios to make
         // sure data doesn't contain an SQL injection
         // attack; if it does,
         // throw a SecurityException
      }
   }
}
```

The idea here is that once the `String` is handed into the `TaintedString`, it must be validated either by using one of the provided validating methods against a particular kind of attack—cross-site scripting and SQL injection are two examples—or by passing in a customized `Strategy` object implementing the `TaintValidator` interface to validate against some other malicious input. Assuming the validation succeeds (i.e., the `validate` method of the `TaintValidator` doesn't throw a `Security Exception`), the `validated` flag is set to `true`, and we can obtain the input via `getString`. If the validation failed or hasn't been called yet, `getString` returns `null` (or, if you prefer, can throw an `Exception`).

The hard part about using this, however, is that developers must have the discipline to take any user input and pass it into the `TaintedString` before using it further. Since neither the Java language nor the JVM itself support `TaintedString`, there's no way to enforce this beyond code reviews and source-code scanners. But if the developers can force themselves into using `TaintedString` for input, they can save themselves from that 3 A.M. phone call, and that's pretty good motivation in my book.

Oh, and for those of you who have taken Item 51 to heart and are using a rich client for your front end and some kind of alternative communication layer back to the server for data exchange, don't think you're out of the woods here. Web Services are fast becoming a favorite way to allow rich-client applications to talk to back-end middleware systems, and to the wily attacker, there is no difference between a Web application serving HTML and a Web Service serving XML. In fact, you must be *more* careful with the Web Service since scrubbing incoming Web Service data for security intrusion attempts is still below the radar of most Web Service developers. Input is still input, whether it's in HTML format, XML format, or RMI/JRMP object-serialization format. If it's coming in from outside this process, validate it every way you can think of, or it's a fair bet you'll be sorry you didn't someday. (*Ring!* "Uh, hi, Mr. CEO, sir. . . . Meeting? With the legal team? Five minutes? " *Gulp.* "Absolutely, sir.")

Regardless of what your front end is, remember that any time you take input directly from the user and feed it into a database query (or any other sort of interaction with a back-end system; I'm firmly convinced that SQL injection attacks are only the most popular of the resource-script-injection attack genre, not the only kind possible), you're taking it upon yourself to be more clever than the attacker, and that's a pretty arrogant assumption. Instead, rely on the mechanisms within the various layers of software you work with, such as the escaping capabilities of the JDBC driver, to protect yourself from malicious user input. And, as a result of reading Item 60, you of course assume that *all* user input is trying to be malicious in some way.

Item 62:   Turn on platform security

Ever since JDK 1.0, one of Java's principal strengths has been its deep relationship with the idea of lacing security directly within the language and environment. The `SecurityManager` and its successor in JDK 1.2 and beyond, the `AccessController`, are a fundamental part of the runtime and environment—myriad actions within the Java environment trigger a security check, such as opening a file, attempting a socket connection to a server, and trying to read a system property.

To make things even better, starting with JDK 1.2, the security mechanism within the platform was extended and opened to allow non-Sun developers to write their own `Permission` classes (representing sensitive actions) and custom `Policy` classes (the class by which allowed permissions are decided and established). No more is Java code constrained to heavy-handed security environments like the applet sandbox. Now, thanks to the default file-based `Policy` implementation that ships with the JDK, developers have tremendous fine-grained control over exactly what sorts of things are allowed within the JVM—which makes it all the more shameful that not only do most J2EE developers ignore it, but so do most of the J2EE specifications and many J2EE container implementations.

For many enterprise Java developers, the Java Security Manager is something to be feared, loathed, and left alone as much as possible. Most developers first run into the `SecurityManager` in RMI code, and it shows up by suddenly throwing `SecurityException` instances everywhere at the worst possible time, usually when trying to put the application into production. Developers quickly learn how to set up a "let everything go by" policy file:

```
grant
{
  permission java.security.AllPermission;
}
```

This, of course, gets them past the immediate problem—if the security policy says to grant everything `AllPermission`, then nothing is ever actually blocked by the `SecurityManager` and we can now live happily ever after again, right?

It's not like we can really blame these poor Java coders, since anything related to the word "security" has huge piles of anxicty associated with it. When the chips are down, and the CEO is breathing down your neck to ship the application yesterday, wrestling with the Java policy file syntax is *not* what you want to be doing.

The problem, however, is that running Java code with this lenient permissions policy effectively gives an attacker a free pass should he or she somehow manage to lure your code into doing something evil. So much for the principle of least privilege (see Item 60). Because the Java Security Manager is no longer able to enforce restrictions, suddenly your servlet or JSP has complete access to anything within the JVM, and an attacker could conceivably start opening sockets, overwriting files on the local filesystem, and wreaking other malicious madness. The most frustrating part of all this is that this is precisely what the security manager was designed to prevent—if you let it.

For example, let's stop and look at the servlet container. From an enterprise perspective, each Web application deployed within a servlet container is intended to be an isolated, self-standing application that has no idea whether it is alone within the container or deployed alongside dozens (or hundreds) of other Web applications. From an Internet service provider's perspective, this is absolutely necessary, or my Web application could conceivably start making method calls on your servlets—this is generally considered a Bad Idea.

So what happens if I write a servlet that takes a relative filename as input and echoes that file back down the pipe as the response content? Intrinsically, nothing here seems amiss, but what happens if I feed it a relative filename (say, something like `../../../../etc/passwd`) that goes right up the directory tree to the parent directory of all the installed Web applications and does a directory listing? Or goes "up and over" into another Web application's deployed directory and lists out its `web.xml` file? Or password files?

If the servlet container is running with an overly permissive Java `Policy` implementation, there's nothing the container can do to stop me; certainly, if I ask for the file through a servlet API, such as `ServletContext`'s `getResourceAsStream`, the servlet container could intercept the request, realize it's outside my Web application, and reject it. Servlet containers might do this; it's not required by the specification that they do so. But what's to stop me if I create a `File` object with that relative path? The servlet container doesn't replace the standard Java runtime library, and since the Java Security Manager is rubber-stamping all requests, I've got a window into any other Web application installed on the system.

Turning the security manager on is a pretty simple thing: when executing the Java launcher (`java.exe`) to start up the J2EE container, set the `java.security.manager` system property by passing it via the -D option; you don't need to set it to anything, just add the JVM command-line parameter `-Djava.security.manager` to the script you use to launch the container. This will turn on the security manager, which in turn uses the `java.policy` file stored in the JRE's `lib/security` directory as the policy for the JVM. Assuming you're using independent JRE instances for the container (see Item 69), any changes required to the policy can be made directly within this file.

As a matter of fact, a number of changes are quite likely; the J2EE environment for the most part assumes that it will be running in a JVM with the security manager turned off, so turning security on will generate `SecurityException` instances pretty quickly; for example, J2EE assumes that the container is free to access system properties at any time, and since accessing a system property is a permission-constrained privilege, this permission needs to be granted to the container itself by explicitly granting it in the policy file. Similarly, if your code needs to reach across the network for any reason (e.g., to connect to a database), socket permissions will need to be granted, and so on.

Given that you're going to have to work out a security policy that describes precisely which permissions need to be granted to the container (as opposed to your component code), and that this is going to take a nontrivial amount of time, assuming your container vendor hasn't already provided you with one, why bother? We all have too much to do and not enough time to do it, so why waste time figuring out security policy? There has to be some legitimate payoff, right?

Assume for a moment that your Web application, running in the servlet container in your company's DMZ, connects to a database running on the server named dbserver.mycompany.com. You've established a security policy that allows for connections to that machine and nowhere else (`permission java.net.SocketPermission "dbserver.mycompany.com", "connect"`). Now an attacker manages to successfully hijack your servlet and wants to execute some arbitrary Java code; despite the fact that he's got control of the thread, when he tries to open a connection to anywhere other than the database server, he's going to run afoul of the security manager, and a `SecurityException` will be thrown. The same will happen if he tries to open a new socket to accept connections on some random high-numbered port, or if he tries to write to the filesystem anywhere outside of your Web application's deployed directory, and so on.

By itself, turning on the security manager within your J2EE container may seem like more work than it's worth, particularly if the vendor implementation doesn't have a security policy definition tuned for its own use. (If your vendor doesn't, consider switching to another vendor product, or put some pressure on the vendor to provide one.) When coupled with using JAAS, however, as described in Item 63, the benefits of the Java platform security model become much clearer.

Item 63:   Use role-based authorization

Authentication is pretty easy to recognize: it's the act of somebody attempting to prove his or her identity to the system, usually by presenting a password (a "secret") that theoretically only that person knows. The login form is a well-known idiom within Web applications, so we're not going to belabor the point here, although we will come back to it later.

Authorization, on the other hand, is a much more nebulous concept. Formally, authorization is the act of ascertaining what actions can be performed within the system. For example, under the normal Java Security Manager, authorization is granted to execute certain "sensitive" actions (such as starting threads, opening connections, and such) based on where the code was loaded from; this is well documented in books like *Inside Java 2 Platform Security* [Gong] and *Java Security* [Oaks]. Nowhere, however, within the standard Java security platform is the concept of *user-based security* discussed.

Most applications, however, have at least a coarse-grained idea of authorization buried within their requirements. Very few applications can treat all users exactly the same. At the very least there are usually three types of users: users, guests, and administrators. For many applications, the authorization model gets extremely complex: there may be dozens of different possible actions within the system and hundreds (if not thousands) of users, each of whom has different access rights to those actions. If we try to code this by hand, the presentation layer (whether servlet or JSP) will quickly become very complex.

Having all this security code laced all throughout the system is a crosscutting concern, something that really has nothing to do with the system's business logic. As a result, the J2EE specifications, most notably the servlet and EJB specifications, include configuration options within the deployment descriptor to try to remove this burden from the developer's shoulders.

To see how complex authorization can get in a real-world system, imagine for a moment a system with tens of thousands of users and hundreds of different unique access rights (not unusual for medium-sized applications). Every time a user is added to the system, a system administrator has to explicitly mark each access right for that user, which becomes more and more time-consuming as the number of access rights goes up. And heaven help your system administrators if you add new permissions to the system in a follow-up phase or release: now they have to go back through the *entire* user database and explicitly add that right to each one of those users that needs it (because you assume the default is that they don't have permission—see Item 60). This *very* quick way to make your system administrators cross with you does not lead to happy developer-administrator relationships.

One way to avoid this kind of administrative and developer security madness is to use a *role-based authorization system,* whereby permissions (rights to execute sensitive actions) are assigned to abstract categories of users called *roles.* The idea is to introduce a layer of indirection between users and the rights they are given. Instead of assigning rights to users directly, rights are assigned to roles, and then users are assigned one or more roles. Permission checks are made simpler because now we only need to consult one of a far smaller collection of roles, and user management is easier because users are simply assigned roles rather than access rights. If new access rights are introduced in a later phase or revision, either these rights can be assigned to existing roles (thus meaning no change to the user base) or new roles can be introduced if necessary.

The J2EE servlet and EJB containers contain sections on security, specifically on authorization and access controls; once the user has authenticated into the system (either by going through the built-in `j_security_check` action in servlet containers or by authenticating via JNDI properties during the EJB bean `Home` lookup), the container can consult a vendor-specific user database to determine the user's configured roles. From here, programmers can allow/restrict access to URL resources (servlets or JSPs) or bean methods (on EJBs) by two methods: (1) by listing those restrictions explicitly in the deployment descriptors of the J2EE component (Web application or enterprise archive), or (2) by using the programmatic APIs provided by both environments, most notably the `isCaller InRole` method. Using the deployment descriptors allows for coarse-grained security controls—for example, doing so on a JSP means users will be granted or denied access to the entire page—whereas using the programmatic APIs allows for a more fine-grained approach.

However, despite the ease and flexibility that the servlet and EJB specifications offer, they miss one important aspect of authorization control: controlling access to resources outside the J2EE sphere of influence. For example, opening a file on the underlying filesystem normally requires an appropriate permission at the Java platform security level. However, because the J2EE security system is entirely orthogonal to Java's Security Manager APIs, there's no way to grant access to the filesystem based on the end-user's role without explicitly putting a check in front of the code that wants to open the file:

```
// EJB bean
EJBContext context = ...;
if (context.isCallerInRole("admin"))
{
  // Do whatever admin-only processing is necessary
  //
}


// servlet
HttpServletRequest request = ...;
if (request.isUserInRole("admin"))
{
  FileOutputStream fos = new FileOutputStream(. . .);

  // Do whatever admin-only processing is necessary
  //
}
```

In many respects, this is a bad situation on multiple levels. First, if an attacker can somehow find a flaw in your code, the underlying platform security model (which is built specifically to prevent such kinds of attacks and thus does a complete stack walk on a security check) won't be able to help stop the attack. More importantly, however, it's too easy for a developer on your team to forget to put the J2EE security check in front of the code to open the file, particularly if it's 3 A.M. and you're supposed to ship the application the next day. Or, worse yet, "I know we should put this security code in here, but it's working now, so let's ship it and fix it later—it's not like an attacker's going to *know* the flaw's here, right?"

What we'd really like to see is an integration of the J2EE role-based authorization security model with the underlying platform security model, so that we can bring the benefits of both security models to bear on our applications' needs. Unfortunately, not only does the J2EE role-based authorization model not hook on to the platform security model, but up through JDK 1.3, the platform security model had no concept of user-based authorization rights.

Between the JDK 1.3 and 1.4 releases, Sun introduced a new API, the Java JAAS, which corrects this egregious oversight. In a sentence, JAAS extends the Java standard security model to include authorization based on *identity*, as well as the code's source. In short, the standard platform security model now understands user-based authorization, which means that integrating role-based authorization into the platform security model is now possible. In case you're wondering whether it's worth reading the rest of this item ("Bah, J2EE security is enough for me"), a new JSR, the Java Authorization Contract for Containers (JSR 115), effectively integrates J2EE security with the underlying JAAS and Java platform security model, so you're going to be here sooner or later anyway. Fortunately, using JAAS is not a difficult thing to do, once you've taken care of some basic overhead. (Other sources, such as *Inside Java 2 Platform Security* [Gong], cover JAAS in detail, so in this discussion I'm just going to walk through some of the high-level steps necessary to use it.)

A JAAS security setup has two elements. First, because JAAS supports a pluggable authentication model, meaning it can support multiple kinds of authentication and authorization systems simultaneously, JAAS needs to know which pluggable modules it will be working with. This is called the *JAAS configuration*, and while it's possible to establish this programmatically (see the `javax.security.auth.login.Configuration` class), it's far more common to use the default `Configuration` implementation that reads a text file identified by the JVM system property `java.security.auth.logon.config`. The contents of this text file look something like the following:

```
MySystem
{
  com.tagish.auth.RdbmsLoginModule Required
    driver="org.gjt.mm.mysql.Driver"
    url="jdbc:mysql://localhost/userdb?user=root";
}
```

(In this particular example, we're using an open-source `LoginModule` provided at http://free.tagish.net/jaas that will use a relational database for its user database. It's possible to build your own `LoginModule` implementations, but that's beyond the scope of this item; either see *Java Security* [Oaks] for details or do a Google search for some of the Internet articles and papers that describe how to do so in greater detail.)

The second part of the setup is the actual assignment of permissions to user roles, which we'll cover later.

Having established the configuration (remember to pass the system property on the container startup command line), upon user entry into the system, we authenticate the user by first creating a `LoginContext` referencing the configuration block we defined previously:

```
// In the servlet acting as the recipient of the
// login.jsp page
//
final String username = request.getParameter("uid");
final String pwd = request.getParameter("pwd");
LoginContext loginCtx =
  new LoginContext("MySystem", new CallbackHandler()
    {
      public void handle(Callback[] callbacks)
        throws IOException,
              UnsupportedCallbackException
      {
        for (int i=0; i<callbacks.length; i++)
        {
          Callback cb = callbacks[i];
          if (cb instanceof NameCallback)
            ((NameCallback)cb).setName(username);
          else if (cb instanceof PasswordCallback)
            ((PasswordCallback)cb).setPassword(pwd);
          else
            throw new
              UnsupportedCallbackException(cb);
        }
      }
    });
loginCtx.login();
```

```
Subject userSubject = loginCtx.getSubject();
HttpSession session = request.getSession(true);
session.setAttribute("userSubject", userSubject);

// userSubject now represents the user
```

A couple of things are happening here at once. The goal is to call `login` on the `LoginContext`, but part of that means we have to pass the authentication credentials to the various modules defined as part of this `Login Context` (which were identified in the configuration file defined earlier). Because JAAS doesn't necessarily know what's needed to do a login ahead of time, it uses a callback approach to gather that information. JAAS doesn't want to make any assumptions about the environment it's executing within; normally, in an interactive application, the callback would pop up some kind of prompt to the user to gather the necessary information, but in a Web application this is obviously not going to work. So, instead, JAAS requires an object that implements the `CallbackHandler` interface to be passed into the `LoginContext` constructor, and then JAAS makes calls on that object to gather its necessary information. In the case of the code above, we provide an anonymous inner-class implementation that simply hands back the strings gathered by the JSP form that fronted this servlet and throw an exception in the event the various authentication systems need something more than username and password.

Once the `LoginContext` has been successfully constructed, we simply call `login` to tell JAAS to authenticate this user against the set of login modules specified in that configuration file. Assuming it is successful (it throws a `LoginException` if it isn't), it returns a `Subject` instance, which essentially represents this user. Cache this thing off—it's a Serializable object for a reason—by storing it into either `HttpSession` or whatever mechanism you're using for per-user data. (This is one case where we have to have some kind of per-user state, so we have to ignore the arguments made in Item 39 and store it in an `HttpSession` or equivalent.) Alternatively, cache off the `LoginContext` itself, since you can always obtain the `Subject` from the `LoginContext` via the `getSubject` call, and the `LoginContext` has another method, `logout`, to close the resources associated with the authenticated user. (As a matter of fact, the `LoginContext` implementation that ships with the Sun JDK has no finalizer, so unless you call `logout`, any external resources allocated to the `Subject` as part of `login` will never be cleaned up; do some profile testing to make sure releasing the last reference to the `LoginContext` doesn't create a resource leak.)

Now, having put the `Subject` into `HttpSession`, on each subsequent JSP and/or servlet access by the user, we can now have the servlet *impersonate* that user for the duration of the HTTP request processing:

```
// Inside the controller servlet or JSP
//
Subject userSubject =
    (Subject)session.getAttribute("userSubject");
Subject.doAsPrivileged(userSubject, new PrivilegedAction()
  {
    public Object run()
    {
      // Do the usual servlet processing logic;
      // inside here, it will be done under
      // userSubject's rights
      //
    }
  }, null);

// Out here, code will execute as the container
//
```

The `Subject.doAsPrivileged` method call essentially tells the executing thread to change its security policy for a bit to mimic that of the user (whose set of available permissions we'll see how to configure in just a moment), so that any calls within the body of the `run` method, which is called by `Subject.doAsPrivileged` once the impersonation is established, are done under the Java platform security semantics. This means that if the servlet attempts to open a file on the filesystem, and the user (or, perhaps more accurately, any roles the user is a part of) doesn't have that permission established, a standard Java `SecurityException` will be thrown. (Within a JSP page, rather than using the plain Java code just listed, it's probably a better idea to write—or download, if one is available, which wasn't the case as of this writing—a JSP custom tag handler to do the impersonation check.)

To configure the authorization policy for a given user role, go to the standard Java security policy file (found at `$JRE/lib/security/java.policy`) and build some authorization blocks in the normal Java platform security fashion. Note that you can do this directly inside this JRE-wide file because you've established an individual JRE just for this container, as recommended by Item 69; if not, you'll need to create a custom policy file and point the servlet container to it via another system property. The policy file looks something like the following:

```
// Java.policy file
//

// Permissions granted to all users
//
grant Principal * *
{
  permission java.security.BasicPermission
    "menuActions","logout";
  // Other permissions here
}


// Permissions granted to users in the "users" role
//
grant Principal com.tagish.auth.TypedPrincipal "user"
{
  permission java.security.BasicPermission "menuActions",
    "save";
  // Other permissions here
}


// Permissions granted to users in the "admin" role
//
grant Principal com.tagish.auth.TypedPrincipal "admin"
{
  permission java.security.BasicPermission "menuActions",
    "delete";
  // Other permissions here
}


// And so on
```

(Again, the `Principal` classes are from the open-source library mentioned earlier.) Now, having granted each role a block of permissions (which are represented by Java `Permission` objects and/or subclasses[4]), we can write code in JSPs and servlets to test whether users have the appropriate permission without having to worry about who the user is, what his or her assigned roles are, or anything beyond the actual `Permission` object required to execute:

```
<%!-- In a JSP page --%>
Menu options:
<% try {
    AccessController.checkPermission(
      new BasicPermission("menuActions","logout");
  %>
<a href="logout.jsp">Logout</a>
<% } catch (SecurityException secEx)
   { /* We ignore this; they don't have access,
       which is OK */ } %>

<%!-- The above is a bit tedious, so we would
      probably replace it with a JSP custom tag
      handler that would look like the following:
   --%>
<taglibrary:checkPermission
     type="java.security.BasicPermission"
     name="menuOptions" actions="save">
   <a href="save.jsp">Save</a>
</taglibrary:checkPermission>

<taglibrary:checkPermission
     type="java.security.BasicPermission"
     name="menuOptions" actions="delete">
   <a href="delete.jsp">Delete</a>
</taglibrary:checkPermission>

<%!-- And so on --%>
```

---

4. See *Inside Java 2 Platform Security* [Gong] or *Java Security* [Oaks] on how to create `Permission` subclasses; it's pretty easy to do.

Again, more information on JAAS is available from the Web and the Java security books mentioned earlier [Gong; Oaks]. As a last comment about JAAS, however, note that the Win32 JDK and Solaris JDK from Sun both include `LoginModule` objects that use the underlying operating system security database to do authentication; never use these for your Web applications. On top of requiring system administrators to do operating system user administration every time a new user wants to use the Web application, using `LoginModule` transmits users' operating system passwords across the HTTP link to the server, so every possible link between the user and the servlet container needs to be locked down in order to avoid Eve (the eavesdropper) sniffing out operating system passwords. In addition, if an attacker manages to guess the password to one system (either the operating system or the Web application), he or she already has a leg up on attacking the other—this is not a defense-in-depth approach (see Item 60).

Item 64: Use `SignedObject` to provide integrity of Serialized objects

Frequently, serializable data travels over media we don't trust inherently (which, by the way, should be all of them—see Item 60). For example, authentication or authorization information that can be spoofed by an attacker could be a powerful way to gain entrance into a system without having to provide the correct credentials—in any situation where authentication or authorization objects are being passed around or stored onto disk, we should make sure the object came from the appropriate server issuing it. In essence, we need to ensure that this token cannot be forged—any modification, benevolent or otherwise, must be immediately detected so that the token can be discarded.

In other words, ask your objects to prove their authenticity to you.

Your first reaction, particularly if you've already read Item 6 and started looking through the Java Object Serialization Specification for ways to use the hook points defined by this specification (see Item 71) might be to provide custom serialization behaviors via `readObject/writeObject` implementations, encrypt the information using the issuer's `PrivateKey` (from the `javax.security` APIs) when the object is first serialized, and deserialize using the issuer's `PublicKey` that travels with the Serialized object. You'd be on the right track, but two things stand in your way: (1) doing all this is tedious and hard, and (2) there's a really good chance that, unless you're a security expert, you'll accidentally leave a hole in the process.

Fortunately, Java already has this covered, via a little-known class in the java.security package called SignedObject. This class wraps a Signature and a Serialized object (actually a copy of the source Serializable object, so future modifications to the Serialized object source won't be reflected in the SignedObject copy), and provides easy methods for verifying the object's authenticity given a PublicKey.

Putting that into code, imagine for a moment that a procedural-first persistence engine (see Item 42) is passing Serialized RowSet objects back and forth between client and server over an ordinary HTTP link. The data isn't confidential, but we need to verify its authenticity as coming from the server—otherwise we could conceivably be receiving replies from some man-in-the-middle process trying to masquerade as the server and influence the results.

In order to circumvent this, create a PrivateKey instance embedded in the server, and serialize the RowSet into a SignedObject by signing it with the PrivateKey:

```
PrivateKey privateKey = getPrivateKey();

RowSet data = ...;

Signature signingEngine =
  Signature.getInstance("SHA1withDSA");

SignedObject signedObject =
  new SignedObject(data, privateKey, signingEngine);

// Serialize the signedObject and ship it
// over the wire
```

The PrivateKey will usually be embedded, probably as a bytestream, somewhere inside the server software resources (usually disguised in some way to avoid being easily discerned as the private key). When serialized, the signedObject instance will contain the digital signature of the private key, and the authenticity of the `signedObject` can be verified by calling the `verify` method with a `Signature` instance that matches the one used to sign the data in the first place and the corresponding public key, again usually embedded as part of the client software footprint:

```
PublicKey publicKey = getPublicKey();

Signature verificationEngine =
    Signature.getInstance("SHA1withDSA");

SignedObject signedObject = ...;
    // Deserialize from server socket

if (signedObject.verify(publicKey, verificationEngine))
{
  RowSet data = (RowSet)signedObject.getObject();
    // We know data was issued under the private key, and
    // that it wasn't tampered with
}
```

As an experiment, use a `java.util.HashMap` instead of the `RowSet`, serialize the `SignedObject` to disk, then modify the contents of the `Signed Object` by using a hex editor. (`SignedObject` provides only integrity, not confidentiality; confidentiality is the province of the `SealedObject`—see Item 65.) When verifying the modified data, the signature won't match, proving that the data was tampered with after the signature was applied. More importantly, unless the attacker has the ability to replace the public key in the client software with a public key of his or her own choosing, we can always ensure that data received from the server is in fact from that server.

Working directly with `SignedObject` can sometimes be onerous to programmers who don't understand its purpose or the need to call `verify` before working with the object itself—in order to hide those details from clients, extend `SignedObject` directly. So, for example, to build a signed authorization context that can be passed around the network, create a `SignedObject` subclass that contains a JAAS `Subject` as its Serializable content, as in the following code:

```
public class AuthorizationToken extends SignedObject
{
```

```
    private static Signature engine =
      Signature.getInstance("SHA1withDSA");

    public AuthorizationToken(PrivateKey privKey,
                                  Subject subject)
    {
      super(subject, privKey, engine);
    }

    public Subject getSubject(PublicKey pubKey)
    {
      if (verify(pubKey, engine))
        return (Subject)getObject();
      else
        throw new
          AuthenticationFailedException("Spoofed!");
    }
}
```

Alternatively, instead of extending SignedObject you could simply compose it (hold it as a field and delegate calls to it directly); either approach works relatively well. Many developers favor the inheritance-based approach because it saves typing, but in this particular case it comes out about the same either way.

By the way, generating a PublicKey/PrivateKey pair is as simple as exercising the KeyPairGenerator class that also comes from the java.security package; a utility that writes out the pair to .publickey and .privatekey files looks like this:

```
import java.io.*;
import java.io.*;
import java.security.*;

public class genkeypair
{
  public static void main(String[] args)
    throws Exception
  {
      KeyPairGenerator kpg =
        KeyPairGenerator.getInstance("DSA");
```

```
    KeyPair kp = kpg.generateKeyPair();
    PrivateKey privKey = kp.getPrivate();
    PublicKey pubKey = kp.getPublic();

    try
    {
      ObjectOutputStream oos =
        new ObjectOutputStream(
            new FileOutputStream(".privatekey"));
      oos.writeObject(privKey);
      oos.close();

      oos = new ObjectOutputStream(
            new FileOutputStream(".publickey"));
      oos.writeObject(pubKey);
      oos.close();
    }
    catch (Exception ex)
    {
      ex.printStackTrace();
    }
  }
}
```

Note that you should never ship software with these keys distributed in this file-based form; it becomes too easy for even basic attackers to replace the files with their own versions on either client or server. The principal concern here is, of course, the keys themselves. An attacker who gets hold of the server's private key could masquerade as your server to any clients. If the attacker can replace the public key value in client systems with a public key of his or her own choosing, the attacker could intercept communications between client and server, resigning data from the server using his or her own private key, which then would verify as authentic to the hacked clients. (This is why digital certificates usually accompany any public key—the certificate acts as a way to verify the authenticity of the public key, by trusting the issuer of the certificate.)

Note, too, that `SignedObject` instances can nest inside of one another (using a `SignedObject` as the data for another `SignedObject`) if multiple signatures are required; the only tricky part of verifying the object is to make sure that the signatures are verified in the reverse order of their signing. (It's reported that a future version of SignedObject will take multiple signatures, but for now stacking them isn't too awkward to work with since the order of signatures could be conveyed as part of the data itself, if desired.)

Again, remember that the purpose of SignedObject is merely to verify the integrity of the data being sent/stored/serialized, to ensure that the data hasn't been tampered with or sent from somebody other than whom we want it from; it provides no confidentiality whatsoever to the data itself. That becomes the responsibility of SealedObject, as described in Item 65.

Item 65: Use SealedObject to provide confidentiality of Serializable objects

Not only do we need to make sure that serialized data isn't tampered with across an insecure medium (see Item 60), but frequently we need to ensure that nobody except the intended recipient can see the contents of the data. It is frequently more necessary to ensure confidentiality of the data than to ensure the integrity of the data in question. Ensuring confidentiality is the province of the javax.crypto.SealedObject class, and it functions in a manner similar to the SignedObject discussed in Item 64.

In this case, rather than using a PublicKey/PrivateKey pair, the Sealed Object needs a SecretKey that is shared somehow between both parties. SealedObject uses a symmetric key to quickly encrypt and decrypt the data because asymmetric key cryptography (public-key/private-key cryptography) takes a huge amount of time to perform. Obtaining the SecretKey in such a way that both parties can safely exchange the key without Eve (the eavesdropper) or Mallory (the malicious in-betweener) subverting the key exchange is beyond the scope of this item, so for now we're going to assume that the SecretKey has been established somehow. (Note, however, that one way you could do this is to effectively replicate the mechanism SSL uses to establish a new session key between recipients on each SSL connection.[5] Another approach is documented in

---

5. In general, it's a Really Bad Idea to try to reimplement existing security infrastructure because it's very likely that you'll accidentally leave holes in the implementation that could be exploited by an attacker. Make sure your threat model is sufficiently covered if you consider rolling your own key-exchange protocol, and as a test for yourself, make sure you can describe how SSL works before even attempting this.

Appendix F of the *Java Cryptography Extension Reference Guide*, included as part of the standard JDK documentation set, using the KeyAgreement class and friends to negotiate the sharing of secret session keys between two parties.)

As with SignedObject, take any Serializable object (and in this case combine it with a Cipher, created from a SecretKey) and construct a Sealed Object passing in both of those objects. The Serializable object is copied by value into the SealedObject and encrypted. Now the SealedObject can be itself serialized, in this case to a file on the local filesystem, and the data within is hidden from prying eyes, unless they happen to have the SecretKey as well.

```
String s = "Greetings";

KeyGenerator keyGen = KeyGenerator.getInstance("DES");
SecretKey key = keyGen.generateKey();
Cipher cipher = Cipher.getInstance("DES");
cipher.init(Cipher.ENCRYPT_MODE, key);

SealedObject sealedObj = new SealedObject(s, cipher);

ObjectOutputStream oos =
  new ObjectOutputStream(new FileOutputStream(".secret"));
oos.writeObject(sealedObj);
oos.close();
```

Obtaining the data inside the SealedObject is a simple matter of calling the getObject method, passing in the SecretKey:

```
ObjectInputStream ois =
  new ObjectInputStream(new FileInputStream(".secret"));
SealedObject sealedObj = (SealedObject)ois.readObject();
ois.close();

String data = (String)sealedObj.getObject(key);
```

While storing data to the filesystem is one use of the SealedObject type, a more common use is to pass SealedObject instances back and forth across JMS message queues, particularly if the data is at all sensitive or if system administrators can view messages residing in the queue. This is actually a more scalable way to achieve confidentiality of JMS messages, since now we don't have to rely on the messaging middleware encrypting the entirety of the traffic, which would most likely be overkill; instead, only the sensitive payload (the message itself) is protected. Just pass the `SealedObject` as the payload of an `ObjectMessage`.

As with its cousins `SignedObject` (see Item 64) and `GuardedObject` (see Item 66), `SealedObject` can be subclassed in order to introduce better strongly typed APIs for use by clients who wish to remain ignorant of the actual security mechanisms in place.

You may be wondering why you should bother with `SealedObject` when other mechanisms, like the `CipherInputStream`/`CipherOutputStream` pair, offer perhaps greater control over the actual encryption and decryption process. The short answer is that when security is involved, the less actual control you have over the implementation, the better—it's too easy to build a roll-your-own security stack that has exploitable flaws. Using `SealedObject` instead lets you focus on simply storing Serializable types into it; the implementation takes care of itself. This is one place you don't want to experiment.

Frequently, however, just the encrypted form isn't, by itself, enough. Encryption by itself doesn't ensure that the object wasn't somehow tampered with—if Mallory can somehow slip into the conversation stream, he can easily use a different secret key between himself and Bob than the one established by Alice in the first place. For this reason, `SealedObject` instances are often combined with a `SignedObject` and sent that way: create and sign the `SignedObject`, then use that to create a `Sealed Object`.

Item 66:   Use GuardedObject to provide access control on objects

So you've read Item 62 and decided to make use of the underlying platform security model to help build authorization into the system (and perhaps you've gone so far as to embrace JAAS for role-based authorization, as described in Item 63). You've created custom permission types, and you've either established a custom `Policy` object or written the policy file (`java.policy`) to reflect the appropriate assignment of permissions. Now you're starting to write the necessary tests for permission ownership before allowing sensitive operations to take place, but you run into a small snag: you've got an object that wraps a sensitive operation, and it needs to travel across the wire to a recipient whose security context may be different from your own.

Consider the problem: in a role-based security environment, a `Person` object may require certain permissions to be held by the requesting principal (in other words, the user on whose behalf the code is currently executing) before allowing the call to go through. For example, recent U.S. legislation declares that certain sensitive personal data like social security numbers can't be accessed by just anybody. This is a perfect place for a JAAS-based permission check:

```
public class Person
{
  private String ssn;

  // . . .

  public String getSSN()
  {
    AccessController.checkPermission(
      new SensitiveDataAccessPermission("ssn",
                                        "read"));
    return ssn;
  }
}
```

In this particular scenario, only this method requires the check, so the cost of making the security stack-walk check is justified.

But what about the situation where even just simple access to the object itself requires permission? For example, in the JDK library itself, any sort of file I/O should be governed by a permission, which means that, in theory, each and every method call on the file-based object (`FileInput Stream`, `FileOutputStream`, and so on) should verify that all of the `ProtectionDomain` instances on the calling thread have the appropriate `FilePermission` in their security context. Under the guidelines noted previously, then, every method in those classes should do the permission check to ensure that the permission is present.

Unfortunately, that's going to "have issues."

The problem is that while the JDK goes to great lengths to minimize the performance impact of the security stack walk, the basic fact is that every

`ProtectionDomain` established on the thread will need to be checked, and each of that `ProtectionDomain`'s permissions will need to be checked to see if it implies the `FilePermission` demanded. This is hardly an inexpensive operation, and to do this on every `FileOutput Stream.write` or `FileInputStream.read` call is going to kill any kind of performance we might desire.

The JDK solves this problem by realizing that if every operation requires the security permission, it makes sense to require it once, at the time of object creation, and thereafter assume that since the caller had to have the permission to create it, they must still have the permission required in order to call the desired methods on it. So, the security check is done once, in the object constructor, and thereafter left out of the other methods.

Unfortunately, this otherwise efficient way to avoid multiple (usually redundant) security checks fails in a very specific and all-too-common scenario—serialization. Remember, as *Effective Java* [Bloch, Item 54] points out, the serialized form of an object effectively presents the class with another constructor, since the process of deserialization means building an object up from a byte array rather than from formal Java arguments.

This becomes dangerous when the object, constructed in a security context that has the appropriate permissions, is serialized and sent to another security context (either across the wire or simply serialized to disk and deserialized back again) that isn't supposed to be able to use this object. But because the security check was already passed in the constructor, and the constructor will never be invoked again for this object (in fact, it can't, by the laws of Java), the object is being used by code that shouldn't be able to use it.

As if this weren't enough to consider, there's also the basic premise that the caller will always have the same permissions in its access control context from the moment the object is constructed to its destruction. In the days before JAAS, this might have been true when the object remained entirely in the same JVM, as long as the object wasn't serialized and deserialized by code in a different `ProtectionDomain`. Now that JAAS is an integral part of the JVM, however, this isn't a fair assumption, and code that makes access control checks needs to take that into account, either within the library classes themselves or in the client code that uses them.

For these reasons, when you want to make sure that only callers with appropriate access use an object, use the java.security.GuardedObject to provide access control. It ensures that access control is checked at least once, by forcing callers to go through a method call to gain access to the protected object.

Using a GuardedObject is much like using its cousins, SignedObject (see Item 64) and SealedObject (see Item 65): create the object to be guarded (which should be Serializable, but doesn't have to be, unless you want to pass it across the wire), and pass it along with the "guarding" object into the constructor of the GuardedObject class. The guarding object itself must be of a type that implements the Guard interface, which requires a single method, checkGuard, to be implemented; this method will be used to verify that the caller has access. Note that even custom Permission objects are acceptable guards, by virtue of the base Permission class that implements Guard and implements the checkGuard method to obtain the SecurityManager and call check Permission on it.

```
public class Person { . . . }

public class PersonPermission extends Permission
{ . . . }

void foo()
{
  Person p = new Person();

  GuardedObject go =
    new GuardedObject(p,
                new PersonPermission("read"));
}
```

The protected object (Person, in this case) doesn't have to be Serializable, but of course if we want to send the GuardedObject over the wire, it will need to be.

Access to the sensitive object can be achieved only by calling getObject on the GuardedObject, which in turn calls the guarding object's check-Guard method. Assuming the guarding object is a Permission type, the caller's security context is checked, rather than assuming that the creator's security context continues to exist.

```
GuardedObject go = getGuardedObject();
Person p = (Person)go.getObject();
  // At this point, if the caller of getObject()
  // doesn't have PersonPermission in its
  // ProtectionDomain, a SecurityException
  // is thrown and access will be denied
```

Again, as with `SignedObject` and `SealedObject`, we can make it marginally easier to work with `GuardedObject` by subclassing it and creating a customized `getObject` method that wraps `getObject` but returns a strongly typed reference to the sensitive object.

This gives us the ability to ensure that a security context check will occur before the recipient of the `GuardedObject` can access the sensitive object in question. Once again, this can be particularly powerful in the form of Message-Driven Beans or simple JMS consumers, since now we can ensure that the caller has the appropriate security context to access the contents of an object even across the wire; for example, we might take the caller's current JAAS security context (the established `Subject`) and pass that as part of the message itself:

```
Message msg = queueSession.createObjectMessage();

Person p = new Person(...);
GuardedObject guardedObj =
  new GuardedObject(p, new PersonPermission("read"));

Subject s = loginContext.getSubject();
  // Obtain the Subject out of the authenticated
  // LoginContext

msg.setObjectProperty("subject", s);
msg.setObject(p, guardedObj);

queueSender.send(msg);
```

Then, when the message is received, we can extract the `Subject`, obtain the `GuardedObject`, and dig the `Person` back out:

```
ObjectMessage objMsg =
  (ObjectMessage)queueReceiver.receive();
```

```
Subject subject =
  (Subject)objMsg.getObjectProperty("subject");
GuardedObject guardedObj =
  (GuardedObject)objMsg.getObject();

Subject.doAs(new PrivilegedExceptionAction()
  {
    public Object run()
      throws Exception
    {
      Person p = (Person)guardedObj.getObject();
        // An access control check is made here; if
        // the Subject doesn't have PersonPermission,
        // a SecurityException is thrown

        // Use p as appropriate; if you got here, you
        // obviously have the necessary permissions
    }
  });
```

Of course, once the object has been retrieved and stored into a Person
reference, no further security checks will be performed when calling into
the Person methods—this permits the "one security check" optimization
desired but ensures that the check still occurs.

Note, as well, that if the holder of the Person reference decides to hand it
out to other callers running in a separate security context, the original
problem remains—unfortunately, there simply is no way to prevent this
without a major change in the Java language and platform. Assuming you
have followed the advice of Item 1 and built components instead of
objects, you can create a dynamic proxy behind the interface exposed to
clients that stores the actual object in a GuardedObject and uses get
Object each time to forward the call on.

Doing this, of course, more or less eradicates the "one security chcck"
optimization that we were looking for in the first place, but remember that this can be done selectively based on factors controlled at runtime, such as knowing whether the object will be used in the same

security context. (At the same time, you can gain a certain measure of knowledge by implementing serialization hooks, as described in Item 71, to serialize the actual data in a `GuardedObject`. Just be careful to avoid infinite recursion as the `GuardedObject` gets serialized, which in turn serializes the protected object, which is to say, the object you wanted serialized in the first place.)

8 System

For the myth is the foundation of life; it is the timeless schema,
the pious formula into which life flows when it reproduces its
traits out of the unconscious.

—Thomas Mann

The Java platform—the Java Virtual Machine plus the libraries—contains a tremendous amount of functionality that J2EE relies on as part of its implementation. For example, the hot deployment capability of servlet engines and EJB containers is due entirely to the ClassLoader architecture of the underlying JVM; without it, bouncing the server would be a necessity to load new versions of the code. Java Object Serialization is used implicitly in a number of places throughout the JDK and so becomes a cornerstone of J2EE. And, of course, in order to allow the container to walk and chew gum at the same time (figuratively), J2EE makes heavy use of the Java threading model to provide concurrent execution of incoming client requests.

As a result, understanding key parts of the Java platform is an absolute "must" for any Java developer who wants to do serious work in the J2EE platform.

Item 67: Aggressively release resources

If anything, a J2EE application is all about accessing resources outside of the JVM: the relational database (JDBC), messaging systems (JMS), other objects running in separate processes (RMI), distributed transaction coordinators (JTA), enterprise integration systems (JCA), and so on. The Java Virtual Machine is great at managing resources within the VM, most notably memory, but unfortunately the JVM's automatic memory management scheme isn't so great at managing resources outside of the JVM (like database connections, result set cursors, and so on). As a result, J2EE programmers need to get into the habit of being as explicit about resource deallocation as we are about allocation. Loosely translated, that means aggressively shutting down resource objects the moment we're finished with them.

This may seem unnecessary at first—after all, Java provides the finalizer mechanism to do per-object cleanup during the whole garbage collection process. So, assuming all of those resource objects (connections, result sets, and so on) have finalizers to shut down whatever resources are held outside of the JVM, we can just let garbage collection take care of it all, right?

Tragically, no. As Item 74 explains, finalizers have some serious issues—in this case, finalizers are entirely nondeterministic and fire "sometime after" the object has been orphaned and left available for collection. The garbage collector doesn't realize that these resource objects are holding resources more precious than just N bytes of memory, however, so the collector won't get around to collecting them until later. As a matter of fact, because these resource objects tend to survive several generational garbage collection passes (see Item 72), they migrate to older generations in a generational collector, which in turn means they won't even be considered for collection until after the entire young generation of objects has been collected and there's still not room left to do an allocation. In a long-running system with the young generation tuned correctly (see Item 68), this means it could be minutes, even hours or days, before those objects get finalized. A system that allocates ResultSet objects at a rate of one per second and never releases them will quickly exhaust the database on the other side, regardless of the database server hardware underneath it.

This in turn means that unless you as a programmer step in to correct this state of affairs, you're going to be in for some nasty high-contention and out-of-resource scenarios. For example, when obtaining ResultSet from a Statement, depending on the transaction isolation level (see Item 35), the database typically has to hold locks against the data in the table the ResultSet is iterating over, because if the ResultSet is scrollable, the ResultSet itself has no idea which data is going to be accessed and used next until it's officially closed. (A forward-only "firehose"-style Result Set at least knows that once data has been read, it can no longer be accessed, which is why many JDBC performance guides suggest using them as often as possible.) As a result, too many open ResultSet objects against a single table could create a situation where other clients seeking to access data in that table are held at bay until some of the open locks are released. That's contention, that hurts scalability, and that's exactly what you need to avoid.

As a result, you need to be as aggressive as you can about releasing any resource objects allocated by the system, in particular, JDBC Connection, Statement (with one notable exception), and ResultSet objects. In an ideal world, all of these objects would be held via WeakReference instances such that as soon as the last strong reference to them is dropped, the object itself could be cleaned up (per Item 74), but that doesn't appear to be happening anytime soon, so as a result you need to ensure you call close on any JDBC resource as soon as you're finished with it. Note that despite not being mentioned until the JDBC 3.0 Specification, calling close on a Connection typically closes all Statement objects created by that Connection, and calling close on a Statement typically closes all ResultSet objects created by that Statement.

Be very careful when writing the code to do the closing, however; you need to ensure that all possible code paths are covered. For example, consider the following snippet:

```
public String[] getFirstNames(String lastName)
{
  ArrayList results = new ArrayList();
  Connection con = null;
  PreparedStatement stmt = null;
  ResultSet rs = null;

  try
  {
    con = getConnectionFromSomeplace();
    String prepSQL =
      "SELECT first_name FROM person " +
      "WHERE last_name = ?";
    stmt = con.prepareStatement(prepSQL);
      // See Item 49 for why we use PreparedStatement
    stmt.setString(1, lastName);
    rs = stmt.executeQuery();
```

```
        while (rs.next())
          results.add(rs.getString(1));
      }
      catch (SQLException sqlEx)
      {
        Logger l = getLoggerFromSomeplace();
        l.fatal("SQL statement failed: " + sqlEx);
        // By the way, don't forget to do something
        // more proactive to handle the error;
        // see Item 7
      }

      if (rs != null) rs.close();
      if (stmt != null) stmt.close();
      if (con != null) con.close();
        // Could also just call con.close if we know
        // that the JDBC driver does cascading closure
        // (which most do), but we'd have to know our
        // JDBC driver (see Item 49) to feel safe doing
        // that

      return (String[])results.toArray(new String[0]);
    }
```

As soon as we're done with the ResultSet (which in turn implies we're done with the Statement and the Connection that prepared it), we call close on them all and we're ready to move on to the next item on our to-do list. Right?

Wrong—there's a hideous bug in here just waiting to bite us later. What happens if an unchecked exception gets thrown from somewhere in the method that's not a SQLException? Because we're not catching anything other than SQLException instances in the try/catch block, we'll never execute the close calls on the Connection, Statement, or ResultSet, and we'll effectively "leak" the resource until the garbage collector gets around to finalizing them.

As a result, we need to change the code above just slightly, to make use of a finally block to do the closures, rather than resting on the good graces of fate to make sure those close calls get made:

```
public String[] getFirstNames(String lastName)
{
  ArrayList results = new ArrayList();
  Connection con = null;
  PreparedStatement stmt = null;
  ResultSet rs = null;

  try
  {
    con = getConnectionFromSomeplace();
    stmt = con.prepareStatement(
      "SELECT first_name FROM person " +
      "WHERE last_name = ?");

      // See Item 61 for why we use PreparedStatement
      // even though we'll lose the "preparation"
      // part of it when the Connection closes

    stmt.setString(1, lastName);
    rs = stmt.executeQuery();

    while (rs.next())
      results.add(rs.getString(1));

    return (String[])results.toArray(new String[0]);
  }
  catch (SQLException sqlEx)
  {
    Logger l = getLoggerFromSomeplace();
      // See Item 12, as well as Item 7
    l.fatal("SQL statement failed: " + sqlEx);

    return new String[0];
      // See Effective Java [Bloch, Item 27]
  }
  finally
  {
    if (rs != null) rs.close();
    if (stmt != null) stmt.close();
```

```
      if (con != null) con.close();
        // Could also just call con.close if we know
        // that the JDBC driver does cascading closure
        // (which most do), but we'd have to know our
        // JDBC driver (see Item 49) to feel safe doing
        // that
    }
}
```

Now, regardless of how execution leaves the `try` block—simple completion, a return statement, or an exception being thrown within it—the `finally` block will always get called, thus ensuring that the JDBC resource objects are always released aggressively.

At first blush, it seems counterintuitive to do this. After all, it's not a free operation to establish the connection in the first place because authentication against the credentials passed in (username, password) has to take place against the database, so why release it just as soon as we've established it? This would seem to be an obvious situation where we would want to cache the connection off someplace, either into `HttpSession` or a stateless session bean.

The problem is that caching off the connection improves performance at the expense of scalability. Most often, a client program using a database connection, or any other form of external resource for that matter, doesn't use 100% of its capacity. Think about the typical enterprise Web- or UI-based application: we present some data to the user, who spends an eternity (to the CPU, anyway) thinking about it and possibly making changes and then submits those changes, which may or may not go directly into the database. In the meantime, we're holding open a connection against the database that no other client can use. If you think about it, a client probably makes use of the database connection it obtains about 5% of the time. Which brings us back to the whole point of moving to the three- or *n*-tier system in the first place: sharing resources. If we can multiplex that connection across 20 clients, that connection gets used to its full 100% capacity, yet only one physical connection is necessary—theoretically, then, we can now support 20 times more concurrent clients against the same hardware resources.

But we're still left with a fundamental problem, that of connection management—we're still facing the overhead of establishing and closing those database connections. In an ideal world, if all clients are somehow routing their database requests through the same JVM, we can pool connections, making it look like the middleware layer has established 20 connections to the database when in fact it's merely multiplexing 20 clients over the same physical connection. Assuming, then, that each client uses the same credentials to connect to the database, the cost of obtaining a connection is amortized across all 20 clients, making it a much more palatable situation.

Even when connection pooling isn't possible, though, we're still generally going to prefer to acquire, use, and release resources aggressively. Granted, it's a performance hit, but most enterprise systems written today are more interested in scalability than in performance. This may seem like an improbable statement at first, but bear in mind that many of the IT projects developed after 1995 are built to sit facing the public via the Internet, and it's a truly embarrassing PR blunder to have your system crumple under a burst load like that produced by the Slashdot effect. Most users won't notice if ordering books online takes a few extra seconds (time that can often be made up by reducing the number of fluffy graphic elements on your Web page—see Item 52), but they'll definitely notice when the service goes down under load.

This acquire-use-release approach is called *just-in-time activation (JITA),* by the way, and is more or less directly modeled by parts of the J2EE Specification, most notably the stateless session bean. Remember, a stateless session bean cannot hold state across method calls, meaning that any resources the bean needs must be acquired at the start of the method and released at the end of the method. It's a great enforcement of the JITA policy, but while it works well for situations where a single stateless session bean method call models a single user interaction session (HTTP request, most often), it creates a lot of "resource churn" when a single user request requires multiple stateless session bean calls—you get an "acquire-use-release-acquire-use-release-acquire-use-release" effect. This is predominantly why, in the case of EJB stateless session beans, multiple authors have suggested that your stateless session bean methods should match (more or less) one-to-one with your system use cases, since that way the resources can be acquired and released once.

What about those situations when we need to keep the data retrieved out of a `ResultSet` around for longer than the scenario above? For example, in a search-results page, we want to hold the search results across page invocations—we don't want to display all the search results at once, obviously, but we don't want to have to go back to the database over and over again to conduct the same search on each successive "Next" request from the search results page, either.

Instead of holding the data in a connected `ResultSet`, put the data into a disconnected `RowSet`, close the `ResultSet`, and use the `RowSet` (which inherits from `ResultSet`, remember, so the API is identical) to display the search page results rather than using the original `ResultSet`. Unfortunately, doing so means taking up more memory in the client process, since all of the result set is now being held in memory inside the `RowSet` instance, where before it was being pulled over in an on-demand fashion via the `ResultSet` APIs. This is a case where you have to make a conscious decision to support scalability at the JVM level (memory being the finite resource in contention) as opposed to scalability at the database (transactional lock) level—for most projects, it's easier to put more memory into the client than to change the transactional policies within the database, but this is a decision you have to make.

Keep an eye, by the way, on JSR-114, the new `RowSet` implementation JSR that will define five different kinds of `RowSet` objects for standard use throughout J2EE applications. (The `RowSet` interface has been a part of J2EE for some time now, but no implementations have been standardized—Sun released several, the `CachedRowSet` and `WebRowSet` being the two most popular, but they remained outside of the formal J2EE Specification.) In addition to supporting the disconnected storage of relational data that we like about the `RowSet`, several new features are being added, such as optimistic concurrency semantics (see `javax.sql.rowset.spi`), XML input/output (see `javax.sql.rowset.spi.XMLReader` and `javax.sql.rowset.spi.XMLWriter`), and the ability to maintain relational relationships across multiple `RowSet` objects (see `javax.sql.rowset.JoinRowSet`). The `RowSet` should be your first choice for offline storage—either use what has already been provided as part of JSR-114, or roll your own `RowSet` implementation to provide the additional semantics you need.

Regardless of whether you store the data into a `RowSet` or a `List` of `Map` instances, pull what data you need across as quickly as you can in order to aggressively release the JDBC resource objects, thereby easing the strain on the JDBC plumbing and database lock management. Note that although not as well-known, this advice applies to other "outside" resources providing connected data feeds, such as distributed transactions or `Connector` resource objects (like `Record` objects).

Item 68: Tune the JVM

With the release of JDK 1.3, Sun made an important enhancement to the Java Virtual Machine: specifically, they released Hotspot, an optimizing virtual machine that promised better garbage collection, better JIT compilation to native code, and a whole slew of other enhancements intended to make Java applications run faster. In fact, two such VMs were created, one for client-based applications and one for server-based applications. The client VM was optimized for short-running applications (like your average Swing application), favoring short-term optimizations to long-term ones; the server VM was optimized in the opposite direction.

Amazing, then, isn't it, that most default installations of Java-based J2EE containers (as opposed to native-code implementations) don't make use of the VM tuned specifically for long-running server operations?

To understand what I mean, we have to take a quick side trip into the JVM invocation code. You can get this as part of the standard J2SDK download if you turn on the Install Sources checkbox during the install. When the installation program finishes installing, a roughly 10MB-sized zip file shows up in the root of the J2SDK directory called `src.zip`. Exploding that zip file yields, among other things, a "launcher" directory, which includes the source code to the `java.exe` launcher. In particular, the core of what we're interested in is the `java.c` source file. (The other C source file, `java_md.c`, is the machine-dependent support routine that varies based on platform: Linux, Win32, or Solaris, depending on which JDK you're currently using.)

The aspects of the java launcher that we're interested in come fairly early in the C file:

```
/*
 * Entry point.
 */
int
main(int argc, char ** argv)
{
    JavaVM *vm = 0;
    JNIEnv *env = 0;
    char *jarfile = 0;
    char *classname = 0;
    char *s = 0;
```

```
      jclass mainClass;
      jmethodID mainID;
      jobjectArray mainArgs;
      int ret;
      InvocationFunctions ifn;
      char *jvmtype = 0;
      jlong start, end;
      char jrepath[MAXPATHLEN], jvmpath[MAXPATHLEN];
      char ** original_argv = argv;

      /* ... Code elided for brevity ... */

      /* Find out where the JRE is that we will be using. */
      if (!GetJREPath(jrepath, sizeof(jrepath)))
      {
        fprintf(stderr,
          "Error: could not find Java 2 Runtime Environment.\n");
        return 2;
      }

      /* ... Code elided for brevity ... */

      /* Find the specified JVM type */
      if (ReadKnownVMs(jrepath) < 1)
      {
        fprintf(stderr,
          "Error: no known VMs. (check for corrupt jvm.cfg file)\n");
        exit(1);
      }
      jvmtype = CheckJvmType(&argc, &argv);

      jvmpath[0] = '\0';
      if (!GetJVMPath(jrepath, jvmtype, jvmpath, sizeof(jvmpath)))
      {
        fprintf(stderr,
          "Error: no '%s' JVM at '%s'.\n", jvmtype, jvmpath);
        return 4;
      }
```

```
/* If we got here, jvmpath has been correctly initialized. */

  /* ... Rest of main() elided for brevity ... */
}
```

For those readers who are a bit rusty in C (who isn't, these days?), `main` essentially calls out to a utility method, also inside this file, called `Read KnownVMs` to determine what the available VM options are within the JDK and to compare against the parameters passed on the `java.exe` command line to discover which one the user wishes to use. Once the VM type, stored in the local variable `jvmpath`, is known, the launcher uses the standard JNI Invocation API to create the JVM, find the class to load, and invoke its `main` method.

Drilling into `ReadKnownVMs` (not shown here) reveals that the list of VMs known to the JDK is controlled by nothing more technically complex than a text file—in this particular case, a text file called `jvm.cfg`, stored in a CPU-specific directory (e.g., for Win32 it's called `i386`) underneath the `lib` subdirectory of the Java Runtime Environment (JRE). This subdirectory structure and filename are hard-coded into the launcher code, by the way; there's no way to change this without writing your own launcher. Under JDK 1.4.1, for example, the `jvm.cfg` file looks like the following:

```
#
# @(#)jvm.cfg  1.6 01/12/03
#
# Copyright 2002 Sun Microsystems, Inc. All rights reserved.
# SUN PROPRIETARY/CONFIDENTIAL. Use is subject to license terms.
#
# List of JVMs that can be used as an option to java, javac, etc.
# Order is important - first in this list is the default JVM.
# NOTE that this both this file and its format are UNSUPPORTED and
# WILL GO AWAY in a future release.
#
# You may also select a JVM in an arbitrary location with the
# "-XXaltjvm=<jvm_dir>" option, but that too is unsupported
# and may not be available in a future release.
#
-client KNOWN
-server KNOWN
```

```
-hotspot ALIASED_TO -client
-classic WARN
-native ERROR
-green ERROR
```

And, in case the comments in the file don't give away the punchline, the key here is that the first option in the list is the default option. This means that unless you specify -server as part of the J2EE server invocation command line, you're running with the client Hotspot VM. (In earlier releases of the JVM, Hotspot was the product name given to the highly optimized JVM, and it was generally recommended for use on client applications; with the release of JDK 1.3, Hotspot had two possible configurations, server and classic, and both are called Hotspot.)

If you're not quite sure which JVM is being invoked, you can see the options the java.exe launcher uses by turning on an undocumented environment variable, _JAVA_LAUNCHER_DEBUG, which will display a collection of interesting details about the JVM and the options used to create it:

```
C:\Prg\Test>set _JAVA_LAUNCHER_DEBUG=1

C:\Prg\Test>java Hello
----_JAVA_LAUNCHER_DEBUG----
JRE path is C:\Prg\java\j2sdk1.4.1\jre
jvm.cfg[0] = ->-client<-
jvm.cfg[1] = ->-server<-
jvm.cfg[2] = ->-hotspot<-
jvm.cfg[3] = ->-classic<-
jvm.cfg[4] = ->-native<-
jvm.cfg[5] = ->-green<-
41768 micro seconds to parse jvm.cfg
JVM path is C:\Prg\java\j2sdk1.4.1\jre\bin\client\jvm.dll
9816 micro seconds to LoadJavaVM
JavaVM args:
    version 0x00010002, ignoreUnrecognized is JNI_FALSE,
                        nOptions is 2
    option[ 0] = '-Djava.class.path=.'
    option[ 1] = '-Dsun.java.command=Hello'
250409 micro seconds to InitializeJVM
```

```
Main-Class is 'Hello'
Apps' argc is 0
317641 micro seconds to load main class
----_JAVA_LAUNCHER_DEBUG----
Hello, world!


C:\Prg\Test>java -server Hello
----_JAVA_LAUNCHER_DEBUG----
JRE path is C:\Prg\java\j2sdk1.4.1\jre
jvm.cfg[0] = ->-client<-
jvm.cfg[1] = ->-server<-
jvm.cfg[2] = ->-hotspot<-
jvm.cfg[3] = ->-classic<-
jvm.cfg[4] = ->-native<-
jvm.cfg[5] = ->-green<-
31218 micro seconds to parse jvm.cfg
JVM path is C:\Prg\java\j2sdk1.4.1\jre\bin\server\jvm.dll
25056 micro seconds to LoadJavaVM
JavaVM args:
    version 0x00010002, ignoreUnrecognized is JNI_FALSE,
                        nOptions is 2
    option[ 0] = '-Djava.class.path=.'
    option[ 1] = '-Dsun.java.command=Hello'
288153 micro seconds to InitializeJVM
Main-Class is 'Hello'
Apps' argc is 0
398426 micro seconds to load main class
----_JAVA_LAUNCHER_DEBUG----
Hello, world!


C:\Prg\Test>
```

The giveaway here is the line `JVM path is`. . . . When running with the client VM, the JVM used is the DLL stored in `jre/bin/client/jvm.dll`, whereas when invoked explicitly with the `-server` flag, the JVM used is `jre/bin/server/jvm.dll`.

To fix this, if you can get at the command line used to invoke the JVM, add the `-server` option into the command-line parameters. If this is somehow hidden from you, simply rearrange the options found in the jvm.cfg file in the JDK to list the -server option first. Bear in mind, however, the comment at the top of the jvm.cfg file: this file format is subject to change and may use a different mechanism sometime in the future. (Case in point: the JDK 1.3 mechanism didn't make use of the keywords following each entry—KNOWN, ALIAS, and so forth.) Future J2SDK releases may change this mechanism, so be prepared to do a little spelunking when J2SDK 1.5 is released.

Note that you can also take a one-time slight performance boost at startup by stripping out the extraneous options in the file (-classic, -native, and -green and the huge comment block at the top); this will reduce the average parse time from around 30,000 microseconds to around 9,000. Not much, but every microsecond counts sometimes.

It's also possible to specify the location of an alternate VM via the use of the -XXaltjvm command-line option, but until alternative JVMs become more of a commodity than they are as of this writing, this won't be of practical use. This is also a Sun JVM-only feature (and undocumented to boot) and may go away in a future release, so use it with caution.

Note that the Hotspot JVM isn't the only option here; in particular, BEA acquired JRockit, a JRE replacement tuned for server operations. JRockit essentially replaces the Sun JRE, so making use of it simply involves pointing your PATH at the java launcher in the JRockit installation tree instead of the Sun JRE.

Once the right JVM is executing, and you've profiled your code to find any obvious bottlenecks or choke points, at some point it becomes an attraction to figure out how to configure the JVM itself to better work with your system at garbage collection, threading policies, and so on. In some cases, this knowledge will reduce the portability of the system since your implementation may depend on the behavior of the underlying JVM, but this may or may not be a bad thing, depending on your reaction to Item 11.

To begin, the JVM spends a tremendous amount of time allocating memory when the system is starting up since the default starting memory footprint for the JVM is a measly 2MB. This is fine for such worthy applications as "Hello, world!" and "Goodbye, world!" but hardly satisfying for an enterprise application running a servlet container or EJB container. Pass a reasonable value to the -Xms option, based on realistic profiling statistics: write a simple servlet to spit back the value from Runtime.

`totalMemory`, deploy that to your servlet container, shut it down, start it back up, and hit that servlet right away. This will give a rough estimation of the servlet container's overhead requirements.

Similarly, the JVM establishes a maximum heap size it will grow to. Many Java resources state that this is the value at which the JVM will begin garbage collection, but the truth is a bit more complex than that. What is true, however, is that the JVM will never grow beyond this value; by default, the JVM establishes 64MB as the upper limit. Use the –Xmx option to bump this value up to something more reasonable, based on profiling statistics (gathered either by using a commercial profiler or the servlet mentioned above) during a reasonable approximation of peak-load testing on your system.

Be very careful with passing large values to –Xmx because as the heap grows larger, it becomes exponentially harder to scan for objects; realistically, if you're looking at maximum heap size parameters of larger than 1GB to the JVM, you might want to experiment with running multiple JVM processes of smaller size rather than one large one. If you're worried about taking the overhead of the JVM multiple times (once per process), be cheered by the fact that (a) most operating systems will silently map code segments in multiple processes to the same physical memory, thus obviating the need to load duplicate code twice into physical memory, and (b) the J2SE 1.5 release is introducing "code sharing" into the JVM itself, to try to avoid the overhead of the loaded-and-defined classes, for example, among other things. Again, you'll want to profile this approach (see Item 10) before committing to it in production.

Another option is to set the starting heap size to the same value as the maximum heap size to avoid resizing the heap as it grows beyond the starting heap size, but this assumes that the JVM will never actually release allocated heap memory when requirements shrink. Although this is the case for Sun JVMs through release 1.4, it's supposedly something that will get fixed "sooner or later," and since it's rare that the JVM is the only application executing on that machine, it's usually polite to return something (like memory) back to its owner (the operating system) when you're not using it anymore.

While we're on the subject of releasing things, sometimes developers will put in calls to `System.gc` in order to force finalization of objects that have external resources that need release. On top of being incredibly wasteful (this will trigger a full garbage collection sweep), the garbage collection pass is never guaranteed to find the unused objects and collect them—as explained in Item 72, garbage collection algorithms may in fact not release the object right away despite its unreachable status. Instead, the far better approach is to explicitly release the object's resources using it's `close` or `dispose` method, assuming it has one. (If it doesn't have one, and it's not using `Reference` objects or shutdown hooks to ensure release, drop it like a hot potato, fire off an angry e-mail to the support department of the vendor you got it from, and find something else to use in its place.)

One tuning parameter that you can also play with comes from the RMI plumbing. RMI over JRMP, thanks to its distributed garbage collection behavior, forces explicit garbage collections periodically, as controlled by the JVM system properties `sun.rmi.dgc.client.gcInterval` and `sun.rmi.dgc.server.gcInterval`, for client and server respectively, and both are set to 1 minute (60,000 milliseconds) by default. In order to avoid such frequent garbage collection passes, set these values higher (recognizing that this will also leave RMI objects that are no longer in use alive for longer before being reclaimed). Think you're not using RMI? Guess again—remember, RMI is the preferred RPC protocol over which EJB operates. (By default, it should be RMI-over-IIOP, but most servers seem to prefer using RMI-over-JRMP since it's more Java-friendly.)

Additionally, as described in more detail in Item 72, a number of garbage collection parameters can be used to make the garbage collector operate in a more efficient manner over your code; using these is an option of secondary resort, however—start playing with these only if you have profiled the code (or seen `verbose:gc` output that seems to indicate a problem) *and* you're not planning to ship the following day.

In general, tuning the JVM is a coarse-grained brush: you're making statements about how your code should execute in broad fashion, and you should expect results of a similar nature. Choosing the client over the server JVM, for example, will have dramatic differences that may (or, ironically enough, may not, depending on your particular application) yield better performance in your enterprise applications. Don't expect orders-of-magnitude results, but don't be surprised during the one or two times when that happens, either.

Item 69: Use independent JREs for side-by-side versioning

One of the touted features of the Microsoft .NET platform has been its support for "side-by-side versioning"—in other words, a successor version of the .NET platform can be installed on the same machine as a previous version without adverse effects. For the first version of an application release, this seems like an overvalued option. Once the second release of an application occurs, however, or another application is deployed into the application server, or two application servers need to coexist side by side, this becomes absolutely critical to ensuring everything runs correctly.

Consider, for example, a company that wrote its first EJB application against an application server bound to the JDK 1.3 a few years ago. This application is still in use and is quite popular with its community of users when the company is acquired by or merges with or acquires another company. Naturally, the first desire is to consolidate the second company's enterprise applications with the first—not an easy task if the second company is using an entirely different application server that requires JDK 1.4. Ideally, it would be possible to take the .ear files from the first application server and run them, untouched, in the second. Unfortunately, it's never that simple.

For starters, the new composite company entity has decided to maintain the first application server vendor as its enterprise application server partner—this means the second application server, the one dependent on JDK 1.4, can't be used going forward. Unfortunately, this leads to another problem. The second enterprise application made use of several JDK 1.4–specific features, like the Preferences and logging APIs.

If this story seems a bit incredible so far, consider another variant: currently, your company makes use of a standalone servlet container to handle all servlet/JSP operations and a separate EJB container for its EJB operations on the same machine (in order to avoid round-trips—see Item 17). When these servers were first deployed to the machine, they both required JDK 1.3; however, a security hole was discovered in the servlet container, and it needs to be upgraded to the latest version, which requires JDK 1.4.

Regardless of which story you find more credible and/or possible, the ultimate issue here is that a single machine is now facing the problem of having to support both JDK 1.3 and JDK 1.4 installations. Or, going forward, JDK 1.4 and JDK 1.5, or JDK 1.4 and JDK 2.0, and so on.

Normally, when Java is installed on a machine, the JDK is deployed to a shared directory, usually `/usr/local/java` on UNIX-based machines. In the case of Win32 boxes, two JRE installations are laid down: the first goes in the location specified by the user during the installation program, the second goes to two other locations. The bulk of the JRE goes in `C:\Program Files\Java\(JRE version)`, but some executable files get copied to `C:\WINNT\SYSTEM32` as well—this is so that "java" can always be accessible from any command prompt since `C:\WINNT\SYSTEM32` (or `C:\WINDOWS\SYSTEM32`, on Win9x or XP or later installations) is intrinsically part of the `PATH` by default.

However, just because the installation program drops Java into a shared location doesn't mean all applications require Java to be run from that shared location; in fact, all the application really needs is the set of files required at runtime, the JRE. As it turns out, all it really needs at startup is to know where the JRE installation root is so that it can find the necessary configuration files to kick-start the JVM.

Go back to the launcher code we examined in Item 68 and take a look at the early parts of the `main` function again. There, the launcher discovers the path to the executing JRE. Remember, this is the code to `java.exe`, so technically the launcher is trying to discover exactly where it was launched from. This discovery comes from the function `GetJREPath`, which isn't defined anywhere inside the `java.c` source file; instead, it is a platform-dependent function whose implementation varies between Solaris, Linux, and Win32 builds of the JDK. It therefore is defined instead in the `java_md.c` source file, in the same directory as `java.c`; the relevant snippets (from the Win32 version in this case) are outlined here:

```
/*
 * Find path to JRE based on .exe's location or registry
 * settings.
 */
jboolean
GetJREPath(char *path, jint pathsize)
{
  char javadll[MAXPATHLEN];
  struct stat s;
```

```c
  if (GetApplicationHome(path, pathsize))
  {
    /* Is JRE co-located with the application? */
    sprintf(javadll, "%s\\bin\\" JAVA_DLL, path);
    if (stat(javadll, &s) == 0)
    {
      goto found;
    }

    /* Does this app ship a private JRE in
       <apphome>\jre directory? */
    sprintf(javadll, "%s\\jre\\bin\\" JAVA_DLL, path);
    if (stat(javadll, &s) == 0)
    {
      strcat(path, "\\jre");
      goto found;
    }
  }

  /* Look for a public JRE on this machine. */
  if (GetPublicJREHome(path, pathsize))
  {
    goto found;
  }

  fprintf(stderr, "Error: could not find " JAVA_DLL "\n");
  return JNI_FALSE;

found:
  if (debug) printf("JRE path is %s\n", path);
  return JNI_TRUE;
}

/* ... Some code elided for brevity ... */

/*
 * If app is "c:\foo\bin\javac", then put "c:\foo" into buf.
 */
jboolean
GetApplicationHome(char *buf, jint bufsize)
```

```
{
  char *cp;
  GetModuleFileName(0, buf, bufsize);
  *strrchr(buf, '\\') = '\0'; /* Remove .exe file name */
  if ((cp = strrchr(buf, '\\')) == 0)
  {
    /* This happens if the application is in a drive root,
     * and there is no bin directory. */
    buf[0] = '\0';
    return JNI_FALSE;
  }
  *cp = '\0';   /* Remove the bin\ part */
  return JNI_TRUE;
}
```

While we could walk through the definitions of `GetApplicationHome` and `GetPublicJREHome`, it's not really necessary to understand the low-level details of what's going on here. When the launcher seeks to discover the path to the JRE, it first checks whether the JRE is co-located with the application; that is, whether the root of the JRE's directory structure is the same directory the application itself runs in. Second, assuming a structure similar to the JRE's isn't found there, it looks to see if the application is running a "private" JRE—the JRE is installed in a subdirectory underneath the application's home directory. Last, assuming neither of those tests pan out to be true, the launcher does a Win32 Registry lookup. It searches for the key `Software/JavaSoft/Java Runtime Environment` under the `HKEY_LOCAL_MACHINE` hive. The value named `Current Version` holds the most recently installed version of the JVM, which in turn acts as the last part of the key; assuming, for example, that the value of `CurrentVersion` is `1.4.1`, the launcher looks up `Software/JavaSoft/Java Runtime Environment/1.4.1` and finds three values: `JavaHome`, where the JRE is rooted in the directory structure; `Micro Version`, which indicates the minor version number of the release (1 in this case since this is JDK 1.4.1); and `RuntimeLib`, the location of the `jvm.dll` file containing the native parts of the JVM itself. Once all this is discovered, the launcher dynamically loads the `jvm.dll` file, uses that to create a JVM instance via the JNI Invocation API, and passes control into the JVM by calling the `main` method of the class specified as a command-line argument.

The key thing to recognize out of all this is the order in which this discovery takes place—in particular, the fact that the launcher first looks to see where the JRE is in relation to the directory in which execution is taking place. This implies that each Java application can in turn have its own JRE without conflict. In fact, it's as simple as copying the entire subdirectory tree of the desired JRE from the JDK (the `jre` subdirectory inside the main JDK installation root) to anywhere underneath the container's installation, and using that java launcher to invoke the container. For example, I routinely run multiple JDKs as well as the Tomcat servlet container on my laptop, so I've got a JRE copied to the root of the Tomcat installation, and the startup batch scripts point to it instead of relying on the `PATH` to identify which `java.exe` launcher to use.

This provides a measure of isolation against accidental or unknown version incompatibilities on that system. Each JRE remains entirely independent of any other JRE installed on the system, meaning that the server or container will continue to run regardless of what JDKs are installed or uninstalled on the box. It can also simplify deployment in some cases, removing the need for the system administrators to know which is the correct version of the JRE to deploy. Simply provide the JRE as a tarball or zip file for them to unpack in the correct place; no other changes are necessary. (The JNLP seeks to handle this transparently for client-side applications.)

By the way, nothing in this item is Win32-specific; I just listed the code for the Win32 version because of its greater complexity (owing to its use of the Registry to look up the location of the "public" JRE). The UNIX version of `GetApplicationHome` is actually much simpler and provides all the information necessary to the launcher to bootstrap the JVM into existence. No reliance on a `GetJREPath` function is necessary at that point. The launcher uses the in-memory address of the `GetApplicationHome` function to look up the dynamic-loader information about the executable (either an executable application or shared library) in which that function resides, then takes that resulting information, which contains the directory in which the executable file resides, and walks back up the known JRE directory structure to determine what the root must be. (See the `dladdr` system call in your system's programmer's API reference for details.) Again, the point is that the lookup is entirely relative to the launcher executable's location.

Now, going into production, the application server, servlet container, Java-powered database, and other Java services can each run under a precisely defined JVM environment. Note that this isolation of JVMs across containers also provides an opportunity to better segregate Java extensions (Java `.jar` files copied into the extensions directory, `jre/lib/ext`) between containers and helps eliminate some confusion with respect to the JDK 1.4 "endorsed standards directory" and XML parsers and CORBA ORBs. By the way, this item isn't limited to just enterprise server containers. I routinely give the most recent Ant installation on my laptop its own JRE to play with, and I install all of the Ant-dependency `.jar` files, like JUnit, into the extensions directory of that JRE, just for simplicity. Each JVM runs with its own settings, its own extensions, and, perhaps most importantly, its own Hotspot configuration file (see Item 68). Changes to one won't affect the others, which is exactly what we want in any kind of production environment.

Item 70: Recognize ClassLoader boundaries

The ClassLoader architecture owns responsibility for the most fundamental task of the JVM, that of loading code into the JVM and making it available for execution. Along the way, it also defines isolation boundaries so that classes of similar package/class naming won't necessarily clash with one another. In doing so, ClassLoaders introduce phenomenal flexibility into a Java server-based environment and, as a result, phenomenal complexity. Dealing with ClassLoader relationships drives developers nuts—just when we think we've got it all figured out, something else creeps in and throws everything up in the air again. Despite our desire to bury our collective head in the sand and pretend that ClassLoaders will go away if we wish hard enough, the brutal fact remains that enterprise Java developers must understand the ClassLoader relationships within their server product of choice.

Consider an all-too-common scenario: a servlet Web application stores Beans (not the EJB kind) in user session space for use during later processing as part of the Web application—classic MVC/Model 2 architecture. At first, the Beans were deployed in a separate `.jar` file to the CLASSPATH of the server product itself—it seemed simpler that way. Unfortunately, doing so meant that the Beans accidentally clashed with other Beans of the same name (how many `LoginBean` classes can we count?) in a different Web application, so the Beans had to move into the

Web application's `WEB-INF/lib` directory, where they're supposed to have been in the first place.

Now, however, whenever a servlet in the Web application changes and the container does its auto-reloading magic, weird `ClassCastException` errors start to creep in. Say you have code like this:

```
LoginBean lb = (LoginBean)session.getAttribute("loginBean");
if (lb == null)
{
    . . .
}
```

The servlet container keeps complaining that the object returned from the `session.getAttribute` call isn't, in fact, a `LoginBean`. You, meanwhile, are pulling your hair out in large clumps because you know for a fact that it is a `LoginBean`; you just put it in there on the previous page. Worse, when you try to verify that it is a `LoginBean`, by calling get `Class.getName` on the object returned, it shows up as `LoginBean`. Better yet, if you restart the server, the problem appears to go away completely, until the next time you change the servlet. You quietly contemplate retirement.

The problem here is one of ClassLoaders, not code.

To be particular, ClassLoaders are used within the Java environment not only as a loading mechanism but also a mechanism for establishing isolation boundaries between disparate parts of the code—in English, that means that my Web application shouldn't conflict in any way with your Web application, despite the fact that we're running in the same servlet container. I can name my servlets and beans by names that exactly match those in your Web application, and the two applications should run side by side without any problems.

To understand why ClassLoaders are used to provide this isolation behavior, we have to establish some fundamental rules about ClassLoaders.

1. *ClassLoaders form hierarchies.* When a ClassLoader is created, it always defaults to a "parent" ClassLoader. By default, the JVM starts with three: a bootstrap loader written in native code to load the runtime library (`rt.jar`), a `URLClassLoader` pointing to the extensions directory (usually `jre/lib/ext` in your JRE directory) called the extensions loader, and another `URLClassLoader` pointing to the

elements dictated by the `java.class.path` system property, which is set via the `CLASSPATH` environment variable. Containers like EJB or servlet containers will augment this by putting their own Class-Loaders into the tree, usually toward the bottom or leaf nodes. The hierarchy is used to delegate loading of code to the parent before trying to load code from the child ClassLoader, thus giving the boot-strap loader first chance at loading code. If a parent has already loaded a class, no further attempt at loading the class is made.

2. *Classes are loaded lazily.* The Java Virtual Machine, like most man-aged environments, wants to minimize the work it needs to do at startup and won't load a class until it becomes absolutely necessary. This means that at any given point, a class may suddenly come across a method it hasn't invoked before, which in turn references a class that hasn't been loaded yet. This triggers the JVM to load that class, which brings up the next rule of ClassLoaders. By the way, this is why old-style non-JNDI JDBC code needed to "bootstrap" the driver into the JVM. Without that, the actual driver would never be loaded since your JDBC code traditionally doesn't directly reference the driver-specific classes, nor does JDBC itself.

3. *Classes are loaded by the ClassLoader that loaded the requesting class.* In other words, if a servlet uses the class `PersonBean`, then when `PersonBean` needs to be loaded the JVM will go back to the Class-Loader that loaded the servlet. Certainly, if you have a reference to a ClassLoader, you can explicitly use that ClassLoader instance to load a class, but this is the exception, not the rule.

4. *Classes are uniquely identified within the JVM by a combination of class name, package name, and ClassLoader instance that loaded them.* This rule means that a given class can be loaded twice into the VM, as long as the class is loaded through two different ClassLoaders. This also implies that when the JVM checks a `castclass` operation (such as the `LoginBean` cast earlier), it checks the two objects to see if they share any common ancestry from a ClassLoader perspective. If not, a `ClassCastException` is thrown. This also implies that since the two classes are considered to be unique, each has its own copy of static data.

Having established these rules, let's take a look at what this means, practi-cally, to enterprise Java developers.

Isolation

In order to support the notion of isolation between Web applications, the servlet container creates a ClassLoader instance around each Web application, thereby effectively preventing the "leakage" of classes from one Web application to the other. Many servlet containers provide a "common" directory in which to put .jar files that can be seen by all Web applications as well. Therefore, most servlet containers have a ClassLoader hierarchy that looks, at a minimum, like the one shown in Figure 8.1.

Notice that this implies that a `LoginBean` class, deployed as part of WebAppA.war and also as part of WebAppB.war, is loaded twice into the servlet container: once through WebApp A and once through WebApp B. What happens if `LoginBean` has static data members?

The answer is simple, rooted in rule 4 mentioned earlier: each `LoginBean` is uniquely identified by its class name and package name (`LoginBean`) and the ClassLoader instance that loaded it. Each Web application is loaded by a separate ClassLoader instance. Therefore, these are two entirely orthogonal classes that maintain entirely separate static data.

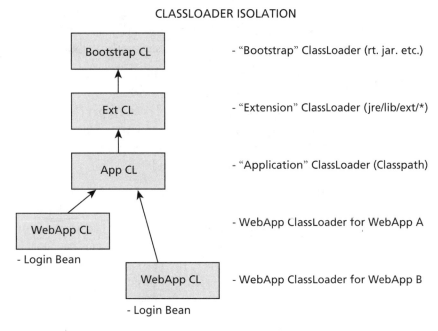

Figure 8.1 | ClassLoader isolation

This has profound implications for servlet developers—consider, for example, the ubiquitous hand-rolled `ConnectionPool` class. Typically this class is written to maintain a static data member that holds the `Connection` instances the pool wants to hand out. If we amend Figure 8.1, putting in `ConnectionPool` in place of `LoginBean`, the unsuspecting developer has *three* `ConnectionPool` instances going, not one, despite the fact that the pool itself was maintained as static data. To fix this, put the `ConnectionPool` class in a jar or ClassLoader higher in the ClassLoader hierarchy. Or, better yet, rely on the JDBC 3.0–compliant driver to handle `Connection` pooling entirely (see Item 73).

Moral: Singletons don't work unless you know where you are in the Class-Loader hierarchy.

Versioning

In order to support hot reloading of servlets, the typical servlet container creates a ClassLoader instance each time a Web application changes—so, for example, when a developer recompiles a servlet and drops it into the Web application's `WEB-INF/classes` directory, the servlet container notes that the change has taken place and creates an entirely new Class-Loader instance. It reloads all the Web application code through that ClassLoader instance and uses those classes to answer any new incoming requests. So now the picture looks something like Figure 8.2.

Let's complicate the picture somewhat: assume SampleWebApp, version 1, created a `LoginBean` and stored it into session space. The `LoginBean` was created as part of SampleWebApp-v1's ClassLoader, so the class type (the unique tuple of package name, class name, and ClassLoader instance) associated with this object is (`unnamed package`)/`LoginBean`/`SampleWebApp-v1`. So far, so good.

Now the developer touches a servlet (or hot deploys a new version of the Web application), which in turn forces the servlet container to reload the servlet, which in turn requires a new ClassLoader instance. You can see what's coming next. When the servlet tries to extract the `LoginBean` object out of session space, the class types don't match: the `LoginBean` instance is of a type loaded by ClassLoader 1 but is asked to cast to a class loaded by ClassLoader 2. Even though the classes are identical (`LoginBean` in both cases), the fact that they were loaded by two different

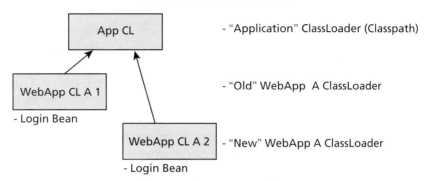

Figure 8.2 | ClassLoaders running side by side to provide versioning

ClassLoader instances means they are entirely different classes, and a `ClassCastException` is thrown.

At first, it seems entirely arbitrary that the same class loaded by different ClassLoaders must be treated as an entirely different class. As with most things Java does, however, this is for a good reason. Consider some of the implications if the classes are, in fact, different. Suppose the VM allows the cast above to take place, but the new version of `LoginBean` doesn't, in fact, have a method that the old version has, or doesn't implement an interface the old version does. Since we allowed the cast, what should the VM do when code calls the old method?

Some have suggested that the VM should compare the binary layouts of the two classes and allow the cast based on whether the two classes are, in fact, identical. This implies that *every* cast, not to mention every reference assignment, within the system would have to support this binary comparison, which would seriously hurt performance. In addition, rules would need to develop to determine when two classes were "identical"—if we add a method, is that an acceptable change? How about if we add a field?

The unfortunate realization is that the pairing of class name and Class-Loader instance is the simplest way to determine class uniqueness. The goal, then, is to work with it, so that those annoying `ClassCastException` errors don't creep up.

One approach is complete ignorance: frequently, when faced with this problem, we try to solve it by bypassing it entirely. In the interests of getting the code to work, we put the `LoginBean` class somewhere high enough in the ClassLoader hierarchy that it isn't subject to reloading, usually either on the container's CLASSPATH or in the container's JVM extensions directory (see Item 69). Unfortunately, that means that if LoginBean *does* change, the server has to be bounced in order to reload it. This can create some severe evolution problems: WebApps A and B depend on version 1 of LoginBean, but WebApp C needs version 2, which isn't backwards-compatible. If LoginBean is deployed high in the hierarchy, WebApps A and B will suddenly "break" when WebApp C is deployed. This is a great way to see how many consecutive 24-hour debugging sessions you can handle.

Worse yet, deploying LoginBean this high in the ClassLoader hierarchy means that other Web applications might also be able to see LoginBean, even if they shouldn't. So WebApp D, which doesn't use LoginBean at all, could still see the class and potentially use it as a means of attack against WebApps A, B, or C. This is dangerous if your code is to be hosted on a server you share with others (as in the case of an ISP); other applications could now use Reflection against your LoginBean class and maybe discover a few things you'd prefer to keep secret.

Don't despair—all isn't lost. A couple of tricks are available.

Trick Number One is to define an interface, say, LoginBean, and put that high in the ClassLoader hierarchy, where it won't get loaded by the Class-Loader that loads the Web application. An implementation of that interface, LoginBeanImpl, resides in the Web application, and any code that wants to use a LoginBeanImpl instead references it as a LoginBean (the interface). When the Web application is bounced, the assignment of the "old" LoginBeanImpl is being assigned to the interface LoginBean, which wasn't reloaded, so the assignment succeeds and no exception is thrown. The drawback here is obvious: every sessionable object needs to be split into interface and implementation. (This is partly why EJB forces this very state of affairs for each bean: this way, EJB can shuffle Class-Loader instances around without worrying about ClassCastException errors. Not coincidentally, this is also why EJB instances are forbidden to have static data members, since statics don't play well with interfaces.)

Trick Number Two is to store only objects from the Java base runtime library (e.g., String and Date objects) into session space, rather than custom-built objects. The Java Collections classes, Map in particular, can be quite useful here as "pseudo-classes" for holding data. Since the bootstrap ClassLoader loads the runtime library, these can never be hot-versioned and therefore won't be subject to the same problems. The danger here, however, is that the Java `Collections` classes will take instances of anything, meaning the temptation to just stick everything into session becomes harder to resist (see Item 39).

Trick Number Three assumes you want or must have your custom objects but can't take the time to break them into interface and implementation pieces. In that case, mark the class as Serializable, then use Java Object Serialization to store a serialized copy of the objects into the session as a byte array. Because Java Object Serialization more or less ignores this problem, and because byte arrays are implicitly themselves Serializable (thus satisfying the Servlet 2.2 Specification requirement/suggestion that only Serializable objects be stored into session), you can store the serialized version of the object, rather than the standard object type, and instead of assigning the session object back to the `LoginBean` reference, deserialize it:

```
// Store in session
LoginBean lb = new LoginBean(...);
try
{
  ByteArrayOutputStream baos = new ByteArrayOutputStream();
  ObjectOutputStream oos = new ObjectOutputStream(baos);
  Oos.writeObject(lb);
  byte[] bytes = baos.toByteArray();
  session.setAttribute("loginBean", bytes);
}
catch (Exception ex)
{
  // Handle exception
}


// Somewhere else, retrieve LoginBean from session
LoginBean lb = null;
try
{
  byte[] bytes = (byte[])session.getAttribute("loginBean");
  ByteArrayInputStream bais = new
    ByteArrayInputStream(bytes);
  ObjectInputStream ois = new ObjectInputStream(bais);
  lb = (LoginBean)ois.readObject();
```

```
}
catch (Exception ex)
{
  // Handle exception
}
```

This third approach carries a significant cost, however: it's somewhat expensive to serialize and deserialize objects, even when you follow Item 71. Fortunately, you shouldn't have to use it very often. Another problem, specifically related to servlet containers, is that byte arrays aren't JavaBean-compliant and so can't be used as targets of the standard JSP bean tags (useBean, getProperty, and setProperty).

The key here, ultimately, is to know exactly how your Java environment sets up ClassLoader relationships, and then work with them, rather than against them. If your environment doesn't tell you straight out, some judicious exploration, via calls to getClass().getClassLoader() and walking the hierarchy, is in order. Failure to do so means mysterious ClassCastException errors when you least want to see them—in production.

Item 71:   Understand Java Object Serialization

Java Object Serialization is a wonderful thing. It allows a Java programmer to take an object and reduce it to a stream of bytes just by implementing the java.io.Serializable interface and passing the object to the writeObject method of ObjectOutputStream. Rebuilding the object back from the bytestream is similarly simple: just call readObject on an ObjectInputStream wrapped around the bytestream. As an example of how wonderful Serialization really is, consider the following:

```
import java.io.*;
import java.util.*;

class Person implements Serializable
{
  public String name;
  public Person spouse;
  public ArrayList children = new ArrayList();
}
```

```java
public class Serial
{
  public Serial()
  { }

  public static void main(String[] args)
    throws Exception
  {
    if (args[0].equals("write"))
    {
      Person youssef = new Person();
      youssef.name= "Youssef";

      Person sheryl = new Person();
      sheryl.name = "Sheryl";

      youssef.spouse= sheryl;
      sheryl.spouse= youssef;

      Person child1 = new Person();
      child1.name = "Johnny";

      Person child2 = new Person();
      child2.name = "Mike";

      youssef.children.add(child1);
      youssef.children.add(child2);
      sheryl.children = youssef.children;


      FileOutputStream fos = new FileOutputStream("people.ser");
      ObjectOutputStream oos = new ObjectOutputStream(fos);
      oos.writeObject(youssef);
      fos.close();
    }
    else
    {
      FileInputStream fis = new FileInputStream("people.ser");
      ObjectInputStream ois = new ObjectInputStream(fis);
      Person youssef = (Person)ois.readObject();
```

```
System.out.println(youssef.name);
System.out.println(youssef.spouse.name);
System.out.println(((Person)youssef.children.get(0)).
  name);
System.out.println(((Person)youssef.children.get(1)).
  name);
System.out.println(((Person)youssef.spouse.children.
  get(0)).name);
System.out.println(((Person)youssef.spouse.children.
  get(1)).name);
    }
  }
}
```

The thing to take careful note of here is that the single call to `write Object` follows the entire object graph: when `youssef` is serialized, so are `sheryl`, `johnny`, and `mike`. Serialization also ensures that each object is deserialized only once, even though the same object may be referenced multiple times throughout the graph. Thus, even though `youssef` refers to `sheryl`, who in turn refers back to `youssef`, each object appears only once, just as it does in the actual object graph. You get all this without having to write a line of code to support it.

Still, when compared to the automatic Serialization capabilities of entity beans or JDO, you may be wondering why as a J2EE programmer you need to worry at all about Serialization. After all, you're not storing data in files, you're storing data in a relational database. So why bother with Serialization?

Because, like it or not, you're using it a great deal.

Serialization is a cornerstone on which other parts of J2EE are built. For example, RMI-over-JRMP uses Serialization as its marshaling framework for making remote calls (see Chapter 3). Servlet containers often use Serialization to store session state to disk when the containers shut down, so they can restore those active sessions when restarting, thus preserving the illusion that the container was never down. Many EJB containers use Serialization to passivate beans to disk between remote (or local) calls. JMS uses Serialization to support the `ObjectMessage`. As a result, developers need to be aware of the ins and outs of the Serialization Specification in order to avoid being "surprised" by some subtle behavior of serialized object data.

For example, one side effect of using Serialization as RMI's marshaling framework is that because Serialization is not concerned with confidentiality, all parameters passed through RMI are done in virtually clear-text fashion. If confidentiality is a concern for an EJB-based system, this is a problem. Unfortunately, the EJB Specification offers no outlines or rules for providing confidentiality between the RMI stubs and the EJB container in a portable fashion; there's no way to customize the channel (socket) used by the RMI plumbing to make the communication between client and server. By taking control over how objects are serialized, however, individual parameter types can be massaged to encrypt (or at least obfuscate) their sensitive data when passed across during an RMI call.

Please note that although many EJB containers may use Serialization for passivation, the EJB Specification does not mandate it, and therefore some containers may not do so in favor of a nonstandardized mechanism. Ideally, such a container would document the mechanism it uses and the reasoning behind it and would provide similar kinds of hook points (see Item 6) for modification. Serialization has a number of hook points that you can (and should, in some cases) take advantage of.

The `serialVerUID` field

The first element of Serialization that every Java programmer should understand is the `serialVerUID` field. When an object is serialized, Java Object Serialization calculates a hash of the entire class based on an exhaustive variety of metadata about the class—the fields in the class, their access scope, their types, the methods of the class, their parameters, the base class, any implemented interfaces, and so forth. This yields an almost-unique value that will be compared at deserialization to ensure that only the same kind of object is deserialized as serialized.

Java classes can precalculate this hash and store the precalculated value in a private static `long` field called `serialVerUID`. During Serialization, if such a field exists, this value will be used rather than calculating the hash. (It's presumed that the value of this field was precalculated using the JDK `serialver` utility, rather than selecting values at random.) While optional for basic Serialization, if a Serialized object evolves, calculating this value is crucial to supporting deserialization of "old" objects into "new" types.

Even for classes that don't require evolutionary support, however, you can obtain a small performance enhancement by precalculating this hash anyway, thereby saving the necessary runtime CPU cycles to generate it.

Customization (`writeObject` and `readObject`)

The simplest way to provide Serialization support and/or customization is to write private `writeObject` and `readObject` methods on the class, each taking a stream argument, `ObjectOutputStream` and `ObjectInput Stream`, respectively. These methods, if present, will be invoked when serialization (`writeObject`) or deserialization (`readObject`) takes place. Within the body of these methods, developers can either take complete control over the serialization of the contents of the class or call the stream's `defaultWriteObject` or `defaultReadObject` method to perform default serialization, then tweak from there.

So, returning to the earlier `Person` example, let's add a `totalWorth` field to track the individual's total net worth. We'd like to keep that value a secret, so we can obfuscate it before serialization and recalculate it on deserialization:

```
import java.io.*;
import java.util.*;

class Person implements Serializable
{
  public String name;
  public Person spouse;
  public ArrayList children = new ArrayList();
  public double totalWorth;

  private void writeObject(ObjectOutputStream oos)
    throws IOException
  {
    totalWorth = obfuscateValue(totalWorth);
    oos.defaultWriteObject();
  }
  private void readObject(ObjectInputStream ois)
    throws IOException
  {
```

```
    ois.defaultReadObject();
    totalWorth = deobfuscateValue(totalWorth);
  }


  private static double obfuscateValue(double originalValue)
  { return originalValue * 2 - 1; } // Imagine your algorithm
                                    // here
  private static double deobfuscateValue(double hiddenValue)
  { return (hiddenValue - 1) / 2; } // Imagine your algorithm
                                    // here
}
```

Obviously in production code we would want a stronger algorithm than the one shown, but it serves our purposes here. Now, when serialized, a `Person` instance's `totalWorth` will be twisted to hide its original value and then untwisted to its original value when deserialized.

Replacement (`writeReplace` and `readResolve`)

At times, simply massaging the data serialized for a given class isn't enough—class evolution or security reasons, for example, sometimes mandate a more drastic measure, that of nominating a different class type for serialization and/or deserialization. This is handled by providing `writeReplace` and `readResolve` methods on the class being serialized.

For example, consider the `CreditCard` class used as part of an online system for e-commerce. Naturally, we want to ensure that the credit card number is sent in encrypted form from the user's Web browser to our receiving servlet, but if we're claiming that the credit card number is truly secure, we also need to ensure it is encrypted across the wire between the servlet and the EJB container (never trust the network, even inside the firewall—see Item 60). Toward that end, we can write the `CreditCard` class to nominate an encrypted replacement, `EncryptedCreditCard`, to be sent across the wire, and `EncryptedCreditCard` can nominate an original `CreditCard` instance when deserialized on the receiving side:

```
class CreditCard implements java.io.Serializable
{
  public CreditCard(Date expiration, String number)
  {
    System.out.println("CreditCard.<init>");
```

```
      this.expiration = expiration; this.number = number;
    }

    public Date expiration;
    public String number;

    private Object writeReplace()
      throws java.io.ObjectStreamException
    {
      System.out.println("CreditCard.writeReplace()");
      return new EncryptedCreditCard(expiration, number);
    }

    public String toString()
    {
      return "CreditCard: " + number + " (" + expiration + ")";
    }
}

class EncryptedCreditCard implements java.io.Serializable
{
    private Date expiration;
    private String encryptedNumber;

    public EncryptedCreditCard(Date exp, String number)
    {
      expiration = exp;
      encryptedNumber = encryptCreditCardNumber(number);
    }

    public Object readResolve()
      throws java.io.ObjectStreamException
    {
      return new CreditCard(expiration,
                   decryptCreditCardNumber(encryptedNumber));
    }

    private String encryptCreditCardNumber(String num) { ... }
    private String decryptCreditCardNumber(String num) { ... }
}
```

The nice thing about this approach is that when working with Credit Card, programmers can ignore the needs of security, at least when transmitting CreditCard instances across the open network wire. In fact, you can design and implement the entire system up front to work entirely with "open" CreditCard instances, then later add the writeReplace/readResolve logic when confidentiality of these objects during serialization becomes an issue. (How to encrypt the data to prevent easy observation is another matter entirely, one beyond the scope of this discussion; see Item 65 for details, or take a look at *Java Security* [Oaks] for more complete discussions on this subject.)

Further details

You can find more information on Java Object Serialization (including discussion of the Serializable fields API and other Serialization functionality) in the standard Java2 SDK documentation bundle or in the books *Component Development for the Java Platform* [Halloway] or *Server-Based Java Programming* [Neward]. You should also have a look at *Effective Java* [Bloch]; in particular, look at Item 54, in which the author points out that marking a class Serializable means you are silently introducing a new constructor on the class, one that takes a byte array as its sole argument. If your class needs to maintain invariants as part of its behavior, make sure the invariants are checked when constructing an object from deserialization, also.

Understanding Serialization has benefits that go beyond just understanding how to use it to work with J2EE; frequently, developers look for ways to store objects or other sorts of data, and Serialization is tailor-made for that sort of thing. Objects can be serialized and stored in BLOB columns in tables, objects can be serialized and sent as the content body of an HTTP request or response, and so on. In fact, one convenient way to store user preferences (if you don't want to or can't make use of the Preferences API) is to put the preferences into a HashMap and serialize the HashMap and its contents. The point is, without understanding how Serialization itself works, you'll end up making decisions—like running all of your RMI traffic over SSL just to protect a few fields—that will hurt you in the long run.

Item 72: Don't fight the garbage collector

We've all heard the conventional wisdom—it has been trumpeted from magazine articles, books, even the conference and lecture circuit: Java object allocation is slow. Minimize the number of objects you create. Unfortunately, those opinions are based on outdated information, and the conclusions they draw as a result lead Java programmers to do exactly the wrong thing.

In the early, version 1.0 days of Java, the JVM garbage collector was truly awful. It was a simple, stop-the-world, mark-and-sweep garbage collector that resulted in frequent visible pauses in execution. The JVM was holding off on all garbage collection activities until it reached its memory maximum threshold, then ripped through the entire JVM heap to find all the objects worthy of collection, marked them as unreachable (and therefore eligible for collection), and executed another pass of the entire heap to collect them all at once. Because the VM needed to keep everything properly correct and synchronized, all executing threads—which were interpreting Java bytecode because we had no JIT yet in those days—had to be stopped while garbage collection was taking place. In many ways, the 1.0 release birthed Java's reputation as a "performance-avoiding platform."

As Java moved through version 1.1 and into its 1.2 release, developers began to find ways to circumvent and bypass the garbage collector—anything we could do to keep the garbage collector from ripping through the heap and doing its odious duty was a blessing. Since object allocation was frequently a place from which a garbage collector could be triggered, it made sense to minimize the number of calls to new as much as possible. A number of ideas were put forth, including the general-purpose object pool (which we'll revisit in a bit).

What happened in the meantime, however, is obvious in retrospect but less so when considering the conventional wisdom: Java garbage collection algorithms and allocation policies got better. By the time of the Hotspot VM release, and particularly with respect to the J2SE 1.4 (and 1.5) releases, no longer can we rely on the assertion that object allocation is expensive. Similarly, with the exception of finalizable objects, it's also not true that object reclamation is expensive. In truth, in modern VMs object allocation and reclamation require a fraction of their former costs;

to understand why, a brief trip through various garbage collection algorithms is in order.

One popular collector is the *copying collector,* so named because it divides the heap into two equal halves, one labeled Fromspace and the other Tospace. Objects are allocated out of the Fromspace, and when a garbage collection pass is called for, the garbage collector does its usual job of starting from the root set of references and looking for referenced objects. This time, however, instead of simply marking the object, it follows the links and slowly *copies* every referenced object from the Fromspace to the Tospace (hence the names), as shown in Figure 8.3.

Having done this, any objects left in the Fromspace are, by definition, unreachable and therefore eligible for reclamation. Therefore the garbage collector can assume the entire Fromspace is eligible for reclamation and can blow the entire space away. Naturally, any finalizable objects in the Fromspace must be dealt with somehow before we can blow away the Fromspace, which once again clarifies what a pain finalizers are to the garbage collector. Modulo the finalizer scenario, however, this all-at-once behavior of the copying collector means it releases allocated objects extremely fast, and as a side benefit it automatically compacts the objects in the Tospace. Once this pass is over, we flip the names, so that the current Tospace becomes the Fromspace, and we wait for the next garbage collection pass.

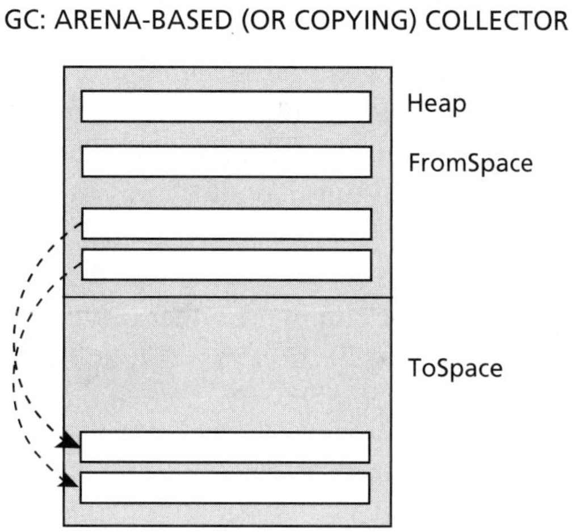

Figure 8.3 Arena-based garbage collection

A copying collector isn't perfect, however, and one of its most notable flaws is pretty easy to spot: the heap requires twice as much memory because we need to maintain enough space to copy the entire heap over to the Tospace. This means that if we have an application that consumes, on average, 128MB of objects, the JVM needs to have at least 256MB allocated just for the heap. This is a bit expensive and not particularly attractive, as you might well imagine.

Another garbage collection algorithm in common use, a *generational collector,* relies on the idea that most objects are short-lived beasts, while a small minority of objects survive for long periods of time. Objects are thus classified by their *generation,* a chunk of memory that contains objects of roughly the same lifetime. Based on this assumption, a generational collector puts newly created objects into a *young generation,* a collection of all objects allocated recently. When a garbage collection pass is requested, then, the collector needs to scan only the first generation looking for unused objects since that's the most likely place they will appear. Only when not enough room is collected from the young generation does the collector begin to move up the generational stack, looking in successively older generations for objects to collect. As an object survives for longer periods of time (usually measured in the number of collection passes successfully survived), it will be moved into successively older generations. Most generational collectors have only a few generations, two or three at the most, although in theory an infinite number of generations could be used (see Figure 8.4).

A generational collector has the immediate and obvious advantage of not having to scan the entire heap during a collection pass, meaning garbage collection passes can be executed more quickly. However, it also suffers the disadvantage that objects in older generations will not be collected for a long period of time, particularly if the young generation remains open enough to satisfy any new allocation requests. In turn, this means that references across generations, particularly an old-to-young reference, will potentially keep objects alive longer than necessary. Finally, depending on the collector, we run the risk that two collections will be necessary, rather than one—if a collection pass through the young generation fails to satisfy allocation requirements, then another pass, this time through the old generation (which may in turn imply a pass through the young generation again) will be necessary, greatly extending garbage collection times.

There are other forms of garbage collection algorithms, including *arena-based collectors* (allocating objects out of *arenas,* chunks of memory from

GC: GENERATIONAL COLLECTOR

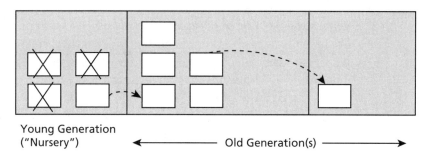

Young Generation
("Nursery") ←————————— Old Generation(s) —————————→

Figure 8.4 Generational garbage collector

which objects are allocated, much as the operating system manages virtual memory in pages), *reference-counting collectors* (which have fallen out of favor because a reference-counting collector cannot handle circular reference scenarios), and others. For more information on garbage collection in general, see *Garbage Collection* [Jones/Lims]; for more information on the Sun collector in general, see the Sun Hotspot documentation available online at http://java.sun.com/docs/hotspot/gc/index.html.

Bearing in mind that mark-and-sweep, copying, and generational collectors are only three of an almost infinite number of possible garbage collection algorithms, it suddenly becomes obvious that programmers' choices that might help one type of garbage collector will hurt another type. In particular, the conventional wisdom that programmers should allocate objects out of object pools in order to speed up allocation depends entirely on the kind of garbage collector running underneath the hood. Therefore, if (after having consulted Item 11) you're trying to write portable code, you can't assume you know anything about the garbage collector under the hood, and as a result, you can't know whether to pool your objects or not. In short, you have to trust the garbage collector to do the right thing.

That doesn't mean you're entirely without options, however. A certain amount of configuration is possible, depending on the JVM you're using—each successive J2SE release since 1.3 has offered greater control over garbage collection behaviors and visibility. The next several paragraphs describe the Sun JVM in some detail, so if you want to preserve your vendor-neutral stance (see Item 11), hold your hands over your eyes and sing loudly until we're done.

Starting with J2SE 1.3, the Sun Hotspot JVM garbage collection mechanism is a hybrid mechanism. It breaks the heap into two arenas, using a generational collector to separate young objects from old objects. Objects are first allocated to a *nursery,* and only when they survive a certain number of garbage collection passes do they migrate up to the old generation. The young generation is managed using a generational garbage collector, consisting of an *eden space,* where objects start, and two *survivor spaces,* where objects are copied to as part of the generational scheme. (The eden space thus acts as a permanent Fromspace, and the survivors switch off as the Fromspace and the Tospace, thus leaving one survivor space empty at any given time between garbage collection passes.)

The old generation, however, because objects allocated within it are far less likely to be ready for reclamation, prefers instead to use a traditional mark-sweep-compact algorithm; the mark-sweep-compact algorithm operates as a standard mark-and-sweep algorithm, except that objects marked for survival are then compacted in order to minimize "holes" in the old generation. Mark-sweep-compact is much slower than a copying collector but has the advantage of being able to use the entire heap, unlike the copying collector, which needs to divide into the Fromspace and the Tospace to work.

In addition, a part of the old generation space is reserved for use by the VM and is called the *permanent space,* since this is where the JVM will allocate Java objects necessary for its own use, such as Reflection objects.

As already described, one of the main advantages of a generational collector is that a complete pass through the entire heap is not necessary—frequently, a single pass through the young generation returns enough free space to satisfy memory requests for the near future. As a result, garbage collection passes within the Sun JVM come in two flavors, a *minor collection* that scours only the young generation and a *full collection* that walks both the young generation and the old generation. The goal, within the Sun JVM, is to keep the young generation free enough that most, if not all, allocation requests can be satisfied within the young generation, since a garbage collection pass there is far less expensive than one through the old generation.

Fortunately, we don't have to guess how the garbage collector is running; using the standard -verbose:gc option to the JVM, we can watch the JVM as it moves through its garbage collection phases because each collection, both minor and full, is written to the java console window as the application executes. Under 1.4.x JVMs, the output of this verbose garbage collection behavior looks something like this:

```
[GC 325407K->83000K(776768K), 0.3400514 secs]
[GC 325816K->83372K(776768K), 0.3054352 secs]
[Full GC 267628K->83769K(776768k), 1.9542351 secs]
```

In this case, we're looking at two minor collections and one full collection. Parsing this output is fairly easy: the number before the arrow indicates the combined size of live objects before and after the garbage collection pass. The third number, in the parentheses, is the total available size of the Java heap, which is the total heap size minus one of the young generation's survivor spaces (because we need that for the copying collector in the young generation to work). Last, of course, is the time taken by this garbage collection pass.

Looking at this output, then, is the first step in seeing how the garbage collector is behaving within your application. If, for example, you see many more `Full GC` entries than `GC` entries, this is a huge red flag telling you that the young generation is getting saturated with objects and can't find enough room to satisfy requests. Part of this may be due to the fact that objects in the young generation, if referenced from objects in the old generation, cannot be reclaimed, which is another argument against using object pools unnecessarily. Whatever the reason, if the heap isn't large enough to honor an allocation request, the JVM will resize the heap by extending its operating system's process footprint by some amount, up to the maximum specified by the –Xmx option to the JVM.

If, however, the old generation has plenty of room and only the young generation is getting saturated, we can resize the young generation by using some underdocumented Sun-specific JVM tuning flags. By default, the young generation is set to be one-quarter the size of the entire heap; if you want to change this ratio, frequently to expand the size of the young generation, you can use the –XX:NewRatio flag, where the value passed to the flag is the ratio of the young generation to the old generation. For example, –XX:NewRatio=3 sets the young generation ratio to be 1:3 to the old generation, which gets us back to the default.

If you're looking for something a bit more fine-grained than a simple multiple of the total heap size, two more flags, NewSize and MaxNewSize, set bounds on the young generation just as the –ms and –mx flags do for the entire heap. Be careful with these values, though—a young generation larger than half of the total size of the heap is allocating a lot of empty space to the young generation. The default `NewSize` on a Solaris JVM is 2172K; on an x86, 640K. `MaxNewSize` is 32M on both platforms, which is typically too small, particularly if you've set the `-mx` option to be larger than 64M (the default). You can do the same for the old generation using the `OldSize` option, set to 1408K by default, and likewise for the permanent space using `PermSize`, 1M by default.

If you're curious about how many passes through the young generation an object has to go before migrating to the old generation, run the application with the `PrintTenuringDistribution` flag turned on (`-XX:+PrintTenuringDistribution`). This exercise is not for the faint of heart and is probably useful only to those developers with more familiarity in this area. On the other hand, getting comfortable with those statistics is a good way to get more familiar with the garbage collector.

This sort of configuration is a lot better than trying to work with things programmatically, by the way. For example, many programmers, believing they know better than the garbage collector when might be a good time to run a garbage collection pass, call `System.gc` on a semi-regular basis, usually when they've released a large object or collection of objects. "I want those objects cleaned up as quickly as possible," they argue, "so I need to tell the garbage collector to run so it'll clean those objects up right away."

This argument has a couple of major flaws. Note that the documentation states that a call to `System.gc` is not a command but a *request* to the garbage collector to run. The garbage collector is free to ignore this call if it feels like doing so. However, before you start spluttering in indignation, "How *dare* they presume such behavior?" stop and think for a moment: If a call to `System.gc` forced a new garbage collection pass, what if the garbage collector were already in the middle of a pass? Should it abandon all its work thus far just to start over because you said so? This would actually result in a *slower* garbage collection time and would work entirely contrary to your stated purpose. More importantly, the collector may not be in a good position to efficiently collect the objects you just released; for example, an arena-based garbage collector may find that the objects you think are eligible for reclamation are still in an arena with reachable objects in it and may decide not to collect those objects. Your "help" here wasn't necessary or appreciated.

As a matter of fact, I know of one Web-based system where programmers littered the code with calls to "force" the garbage collector to run when they thought it was appropriate. On a suggestion from one of the senior developers, they tried running a version of the code with all those calls commented out and found it ran roughly 20% *faster* than it did before, with a smaller memory footprint. Even the Sun documentation points out scary facts behind the `System.gc` call: "These calls force major collection, and inhibit scalability on large systems."[1] For this reason, the Sun JVM has an option to disable the `System.gc` call entirely (the "unsupported" option `-XX:+DisableExplicitGC`), which I strongly suggest you consider using, just in case a few of your more zealous Java developers still drop `System.gc` into their code.

As another example, consider again the conventional wisdom of object pools: "the cost of allocating a Java object is hideously expensive." Actually, as it turns out, under the Hotspot VM from Sun, the cost of constructing a new object is around ten native CPU instructions[2] plus whatever time is spent in the object's constructor(s). This is easily on par with the best C++ compilers and hopefully puts to rest the idea that allocating objects is expensive—as long as the constructors in the objects being constructed aren't slow or complex, the cost of creating a new object is far more efficient than obtaining an object out of a pool. (Remember, even once the object has been retrieved from the pool it still needs to be initialized to a good starting state, which is what a constructor typically does anyway, so the pool only really avoids the cost of construction—which we've already seen is negligible.)

This isn't to say that *all* object pooling is bad, only that it's not the panacea it's made out to be by magazine articles more focused on showing off a particular pooling implementation than on discussing when a pool is best used. For example, J2EE goes to great lengths to provide connection pooling of expensive connections (like database connections, the poster child for resource pooling) because the cost of acquiring a database connection can be an expensive operation—not because creating the object itself takes time but because of the work performed under the hood, making the trip(s) across the network, negotiating authentication credentials, and so on.

---

1. Quoted from http://java.sun.com/docs/hotspot/gc/index.html.
2. Based on information presented by Y. Srinivas Ramakrishna, "Automatic Memory Management in the Java Hotspot Virtual Machine," at JavaOne 2002.

In fact, object pooling—or rather, *resource object management,* since that's the more generic term for what we're describing—falls into several major categories.[3]

- *Object factories:* An object factory, typified by a static method used to simplify object creation and construction by clients, manages infinite, cheap resources. The JAXP API, for example, describes an object factory to create instances of SAX and DOM XML parsers. There is no inherent cost (other than memory, of course) to creating more than one parser, so assuming we didn't care about the ability to swap XML parser instances in and out without changing code, we could go back to using straightforward constructor calls. Instead, the object factory approach allows the client to remain ignorant of the actual instance created. No pooling, per se, occurs.
- *Object banks:* Where a resource is infinite but expensive to create, an object bank allows clients to create and store resource objects for later use, thus avoiding unnecessary creation or destruction of these objects. Object banks aren't used much because most resources that are expensive to create are also finite (and thus fall more typically in the object pool category, below). However, one possible example is an object bank that manages active socket connections to a server, since sockets are for the most part infinite yet require network coordination to create and are thus somewhat expensive.
- *Finite object managers:* Sometimes resources are finite yet cheap to create and destroy. In those situations, a finite object manager chooses to create and destroy objects because it's faster to just allocate and deallocate them than to pool them, but the finite object manager itself is necessary to keep track of the resources allocated in order to ensure that client requests don't exceed the resource maximum. License managers often fall into this category because they want to throttle the usage of a given type of object to a certain upper bound (unless you buy a larger license, of course).
- *Object pools:* When a finite resource is also expensive to create, it makes sense not only to throttle the number of resource objects allocated but also to hang on to the objects already created (when clients are no longer using them) so as to reuse them for interested clients later. The canonical example for object pooling is database connection

---

3. Thanks to Brian Maso, who first came up with this classification and graciously allowed me to "leverage" it.

pooling—most databases now charge licensing fees based on the number of concurrent connections allowed to the database instance, and each connection itself requires a certain amount of negotiation when opened for use.

The ironic part about this discussion is that when broken out this way, it becomes apparent that the EJB Specification makes something of a mistake by placing such heavy emphasis on object pooling—a stateless session bean is a cheap resource to create because it holds no state on behalf of any client, so pooling stateless session bean instances is probably unnecessary. Instead, a container would probably be better off trusting the garbage collector and simply creating new instances of session beans on demand and letting old ones fall into the garbage collector's clutches when the demand drops. (In the interests of safety and security, the object factory used to create the stateless bean instances should probably have an upper boundary on the number of bean instances it will create, in order to avoid denial-of-service attacks from attackers creating an excessive number of stateless calls simultaneously; most EJB implementations provide for this.)

Some readers will undoubtedly look at this list and casually dismiss all four categories as nit-picking over the whole "object pooling" concept; before doing so, however, remember that each one deals with a different scenario and uses different algorithms underneath in accordance with the relative expense and finiteness of the resources they represent. (For details on how to build an effective object pool, see Item 74.)

So, after all that, what now? How exactly are we supposed to write memory-efficient code?

For starters, if you plan to write vendor-neutral code, you have to trust the garbage collector. It's really that simple, and it actually turns out to be the best situation in most cases. Look at it this way: the developers writing the JVM implementations are writing garbage collectors that will work best in "normal" situations and will likely run into problems when faced with tricky and/or bizarre object lifecycle scenarios. Code intentionally—don't try to fool the garbage collector because you'll only confuse it and produce worse results overall.

If you already know the JVM you're working against, however, this isn't necessarily *carte blanche* to pool objects left and right (assuming your JVM recommends it, which the Sun Hotspot team doesn't for its JVM).

It's usually still better to code intentionally, only managing resource objects when they become finite, expensive, or both; the garbage collectors in most JVMs are optimized to deal with the far more common case, that of objects that have no special needs with respect to outside resources.

The overall point here is to try to avoid "tricks" that you believe will make your garbage collection scenario more efficient, at least not without some hard scientific evidence that it's necessary or worthwhile (see Item 10). For example, when was the last time you actually profiled string concatenation, to see if using `StringBuffer` is actually more efficient than just adding two `String` instances together?

Item 73: Prefer container-managed resource management

Java developers coming from the servlet/JSP environment into the EJB environment are frequently surprised to learn how restrictive, by comparison, the EJB environment is. Enterprise beans are not permitted to start threads. Enterprise beans are not permitted to do file-based I/O. Enterprise beans are not permitted to manually implement any sort of synchronization behavior. Enterprise beans are not allowed to establish server sockets, or Reflect, or load a native library, or. . . .

It leaves you wondering precisely what you *can* do.

There is, of course, a reason for all these restrictions. In order to maintain a system that's as scalable as possible, the container seeks to take on resource management as part of its duties. It does this because, as a unifying force across all sorts of different programs and enterprise systems, the container often has a better picture of the overall resource needs, as opposed to your code's rather localized view of the world.

For example, consider threading: it's not uncommon in many servlet books to see a servlet creating a daemon thread to do some kind of processing in the background when the servlet starts up. Think about what this implies for the servlet container. The servlet container itself needs to manage threads in order to take incoming requests on port 80 or 443 (or any other port, for that matter) and fire them down the appropriate filter chain and servlet code. Intuitively, we know that we want the servlet container to do this—or, more specifically, we want the servlet container to keep a tight lid on the maximum number of executing servlets, since to do otherwise would mean opening the servlet container to a denial-of-service attack.

(If that connection isn't obvious to you, consider the following scenario. Suppose I have a servlet framework that creates a new thread on each incoming request. An attacker creates a small program that loops infinitely, creating HTTP requests against the Web application. The servlet framework continues to spin off new threads until the machine crumples due to too many threads executing simultaneously.)

But now you start firing up threads from your servlets. Because the Servlet specification provides no way for a servlet developer to integrate with the servlet container's thread-management scheme, these threads are, by definition, outside the servlet container's control. So if the system administrator sets a thread pool limit of N threads in the servlet container because he has figured out, after much tuning and testing, that N is the optimal number for this particular container and platform, the underlying virtual machine is actually running $N+1$ threads—the N threads the servlet container knows about and the one it doesn't, your servlet's thread. Suddenly, you're past the point of optimal usage and starting down the road of diminishing returns. If that one becomes two or more, you could very quickly get into a situation where the thread-switching time outnumbers the actual work time.

This story gets even worse if this rogue thread is created when the servlet context is started up but the programmer (due to a bug, ignorance, or apathy) doesn't shut down the thread on servlet context shutdown. This means that on every servlet context restart (which can happen for a variety of reasons as the system administrator requires), a new thread is being spun off without reaping the old one. Garbage collection won't help here—threads are one of the very few resources that will continue to live even if all formal references to the object are dropped. (The Thread object will not be collected until the thread itself dies *and* all strong references are gone.) In addition, any objects referenced from that thread will continue to be strongly referenced, meaning they cannot be garbage collected, meaning the JVM now has a larger memory footprint than it should; also, these Thread objects represent thread resources within the operating system itself that are heavier than simple memory-based objects, and ... well, you get the idea.

What's more, we haven't even begun to discuss whether the servlet spinning off threads should do so from a thread pool or not; that subject is covered in more detail in Item 68. The long and the short of it is, however, how can you know whether it's better to use a thread pool or not on a given system until you've tested that particular VM? Certain JVMs use a threading system that works better when using thread pools, others pool threads under the hood and are in fact more inefficient when Java code itself pools the threads.

J2EE specifies resource management for a number of reasons, chiefly because when working within a container-based environment, it's more efficient and scalable to let the container keep track of those resources and to have components borrow them as necessary. In some cases, as seen within the EJB Specification, giving this ability to the developer would actually create more harm than good; managing threads directly is not the simplest of tasks and introduces all sorts of synchronization concerns that the EJB Specification is trying to get out of the developer's way. (While the Servlet Specification takes a more permissive perspective about this, developers are still discouraged from creating or manipulating threads directly.) Similarly, trying to manage component lifecycle directly often interferes with whatever lifecycle policies the container wishes to introduce.

It's understandable why so many books and articles suggest spinning a thread off from a servlet; one facet that was missing from the J2EE space for a long time was the ability to give J2EE components any sort of "active" status. All of the "traditional" J2EE components (servlets, EJBs, JMS) require a logical thread of control from the client—they require that a client call them in order to borrow a thread from the container to carry out some action. Prior to the EJB 2.1 Specification, there was no way to create an active thread that would tie into a J2EE component without making the thread some kind of client to the component. For example, you couldn't "wake up" a bean within the EJB container every ten minutes or so and check a database table for new entries.

The closest approximation was to create a client process, running on the same machine as the EJB container, that would call into the bean every ten minutes or so. Not exactly the most elegant of solutions, but you do what you have to do. The only other alternatives were to either find EJB containers that were more lax about these resource-management rules, thus allowing them the ability to spin off a thread despite the Specification's prohibition against doing so (thus eliminating any portability), or create the daemon or service application process described earlier that would call into the EJB container when desired.

Only now, as part of EJB 2.1, do programmers have any sort of relief, in the form of the Timer Service, which allows you to register a request for an activity to be created by the EJB container—you create a Timer, either keyed to a periodic recurring sequence of calls (e.g., every five minutes) or to a particular time (e.g., five minutes from now), and the bean you wish the container to call in to; then the container, when the appropriate time elapses, makes the call as necessary. Thanks to this, there is no compelling reason for any of the J2EE specifications to spin off their own threads for polling or timeout purposes.

This *laissez-faire*[4] attitude reaches beyond just threads. Network connections are another good resource to leave alone; unless you're somehow tying into the container's connection-management mechanism, don't open and close sockets yourself. On top of the fact that there's an outside possibility you'll open a socket port that the container itself will want to listen on later, most post–JDK 1.4 containers use the `java.nio` libraries to efficiently handle incoming connections, and your meddling here will create more problems than solutions. If you want to listen to outside communications, either use one of the established communications layers already present in J2EE (RMI, JMS, or an established Internet protocol like servlets/HTTP or JavaMail/SMTP) or do your communications outside of a container and bridge to RMI, JMS, servlets, or JavaMail.

The classic "other" resource the container will manage for you is database connections (which includes other connection-style resources, such as `Connector` connections and JMS connections). Frequently, this isn't an issue within EJB containers, but when working from a servlet container or an application that deals directly with JMS `Queue` and `Topic` instances, the EJB container isn't there to do all that wonderful database connection pooling for you. The same is true of working from client Swing applications, or at least it would seem that way.

Because of the widespread belief, not unfounded but not always correct (see Item 72), that pooling is good, servlet developers who worry about extraneous database connections start writing their own database connection pool system or download an existing one (the implementation

---

4. French for "keep your hands off," more or less.

found in the Jakarta Commons project is a popular one, for example). They deploy the connection pool implementation into their Web application and breathe a sigh of relief knowing that all database connections are now being recycled and that their system is now scalable where before it wasn't.

Unfortunately, things aren't necessarily as idyllic as they might seem. First, it's highly likely that the connection pool, if deployed into the Web application itself, is pooling connections only for that particular Web application—because of ClassLoader boundaries (see Item 70 for details), in most cases each connection pool has its own static collection of connections. This means that there are many more `Connection` instances out there than desired. Second, depending on how the connection pool is coded, it's entirely possible that connections are being lost—if the pool doesn't make use of `Reference` objects (see Item 74 for details), any code that doesn't explicitly return a `Connection` to the pool is "leaking" a `Connection` that cannot be recycled or garbage collected. Third, when using the latest JDBC drivers, depending on the details of the driver, you don't need to use an external connection pooling implementation. The JDBC 3.0 Specification suggests that drivers can and should pool connections directly, even without having to go through a JNDI-hosted `Data Source` to do so.

With few exceptions, there is little reason for developers to manage resources in the J2EE containers "by hand"—the underlying implementation of the specification or the containers themselves will typically do a much better job, owing to more knowledge about how the resource operates internally. By stripping out the pooling, you'll also potentially reduce the workload on the garbage collector because there are fewer long-lived objects to keep track of within your code.

Item 74: Use reference objects to augment garbage collection behavior

So, having read Item 72 and facing a situation where just waiting for the garbage collector isn't going to work—you need to know when the object is no longer referenced in order to aggressively release resources (see Item 67)—what's a good Java programmer to do?

Your first reaction might be to go back to the Java Language Specification to see what sort of facilities are available within the language—after all, if you needed to initialize something (which is what constructors do), then certainly you must need to clean it back up, right? And sure enough, Java provides a concept of a *finalizer*, a method invoked by the garbage collector when the object is cleaned up. But before you run off to start writing finalizers everywhere, take a deep breath and keep reading.

As Joshua Bloch discusses in his excellent *Effective Java*, finalizers are typically a bad idea all around. For starters, you have no guarantees when—if ever—a finalizer will be executed. If the JVM is shutting down, for example, it's entirely possible that objects waiting to be finalized will simply be ignored and never called; it would be redundant and unnecessary because the JVM is going down anyway. Second, finalizers create more work for the garbage collector; now, instead of simply placing the allocated object back within the pool of available memory (depending on how the garbage collection algorithms are implemented, of course; see Item 72), the object must be placed within a queue of other objects that must have their finalizers invoked. This slows down not only deallocation but allocation as well because this need is flagged at the time the object is created. This also means that those objects requiring finalization are kept around longer, which in turn yields a larger memory heap footprint for the JVM process than might otherwise be required. One story tells of a Java programmer who consistently ran into `OutOfMemoryError` instances from a given program run. As it turned out, too many objects were being finalized, and the finalizer thread simply couldn't keep up—eventually the JVM ran out of free heap to honor new allocation requests.

More importantly, from a server-side perspective, the JVM offers no guarantees about the order or timing a finalizer is invoked around. For example, given three objects, A, B, and C, where A references B, and B references C, if each object has a finalizer, it might seem logical that the JVM would invoke the finalizers in the order A, B, and C; not so. In fact, it's entirely possible that C's finalizer will be invoked first, then B's, then A's, meaning that if B calls into C within B's finalizer, we're invoking methods on an object that by all measures should be dead.

As if all that weren't bad enough, what happens in the following situation?

```
public class Resurrector
{
  private static ArrayList deadObjects = new ArrayList();

  protected void finalize()
```

```
{
  try
  {
    deadObjects.add(this); // Arise, Lazarus!
  }
  finally
  {
    super.finalize();
  }
}
```

Because within the finalizer we're making the object reachable again from a root set of references, we're effectively resurrecting a dead object. But like all good horror flicks, resurrection isn't everything it's cracked up to be; in this case, this object has already been finalized once, and resurrecting it doesn't change that—so now you have an object that already has one foot in the grave, just waiting for that last reference to be dropped. Once that happens, the object will immediately be released, without the finalizer being invoked again, giving it no chance to do any sort of cleanup. Ouch.

See *Effective Java* [Bloch] for tips on how to implement finalizers correctly; but for the most part, enterprise Java developers will want to avoid finalizers entirely. So now what?

In some cases, the various J2EE specifications offer event methods to tell you when objects are being destroyed. For example, servlets have an `init` method that is fired just before the servlet is handed its first request, and a `destroy` method that is fired just before the servlet container is about to hand the servlet instance off to the garbage collector for recycling. Starting with the Servlet 2.3 Specification, we can also know the lifetime of the entire Web application itself by creating a `ServletContextListener` that the container guarantees it will call at startup and shutdown. EJB beans have similar support via the `ejbCreate` and `ejbRemove` methods, although only on a per-bean basis.

Unfortunately, not all objects whose lifecycles we're interested in are tied to those particular J2EE objects—for example, we may want to create a cache of data in order to speed up processing (see Item 4), and this cache is shared across servlet and/or EJB instances. We could conceivably create some kind of counting scheme within the cached objects, but we'd have to do this for every single object we want to hold in the cache, and this scheme could very quickly break down if we don't get everything exactly correct.

Starting with the JDK 1.2 (Java 2) release, Sun realized that Java programmers needed better interaction with the garbage collector in the JVM, and the company provided it via the `Reference` object types declared in the `java.lang.ref` package. Although their use may seem a bit esoteric, in many cases it offers up the very sort of functionality we're looking for.

Java offers up three kinds of `Reference` objects: `SoftReference`, `WeakReference`, and `PhantomReference`. All are subclasses of the base class `Reference`, and each has the basic property that they "wrap" another object, called the *referent*. You can access this referent from the `Reference` object via the `get` method on the `Reference` object (with one exception, the `PhantomReference` type, which we'll talk about in just a bit).

Reference objects reduce the "strength" of a reference to an object. Normally, when we write something like the following code, the reference declared on the stack, in this case, `strongRef`, means the object on the other side of the reference could still be used:

```
Person strongRef = new Person();
while (true)
{
  // Do some work with the Person object here
}
return;
```

Therefore, by Java Language Specification law, the object cannot be garbage collected. Only when that object is no longer strongly reachable, in this case, when we return from the method (since the local variable reference will no longer exist), can it be collected.

`Reference` objects give us more flexibility in interacting with the garbage collector. An object held on the other side of a `Reference` object, the referent, assuming it is not strongly referenced elsewhere, is now either weakly, softly, or phantomly reachable. The upshot is that the garbage collector is now free to collect the referent, depending slightly on the semantics of the reference object itself.

At first, this doesn't seem like much of an advantage; however, the story doesn't end here. In addition to marking the referent as eligible for collection, a `Reference` object also provides a notification mechanism, called a `ReferenceQueue`. When a `ReferenceQueue` is passed into the `Reference` object's constructor, the garbage collector guarantees to put the `Reference` object into that queue (it will *enqueue* the reference), and interested parties can pull the `Reference` object out of the `Reference Queue` to know whether that `Reference` object's referent is no longer with us and, if so, when it was collected.

Having gone through the basics of `Reference` objects, we'll take a look at each kind in turn.

SoftReference objects

At some point in your life as a Java programmer, somebody (usually the Big Boss) comes by your cubicle and starts talking about what great work you're doing, how glad he or she is that you work for the company, and so on. Right about the time you start wondering where this is going, he or she drops the other shoe: the application is too slow, and you need to speed it up, fast.

Particularly for servlet-based applications, the immediate response comes in a single word: *cache*. It's not uncommon for a developer facing performance problems to quickly decide (based on intuition, which is bad—see Item 10) that a cache is needed to speed up processing. In particular, the programmer has intuited that the system is spending too much time accessing data from some other location, such as disk or database, and that the data doesn't change very often. Therefore, caching the data in memory, to avoid the slow I/O of disk or database access, will help speed things up.

Be very careful here when coming to this conclusion—the performance of your application may not have anything to do with the speed of accessing data from disk or database at all but instead may be suffering from a bottleneck due to contention over a shared resource. Caching in this situation won't help one iota. Only if you've profiled your system, eliminated bottlenecks, and found that the latency of the application is still unacceptable—only then, perhaps, caching is an answer. This is a deliberate tradeoff, however: you're trading scalability on the server-side system in exchange for less latency in obtaining results.

So you start caching everything you can: output results, generated images, generated objects, anything you can keep around from one request to another one so that you don't have to recreate the duplicate object the second time. In some cases, programmers have been known to even cache `String` objects, despite the fact that `String` objects are often cached under the hood by the JVM.

This all works well, for a while. You test the code and find that the system can now handle *N* clients much faster than it could before. And this code works great, until you get to that *N*+1 client accessing the system; that is, at some point, as the system adds more and more clients, sooner or later you're going to run out of memory, and the request will fail. The rejected client will be forced to try again until an existing client drops its connection, thereby releasing the resources, including the cached data, used by the server-side code on behalf of that client. "Alas," you tell your boss, "it's time to buy some more hardware to deal with those rare situations when we get that *N*+1 client. Yeah, it's a shame that it was the big multimillion-dollar client demo, but remember, we wanted those calls to be faster than they were before, so we cached the data. That's the tradeoff between latency and scalability, boss—can't do anything about it."

This isn't a great state of affairs. The cache was intended to reduce latency, not reduce scalability. What's happening here is fairly obvious: each client on the system is suddenly soaking up more in the way of resources, and that in turn reduces the number of clients you can support on a given hardware node. This will be the case even if the cache is somehow global in nature, shared across all clients; it's rare that a server-based application can cache data across users, and even where only shared objects are cached, they still take up a certain amount of memory that is no longer available for client processing. Unfortunately, as a result, this means that the cache, data that, by definition, you could recreate if you had to, is acting as a roadblock to further scalability.

In many ways, what programmers really want in situations like this is for the cache to empty itself out under low-memory conditions, since we can always go back and recreate objects and recalculate data if necessary. This is precisely what the `SoftReference` does: when a `SoftReference` is created around an object, that object is now softly reachable, meaning that if no other strong (normal) references are held to the object, under low-memory conditions the JVM will release the softly referenced object, thus hopefully making more room for object allocations. When this happens, the `SoftReference` will no longer hold a valid reference to its object and will return `null` when asked for its referent.

Using a `SoftReference` is actually quite simple: for any object that we wish to be softly referenced, we can create a `SoftReference` around that object and hold the `SoftReference`. So, for example, a generic cache implementation based loosely on the `java.util.Map` interface would look something like this:

```
public class Cache
{
  private Map cachedItems = new HashMap();

  public Cache()
  { }

  public void put(Object key, Object data)
  {
    cachedItems.put(key, new SoftReference(data));
  }
  public Object get(Object key)
  {
    SoftReference sr = (SoftReference)cachedItems.get(key);
    return sr.get();
  }
}
```

Notice that the cache hands out strong references to the softly referenced objects; if code has asked the cache for an object, we don't want the object to suddenly disappear once the object has been returned. The returned strong reference will keep the softly referenced object alive until that strong reference has been dropped, and once that has happened the object will be eligible for collection under low-memory conditions once again.

In the case of the `Cache` class, in the code above, notice that if a softly referenced object does get collected, we may want to remove the key for that object as well. This means that we need to somehow register with the JVM to be notified when a `SoftReference` gets cleared out; fortunately, this exact behavior is possible using a `ReferenceQueue`.

When we create the `SoftReference` (or any `Reference` object, for that matter), we can pass in an instance of a `ReferenceQueue` that the `Cache` knows about. When the `SoftReference` is cleared, the JVM will enqueue the `SoftReference` instance into the `ReferenceQueue`, where we can fetch it from the `ReferenceQueue` by calling `remove` (which blocks until an enqueued reference is available or a timeout expires) or `poll` (which returns immediately with either `null` or an enqueued `Reference`). So we can amend the `Cache` implementation shown earlier by making it more aware of when the softly reachable value objects are collected; in this case, we'll poll for enqueued references on each call to `get` or `put`, so that way we don't have to worry about setting up a separate `Thread` to do the blocking `remove` calls.

So now we can cache off objects as much as we like, knowing that if the JVM starts to run tight on memory, it will start reclaiming objects from the cache as necessary until either the cache is empty or the need for memory has been met. If that happens, we can always go back and repopulate the cache when the memory situation is friendlier, but be careful—we don't want to repopulate the cache *until* there's more room in the heap, or we'll just start thrashing the garbage collector in a big way. In a production implementation, the `Cache` class should take a threshold parameter in the constructor—if the available heap is less than that threshold, it won't bother trying to hold the cached items but will just throw the references away (since, we presume, the garbage collector is just going to clear the `SoftReference` in a few milliseconds anyway).

WeakReference objects

`WeakReference` objects, as the name implies, make their referents weakly reachable, which essentially means the referents are eligible for collection at any time, assuming they're not strongly reachable through some other reference. As with `PhantomReference` objects (discussed next), the power of the `WeakReference` object lies not so much in the fact that we're allowing the referent to be collected as in the fact that we can be notified when the garbage collector wants to collect the referent. To understand why this is useful, we have to take a step back for a moment and talk about object pools again.

Recall from Item 72 that when a resource is both finite and expensive to create, we want to create an object pool around it to mitigate the cost of allocation and cleanup as well as to keep track of how many of these objects have been created. Implicit with this, however, is not only knowing when to *create* an instance of the resource object in question but also knowing when the borrowed resource object is no longer in use. In traditional object pool implementations, this responsibility is left to the programmer, via some kind of return or cleanup method on the pool, passing the pooled instance back into the pool for reuse.

Unfortunately, both you and I know that this sort of policy requires programmers to be vigilant and disciplined, and the brutal fact is that under tight deadlines and impossible requirements specifications, vigilance and discipline tend to be the first casualties of the development team. This means that we run the very real risk of objects *not* being returned to the pool, and now we're back to relying on the pooled objects' finalizers being triggered as the only means by which we can know the client is done with the pooled object.

Fortunately, there's a better way, and as you might have guessed by now, it uses the `WeakReference`. Because a `WeakReference` doesn't keep an object alive, we can build an object pool by handing out strong references to pooled resources. When the client is finished, it simply drops the strong reference, which in turn leaves the object weakly reachable, and on the next garbage collection pass, the object will be collected and (by catching the `ReferenceQueue` notification) the resource can be returned to the object pool.

The key to making this work, then, is handing out objects that can be freely recycled and thereby notifying the object pool; the classic way to make this work is to have the object pool itself hold the finite collection of objects in the pool, and instead of handing out references to these objects, hand out references to proxies. When the client drops the reference to the proxy (weakly referenced by our pool), the `WeakReference` to the proxy gets enqueued. That in turn means we can detect the drop thanks to the `ReferenceQueue` held inside the pool, and thus return the resource object on the other side of the proxy back to the pool.

Because the client always interacts with the proxy (and not our `Weak Reference` itself), normally this means that we want an interface for both the resource objects managed by the pool as well as the proxies to implement (see Item 1).

Note that an object pool implementation could also be done with `Phantom Reference` objects, and code that does so (generously donated by Vlad Roubtsov, *JavaWorld* columnist) appears on the book's accompanying

Web site. Practically speaking, from a client perspective, there's no functional difference; the only real change is that PhantomReference objects are signaled at a different time in the object lifecycle than WeakReference objects are.

PhantomReference objects

According to the documentation for PhantomReference objects, "PhantomReferences are most often used for scheduling pre-mortem cleanup actions in a more flexible way than is possible with the Java finalization mechanism." Quite honestly, after reading the earlier paragraph on finalizers and realizing just what a bad idea they are, you may think that anything that makes object cleanup easier seems like a good idea.

(I really should be fair here and point out that it's not finalization that's so bad but the fact that it's entirely nondeterministic, unordered, and unreliable. This isn't really something that Java itself can correct, and any automatic reclamation system must deal with it. For those of you keeping score at home, .NET has the exact same problem.)

The problem is, PhantomReference objects don't seem that useful at first; they are unique among the three reference types in that they don't actually hold a reference to their referent, meaning that when get is called on a PhantomReference, it returns null. Or, to be more specific, calling get *before* the PhantomReference is enqueued returns null—all three Reference types return null after the Reference has been enqueued/signaled. The documentation points out that we can create subclasses of PhantomReference, but if we actually put a reference to the object on which we want to invoke a close method in the PhantomReference subclass, that reference will be a strong one, and the PhantomReference itself will never be enqueued.

Using PhantomReference objects requires a bit more subtlety. Here's an example of how we can use the PhantomReference to do cleanup when an object is no longer strongly reached:

```
// Example showing use of PhantomReference
//
import java.lang.ref.*;
import java.util.*;
```

```java
class CleanThisUp
{
  // The resource we need to finalize; for simplicity's sake,
  // I'm not actually going to show the connection, but it's
  // pretty easy to see how this would work in practice
  //
  private java.sql.Connection conn =
    getConnectionFromSomeplace();


  public CleanThisUp()
  {
    System.out.println("CleanThisUp created: " + hashCode());

    // Create our PhantomReference to do the cleanup and
    // register it so the PhantomReference itself doesn't get
    // lost
    refList.add(new CTUPhantomRef(this, conn, cleanupQueue));
  }


  private static class CTUPhantomRef extends PhantomReference
  {
    private java.sql.Connection connToClose;

    public CTUPhantomRef(CleanThisUp referent,
                         java.sql.Connection conn,
                         ReferenceQueue q)
    {
      super(referent, q);

      this.connToClose = conn;
    }
    public void clear()
    {
      try
      {
        super.clear();
      }
      finally
```

```
    {
      // Now do our own cleanup
      //
      try
      {
        if (connToClose != null)
          connToClose.close();
        System.out.println("I cleaned up a connection!");
      }
      catch (java.sql.SQLException sqlEx)
      {
        // Log this, ignore it, whatever—it's never exactly
        // clear what should be done in the event of an
        // exception on a close() call. Regardless, don't
        // just ignore it.
        //
        sqlEx.printStackTrace();
      }
    }
  }
}


private static ReferenceQueue cleanupQueue =
  new ReferenceQueue();
private static List refList =
  Collections.synchronizedList(new ArrayList());
private static Thread cleanupThread;
static
{
  cleanupThread = new Thread(new Runnable()
    {
      public void run()
      {
        try
        {
          Reference ref = null;
          while (true)
          {
            ref = cleanupQueue.remove();
```

```
                   refList.remove(ref);
                   ref.clear();
                }
             }
             catch (InterruptedException intEx)
             {
                return;
             }
          }
        });
      cleanupThread.setDaemon(true);
      cleanupThread.start();
   }
}


public class PhRefTest
{
   public static void main (String args[])
   {
      for (int i=0; i<100; i++)
      {
        CleanThisUp[] ctuArray = new CleanThisUp[10];
        for (int j=0; j<10; j++)
           ctuArray[j] = new CleanThisUp();
        ctuArray = null;
      }
   }
}
```

There's a lot going on here. To start, we have a class that requires some kind of cleanup—in this case, it's holding a database connection that we want to ensure gets closed in a timely fashion, ideally as soon as the object itself gets released. While the garbage collector can't guarantee that it will react as soon as the last strong reference to the CleanThisUp instance is dropped, we can get the garbage collector to tell us right before it's going to blow this object away using a PhantomReference. So, in the constructor of CleanThisUp, we create a PhantomReference instance (a private derived type of PhantomReference, in fact) with a ReferenceQueue held within the CleanThisUp class's static data area.

Remember, however, that the `PhantomReference` itself can't hold a reference to the `CleanThisUp` instance, which is why the `CTUPhantomRef` class is declared as a static nested class within `CleanThisUp`[5]—unless it's declared static, a nested class instance holds a reference to its enclosing class instance (the "outer this," in Java parlance). This would be enough to keep the `CleanThisUp` instance strongly reachable, which means it would never be enqueued by the garbage collector, and our better-than-a-finalizer cleanup scheme would fail miserably.

Notice that we also keep track of the `CTUPhantomRef` instances in an `ArrayList` held within a `CleanThisUp` static field (which must be synchronized, by the way, because this `ArrayList` is going to get pummeled by multiple threads). We need to keep the `PhantomReference` itself alive, but this strong reference to the `PhantomReference` has no bearing on the reachability of the referent (the `CleanThisUp` instance).

Down in the `PhRefTest` class, the driver for this example, we loop 100 times, creating an array of 10 `CleanThisUp` instances and releasing the reference to the array (thus releasing our strongly referenced link to the instances inside the array). This in turn means those instances are only phantomly reachable; remember, we're still holding the `CTUPhantomRef` instances in that static `ArrayList` inside `CleanThisUp`. The garbage collector is encouraged to do a full collection (despite the fact that it's generally a bad idea to coerce the garbage collector this way—see Item 72), and we execute the next iteration of the loop.

When the garbage collector decides to collect our orphaned and phantomly reachable `CleanThisUp` instances, it first enqueues the `CTUPhantomRef` instances on the `ReferenceQueue` we passed in when we constructed it. As far as the garbage collector is concerned, that's all it needs to do, but we have a daemon thread looping infinitely, blocking until a reference is available on that `ReferenceQueue`. We pull the `Reference` out of the queue, remove the `Reference` from the `ArrayList`, and then call `clear` on it. (We have to do this because otherwise, `PhantomReference` instances will never clear and thus never actually collect their referent. It's another of those "quirks" of the `PhantomReference` class.) By overriding `clear` on `CTUPhantomRef`, then, we have an opportunity to do our cleanup before the CleanThisUp instance gets released back to the pool of available memory.

---

5. We want to keep this sort of implementation detail hidden from the clients of `Clean ThisUp`, so we make it a nested class and mark it private to keep prying eyes away.

We still have to be a bit tricky here, however—we can't hold a reference back to the CleanThisUp instance the CTUPhantomRef holds as a referent because that would keep the referent strongly reachable and then we'd be back to "will never be enqueued" status again. Instead, we pass the CleanThisUp resources themselves into the CTUPhantomRef for cleanup; in this case, we give the CTUPhantomRef a copy of the JDBC Connection instance CleanThisUp is holding so that in the overridden call of clear on CTUPhantomRef we can close it.

Sure enough, if you run this, you'll see a whole slew of CleanThisUp instances created, and after a few moments, calls to the CTUPhantomRef's clear method start to intermingle in the display. Take careful note, though—if you're paying close attention, you'll quickly notice that not every object created gets cleaned up. This is because our Thread is a daemon thread, and even though the objects are, in fact, enqueued in the ReferenceQueue, the main thread has exited and our daemon thread isn't enough to keep the JVM alive, so we shut down with some instances still awaiting cleanup. If you absolutely, positively require those objects to be cleaned up, mark the Thread as a nondaemon thread, and figure out some way to kill it when it's time to shut down the JVM.

The key drawback to this sample is the Thread spun off from within the CleanThisUp class; in a J2EE environment, it's not always an easy matter to just arbitrarily spin off a Thread (see Item 73 for why the container wants to shoulder thread management). Other possibilities come to mind: create a static method on CleanThisUp that takes a Thread reference for the ReferenceQueue-listening Runnable to use, or return that Runnable from a static method to hand into the container to execute on a Thread. Alternatively, you could periodically hijack a client's thread and use the poll method on ReferenceQueue to see if there are any Reference instances to listen to, but this requires more complexity within the CleanThisUp class.

Finally, however, we have a way to do cleanup in a better fashion than using a finalizer; it's more work, certainly, but nothing worth doing is easy.

Take careful note of what we're doing with these three examples: in each case, we're offering hints to the garbage collector about how it should behave in certain situations and scenarios. In the case of Phantom Reference objects, we're asking for some kind of postmortem cleanup to take place after the object's ready for reclamation. Because the actual cleanup is happening on our own thread, rather than the finalizer thread, we can make conscious decisions about cleanup and thread deadlock that the finalizer thread, since it's encoded deep inside the JVM, can't do. With `WeakReference` objects, we're asking the garbage collector to send a notification when the last reference to an object has been dropped, which in turn gives us the ability to perform some kind of reclamation of the object on the other side of the `WeakReference`. And with `Soft Reference` objects, it's a direct signal to the garbage collector that the object on the other side of the reference isn't worth keeping around in low-memory situations. In each case, we're offering more information to the garbage collector than we could in earlier releases of Java; use them as appropriate.

Item 75: Don't be afraid of JNI code on the server

For years, Java developers have had something of a love/hate relationship with code outside the JVM. Quite frequently, we need to get at that code, but doing so from within the JVM is something of an art form at best, a quick way to a crashed process at worst.

The problem, of course, is that accessing anything outside the purview of the Java environment requires using the JNI, which typically means we're back to pointers, unmanaged code, and C/C++. While most Java programmers really don't have anything personal against C/C++ compilers, there's a *reason* we like to write code in Java: automatic memory management, a virtual machine that pretty much eliminates wild pointers and process crashes if we accidentally dereference a null pointer, and so on.

It's a hard fact of the Java programmer's life, however, that the Java environment doesn't cover everything, despite Sun's efforts to the contrary. At times we will need to access something from Java that requires going through a C/C++-based API to do it, and that brings us directly back to JNI. When that happens, take a deep breath, put your courage to the sticking place, and dive right in.

The truth is, JNI really isn't as bad as it seems; in fact, assuming you're already comfortable with C/C++ in general, the hard part about JNI isn't writing (and debugging!) the code. It's trying to figure out why the JVM won't load your shared library from within your J2EE environment that typically drives the Java developer mad.

First things first, however. When faced with the task of writing JNI code, there are basically two ways to go about it: the hard, low-level way, and the easier, high-level approach. The hard, low-level way is to write JNI code as defined by the JNI Specification. Write your Java class with methods defined using the `native` keyword, use the javah utility to generate C header stubs (which can then be cut and pasted as the starting point for the C/C++ implementation), and then write a shared library (`.dll` under Win32, `.so` or similar construct under most flavors of UNIX) that contains the implementation of the `native` method, using the `JNIEnv` structure to get function pointers that allow for calling back into the JVM when necessary. Want to allocate a Java string as part of your `native` method? Call back into the JVM to take the C character string and turn it into a Java string. Want to turn a passed Java string into a C-style `null`-terminated character array? Call back into the JVM to do it. Want to allocate a Java object? You guessed it—call back through that `JNIEnv` structure into the JVM again. Oh, and don't forget to check for a Java exception at every step, just in case the JVM runs into a problem (like an `OutOfMemoryError` or a `ClassNotFoundException`). Doing this gets tedious, and anything that a programmer finds tedious very quickly turns error-prone.

There's a better way, however, and it comes in a variety of flavors: let somebody else do the low-level code for you. A number of toolkits, both commercial and open-source, that litter the Internet can take much of the onerous parts of JNI code off your hands. Some of the open-source alternatives include Sheng Liang's "Shared Stubs" code from his book *The Java Native Interface* [Liang], Stu Halloway's Jawin (Java-Windows) library from his book *Component Development for the Java Platform* [Halloway], and JACE, an open-source project that provides C++ wrappers around Java objects in order to make calling those Java object methods easier from within native code. Take full advantage of these toolkits when you can—most have flexible licensing schemes that will accommodate even the stingiest managers and the most inflexible lawyers, and should the open-source community not serve your needs, a number of companies provide commercial alternatives.

Whichever way you get your JNI code written, now the hard part comes: precisely where do you *put* this shared library so that the JVM will pick it up, even from within a J2EE container? The answer comes in two parts. First, the JVM looks for shared libraries in the manner common to the operating system, meaning it uses the dynamic-loading policies of the underlying operating system; on a Win32 box, for example, consult the LoadLibrary Win32 API for details of exactly where the Win32 loader will look for a DLL (it includes the PATH, the WINNT directory, the WINNT/SYSTEM32 directory, and the current directory). However, the JVM also augments this collection of locations with one other, "portable" location: within the JRE's lib directory, there is a CPU-specific directory into which shared libraries can go. For example, on a Win32 JVM, the lib directory contains an i386 directory. Normally, the only file there is a configuration file (see Item 68 for details), but if you drop a native-library DLL in here, it's automatically part of the path the JVM will search for native libraries when using the System.loadLibrary call—yet another reason to use separate JRE instances (see Item 69).

In fact, part of the path the JVM searches, which includes those directories specified by the underlying operating system, is controlled by a JVM system property, the java.library.path property. Changing this at the Java launcher command line via the standard -D option replaces the JVM's default (which is the bin directory of the JRE, the current directory, and the PATH value on a Win32 box, for example).

However, it's important to point out that J2EE containers support the hot deployment of components, meaning that we can insert, remove, and upgrade components deployed into a J2EE container without taking the server down. If the container is already handling requests from clients, this implies that two versions of the component could exist simultaneously in the JVM, as long as they are loaded by separate ClassLoader instances. Unfortunately, this isolation provided by ClassLoaders doesn't extend to native libraries, and most operating systems will load a dynamic library only once. Requests to load the same library, typically differentiated only by the library's name, will essentially no-op.

To the JNI programmer, this means that once a native library is loaded, we're pretty much done for the day—getting a JVM to unload a native library is an exercise in utmost frustration. The JNI Specification states that a native library will be unloaded when the ClassLoader associated with the class it provides the implementation to is unloaded, but trying to force a ClassLoader to unload is virtually impossible within the JVM.

As a result, if you're writing native libraries that will need to be hot deployed into a J2EE container (like a servlet container), make sure that each library has a differentiating name based on its version number; this will fool most operating systems into believing these are separate libraries and therefore will allow them to be loaded when the new version of the component is hot deployed into the container. The drawback, of course, is that if the component gets hot deployed multiple times, it's highly likely that multiple copies of the same native library will be loaded into the process, making the overall footprint of the JVM process that much larger.

Obviously, "going native" in Java is not the optimal case. Your code loses some portability (if portability is important to you; see Item 11), it weakens the stability of the JVM because it opens the possibility of unmanaged code (i.e., non-Java code) accidentally trashing parts of the process, it weakens the secure environment Java code executes in because unmanaged code has no `SecurityManager` and/or `Permissions` model to protect it, and so on. But for those scenarios where you absolutely, positively must escape the JVM, JNI (and the assorted higher-level toolkits) give you the power to do so.

Bibliography

—If I have seen further, it is because
I have stood on the shoulders of giants.

—Sir Isaac Newton

Books

[Alur/Crupi/Malks] *Core J2EE Patterns* (2nd ed.), by Deepak Alur, John Crupi, and Dan Malks. Boston, MA: Addison-Wesley, 2003. A good collection of implementation idioms specific to the J2EE platform. The second edition includes revisions to reflect common terminology, among other things. The first edition, which contains some patterns not included in the second edition, was published in 2001.

[AJP] *Applied Java Patterns*, by Stephen Stelting and Olav Maassen. Palo Alto, CA: Sun Microsystems Press, 2002.

[Bernstein/Newcomer] *Principles of Transaction Processing*, by Philip A. Bernstein and Eric Newcomer. San Francisco: Morgan Kaufman, 1997. The first book to read to understand transactional processing, what it's for, and why it's so critical to enterprise systems. A bit dated in its technology examples and descriptions, but the concepts are timeless.

[Bloch] *Effective Java*, by Joshua Bloch. Boston, MA: Addison-Wesley, 2002. Required reading for any Java developer. 'Nuff said.

[Box] *Essential COM*, by Don Box. Reading, MA: Addison-Wesley, 1997. The first chapter is quite possibly the best piece of technical writing ever conceived and a great explanation for why developers should prefer component-oriented designs. An inspiration for Item 1.

[Brown] *AntiPatterns*, by William J. Brown. New York: Wiley, 1999. A pattern describes a solution to a problem in a certain context that yields

449

certain consequences; antipatterns describe how to recover from negative situations.

[Brown] *Programming Windows Security,* by Keith Brown. Boston, MA: Addison-Wesley, 2000. Understanding security in the Windows operating system turns out to be more important than most Java developers would think, particularly when running Java code as a Windows background service.

[Celko97] *SQL Puzzles and Answers,* by Joe Celko. San Francisco: Morgan Kaufman, 1997. Think you know SQL? Try these on for size.

[Celko99] *Data and Databases: Concepts in Practice,* by Joe Celko. San Francisco: Morgan Kaufman, 1999. Joe Celko is by far one of the most insightful writers about relational technology today. In this work, he explains the relational model in clear, precise terms.

[Celko00] *SQL for Smarties: Advanced SQL Programming* (2nd ed.), by Joe Celko. San Francisco: Morgan Kaufmann, 2000. After reading *Data and Databases: Concepts in Practice* [Celko99], move on to this book to take things to the next level.

[Cooper99] *The Inmates Are Running the Asylum,* by Alan Cooper. Indianapolis, IN: SAMS Publishing, 1999. An excellent treatise on why user interfaces designed by programmers tend to remain incomprehensible to the rest of the world.

[Cooper03] *About Face 2.0,* by Alan Cooper. New York: Wiley, 2003. The second edition of his groundbreaking work on building end-user-friendly user interfaces.

[Date] *Introduction to Database Systems* (8th ed.), by C. J. Date. Boston, MA: Addison-Wesley, 2004. By far the best—and the most intense—discussion of relational database systems ever written. Very conceptual, discussing the theory of relational systems much more than any one particular dialect of SQL or implementation.

[EAI] *Enterprise Integration Patterns,* by Gregor Hohpe and Bobby Woolf. Boston, MA: Addison-Wesley, 2004. A collection of dozens of patterns specific to messaging systems, nominally in the context of enterprise application integration. Ignore the title and read it for a great look at messaging and its flexibility and power.

[Ewald] *Transactional COM+*, by Tim Ewald. Boston, MA: Addison-Wesley, 2001. Despite its COM+ focus, a great discussion of transactional processing in modern object-oriented context. His discussion of identity in Chapter 1 is pure goodness and the inspiration for Item 5. Ignore the code examples and focus on the concepts.

[Falkner/Jones] *Servlets and JavaServer Pages,* by Jayson Falkner and Kevin Jones. Boston, MA: Addison-Wesley, 2004. The best discussion of servlets and JSP for Java programmers on the planet, bar none.

[Ferguson03] *Practical Cryptography,* by Niels Ferguson and Bruce Schneier. New York: Wiley, 2003. A great distillation of [Schneier95] into a much more compact and consumable form. Required reading for anyone looking to learn more about cryptography in general (but remember, cryptography is not all there is to security.)

[Fowler] *Patterns of Enterprise Application Architecture,* by Martin Fowler. Boston, MA: Addison-Wesley, 2002. A good breakdown of the enterprise application space and technology-agnostic patterns used therein. Note that Fowler tends to shy away from EJB and other "heavyweight" J2EE technologies, so read this for the conceptual knowledge, not as a guide to J2EE (or .NET, for that matter).

[Friedman-Hill] *JESS in Action,* by Ernest Friedman-Hill. Greenwich, CT: Manning Press, 2003. An excellent introduction and reference on JESS, the Java Expert System Shell, and on rules-based systems in general.

[GOF] *Design Patterns,* by Erich Gamma, Richard Helm, Ralph Johnson, and John Vlissides. Reading, MA: Addison-Wesley, 1995. The gold standard of patterns books—every developer's required primer for designing software in object-oriented languages.

[Gong] *Inside Java 2 Platform Security,* by Li Gong, Gary Ellison, and Mary Dageforde. Boston, MA: Addison-Wesley, 2003. The second edition is even better than the first and incorporates discussion of the baseline platform security model, the GSSAPI, a light discussion of Kerberos, and the source for Items 64, 65, and 66.

[Gray/Reuter] *Transaction Processing,* by Jim Gray and Andreas Reuter. San Francisco: Morgan Kaufman, 1993. The book to read after [Bernstein/Newcomer] if you're still looking for the Zen of transactional processing. Great for historical perspective, if nothing else.

[Gulutzan/Pelzer] *SQL Performance Tuning,* by Peter Gulutzan and Trudy Pelzer. Boston, MA: Addison-Wesley, 2003. Tuning SQL is by far one of the most important things an enterprise developer can do to build effective systems. But more importantly, this book points out the relative merits of each tuning approach for eight popular databases, showing that for many tuning options, one size doesn't fit all.

[Halloway] *Component Development for the Java™ Platform,* by Stuart Dabbs Halloway. Boston, MA: Addison-Wesley, 2001. An awesome discussion of ClassLoaders, Serialization, Java Native Interface, and general advice on components.

[Henderson] *The Guru's Guide to SQL Server Stored Procedures, XML, and HTML,* by Ken Henderson. Boston, MA: Addison-Wesley, 2005.

[Howard/LeBlanc] *Writing Secure Code* (2nd ed.), by Michael Howard and David C. LeBlanc. Redmond, WA: Microsoft Press, 2003. Despite its Windows-centric nature, this is a gold mine of gotchas and concerns in code. For example, use the regular expression on page 430 to avoid cross-site scripting attacks.

[Jones/Lims] *Garbage Collection,* by Richard Jones and Rafael Lims. New York: Wiley, 1996. The canonical reference on how garbage collectors work.

[Kaye] *Loosely Coupled: The Missing Pieces of Web Services,* by Doug Kaye. Kentfield, CA: RDS Press, 2003.

[Kreger/Harold/Williamson] *Java and JMX,* by Heather Kreger, Ward Harold, and Leigh Williamson. Boston, MA: Addison-Wesley, 2003. A great comprehensive discussion of the Java Management Extensions API and standard.

[Lea] *Concurrent Programming in Java* (2nd ed.), by Douglas Lea. Boston, MA: Addison-Wesley, 2002. A high-powered discussion of concurrency and synchronization for the Java platform. Highly recommended if you're not sure what the "synchronized" keyword in Java does.

[Liang] *The Java Native Interface,* by Sheng Liang. Boston, MA: Addison-Wesley, 1999. While a bit old (it was released during the JDK 1.1 timeframe), Sheng's book nevertheless stands as the seminal reference for JNI. It also contains an explanation of his Shared Stubs library (available online), which acts as a simpler native code invocation mechanism.

[Marinescu] *EJB Patterns,* by Floyd Marinescu. New York: Wiley, 2001. An early collection of EJB idioms.

[Meyers95] *Effective C++*, by Scott Meyers. Reading, MA: Addison-Wesley, 1995. Despite its C++ focus, still a great source of ideas and concepts. The inspiration for this book.

[Meyers97] *More Effective C++*, by Scott Meyers. Reading, MA: Addison-Wesley, 1997. Great follow-up with discussions of higher-level language elements, such as lazy-evaluated and eager-evaluated values within a class.

[Mitnick] *The Art of Deception,* by Kevin Mitnick. New York: Wiley, 2003. If ever you or a coworker need to be convinced that security is much more than just code, read this book. The most secure cryptographic protocol in the world can't protect against a simple con man, and Mitnick shows you how the most innocuous conversation can reveal critical attack secrets.

[Neward] *Server-Based Java Programming,* by Ted Neward. Greenwich, CT: Manning Press, 2000. A previous attempt at discussing enterprise Java development that focuses more on how an application server works. A bit dated by this point, but parts are still relevant.

[Nock] *Data Access Patterns,* by Clifton Nock. Boston, MA: Addison-Wesley, 2004. Quite possibly one of the best books on generic (i.e., not tied to any particular technology) relational data access patterns. The examples in Java are just a bonus. The inspiration for Items 33 and 34.

[Oaks] *Java Security* (2nd ed.), by Scott Oaks. Sebastopol, CA: O'Reilly, 2001. Understanding the Java platform security model is crucial to building secure Java systems; reading this book is a great first step to understanding the Java security model.

[PLOPD2] *Pattern Languages of Program Design 2,* edited by John Vlissides, James O. Coplien, and Norman L. Kerth. Reading, MA: Addison-Wesley, 1997. Collected from the patterns conference of the same name, a good collection of patterns useful for enterprise systems.

[PLOPD3] *Pattern Languages of Program Design 3,* edited by Robert Martin, Dirk Riehle, and Frank Buschmann. Reading, MA: Addison-Wesley, 1998. Like its predecessor, a good collection of patterns in all sorts of systems, much of it about enterprise systems. More code-centric than previous volumes.

[PLOPD4] *Pattern Languages of Program Design 4,* edited by Neil Harrison, Brian Foote, and Hans Rohnert. Boston, MA: Addison-Wesley, 2000. Like the earlier volumes in this series, a good collection of patterns useful to enterprise architects and developers. Very code-centric.

[POSA1] *Pattern-Oriented Software Architecture* (vol. 1), by Frank Buschmann, Regina Meunier, Hans Rohnert, Peter Sommerlad, and Michael Stal. New York: Wiley, 1995. One of the original patterns works, shipped just before [GOF]. Notable for its division of patterns into different tiers: architecture, patterns, and idioms. (Note: When it first shipped, it wasn't labeled as vol. 1 because vol. 2 wasn't shipped until eight years later. Wiley reprinted this work in 2002 to accompany vol. 2, below.)

[POSA2] *Patterns of Software Architecture* (vol. 2), by Douglas Schmidt, Michael Stal, Hans Rohnert, and Frank Buschmann. New York: Wiley, 2002. A great follow-up to vol. 1, with patterns dealing with concurrency, communications, and networking.

[Raymond] *The Art of UNIX Programming,* by Eric S. Raymond. Boston, MA: Addison-Wesley, 2004. Just as understanding the Windows platform is important to understand how to best build systems that run on it, understanding the UNIX platform is equally important. While this isn't a book that explains the internals of UNIX, it covers the more important aspect—the philosophy of UNIX itself.

[Schneier95] *Applied Cryptography* (2nd ed.), by Bruce Schneier. New York: Wiley, 1995. The last word on cryptographic algorithms and secure data exchange. I recommend reading [Schneier03] as a primer before tackling this book.

[Schneier01] *Secrets and Lies,* by Bruce Schneier. New York: Wiley, 2001. This is every developer's, project lead's, architect's, and manager's primer on security and why it must be taken seriously from the beginning. Inspiration for most of Chapter 7 on security.

[Stevens] *UNIX Network Programming* (3rd ed., vols. 1, 2, and 3), by W. Richard Stevens. Boston, MA: Addison-Wesley, 2004 and forthcoming. Stevens' books have long been the Last Word on TCP/IP communications, and his books are being revised for modern developments despite Stevens' death. Required reading for anyone who wants to understand the TCP/IP software stack and applications.

[Szyperski] *Component Software* (2nd ed.), by Clemens Szyperski. Boston, MA: Addison-Wesley, 2003. The holy canon of component-oriented designs. If Item 1 still doesn't make sense to you, this is the book for you.

[Tanenbaum] *Distributed Systems: Principles and Paradigms,* by Andrew S. Tanenbaum and Maarten van Steen. Upper Saddle River, NJ: Prentice

Hall/Pearson Education, 2002. A great conceptual discussion of distributed systems in general.

[Tate] *Bitter Java*, by Bruce Tate. Greenwich, CT: Manning Press, 2002. Antipatterns for Java and J2EE. Definitely a good companion for this book.

[Tate/Clark/Lee/Lindskey] *Bitter EJB*, by Bruce Tate, Mike Clark, Bob Lee, and Patrick Lindskey. Greenwich, CT: Manning Press, 2003. An EJB-specific follow-up to [Tate]; another good companion to this book.

[Van Duyne/Landay/Hong] *The Design of Sites,* by Douglas K. Van Duyne, James Landay, and Jason I. Hong. Boston, MA: Addison-Wesley, 2002. Constructing an HTML-based user interface is more art than science; this book is the best description of patterns for Web site design available.

Web Sites

[http://www.alphaworks.ibm.com/tech/hyperj] The home page of IBM's Hyper/J language and framework.

[http://aspectj.eclipse.org] The home page of the AspectJ AOP programming language.

[http://aspectwerkz.codehaus.org/] The home page of AspectWerkz, an AOP framework.

[http://www.enterpriseintegrationpatterns.com] The Web site on which [EAI] was workshopped and developed. Not all patterns made it to the book, and active discussion continues on its wiki.

[http://nanning.codehaus.org] The home page of Nanning, an AOP framework.

[http://www.neward.net/ted] The author's Web site and blog.

[http://www.ncward.net/ted/EEJ] The book's supplemental Web site; stay tuned here for errata and updates.

[http://www.owasp.org] The home page of the Open Web Application Security Project, an open-source collection of security tools, articles, and discussion.

[http://www.theserverside.com] The preeminent J2EE community and discussion portal on the Internet.

Index

Note: Italicized page locator indicates figure/table.